Learning to Fight

Learning, innovation, and adaptation are not concepts that we necessarily associate with the British Army of the First World War. Yet the need to learn from mistakes, to exploit new opportunities, and to adapt to complex situations is enduring and timeless. This revealing work is the first institutional examination of the army's process for learning during the First World War. Drawing on organisational learning and management theories, Aimée Fox critiques existing approaches to military learning in wartime. Focused around a series of case studies, the book ranges across multiple operational theatres and positions the army within a broader context in terms of its relationships with allies and civilians to reveal that learning was more complex and thoroughgoing than initially thought. It grapples with the army's failings and shortcomings, explores its successes, and acknowledges the inherent difficulties of learning in a desperate and lethally competitive environment.

AIMÉE FOX is a Lecturer in Defence Studies at King's College London. Her research interests centre on organisational learning, change, and administration in the British Army of the First World War.

Cambridge Military Histories

Edited by

HEW STRACHAN, Chichele Professor of the History of War, University of Oxford and Fellow of All Souls College, Oxford

GEOFFREY WAWRO, Professor of Military History, and Director of the Military History Center, University of North Texas

The aim of this series is to publish outstanding works of research on warfare throughout the ages and throughout the world. Books in the series take a broad approach to military history, examining war in all its military, strategic, political and economic aspects. The series complements Studies in the Social and Cultural History of Modern Warfare by focusing on the 'hard' military history of armies, tactics, strategy and warfare. Books in the series consist mainly of single author works – academically rigorous and groundbreaking – which are accessible to both academics and the interested general reader.

A full list of titles in the series can be found at:
www.cambridge.org/militaryhistories

Learning to Fight

Military Innovation and Change in the British Army, 1914–1918

Aimée Fox

King's College London

CAMBRIDGE
UNIVERSITY PRESS

University Printing House, Cambridge CB2 8BS, United Kingdom

One Liberty Plaza, 20th Floor, New York, NY 10006, USA

477 Williamstown Road, Port Melbourne, VIC 3207, Australia

314-321, 3rd Floor, Plot 3, Splendor Forum, Jasola District Centre, New Delhi - 110025, India

79 Anson Road, #06-04/06, Singapore 079906

Cambridge University Press is part of the University of Cambridge.

It furthers the University's mission by disseminating knowledge in the pursuit of education, learning and research at the highest international levels of excellence.

www.cambridge.org
Information on this title: www.cambridge.org/9781107190795
DOI: 10.1017/9781108120210

First published 2018

Printed in the United States of America by Sheridan Books, Inc.

A catalogue record for this publication is available from the British Library

ISBN 978-1-107-19079-5 Hardback

Cambridge University Press has no responsibility for the persistence or accuracy of URLs for external or third-party internet websites referred to in this publication, and does not guarantee that any content on such websites is, or will remain, accurate or appropriate.

Contents

Figures

Acknowledgements

I underestimated the challenge of penning acknowledgements: it turns out that there really is something more difficult than writing your first book. The paragraphs of thanks that follow are poor recompense for the generosity and support I have experienced in the researching and writing of this book. First and foremost, I would like to thank Dr Jonathan Boff. He supervised the doctoral thesis upon which this book is based. Back in 2012, he took me on as his first PhD student, demonstrating a cheerful patience every time I updated my colour-coded, three-year work plan. He has been a constant source of inspiration, advice, and guidance, challenging and motivating me to become a better historian. His patience, support, and friendship have been unwavering and invaluable. I also owe a great debt to Professor John Bourne and Dr Rob Thompson, who were able to see the potential in a painfully self-conscious, shy, nineteen-year-old undergraduate at Birmingham all those years ago. They nurtured my interest in the First World War, encouraging me to pursue post-graduate study. Without the support and input of these three inspirational historians, this book would never have been written.

The research and writing of this book took place at two academic institutions: the University of Birmingham and King's College London. My time as both a student and staff member in the Department of History at Birmingham brought me into contact with inspiring colleagues and wonderful students. Since moving 'down south', I have been humbled by the generosity of my colleagues in the Defence Studies Department at King's College London. They have welcomed me with open arms, giving up time to talk through my ideas and listen to my thoughts on innovation. The opportunity to work with my military students has been invaluable. They live and breathe some of the challenges and opportunities raised in this book, often providing a welcome sounding board for the ideas contained within.

I have also been the beneficiary of much kindness, generosity, and positivity from a number of individuals – both inside and outside the academy – over the last five years, whether at formal conferences and seminars, the inevitable networking that follows, chance encounters in a library or archive, or through the glorious medium of Twitter and the #twitterstorians network. For their time, input, emotional support, and encouragement, I would particularly like to thank Jim Beach, John Bourne, Tim Bowman, the Chicks of War network, Tessa Cockcroft, Mark Connelly, Tony Cowan, Rhys Crawley, Huw J. Davies, Doug Delaney, Andrew Duncan, Ashley Ekins, Ed Erickson, Robert Foley, Matthew Francis, Peter Gray, Steven Gray, the late Jeff Grey, Stuart Griffin, Meleah Hampton, Paul Harris, Lynelle Howson, Spencer Jones, James Kitchen, Roger Lee, Ross Mahoney, Helen McCartney, Sarah McCook, Stuart Mitchell, Aaron Pegram, Chris Phillips, William Philpott, James Pugh, Chris Roberts, Gary Sheffield, Peter Simkins, Michael Snape, Bob Stevenson, Christian Tripodi, and Dan Whittingham. I would also like to thank Tim Godden, who played an important role during the early phases of the book. Special praise is reserved for David Morgan-Owen and Andy Simpson, who read the manuscript in its entirety; I am incredibly grateful for their support, comments, and criticisms.

Professors Sir Hew Strachan and Gavin Schaffer examined my doctorate, and the comments and encouragement that they provided during the viva and in subsequent conversations afterwards were invaluable in preparing the thesis for publication. As one of the editors of the Cambridge Military Histories series, Professor Strachan deserves an additional special mention for his advice, support, and belief in this project. I would also like to thank the two anonymous readers commissioned by Cambridge University Press to review the first draft of the manuscript. Their incisive comments and criticisms have certainly enabled me to both strengthen and round out the monograph, for which I am grateful. Naturally, any errors or omissions that remain are my own. Michael Watson, Melissa Shivers, Claire Sissen, and the team at Cambridge University Press made the path from proposal to publication a smooth one. Nothing was too much trouble, and they were always on hand to offer support and guidance.

I am grateful to the Arts and Humanities Research Council, who funded much of the research upon which this book is based. Thanks are also due to the National Army Museum and the Universitas 21 scheme for additional research bursaries and scholarships. The research for this book was facilitated by the invaluable assistance of the staff at the numerous archives and institutions that I visited to conduct the research. For permissions to quote from materials in their care, I would like to thank the British Library; the Trustees of the Churchill Archives Centre and Cynthia Bonham-Carter, Graeme Bonham-Carter, and Catherine

Maddocks; the Trustees of the Imperial War Museum and Lord Chetwode, Rupert Dawnay, Neil Kermack, John Martin, Joan Micklem, and Alisdair Murray; the archive of the Institution of Civil Engineers; the Trustees of the Liddell Hart Centre for Military Archives and the Robertson family; the Liddle Collection at the University of Leeds; the Modern Records Centre at the University of Warwick; the National Archives of the United Kingdom; the Council of the National Army Museum; the Royal Artillery Historical Trust; the Australian Army History Unit; the Australian War Memorial and Michael Bennett, Mark Derham, and Janverin McCombe; the National Library of Australia; and the State Library of New South Wales. I would also like to thank Katherine Davies (née Swinfen Eady) and Sally McLaren for allowing me to quote from the Mynors Farmar papers for which they hold the copyright. Every effort has been made to contact copyright holders to secure necessary permissions. Any omissions or lapses are unintentional.

Unsurprisingly, my deepest gratitude is reserved for my family. I thank my parents, whose bottomless love and moral support have spurred me on throughout my career. From an early age, they encouraged my passion for history and demonstrated the greatest forbearance when their only daughter decided to leave a 'job for life' to embark on a career in academia. My brother Tom also offered his support whilst undertaking his own post-graduate studies. Without my family's support, I would not have started, nor got anywhere near to finishing, this book. This book is dedicated to Team Fox, with my love and gratitude.

Abbreviations

AA&QMG	Assistant Adjutant and Quartermaster-General
AAG	Assistant Adjutant-General
AIF	Australian Imperial Force
AIT	Assistant Inspector of Training
ANZAC	Australian and New Zealand Army Corps
APSS	Army Printing and Stationery Service
AQMG	Assistant Quartermaster-General
ASC	Army Service Corps
ASE	Amalgamated Society of Engineers
BCM	Bureau Central Météorologique
BEF	British Expeditionary Force
BGGS	Brigadier-General, General Staff
BGRA	Brigadier-General, Royal Artillery
BSF	British Salonika Force
CBSO	Counter-battery Staff Officer
CDS	Central Distribution Section
CEF	Canadian Expeditionary Force
CGS	Chief of the General Staff
CIGS	Chief of the Imperial General Staff
CinC	Commander-in-Chief
CMF	Commonwealth Military Force
CO	Commanding Officer
CRA	Commander Royal Artillery
CRE	Commander Royal Engineers
DDW	Deputy Director of Works
DFW	Director of Fortifications and Works
DGT	Director-General of Transportation
DMC	Desert Mounted Corps
DSD	Director of Staff Duties
DST	Director of Supplies and Transport
EEF	Egyptian Expeditionary Force
ERSC	Engineering and Railway Staff Corps

ESR	Egyptian State Railways
FFI	Force Françaises en Italie
FSR	*Field Service Regulations*
GCT	Groupe de Canevas de Tir
GHQ	General Headquarters
GOC	General Officer Commanding
GSO1	General Staff Officer (First Grade)
GSO2	General Staff Officer (Second Grade)
GSO3	General Staff Officer (Third Grade)
IAE	Institution of Automobile Engineers
ICE	Institution of Civil Engineers
IEF	Italian Expeditionary Force
IGC	Inspector-General of Communications
IGF	Inspector-General of the Forces
LSE	London School of Economics
MEF	Mediterranean Expeditionary Force
MGC	Machine Gun Corps
MGGS	Major-General, General Staff
MGRA	Major-General, Royal Artillery
NCO	Non-commissioned officer
OC	Officer Commanding
OR	Other rank
psc	Passed Staff College
PWD	Public Works Department
QMG	Quartermaster-General
RAF	Royal Air Force
RE	Royal Engineers
REC	Railway Executive Committee
RFC	Royal Flying Corps
RUSI	Royal United Services Institute
SGA	Service Géographique l'Armée
SMR	Sudan Military Railways
SOP	Standard Operating Procedure
SS	Stationery Service

Introduction

Reflecting back on his experience of overseeing the nation's war effort during the First World War, David Lloyd George lamented the 'rigidity and restrictiveness about the methods employed', which he felt had 'allowed no play for initiative, imagination and inventiveness'. The war, he observed, revealed that

independent thinking is not encouraged in a professional Army. It is a form of mutiny. Obedience is the supreme virtue. Theirs not to reason why. Orders are to be carried out and not canvassed. Criticism is insubordination...Such an instinctive obedience to the word of command...makes an 'officer and a gentleman' but it is not conducive to the building up of an alert, adaptable and resourceful leader of men.[1]

A strident critic of the British military and its senior commanders, Britain's former wartime prime minister pointed to what he saw as serious cultural deficiencies within the British army. There were fundamental problems within the institution. While the army had many qualities, such as meritocracy and objectivity, for Lloyd George, it was a bureaucracy in the worst sense of the word: rigid, hierarchical, incapable of adaptation, and averse to change. Lloyd George was not the only critic of the army's cultural and intellectual foundations. Basil Liddell Hart, though less vociferous, was no less scathing with his assessment that 'the only thing harder than getting a new idea into a military mind is to get an old idea out'.[2] For Lloyd George and Liddell Hart, the army was institutionally and culturally deficient when it came to innovation and adaptation.

These negative perceptions have become a mainstay in popular perceptions of the British army in the First World War. While the centenary commemorations have enhanced awareness of the war more broadly, notions of military competency and effectiveness are not as palatable to

---

[1] D. Lloyd George, *War Memoirs*, II (2 vols, London: Odhams Press, 1938 [1936]), pp. 2040–2041.

[2] B. H. Liddell Hart, *Thoughts on War* (London: Faber and Faber, 1944), v.

1

the general public as those of pity and futility.[3] The narrative of tragedy is hard to dislodge, particularly in Britain, where the conflict has become a byword for military misadventure. As one esteemed historian reminds us, the idea of a British army 'learning curve' – a term lifted from the business world – 'sticks in the gullet of many people in Britain because the curve was so liberally greased with soldiers' blood'.[4] Put simply, innovation and adaptability are not concepts that we necessarily associate with the seemingly unwieldy behemoth that was the British army of the First World War. Instead, they are notions that we are more likely to ascribe to the small, agile military forces of the post–National Service period.

Words like innovation, adaptability, and responsiveness litter modern defence reviews and policies alike. They are the watchwords of increasingly lean forces. In an age of austerity, innovation and entrepreneurialism have become all the more desirable. Yet, whilst smaller budgets may necessitate improvements in tactics, techniques, and procedures, these efficiencies are often more aspirational than tangible or deliverable. Western militaries in particular have grappled with the goal of becoming a Peter Senge-style 'learning organisation' – an ideal that is more myth than reality.[5] The drive for greater innovative capabilities can be seen in Australia's 2008 'Adaptive Army' initiative with its restructuring of higher command and control arrangements to ensure that learning and adaptation is more integral to the structure and culture of the Army.[6] The US's 'third offset strategy' and its 2014 quadrennial review reaffirmed that 'innovation ... is a central line of effort ... [and] is paramount given the increasingly complex warfighting environment we

[3] See M. Hough, S. Ballinger, and S. Katwala, *A Centenary Shared: Tracking Public Attitudes to the First World War Centenary, 2013–16* (London: British Future, 2016).

[4] D. Reynolds, 'Britain, the Two World Wars, and the Problem of Narrative', *Historical Journal* 60 (1) (2017), p. 222.

[5] P. Senge, *The Fifth Discipline: The Art and Practice of the Learning Organization* (New York: Doubleday, 1990). For the appropriation of the 'learning organization' in a military context, see J. Nagl, *Learning to Eat Soup with a Knife: Counterinsurgency Lessons from Malaya and Vietnam* (Chicago: Chicago University Press, 2005 [2002]); A. J. DiBella, 'Can the Army become a Learning Organization? A Question Reexamined', *Joint Force Quarterly* 56 (1) (2010), pp. 117–122; G. A. Daddis, 'Eating Soup with a Spoon': The US Army as a 'Learning Organization' in the Vietnam War', *Journal of Military History* 77 (2013), pp. 229–254; R. Di Schiena, G. Letens, E. Van Aken, and J. Farris, 'Relationship between Leadership and Characteristics of Learning Organizations in Deployed Military Units: An Exploratory Study', *Administrative Sciences* 3 (2013), pp. 143–165. For some of the weaknesses of the 'learning organization' concept more broadly, see S. Kerka, *The Learning Organization: Myths and Realities* (Washington, DC: Office of Educational Research and Improvement, 1995); C. Hughes and M. Tight, 'The Myth of the Learning Society', *British Journal of Educational Studies* 43 (3) (1995), pp. 295–296, 299–300.

[6] J. Blaxland, *The Australian Army from Whitlam to Howard* (Melbourne, VIC: Cambridge University Press, 2014), pp. 352–353.

expect to encounter'.[7] In Britain, the Ministry of Defence's 'Defence Innovation Initiative', launched in 2016, drives home the point that 'innovation is key to maintaining our military advantage, and that to realise this a 'culture that is "innovative by instinct"' is required, which emphasises the willingness to accept risk.[8] The British army's ongoing 'Army 2020' review is predicated upon the need to be 'an integrated, adaptable and sustainable Force for the future'. One of the review's key themes is 'versatile by design', which enables the army to hark back to its 'proud record of adapting quickly to meet any crisis'.[9]

While expressions like 'innovative by instinct', 'adaptable forces', and 'learning organisations' might carry an air of modernity, this book shows that learning, innovation, and change are not just twenty-first-century concerns. The need to learn from mistakes, to exploit new opportunities, and adapt to complex situations in order to defeat an adversary on the 'other side of the hill' are enduring and timeless. This book takes the British army of the First World War as its case study. Moving beyond the operational focus of existing studies, it examines the army's institutional process for learning and adaptation more broadly. It poses a number of questions: how effective was the army's learning process? Did a 'culture of innovation' exist within the army? If such a culture existed, to what extent was this maintained during the First World War? How do we reconcile the relationship between learning and performance?

This book does not seek to whitewash the British army's performance during the First World War. Costly mistakes were made. Blimpish pockets existed. Certain individuals were overpromoted, ill-equipped to deal with the war they faced. Irrational choices were made without sufficient forethought. These aspects ought not to be ignored or marginalised. Instead, they need to be integrated into any discussion of learning and change, adding much-needed realism to our understanding of an inherently messy process. This process – the continual series of actions and steps taken – is often reduced to cause and effect, input and output. The expansive nature of learning is overlooked, as well as the ways and means that facilitate it. This book aims to reinstate some of the complexity and messiness associated with learning. It grapples with the army's failings and shortcomings, explores its successes, and acknowledges the inherent

---

[7] Department of Defense, *Quadrennial Defense Review 2014* (Washington, DC: Department of Defense, 2014), p. 22.

[8] Ministry of Defence, *Advantage through Innovation: The Defence Innovation Initiative* (London: Ministry of Defence, 2016), pp. 2, 4.

[9] Ministry of Defence, *Transforming the British Army: An Update – July 2013* (London: Ministry of Defence, 2013), pp. 29, 28. Following the 2015 National Security Strategy and Strategic Defence and Spending Review's amendments to 'Army 2020', it is now known as 'Army 2020 Refine'.

difficulties of learning in a desperate and lethally competitive environment. In short, it reveals that failure to understand how the army learned obfuscates our understanding of how the army changed as an institution. A better understanding of this relationship has profound implications for our historical memory of the First World War, forcing us to acknowledge the importance of learning and the myriad difficulties that the British military faced, not least of which was the efficacy of its adversary.

Although the book necessarily engages with operational and tactical learning, it also has a broader remit. It considers the army's institutional openness to learning and change, of which operations were only one facet. It is as much about what (and how) the army learned from different disciplines, nations, and walks of life, as it is about those tactical lessons gleaned from the battlefield. By taking a more holistic approach, the book recasts learning and innovation as a type of bricolage: a reconfiguration of different knowledges resulting from encounters between different cultures.[10] Concerned with the movement, reinterpretation, and transformation of expertise, knowledge, and lessons, the book is as much an institutional study of the British army in the First World War as it is a study of *transfert culturel* within a military context.[11]

How, and if, militaries learn has been of long-standing interest to historians and social scientists alike. The observation that militaries are averse to change is not one limited to former British prime ministers. It is a view that has proved an important element of scholarship in the field of military innovation studies. Early writings identified the hierarchical, rule-bound nature of the military as a barrier to change; that the absence of innovation was the natural state for the military as a bureaucracy. Commentators suggested that militaries needed to be goaded into change, usually by outside involvement.[12] One critic went so far as to suggest that the military required a good 'kick in the pants' if it was to innovate.[13] Recent scholarship – primarily focused on post-1945 militaries involved in a single campaign – has challenged this change-averse view.[14] James Russell's examination of the US Army in Iraq showed how

---

[10] P. Burke, *A Social History of Knowledge: From the Encyclopédie to Wikipedia* (Cambridge: Polity, 2012), p. 86.

[11] See M. Espagne, 'La notion de transfert culturel', *Revue Science / Lettres* 1 (2013) (Published Online 1 May 2012. DOI: 10.4000/rsl.219), pp. 1–9.

[12] See e.g. B. Posen, *The Sources of Military Doctrine: France, Britain and Germany between the World Wars* (Ithaca, NY: Cornell University Press, 1984); K. Zisk, *Engaging the Enemy: Organization Theory and Soviet Military Innovation, 1955–1991* (Princeton, NJ: Princeton University Press, 1993); D. Avant, *Political Institutions and Military Change: Lessons from Peripheral Wars* (Ithaca, NY: Cornell University Press, 1994).

[13] Posen, *Military Doctrine*, p. 226.

[14] J. A. Russell, *Innovation, Transformation and War: Counterinsurgency Operations in Anbar and Ninewa Provinces, 2005–2007* (Stanford, CA: Stanford University Press, 2011), p. 211.

'a collection of hierarchically structured organisations' became the 'kind of agile and adaptive structures thought only to exist in certain parts of the private sector', while Nina Kollars has recently argued that military organisations tend to become fluid when exposed to Clausewitzian friction.[15] Indeed, decisions made in wartime do not always reflect a 'cautious, bureaucratic approach'.[16]

Scholarship on innovation can be broadly grouped into three main areas of enquiry, which will be summarised here and further explored throughout the course of the book.[17] First, we have where and how innovation (or adaptation) takes place. This can be broken down into three vectored approaches: top-down, bottom-up, or horizontal. The top-down approach has generally focused on innovation in peacetime, thus ignoring the 'adapt or die' dilemma that accompanies the victory imperative of war.[18] It is also concerned with organisation-wide revolutions, disruptive technological change, and elite-driven politics. Such interpretations tend to argue that only civilians or senior military leaders can effect innovation, removing practitioners from this narrative. This contributed to the emergence of the second major strand of literature: the bottom-up approach, which sought to incorporate the role of practitioners in this process.[19] There was a drive to re-establish the relationship between human behaviour, particularly lower down the hierarchy, and organisational behaviour. Emerging from this bottom-up scholarship was the concept of military adaptation. Underpinned by organisational learning theory, studies on adaptation have tended to focus on modern, Western militaries during counter-insurgency operations with the aim of distilling lessons for future conflicts.[20] The final

---

[15] N. A. Kollars, 'War's Horizon: Soldier-Led Adaptation in Iraq and Vietnam', *Journal of Strategic Studies* 38 (4) (2015), p. 550.

[16] Russell, *Innovation*, pp. 208–209.

[17] For a recent overview of the 'state of play' in military innovation studies, see S. Griffin, 'Military Innovation Studies: Multidisciplinary or Lacking Discipline?', *Journal of Strategic Studies* 40 (1–2) (2017), pp. 196–224. See also A. Grissom, 'The Future of Military Innovation Studies', *Journal of Strategic Studies* 29 (5) (2006), pp. 905–934.

[18] For examples of this top-down approach, see Posen, *The Sources of Military Doctrine*; S. P. Rosen, *Winning the Next War: Innovation and the Modern Military* (London: Cornell University Press, 1991); Zisk, *Engaging the Enemy*; Avant, *Political Institutions*; E. Kier, *Imagining War: French and British Military Doctrine between the Wars* (Princeton, NJ: Princeton University Press, 1997); T. G. Farrell and T. Terriff (eds), *The Sources of Military Change* (Boulder, CO: Lynne Rienner, 2002).

[19] E. A. Cohen, 'Change and Transformation in Military Affairs', *Journal of Strategic Studies* 27 (3) (2004), pp. 395–407; Grissom, 'Future'.

[20] See e.g. T. G. Farrell, 'Improving in War: Military Adaptation and the British in Helmand Province, Afghanistan, 2006–2009', *Journal of Strategic Studies* 33 (4) (2010), pp. 567–594; S. Catignani, '"Getting COIN" at the Tactical Level in Afghanistan: Reassessing Counter-Insurgency Adaptation in the British Army', *Journal of Strategic Studies* 35 (4) (2012), pp. 513–539; Kollars, 'War's Horizon'; R. Marcus, 'Military Innovation and Tactical Adaptation in the Israel-Hizballah Conflict: The

approach – horizontal innovation – is influenced by adaptation scholarship and pioneered by Robert Foley with his work on the German Army in the First World War.[21] This approach adds another dimension to our understanding of learning that moves beyond the vertical polarity of top-down and bottom-up. Recent scholarship has added nuance to this process, highlighting the 'dynamic interplay' between different learning approaches, as well as the importance of the military's 'tolerance of creativity'.[22]

Secondly, scholarship has grappled with the dynamics of organisational culture and the role that it plays in facilitating or hindering innovation. While some scholars saw the military as rigid and inflexible, particularly in peacetime, others have suggested that, in time of war, the military becomes far more decentralised and fluid.[23] It is not rigidity that undermines efforts to change, but rather the military's struggle with 'the knowledge generated by its practitioners'.[24] Culture can determine how an organisation approaches learning, shaping the ways and means used. Foley, for example, has considered the importance of distinct learning cultures to British and German adaptation during the First World War.[25] This book suggests that, while pioneering in approach, Foley's work in important ways needs revision, not least of which his contention that the British army was more likely to use 'non formal' methods to learn.

The final strand of scholarship tackles the challenges of capturing and converting low level, informal learning into organisational learning. For our purposes, organisational learning – a notoriously difficult concept to pin down – may usefully be defined as 'the process of improving actions through better knowledge and understanding'.[26] Much of the

Institutionalization of Lesson-Learning in the IDF', *Journal of Strategic Studies* 38 (4) (2015), pp. 500–528; K. A. Harkness and M. Hunzeker, 'Military Maladaptation: Counterinsurgency and the Politics of Failure', *Journal of Strategic Studies* 38 (6) (2015), pp. 777–800.

[21] R. T. Foley, 'A Case Study in Horizontal Military Innovation: The German Army, 1916–1918', *Journal of Strategic Studies* 35 (6) (2012), pp. 799–827.

[22] Marcus, 'Institutionalization of Lesson-Learning', p. 500; Kollars, 'War's Horizon', p. 21.

[23] For studies on organisational flexibility, see R. D. Doubler, *Closing with the Enemy: How GIs Fought the War in Europe, 1944–1945* (Lawrence: University Press of Kansas, 1994); J. Buckley, *British Armour in the Normandy Campaign 1944* (London: Routledge, 2004), pp. 9–11, 92–98; J. Buckley, 'Tackling the Tiger: The Development of British Armoured Doctrine for Normandy 1944', *Journal of Military History* 74 (2010), pp. 1161–1184; Russell, *Innovation*.

[24] Kollars, 'War's Horizon', p. 534.

[25] R. T. Foley, 'Dumb Donkeys or Cunning Foxes? Learning in the British and German Armies during the Great War', *International Affairs* 90 (2) (2014), pp. 279–298.

[26] C. M. Fiol and M. A. Lyles, 'Organizational Learning', *Academy of Management Review* 10 (4) (1985), p. 803.

scholarship in this subset concerns itself with the relationship between informal and formal learning.[27] When we talk about informal learning, we are generally referring to that which occurs through practice and experience. It is tacit in nature, often unintended and opportunistic.[28] Formal learning, on the other hand, is 'institutionally sponsored', occurring in an organised and structured context.[29] Yet, even in the most bureaucratic institutions, there is much that is unwritten, unsaid, and informal in nature.[30] Informal methods are often key sites for adaptation, but the failure to integrate these into the formal learning system can lead to 'adaptation traps', increasing the likelihood of solutions being 'lost, reinvented, or duplicated under the fog of war'.[31]

While existing research has enhanced our understanding of the interplay between informal and formal learning, this book challenges this largely binary approach, suggesting new ways of understanding organisational learning in a military context. Drawing upon the various theories of military innovation, the book argues, instead, for a more complex, integrated view of learning. The networked model of learning developed in this book points to the importance of the interconnectedness between top-down, bottom-up, incidental, and horizontal approaches. How learning is diffused is contingent on the size and extent of the networks involved. This model puts the individual front and centre, demonstrating the importance of human choice, behaviour, and action to the transfer of knowledge, as well as the importance of organisational culture or ethos in influencing the shape and evolution of British army learning.

Unlike military innovation studies, learning in the First World War has not been subject to the same level of sustained analysis. With the

---

[27] This is a burgeoning and exciting area of scholarship. See K. B. Bickel, *Mars Learning: The Marine Corps' Development of Small Wars Doctrine, 1915–1940* (Boulder, CO: Westview Press, 2001); R. T. Foley, H. McCartney, and S. Griffin, '"Transformation in Contact": Learning the Lessons of Modern War', *International Affairs* 87 (2) (2011), pp. 253–270; P. O'Toole and S. Talbot, 'Fighting for Knowledge: Developing Learning Systems in the Australian Army', *Armed Forces and Society* 37 (1) (2011), pp. 42–67; C. C. Serena, *A Revolution in Military Adaptation: The US Army in the Iraq War* (Washington, DC: Georgetown University Press, 2011); S. Catignani, 'Coping with Knowledge: Organizational Learning in the British Army?', *Journal of Strategic Studies* 37 (1) (2013), pp. 30–64.

[28] M. Eraut, 'Informal Learning in the Workplace', *Studies in Continuing Education* 26 (2) (2004), p. 250.

[29] D. McGuire and C. Gubbins, 'The Slow Death of Formal Learning: A Polemic', *Human Resource Development Review* 9 (3) (2010), p. 250.

[30] D. H. Kim, 'The Link between Organizational and Individual Learning', *Sloane Management Review* 35 (1) (1993), p. 45.

[31] Catignani, 'Coping with Knowledge', pp. 32, 38–39; Kollars, 'War's Horizon', p. 548.

exception of a single study on 'military effectiveness' in the First World
War, studies on British military learning have been isolated and fragmen-
tary despite the burgeoning literature that is broadly aligned with the
concept of a 'learning curve' or 'learning process'.[32] This Anglocentric
concept is used to describe the evolution of the British army from a small,
colonial *gendarmerie* in 1914 to a mass citizen army capable of waging
sophisticated operations in industrial warfare in 1918.[33] Historians associated with this concept have used the term to convey the belief that
the army learned from its mistakes at the operational and tactical levels
of war, attaining a high level of proficiency that manifested itself during the Hundred Days offensive of 1918.[34] Scholarship associated with
the learning curve has tended to focus on British, Western Front operational and tactical considerations, including studies on command, new
technologies, and the important role of Imperial forces.[35] More recent
additions to this canon have grappled with the less glamorous aspects

---

[32] A. R. Millett and W. Murray (eds), *Military Effectiveness, Vol. 1, The First World War*
(New York: Cambridge University Press, 2010 [1988]). This single study, funded by
the Office of the Secretary of Defense, sought to understand the problems facing the
US military in the 1980s. As a result, Millett and Murray chose case studies that very
much reflected the strategic environment of the early 1980s. Paul Kennedy's chapter on
Britain and the First World War offers a largely condemnatory account of the British
army, arguing that its effectiveness was only 'moderately good' and that it 'might have
done better'. See P. Kennedy, 'Britain and the First World War', in Millett and Murray
(eds), *Military Effectiveness*, pp. 31–79.
[33] A handful of scholars have considered learning in other belligerent armies. See M. Goya,
La Chair et L'Acier. L'Armée Française et L'Invention de la Guerre Moderne 1914–1918
(Paris: Tallandier, 2004); C. Stachelbeck, *Militärische Effektivität im Ersten Weltkrieg: die
11. Bayerische Infanteriedivision 1915 bis 1918* (Paderborn: Ferdinand Schöningh, 2010);
Foley, 'Horizontal'; Foley, 'Dumb Donkeys'.
[34] Forefathers of the 'learning curve' include J. Terraine, *Douglas Haig: The Educated Sol-
dier* (London: Hutchinson, 1963); S. Bidwell and D. Graham, *Fire-Power: The British
Army Weapons and Theories of War 1904–1945* (reprint, Barnsley: Pen and Sword, 2004
[1982]). Early proponents of the concept include B. Rawling, *Surviving Trench Warfare:
Technology and the Canadian Corps, 1914–1918* (Toronto, ON: University of Toronto
Press, 1992); P. Griffith, *Battle Tactics of the Western Front: The British Army's Art of
Attack 1916–18* (London: Yale University Press, 2000 [1994]).
[35] For command and generalship, see S. Robbins, *British Generalship on the Western Front
1914–1918: Defeat into Victory* (London: Frank Cass, 2005); G. D. Sheffield, *The Chief:
Douglas Haig and the British Army* (London: Aurum, 2011); A. Simpson, *Directing Operations: British Corps Command on the Western Front 1914–1918* (Stroud: Spellmount,
2006); P. E. Hodgkinson, *British Infantry Battalion Commanders in the First World War*
(Aldershot: Ashgate, 2015). For technology, see S. Marble, *British Artillery on the West-
ern Front in the First World War* (Aldershot: Ashgate, 2013); A. Palazzo, *Seeking Victory
on the Western Front: The British Army and Chemical Warfare in World War I* (London:
University of Nebraska, 2000). For Dominion forces, see Rawling, *Surviving Trench
Warfare*; G. Morton-Jack, *The Indian Army on the Western Front: India's Expeditionary
Force to France and Belgium in the First World War* (Cambridge: Cambridge University
Press, 2014).

of the army's war machine, such as intelligence, communications, and logistics.[36]

The 'learning curve' has certainly added colour and depth to our understanding of the myriad changes taking place at different levels of command, in different branches, and behind the lines. Yet while efforts have been made to understand the disjointed nature of learning in wartime, these efforts remain sporadic.[37] There are also significant gaps in the historiography, not least of which is the concept's highly Anglocentric, Western Front bias.[38] The experience and influence of Britain's enemies and allies have been marginalised in the historiography with only a handful of truly comparative works.[39] Similarly, while recent scholarship has reassessed theatres beyond the Western Front, these theatres are still analysed singly, often resulting in a skewed picture of progress and development, thus failing to demonstrate the complex evolutionary processes at work.[40] One of the clearest shortcomings of the 'learning curve' has been the simplistic and, at times, reductionist linkage between the army's ability and willingness to learn and its battlefield performance. The binary association between learning and performance has obscured the reality of how the army learned by hitching it to the much more complex issue of success on the field of battle. Seductive as the notion that learning improves combat power may be, it must be acknowledged that myriad other concerns – terrain, weather, supply, morale, the enemy, relative balance of force (across all arms) – all complicate the association between the two to the extent that attempting to gauge how the army learned by focusing upon how it fought becomes impossible. Indeed, it is by moving past this linkage that this book presents the first thoroughgoing appreciation of how the army – across its multiple branches and theatres – learned during the First World War.

---

[36] See e.g. J. Beach, *Haig's Intelligence: GHQ and the German Army 1916–1918* (Cambridge: Cambridge University Press, 2013); B. N. Hall, *Communications and British Operations on the Western Front, 1914–1918* (Cambridge: Cambridge University Press, 2017); I. M. Brown, *British Logistics on the Western Front 1914–19* (Westport, CT: Praeger, 1998); C. Phillips, 'Managing Armageddon: The Science of Transportation and the British Expeditionary Force, 1900–1918', Unpublished PhD Thesis, University of Leeds, 2015.

[37] J. Boff, *Winning and Losing on the Western Front: The British Third Army and the Defeat of Germany in 1918* (Cambridge: Cambridge University Press, 2012).

[38] H. Strachan, 'The First World War as a Global War', *First World War Studies* 1 (1) (2010), pp. 3–14.

[39] See e.g. Robert Foley's scholarship.

[40] A handful of inter-theatre scholarship exists. See e.g. M. Harrison, *The Medical War: British Military Medicine in the First World War* (Oxford: Oxford University Press, 2010); P. Strong and S. Marble, *Artillery in the Great War* (Barnsley: Pen and Sword, 2011); Hall, *Communications*.

Beyond offering the first institutional study of the army's process for learning, the contribution of this book is three-fold. First, the book moves beyond the standard Western Front narrative of learning. Examining the army as an institution requires us to look beyond the British Expeditionary Force in France and Flanders, turning our gaze to the various British forces that fought in Egypt, Gallipoli, Italy, Palestine, and Salonika. Employing a multi-theatre approach also enables us to examine the important role that allies, enemies, and civilians played in the army's learning process. As such, we are rewarded with an enhanced understanding of the multiplicity of learning processes and modalities within a single institution.

Secondly, it changes the dialogue about learning, challenging the imprecision of the language and terminology used. Learning as a term and concept has been misapplied to the British army of the First World War. This book provides a necessary corrective. To date, discussion of organisational learning or the army as a 'learning organisation' is something of a misnomer when such discussions are merely confined to one front, one branch, or one formation.[41] An institutional focus enables us to better understand and interrogate these concepts, charting the relationship between individual, group, and organisational learning. Furthermore, while scholars have spilt ink over whether the army learned, not enough has been spent on the higher question of how it learned. To date, the processes of institutional learning that enabled the army to rise to the challenges of modern war have been poorly served by existing scholarship.[42] Engaging with this 'how' question has broader implications for our understanding of the nature of the army as an institution. It also helps us to understand why learning is not always successful. By re-establishing the importance of human agency to the learning process and unpacking the various ways and means of learning, we come closer to understanding why and how the army learned in the way that it did.

Finally, it moves away from the 'one campaign' approach that typifies most studies on innovation. It is impossible to determine how and to what extent doctrine and practice developed over time by focusing on a single campaign.[43] Grounding the army's learning experience in a pre-war context forces us to understanding learning as a continuous

---

[41] See e.g. E. Erickson, *Ottoman Army Effectiveness in World War 1: A Comparative Study* (London: Routledge, 2007); Hall, *Communications*; C. Forrest, 'The 52nd (Lowland) Division in the Great War', Unpublished PhD Thesis, University of Salford, 2010.

[42] W. Philpott, 'L'histoire militaire un siècle après la Grande Guerre', *Revue Française de Civilisation Britannique* 20 (1) (2015), pp. 1–2.

[43] D. French, *The British Way in Counter-Insurgency, 1945–1967* (Oxford: Oxford University Press, 2011), p. 7.

process – one of ups and downs, of steps forward and steps back. While the luxury of hindsight affords us the opportunity of identifying 'turning points' in the process, this can be artificial and unhelpful.[44] By placing the army's attitude towards learning and innovation in a broader context, conclusions can be drawn as to the flexibility and, indeed, the continuing relevance of its ethos.

The approach taken is a thematic examination of the army's process of learning. Naturally, some self-imposed limitations have been necessary to bind such an expansive topic. First, the book is fundamentally concerned with learning in the British army (including Dominion forces). Where possible and appropriate, contrasts have been drawn with the experiences of other belligerents, including France, Germany, and Italy. The presence of these belligerents is a constant, often shaping *what* the British army learned. However, this book is primarily concerned with the *how* and the *why*. It does not purport to be a comprehensive study of the British army's relationship with its enemies and allies. A second self-imposed limitation relates to the choice of operational theatres. The book's focus on the British army's expeditionary forces precluded detailed discussion of both the Mesopotamian and East African theatres, which were primarily fought by Indian expeditionary forces.

The book is based upon research conducted in a variety of archives in the UK and abroad. The majority of sources have been drawn from the National Archives [TNA] at Kew and include, inter alia, records from the War Office, Cabinet Office, Foreign Office, and Ministry of Munitions. Examining records from a number of different government departments highlights the complexity of arrangements required to support and supply the army with knowledge, matériel, and personnel throughout its various theatres. The war diaries held in WO 95 have provided the core of this study's operational analysis. Diaries from General Headquarters [GHQ] down to battalion level have been consulted to furnish detail on the development and subsequent impact of training and integration methods. Owing to bomb damage sustained during the Second World War and official 'pruning', some records are incomplete, while others are non-existent.[45] Records from the various training schools, for instance, both on and beyond the Western Front are sparse. Fortunately, some

---

[44] For examples of these 'turning points', see Griffith, *Battle Tactics*; P. Simkins, *From the Somme to Victory: The British Army's Experience on the Western Front, 1916–1918* (Barnsley: Pen and Sword, 2014).

[45] M. Seligmann, 'Hors de Combat? The Management, Mismanagement and Mutilation of the War Office archive', *Journal of the Society for Army Historical Research* 84 (337) (2006), p. 53.

gaps can be filled by reference to duplicate files held by the Australian War Memorial.

No official could reach the top unless they were 'effective in the little private and informal conferences, committees, and interviews where the real decisions are taken'.[46] Where questions of policy were concerned, 'probably the most important work is done outside the formal committee structure by personal discussion and exchange of views'.[47] The personal testimony and correspondence of politicians, generals, officers, men, and civilian experts has, therefore, been used to supplement the official record. The well-used papers of prominent commanders provide the backbone, but some of the richest material can be found at the middle and lower levels of command: from Arthur Lynden-Bell's gossipy letters to Frederick Maurice, through Robert Anderson's resigned frustration as an Australian civilian working in military uniform, to Philip Howell's critical perspective on the difficulties of global and coalition warfare. These papers have been used to fill gaps within the official record, but also to uncover attitudes towards certain individuals or formations, the strengths and weaknesses of existing systems, or simply to gauge morale within the various forces. Often unfettered by bureaucratic protocols, these diaries and private papers provide useful details on the personality and perceived effectiveness of some individuals. Unsurprisingly, there are weaknesses to this personal testimony. Personal recollection can 'mislead or conceal as much as it reveals. Without any lies being told, information can be simply incorrect'.[48] Given the importance of social networking and the social ethos of the army, personal testimony and correspondence have proved vital to understanding how and why the army acted the way it did during the war.

Weaving together official and personal records, the book creates a tapestry that illustrates an institution in a time of change. We can take this tapestry analogy further. On the surface, the depiction is clear, ordered, and detailed. Each thread adds nuance and colour to the whole. There is a clear plan. However, turn the tapestry over and you are greeted with a different prospect: it is knotted, messy, and full of loose ends. Notwithstanding the threads used, the back of the tapestry gives no clue to the polished needlepoint on the front. However, without this messy,

---

[46] R. Lowe, 'Plumbing New Depths: Contemporary Historians and the Public Record Office', *Twentieth Century British History* 8 (2) (1997), pp. 247–248. For the strengths and weaknesses of TNA records, see A. McDonald, 'Public Records and the Modern Historian', *Twentieth Century British History* 1 (3) (1990), pp. 341–352; S. J. Ball, 'Harold Macmillan and the Politics of Defence', *Twentieth Century British History* 6 (1) (1995), pp. 78–100.
[47] Lowe, 'Plumbing New Depths', pp. 247–248.   [48] Ball, 'Harold Macmillan', p. 99.

seemingly chaotic underpinning, the tapestry would not exist. This analogy is just as applicable to the historian's craft as it is to the process of learning within the army itself.

The book is split into two main sections. Part I examines the practice of learning within the British army, teasing apart the complexities and nuances of its approach. Concerned with the conceptual underpinnings of the army's learning process, this section focuses on organisational culture, the army's strategy for learning, and its methods for learning. Chapter 1 provides necessary context to the army's First World War experience, establishing the common character or ethos of the army pre-war, which proved vital to its wartime resilience. Benchmarking the army's experience from the mid-nineteenth century onwards, the chapter considers the influence of geostrategy, nationalism, demography, as well as broader societal values on the army's twinned intellectual and social ethos.

Having established the ethos of the army, Chapters 2 and 3 add to this conceptual framework with an examination of the army's ways and means of learning, respectively. The distinction between ways and means is important, and one that has been overlooked in the current literature. This distinction can be understood as the difference between how the army learns and the methods by which it does this. Chapter 2 focuses on the 'how' question, revealing that our understanding of this process has hitherto been binary, neatly split between formal and informal. Instead, it argues for a new way of looking at learning – as a kaleidoscopic network – with the various strengths and fragilities that such a model entails. Moving away from the highly vectored language of learning prevalent in much of the literature, the chapter details the interconnected, hybrid nature of learning whether incidental, top-down, bottom-up, horizontal, or external in nature. Chapter 3 provides the final piece of this conceptual structure, analysing the means through which the army learned. The changing demography and commitments of the army demanded the use of diverse learning methods, ranging from publications to training schools to dialogue. The increasing complexity of war forced the army to grapple with increased bureaucracy when recording and disseminating learning. That the army was willing to recalibrate its approach to learning, blending different methods, demonstrates the relevance and flexibility of its ethos. However, at the heart of this chapter lies an ongoing and, for the most part, unresolved tension for the army: the need for uniformity versus the continuing importance of initiative and individual action.

Part II builds on this conceptual framework and considers the army's attempts to learn in practice. The various learning networks and inputs identified in the first part of the book are pulled through into this second half with chapters that concern themselves with the extent and efficacy of learning in a variety of different, wide-ranging contexts. Chapter 4 considers learning in an inter-theatre context, engaging with the 'global turn' in First World War studies, to show how different British expeditionary forces engaged in the learning process. It argues that the army's ability and, more importantly, its desire to learn from its experiences in different theatres was subject to certain constraints or frictions. It also exposes the potency of the army's ethos, highlighting some of the limits to the usefulness of initiative.

Chapters 5 and 6 are primarily concerned with learning from external sources. Inter-allied learning is the subject of Chapter 5, which picks up on some key themes established in previous chapters, namely the importance of the individual as a conduit for learning, the limitations of initiative, and the friction associated with knowledge generated beyond local confines. The primary focus here is the long-standing relationship between Britain and France, with reference made to the two allies' relationship with Italy and the US, respectively. The chapter demonstrates that, while a permissive environment for the exchange of ideas was encouraged by the British, inter-allied learning was often most successful at a local level, predicated on pre-existing or localised relationships between individuals. Chapter 6 focuses in depth on the army's use of civilian expertise. The relationship between civilian and combatant increasingly blurred during the war. Concentrating on the transport and engineering professions, the chapter explores the formal links, many of them with pre-war origins, which enabled the systematisation of skills acquired outside the army and their effective use within it.

While previous chapters focused on acquiring knowledge from various inputs, Chapter 7 rounds out our understanding of learning by examining how knowledge was imparted to newcomers, using the Australian Imperial Force [AIF] as its case study. We once again see the army's organisational flexibility coming to the fore through the promotion of 'self-integration'. While there was commonality in the methods used, the process was kaleidoscopic, varying between theatres, forces, and, often, formations – a theme present throughout the army's wartime learning experience.

Finally, the conclusion pulls the monograph's findings together and argues that, through a combination of its pre-war ethos and increased fluidity in wartime, the army displayed organisational and cultural flexibility, promoting informal learning and encouraging individuals to innovate. While there were instances of snobbery and resistance, common within any complex organisation, the army nurtured a culture of innovation, rather than one of inertia. Rather than promoting restrictiveness and rigidity, the army demonstrated imagination and inventiveness, acting on the experience of its allies, as well as promoting the ideas of soldier-innovators and civilian experts in order to enhance its operational effectiveness. The book concludes by suggesting the broader implications of this work on our understanding of military innovation, the British army, and other traditionally bureaucratic institutions where learning and change are concerned.

Part I

The Practice of Learning

1 The Legacy of the Past

Reflecting on pre-war British military education in mid-1916, General Sir William Robertson (Chief of the Imperial General Staff [CIGS], 1915–1918) noted that the 'situation is now better than it has ever been before and all that is needed is the use of common-sense, careful methods, and not to be too hidebound by the books we used to study before the war'.[1] Robertson's remarks provide a snapshot of the army's ethos, highlighting the importance of prioritising initiative and experience over conformity. However, the army of July 1916 was very different to the one that took the field in August 1914 and, indeed, to the one that ended the war in November 1918. At the outbreak of war, the British army was a small, professional *gendarmerie*, totalling 247,432 officers and men.[2] By the eve of the Somme, the army's establishment stood at 1,873,932 in all theatres. It was no longer a homogeneous force, but a mixture of Territorial, Kitchener's New Armies, Indian Army, and Dominion units. By the end of hostilities, the army's strength across its various expeditionary forces totalled 2,668,736 officers and men – a vast citizen force, largely conscript in nature. It would not be unreasonable to expect that the army's rapid expansion and altered composition would have had a considerable impact on the survival and relevance of any pre-war ethos. Yet it would be to deny the nature of a hierarchical bureaucracy to suggest that the structures and ideas of the decades before 1914 simply vanished at the outbreak of hostilities. This chapter provides an overview and context for the subsequent discussion of the army's ability to learn during the war, offering a preview of the army's First World War experience. What was the army's ethos in 1914? Was there more than one? What factors shaped it? How, if at all, did it survive the First World War?

---

[1] Liddell Hart Centre for Military Archives [LHCMA], Papers of Field Marshal Sir W. R. Robertson, 8/4, Robertson to Rawlinson, 26 July 1916.

[2] War Office, *Statistics of the Military Effort of the British Empire during the Great War 1914–1920* (London: HMSO, 1922), pp. 30, 62–63, 64. This figure does not include the reservists.

Ethos and Doctrine

Ethos refers to what a human group does and how it does it.[3] It can be both unspoken and overt. It is implicitly assumed in every single interaction, as well as explicitly defined in military training, regulations, routines, and practice. Rather than doctrine and the rigidity that it implies, the British army used the institutional ethos of its members to interpret the nature of war, identify problems, pose solutions, and implement change.[4] This viewpoint is contentious within the historiography of the British army, that the split between doctrine and ethos is unnecessarily complicated. Much of the debate comes down to how one defines doctrine. It has been variously defined as 'a set of beliefs about the nature of war and the keys to success on the battlefield', as the 'central idea of an army', and as 'guidance for the conduct of battle approved by the highest military authority'.[5] The nuances in these various definitions, ranging from a formal framework to a more abstract set of ideals, ensure that doctrine, particularly where the historic British army is concerned, is difficult to pin down. While some officers pre-1914 believed the army to have a doctrine in the form of *Field Service Regulations*, it was not universally recognised as such.

Historically, the army was an institution averse to doctrine. Prior to the 1989 publication *Design for Military Operations – The British Military Doctrine*, it had opted for a 'doctrine of no doctrine'. This long-standing reluctance was based on the perception that doctrine would 'prepare the army to face the wrong army at the wrong time and in the wrong place'.[6] Writing in 1912, Brigadier-General Thompson Capper posed the following: 'can we imagine a "doctrine" which will meet the ever varying conditions in which a British army, with its many degrees of organisation, composition, qualities of individuals, standards of training, [and] possible theatres of operations, may find itself?' For Capper, 'a doctrine of procedure, of necessity, leads to one type and one system'. Adherence to a single doctrine that 'attempts to apply itself to every possible and

---

[3] A. King, 'The Ethos of the Royal Marines: The Precise Application of Will', Report Commissioned by the Royal Marines, 2004, https://ore.exeter.ac.uk/repository/bitstream/handle/10036/58653/RMethos4.pdf, p. 2.

[4] D. French, *Raising Churchill's Army: The British Army and the War against Germany 1919–1945* (Oxford: Oxford University Press, 2000), pp. 21–22, 50; Palazzo, *Moltke to Bin Laden*.

[5] J. Snyder, *The Ideology of the Offensive: Military Decision Making and the Disasters of 1914* (Ithaca, NY: Cornell University Press, 1984), p. 27; J. F. C. Fuller, *The Foundations of the Science of War* (London: Hutchinson, 1926), p. 254; T. T. Lupfer, *The Dynamics of Doctrine: The Changes in German Tactical Doctrine during the First World War* (Fort Leavenworth, KS: Combat Studies Institute, 1981), vii.

[6] H. Høiback, 'What Is Doctrine?', *Journal of Strategic Studies* 24 (6) (2011), p. 890.

universal requirement' was dangerous.[7] For the inter-war military theo-rist J. F. C. Fuller, doctrine could lead to dogma. It could be 'seized upon by mental emasculates who lack virility of judgment, and who are only too grateful to rest assured that their actions, however inept, find justi-fication in a book'.[8] Unlike its continental neighbours, the British army could not predict where it might next be deployed with any degree of certainty. While realising that certain principles needed to be articulated in print, it did not promote a formal doctrine, relying instead on its ethos or 'common character' for unity. Rather than an example of entrenched anti-intellectualism, the army's lack of doctrine was something of a delib-erate policy decision.[9] Ethos provided an alternative, equivalent struc-ture for the decision-making process. Based on the cultural values of the nation and the army, this ethos was institutionalised within the officer corps, its continuation assured by the use of mechanisms such as the regimental tradition to pass it on to the next generation.[10]

Given its link to national and cultural values, it is tempting to equate ethos with tradition. However, to do this implies that ethos is inflexible and intolerant of change. This particular viewpoint resonates with out-dated ideas around military conservatism: that an army's ethos, or its cul-tural construct, may act as a brake on innovation.[11] Existing procedures can become routine, even ritualised, and lose touch with their original purpose. Given the military's veneration of tradition, this can become a self-reinforcing cycle.[12] Yet this view is predicated on the belief that ethos is static. In the case of the pre-1914 British army, while influenced by past conflicts and national identity, ethos was not so rigidly inflexible. Rather, it provided the army with the ability to adequately examine new ideas and situations. In short, it enabled the army to respond fully to the need for adaptation and innovation.[13]

On the outbreak of the First World War, the army's ethos focused on a preference for amateurism, a distaste for prescription, and an emphasis on the character of the individual. It was shaped and propagated by a

[7] LHCMA, Papers of Brigadier-General T. Capper, 2/4/20, Draft of 'The Doctrine of a "Doctrine"', n.d. (c. 1912), pp. 3, 5, 9.
[8] Fuller, *Foundations*, p. 254.
[9] T. Travers, *The Killing Ground: The British Army, the Western Front, and the Emergence of Modern War 1900–1918* (reprint, Barnsley: Pen and Sword, 2003 [1987]), p. 38; Palazzo, *Seeking Victory*, pp. 8–19.
[10] Palazzo, *Seeking Victory*, p. 10.
[11] T. G. Farrell, 'The Dynamics of British Military Transformation', *International Affairs* 84 (4) (2008), p. 783.
[12] P. H. Wilson, 'Defining Military Culture', *Journal of Military History* 72 (2008), pp. 31–32.
[13] Palazzo, *Seeking Victory*, p. 17.

number of different factors, including, inter alia, perceptions of national character, geostrategic policies, military initiatives, and the social make-up of the officer corps. The influence of these factors would result in the endurance of this ethos during the First World War.

Britain's National Character

Writing in 1911, Major Ladislaus Pope-Hennessy, a regular officer and an advocate for 'definite doctrine', remarked that 'the character of a nation is woven closely into the texture of a national conception of war'.[14] Armed forces reflect, like a time capsule, the values, beliefs, and social order of the society from which they spring.[15] Naturally, the army's ethos reflected some of the broader characteristics and self-perceptions of what it meant to be British. Questions around national character, 'nation-ness', 'Britishness', and the increasing popularity of 'Four Nations' history have generated considerable debate in recent years.[16] For our purposes, it is sufficient to appreciate that the term *nation* refers to more than an institution or space. It expresses a sense of belonging reaffirmed by the values or practices of the community and rests in the hearts, minds, and activities of its members.[17] Regardless of inequalities that prevail, the nation is conceived of as a 'deep, horizontal comradeship'. This 'imagined community' is constituted, in part, by discourses of national identity.[18] These discourses are stories that all nations tell themselves: stories about the nation's origins, its struggles, its triumphs, its character, its values, and its past.[19] It is unsurprising, then, that these national discourses shaped the culture and mentality of the army itself.

Since the eighteenth century, the British had defined their own national identity by contrasting themselves with their continental

---

[14] L. H. R. Pope-Hennessy, 'The British Army and Modern Conceptions of War', *Edinburgh Review* 213 (436) (1911), p. 332.

[15] G. Sloan, 'Haldane's Mackindergarten: A Radical Experiment in British Military Education?', *War in History* 19 (3) (2012), p. 328.

[16] See e.g. R. Colls and P. Dodd (eds), *Englishness: Politics and Culture 1880–1920* (London: Croom Helm, 1986); R. Samuel (ed.), *Patriotism: The Making and Unmaking of British National Identity* (3 vols, Abingdon: Routledge, 1989); L. Colley, *Britons: Forging the Nation 1707–1837* (London: Pimlico, 2003 [1992]); P. Mandler, *The English National Character: The History of an Idea from Edmund Burke to Tony Blair* (New Haven, CT: Yale University Press, 2006).

[17] E. Amenta, K. Nash, and A. Scott, *The Wiley-Blackwell Companion to Political Sociology* (Oxford: Wiley-Blackwell, 2012), pp. 277–278.

[18] B. Anderson, *Imagined Communities: Reflections on the Origins and Spread of Nationalism* (new edn, London: Verso, 2006 [1983]), p. 7.

[19] J. Hogan, 'Genderised and Racialised Discourses of National Identity in Baz Luhrman's "Australia"', *Journal of Australian Studies* 34 (1) (2010), p. 63.

neighbours, particularly France and Germany. British national identity was an 'invention forged above all by war'. The succession of wars
against France brought Britons into confrontation with a hostile 'other',
encouraging them to define themselves collectively against it.[20] To the
British, France represented cosmopolitanism, artificiality, and intellectual deviousness. In contrast, the British saw themselves as bluff,
forthright, and morally serious.[21] Such differences manifested themselves in the contrasting philosophies of the French Rationalist René
Descartes and the Scottish Empiricist David Hume. They were also
realised through Britain's dominant liberal political culture that emphasised the right of the individual to live his or her life with the mini-
mum of state interference and to take responsibility for his or her own
well-being.[22]

These self-perceptions leached into the Victorian period. Unlike their
continental neighbours, the British perceived that actions were not to
be governed by abstract reason. Instead, character was thought to be
more important than intelligence, while improvisation was considered a
great benefit to the nation.[23] Character was a central feature of Victorian political thought, particularly during the mid-nineteenth century. It
was usually concerned with the idea of an isolated individual maintaining his will in the face of adversity.[24] Such adversity was often cast as
military or sporting in nature. From the 1830s onwards, the rise in the
popularity of organised games was well under way. Cricket, for example, was a 'national symbol' for the Victorians because it was 'unsullied
by oriental or European influences'. British character in the Victorian
and Edwardian periods could be typified by the phrase 'it's not cricket'.
Loaded and emotive, this phrase was used to denote any act that was
'immoral, ungentlemanly, or improper'; essentially, any act deemed to
be 'un-British'.[25]

Tied to the rise of organised sports were concepts such as the
'Corinthian Spirit' and the 'Gentleman Amateur', along with the ideologies of athleticism and Muscular Christianity. This latter ideology
considered that participation in sport could contribute to the development of Christian morality, physical fitness, and manliness. However,

---

[20] Colley, *Britons*, p. 5.   [21] Ibid., p. 252.
[22] French, *Raising Churchill's Army*, p. 21; W. Funnell, 'Social Reform, Military Accounting and the Pursuit of Economy during the Liberal Apotheosis, 1906–1912', *Accounting
History Review* 21 (1) (2011), p. 72.
[23] French, *Raising Churchill's Army*, p. 21.
[24] S. Collini, 'The Idea of "Character" in Victorian Political Thought', *Transactions of the
Royal Historical Society* 35 (1985), pp. 33, 47.
[25] K. A. P. Sandiford, 'Cricket and the Victorian Society', *Journal of Social History* 17 (2)
(1983), p. 303.

manliness was not simply the outward display of physical strength; it also signified duty and moral courage and, for some commentators, was intrinsically linked to imperial preservation and expansion.[26] These ideologies nurtured the 'mind-set of the Empire's ruling elites'.[27] The physical and moral value of sport in the public consciousness was promoted by the public school system, idealised by Thomas Hughes in his Tom Brown books. For Hughes, sport was designed 'to try the muscles of men's bodies, and the endurance of their hearts, to make them rejoice in their strength'.[28] In the final cricket match in *Tom Brown's School Days*, for example, the eponymous hero discussed the benefits of the game with his friend George Arthur and one of the masters:

'. . . But it's more than a game. It's an institution', said Tom.
    'Yes', said Arthur, 'the birthright of British boys old and young, as *habeas corpus* and trial by jury are of British men'.
    'The discipline and reliance on one another which it teaches is so valuable, I think', went on the master, 'it ought to be such an unselfish game. It merges the individual in the eleven; he doesn't play that he may win, but that his side may'.[29]

The pre-eminence of organised games, particularly in the public schools, also gave rise to the belief that sport and war were in some sense comparable endeavours.[30] Sport was war without the adversity, while war was simply the 'greater game' as immortalised in the second verse of Sir Henry Newbolt's poem 'Vitaï Lampada':

The sand of the desert is sodden red, –
Red with the wreck of a square that broke: –
The Gatling's jammed, and the Colonel's dead,
And the regiment blind with dust and smoke.
The river of death has brimmed his banks,
And England's far, and Honour's a name,
But the voice of a schoolboy rallies the ranks:
'Play up! play up! and play the game!'

---

[26] See e.g. P. McDevitt, 'The King of Sports: Polo in Late Victorian and Edwardian India', *International Journal of the History of Sport* [hereafter *IJHS*] 20 (1) (2003), pp. 1–27; J. A. Mangan and C. McKenzie, 'Martial Conditioning, Military Exemplars and Moral Certainties: Imperial Hunting as Preparation for War', *IJHS* 25 (9) (2008), pp. 1132–1167.

[27] M. Huggins, *The Victorians and Sport* (London: Palgrave Macmillan, 2004), p. 221.

[28] T. Hughes, *Tom Brown's School Days* (London: Macmillan, 1900 [1857]), p. 33.

[29] Ibid., p. 289.

[30] T. Mason and E. Riedi, *Sport and the Military: The British Armed Forces, 1880–1960* (Cambridge: Cambridge University Press, 2010), pp. 3–4. For an opposing view, see W. Vamplew, 'Exploding the Myths of Sport and the Great War: A First Salvo', *IJHS* 31 (18) (2014), pp. 2297–2312.

The values of teamwork and self-reliance, of concentration and courage, of obedience and initiative, were presented as essentially compatible.[31] As we shall see, this was often far from the case, particularly where the latter pairing was concerned. During the First World War, individuals like the newspaper magnate Lord Northcliffe used the British predilection for organised sports as propaganda to explain why the British were superior to their German adversary. According to Northcliffe:

> Our soldiers are individual. They embark on little individual enterprises. The German . . . is not so clever at these devices. He was never taught them before the war, and his whole training from childhood upwards has been to obey, and to obey in numbers. He has not played individual games. Football, which develops individuality, has only recently been introduced into Germany in comparatively recent times. His amusements have been gymnastic discipline to the word of command.[32]

Unlike the perceived German 'gymnastic discipline' to command, the British were seen to be devoted to 'amateurishness'.[33] For some outsiders, this tendency towards 'muddling through' was an intriguing and very British phenomenon. One American literary critic noted in 1904 that the glorification of amateur qualities 'is all the more curious because of our pronounced national distaste for ineffectiveness. The undisguisedly amateurish traits of unskillfulness and desultoriness have not been popular here'.[34] Britain's Boer War bungling in autumn 1900 led to the 'nation of shopkeepers' being described as the 'nation of amateurs'. It marked the point where the nation's way of business began to be described as 'muddling through' – a more critical observation than it would become after the First World War.[35]

For the army, its poor performance during the Boer War resulted in reform and soul searching. For some, its failings signified the need to embrace a formal doctrine. However, this need was tempered by the pre-eminence of the regular soldier's character and, as we shall see, Britain's geostrategic realities. That the army did not develop a formal doctrine following the Boer War was not a case of amateurism winning out over professionalism. The army's re-emphasis on values such as

---

[31] Collini, 'Idea of "Character"', p. 49.
[32] A. C. W. Harmsworth (1st Viscount Northcliffe), *Lord Northcliffe's War Book* (New York: George H. Doran, 1917), p. 86.
[33] T. W. Heyck, 'Myths and Meanings of Intellectuals in Twentieth-Century British National Identity', *Journal of British Studies* 37 (2) (1998), p. 199; R. Scruton, *England: An Elegy* (London: Pimlico, 2001), pp. 57–59.
[34] B. Perry, *The Amateur Spirit* (Boston: Houghton Mifflin, 1915 [1904]), p. 18.
[35] Mandler, *English National Character*, p. 138.

initiative, common sense, instinct, and determination provided a framework that better suited its myriad commitments. Flexibility was the army's watchword, particularly given the tension between its myriad roles in India and across the colonies.

Britain's Geostrategic Considerations

Unlike its continental neighbours, the British army had to be prepared for deployments across the globe. It had to envisage numerous different roles against different enemies in diverse geographical and cultural environments throughout its global empire.[36] The proceedings of the 1911 General Staff conference neatly summed up the implications this uncertainty had for the army:

> We must remember that our officers must be prepared to fight in every country on the globe. Arrangements that are desirable in England, or even on the continent of Europe, will be very different from those which will be necessary in South Africa, or on the North Western Frontier of India.[37]

As a result, successive governments had failed to provide a clear statement of what they saw as the army's priorities. In fact, the 1888 Stanhope Memorandum provided the most recent outline of the army's responsibilities. On that occasion, aid to the civil power in the UK was placed first, while the employment of an expeditionary force on the continent occupied last place. At the time, such an ordering made political and military sense. Fenian activities and agitation were still a threat to the safety of the nation with attacks on the mainland a regular occurrence from 1881 to 1885.[38] According to William Robertson, however, this focus on aid to the civil power meant that 'mobilisation plans dealt principally with home defence, and that broad military plans essential for the defence of the Empire as a whole received no adequate treatment'.[39] The growing difficulties of using the army against Russia anywhere but the Indian Frontier and the size of the French and German armies suggested that provision of an expeditionary force for the continent was increasingly unnecessary. The tension in military policy during this period became one between those who wished to prepare for relatively minor operations against enemy colonies and those who fixated on the North West Frontier. Yet, British military thought during this period

---

[36] Palazzo, *Moltke to Bin Laden*, p. 24.
[37] TNA, WO 279/42, General Staff officers conference, 9–12 January 1911, p. 7.
[38] I. F. W. Beckett, *Victorians at War* (London: Hambledon Press, 2003), pp. 153–154.
[39] W. R. Robertson, *From Private to Field Marshal* (London: Constable, 1921), p. 92.

soon took on an increasingly continental aspect owing to the defence of India against Russian encroachment.[40]

Its multiple commitments meant that the army was loth to privilege one set of priorities over another. It also appeared reluctant to apply the experiences drawn from its nineteenth-century small wars to a larger conflict against a major continental power. General Sir Frederick Roberts's troops, for instance, had gained considerable experience in hill warfare against Afghan irregulars in 1878–1880. However, many officers who took part in the Second Afghan War were cautious about applying the experiences of that campaign to the quite different circumstances they might encounter if confronting a regular Russian army across the same terrain.[41]

The tensions between colonial and continental modes of thought underscored the complexities of military opinion in the late nineteenth century. Three main schools underpinned this complexity: the 'continentalists', whose position was defined by their conviction that the army should prepare for European war; the 'traditionalists' who demonstrated a 'profound antagonism' towards the Cardwell reforms; and finally, the 'imperial school', distinguished by their appreciation of the significance of colonial warfare.[42] Continentalists such as Colonel Lonsdale Hale, for example, observed that:

An officer who has seen service must sweep from his mind all recollections of that service, for between Afghan, Egyptian, or Zulu warfare and that of Europe, there is no similarity whatever. To the latter the former is merely the play of children.[43]

For Hale, the German official account of the Franco-Prussian War 'should be studied page by page, paragraph by paragraph, line by line', on the basis that continental war against a European power was a fundamentally different endeavour to imperial policing.[44] Germany was held up as an inspiration in this regard. Captain Frederick Maude, a fellow continentalist, believed the German Army 'to be the most perfect engine of war every yet put together'. For those officers so minded, Britain's

---

[40] J. Gooch, 'The Weary Titan: Strategy and Policy in Great Britain, 1890–1918', in W. Murray, M. Knox, and A. Bernstein (eds), *The Making of Strategy: Rulers, States, and War* (Cambridge: Cambridge University Press, 1994), pp. 287–289.

[41] D. French, *Military Identities: The Regimental System, the British Army, and the British People, c. 1870–2000* (Oxford: Oxford University Press, 2005), p. 65.

[42] H. Bailes, 'Patterns of Military Thought in the Late Victorian Army', *Journal of Strategic Studies* 4 (1) (1981), pp. 29–45.

[43] Quoted in E. Spiers, *The Late Victorian Army, 1868–1902* (Manchester: Manchester University Press, 1992), p. 246.

[44] Bailes, 'Military Thought', p. 30.

small wars were often the 'worst possible experiences' for the army, as they made 'us think we have reached a high pitch of excellence, when as a matter of fact, we are far from it'.

While following continental developments with interest, the 'imperialists' were primarily concerned with the organisation and training required for imperial defence. This concern often manifested itself in nationalistic grandstanding against the perceived excessive advocacy of German practices. G. F. R. Henderson remarked that 'we have no need to ask another nation to teach us to fight', while Major-General Sir Henry Brackenbury suggested that Britain no longer draw from the 'poisonous wells of French military history'. Colonel H. H. Knollys, editor of the *United Services Magazine* and a noted reformer, thought that Britain's imperial experience was of 'more immediate and practical use' than that associated with continental warfare: 'regular warfare is with us exceptional, while a campaign against a [*sic*] uncivilized foe in some parts of the world may be considered chronic'.[45] However, the variety of these colonial campaigns and their small scale tended to leave little mark on the army as a whole.[46] Despite vigorous discussion around appropriate colonial tactics, it had little appreciable impact on official training in Britain or India. Even dispersed infantry tactics, learned from the Tirah Expedition, were largely overlooked by the military authorities.[47] For the British army outside of India, there was a tendency to refocus on the continental lessons of Plevna or Gravelotte, rather than those of the Tirah. This tendency cast a long shadow: it was by no means limited to the pre-war army.

The sheer diversity of conditions meant that tactics required for one war could be markedly different for the next. General Sir Neville Lyttelton, the first Chief of the General Staff [CGS], remarked that

Few people have seen two battles in succession in such startling contrast as Omdurman and Colenso. In the first, 50,000 fanatics streamed across the open regardless of cover to certain death, while at Colenso I never saw a Boer all day until the battle was over, and it was our men who were the victims.[48]

The army had to be flexible, yet this often led to an incomplete and far from uniform approach to waging war. Many of the initial lessons

---

[45] Quoted in T. R. Moreman, *The Army in India and the Development of Frontier Warfare, 1849–1947* (London: Palgrave, 1998), p. 41.

[46] S. Jones, *From Boer War to World War: Tactical Reform of the British Army, 1902–1914* (Norman: University of Oklahoma Press, 2012), pp. 20–21.

[47] T. R. Moreman, 'The British and Indian Armies and North-West Frontier Warfare, 1849–1914', *Journal of Imperial and Commonwealth History* 20 (1) (1992), pp. 58–59.

[48] N. Lyttelton, *Eighty Years: Soldiering, Politics, Games* (London: Hodder and Stoughton, 1927), p. 212.

learned fighting Pathan tribesmen or irregulars in the hill warfare of the North West Frontier were not readily available or circulated to regular Indian or British formations.[49] Charles Callwell, author of *Small Wars*, went further, suggesting there was an official 'conspiracy of silence' regarding mountain warfare tactics.[50] In a less conspiratorial vein, the duration of service aboard, particularly for those in India, often made the transfer of experiences at lower levels far more difficult. Regardless, the resulting lack of uniformity from the army's myriad commitments led to a highly personalised approach to operations. Those units which had served on the North West Frontier, for example, focused on the individual soldier's initiative and marksmanship, placing a premium on fighting in open order. General Sir Ian Hamilton's successful attack at Elandslaagte in 1899 involved infantry in open-order formation, a flanking manoeuvre, and cavalry.[51] A veteran of the North West Frontier, Hamilton recognised some of the similarities between Boers and Afghans. In contrast, while not an exact science, some units or commanders who had experienced warfare in the Sudan against the Mahdi's forces often continued to rely on close order, volley firing, and the bayonet.[52] Major-General Arthur Fitzroy Hart, a veteran of the Zulu and Sudan wars, typified this approach at Colenso in 1899. Unlike Hamilton, Hart advanced his 5th Brigade in close order quarter columns up to the Boer lines with disastrous results. As the examples of Hamilton and Fitzroy Hart show, the army's support for personalisation could cut both ways.

Establishment of the General Staff

The army's conflicting geostrategic priorities were further compounded by organisational initiatives, such as the establishment of the General Staff in 1906, which served to reinforce rather than curb the army's initiative-driven ethos. Its limitations were partly due to initially ineffective leadership by its first chief, Lyttelton, and its own confused raison d'être. Unlike the German General Staff, the British General Staff lacked power, status, and the controlling influence over the army itself. Germany had a 'capital General Staff' – an institution whose intellectual

---

[49] Moreman, 'British and Indian Armies', p. 42.

[50] C. Callwell and J. Headlam, *History of the Royal Artillery from the Indian Mutiny to the Great War*, I (3 vols, Woolwich: Royal Artillery Institute, 1931), p. 266.

[51] M. Ford, 'The British Army and the Politics of Rifle Development, 1880 to 1986', Unpublished PhD thesis, University of London, 2008, pp. 30, 89–90.

[52] M. A. Ramsey, *Command and Cohesion: The Citizen Soldier and Minor Tactics in the British Army, 1870–1918* (Westport, CT: Praeger, 2002), p. 92.

coherence created an institutional and politically independent entity.[53] Britain did not. The question of whether the army should adopt a German model General Staff was an important consideration throughout the late Victorian era. In 1887, Henry Brackenbury lamented that 'want of any such great central thinking department is due to that want of economy and efficiency which to a certain extent exists in our army'.[54] The Hartington Commission in 1889–1890 had called for the establishment of a chief of staff, but this was rejected for a number of reasons, including financial implications, Liberal opposition, and fear that a General Staff might engender Prussian militarism. In line with the differences in military opinion, there was also concern that a General Staff would prepare for continental war, rather than respond to imperial crises.[55] Published on the same day as the Hartington Commission's report, Spenser Wilkinson's *The Brain of an Army* was vocal in its call for a General Staff. For Wilkinson, the commission's proposals did not go far enough. He feared that a chief of staff would be given 'no authority over the army', merely the 'general power to meddle'.[56] When the General Staff was finally instituted, it was structured along different lines to the German model. The Chief of the General Staff was *primus inter pares* with the Adjutant-General, Quartermaster-General, and the Army Council: he neither inherited nor acquired the same authority that Commanders-in-Chief had enjoyed in the past. Wilkinson's earlier fears proved to be correct.

The eventual establishment of the General Staff suggested a growing professionalism within the army. However, the General Staff lacked a clear remit and a clear direction. Even had it wanted to, the army was unable to model its General Staff on the German system, and therein lies the rub: the British General Staff was not a dominant institution like its German counterpart. Furthermore, despite calls from Wilkinson and Brackenbury, it was neither able nor designed to serve as the brain of the army and lacked the power to develop and enforce doctrine. Underpinning the differences between the two General Staffs were the geostrategic realities of each country. Germany's strategic problem was

---

[53] H. Strachan, 'The British Army, Its General Staff and the Continental Commitment, 1904–1914', in D. French and B. Holden Reid (eds), *The British General Staff: Reform and Innovation c. 1890–1939* (London: Frank Cass, 2002), p. 86.

[54] S. Wilkinson, *The Brain of an Army* (2nd edn, London: Archibald Constable, 1895), p. 39.

[55] H. Kochanski, 'Planning for War in the Final Years of Pax Britannica, 1889–1903', in French and Holden Reid (eds), *The British General Staff*, pp. 11, 12.

[56] J. Luvaas, *The Education of an Army: British Military Thought, 1815–1940* (London: Cassell, 1965), pp. 261–262.

relatively clear-cut: it had to defend its eastern and western frontiers.[57] In Britain's case, the sheer number of scenarios it might face, given its hugely diffuse empire, precluded any simple, narrow definition of purpose and aim.[58] The General Staff was in a lose-lose situation. First, it had been formed when the possibility of war against France was still on the horizon. Within eighteen months of the Esher Committee, war with Germany was the more likely scenario. Secondly, even if it had been better conceived, it was unlikely to have been able to solve the inherent continental-colonial tensions, which proved increasingly difficult to negotiate.

Further undermining the General Staff's influence was the army's lack of scale and political visibility, particularly when compared to the Royal Navy. Successive governments demonstrated an increasing unwillingness to spend the same level of money on the army as the Royal Navy. As First Sea Lord, Admiral Sir John 'Jacky' Fisher lamented that 'every penny spent on the army is a penny taken from the Navy'. This unwillingness to spend was also underpinned by traditional liberal distrust of the army, as well as the Liberal party's commitment to social reforms at the expense of military spending. Without a clear role, the General Staff was far removed from Wilkinson's original conception: that it can only 'perform its functions . . . in connection with a body adapted to its control, and united with it by the ramifications of a nervous system'.[59] From the beginning, the General Staff fought for acceptance within an army that prioritised individual initiative and ultimately sought a universal, rather than a purely continental, approach to war.

Field Service Regulations (1909)

The army's lack of common strategic purpose, coupled with the embryonic nature of its General Staff, precluded the development of a clear doctrine. As we have seen, the production of an over-specific doctrine was considered by many to be a positive danger. Instead, the army stressed pragmatism and flexibility, rather than formalism and rigidity. It was against this backdrop that *Field Service Regulations* [FSR] (1909) was formulated. *FSR* has been held up by some to be a work 'of the greatest value for the inculcation of one central doctrine'.[60] For one

---

[57] Strachan, 'Continental Commitment', p. 86.
[58] T. Bowman and M. Connelly, *The Edwardian Army: Recruiting, Training, and Deploying the British Army, 1902–1914* (Oxford: Oxford University Press, 2012), pp. 65–66.
[59] Wilkinson, *Brain of an Army*, p. 97.
[60] J. Dunlop, *The Development of the British Army, 1899–1914* (London: Methuen, 1938), pp. 291–292.

captain, it was 'the Bible of the Army'.[61] Whether *FSR* can or should be perceived as formal or semi-formal doctrine, it was designed as a loose conceptual framework, adaptable to any of the situations that the army might find itself.[62]

Prior to 1909, the army began to move from an organisation focused on drill and obedience to one that stressed initiative. Guided by Jominist principles and following the army's poor performance during the Boer War, the training manuals produced from 1902 onwards pushed for greater initiative and less rigidity. This did not alleviate the difficulties of balancing initiative and control, however. The preface to *Combined Training* (1902), the army's first 'modern all-arms manual', stressed that the principles within 'have been evolved by experience as generally applicable to the leading of troops in war'. Such principles were to 'be regarded as pointing out the dangers involved rather than as precepts to be blindly obeyed'.[63] These publications emphasised thought, principles, and cooperation, but they were not prescriptive in nature.[64] *Infantry Training* (1905), for example, stated that it was 'impossible to lay down a fixed and unvarying section of attack or defence . . . It is therefore strictly forbidden either to formulate or to practise a normal form of either attack or defence'.[65]

The reluctance to embrace one single, authoritative doctrine was reinforced by the publication of *FSR* in 1909. The document was split into two parts: Part I [*FSR1*] dealt with operations, while Part II [*FSR2*] focused on organisation and administration. Both parts of *FSR* emphasised flexibility and initiative, providing a documented snapshot of the army's ethos prior to the First World War. This flexibility proved a double-edged sword: it privileged individual action, whilst allowing for a proliferation of different methods that undermined unity of purpose and effort.

FSR1 did not provide a uniform doctrine. The introduction spoke of principles rather than prescription, but such principles 'should be so thoroughly impressed on the mind of every commander that, whenever he has to come to a decision in the field, he instinctively gives them

[61] R. H. Beadon, 'The Business Man and the Army', *Journal of the Royal United Services Institute* [hereafter *JRUSI*] 62 (1917), p. 288.

[62] A. Simpson, 'Launcelot Kiggell and Herbert Lawrence', in D. T. Zabecki (ed.), *Chief of Staff: Napoleonic Wars to World War I*, I (2 vols, Annapolis, MD: Naval Institute Press, 2008), p. 201.

[63] War Office, *Combined Training (Provisional)* (London: HMSO, 1902), pp. 3–4.

[64] N. Evans, 'From Drill to Doctrine: Forging the British Army's Tactics 1897–1909', Unpublished PhD thesis, University of London, 2007, p. 316.

[65] War Office, *Infantry Training* (London: HMSO, 1905), p. 123; Jones, *Boer War to World War*, p. 52.

their full weight'.[66] The focus here was on instinct and initiative. This was explored further in *FSR1*'s second chapter, 'Inter-Communication and Orders', which stressed the flexibility, individuality, and freedom afforded to junior commanders. It advised that

> an operational order ... should tell him nothing which he can and should arrange for himself. The general principle is that the object to be attained ... should be briefly but clearly stated; while the method of attaining the object should be left to the utmost extent to the recipient, with due regard to his personal characteristics ... It is usually dangerous to prescribe to a subordinate at a distance of anything that he should be better able to decide on the spot, with a fuller knowledge of local conditions, for any attempt to do so may cramp his initiative.[67]

It was clear that the army understood the importance of decentralised command, at least on paper. However, the discussion lacked specifics. How would this decentralisation actually work on the battlefield? At what level of command could subordinates sensibly exercise initiative?[68] Such questions were left unanswered. Sections on all-arms cooperation, the principles of envelopment, and planning an offensive were presented in a clear and tangible manner, yet some contemporaries expressed concern at their content.[69] At the 1910 General Staff conference, Colonel William Bridges, then commandant at Australia's Royal Military College at Duntroon, argued that 'Field Service Regulations ... have become more abstract with each edition, that is to say, they lay down principles but the application is concrete; illustrations of their application are omitted'.[70] Other commentators, such as Brigadier-General Launcelot Kiggell, were strongly opposed to any additional prescription. Defending *FSR1* against Bridges's criticism, Kiggell reaffirmed that 'the problems of war cannot be solved by rules, but by judgement based on a knowledge of general principles'. To lay down rules would 'tend to cramp judgement, not to educate and strength it. For that reason our manuals aim at giving principles but avoiding laying down methods'.[71] Kiggell's view was shared by Capper who thought *FSR1* an 'excellent and sufficient

---

[66] General Staff, *Field Service Regulations Part 1* (London: HMSO, 1909), p. 13.

[67] Ibid., p. 27.

[68] Problems relating to initiative were not limited to the army. For similar concerns in the Royal Navy, see A. Gordon, *The Rules of the Game: Jutland and British Naval Command* (London: John Murray, 2005 [1996]), pp. 155–192, 593–595.

[69] General Staff, *Field Service Regulations*, pp. 14, 129–130, 22–23; S. B. T. Mitchell, 'An Inter-Disciplinary Study of Learning in the 32nd Division on the Western Front, 1916–1918', Unpublished PhD Thesis, University of Birmingham, 2013, pp. 41–43.

[70] TNA, WO 279/496, General Staff officers conference, 17–20 January 1910, pp. 53–54.

[71] TNA, WO 279/48, General Staff officers conference, 13–16 January 1913, p. 17.

guide'. They 'describe . . . which method may *probably* be found generally most suitable . . . and they provide clear and simple principles for the application of *any* method'.[72]

Although *FSR* was formulated against the backdrop of colonial warfare, it was intended for use in all situations, including operations against a major power on the continent.[73] Indeed, the army's decision to produce its own regulations could be seen as an attempt to emulate equivalent continental publications.[74] At the 1913 General Staff conference, Colonel James Edmonds recalled that the army's first *Field Service Manual* was derived from the German Army's *Felddienstordnung* and translated 'with artistic merit' for British use.[75] Certainly, for Field Marshal Sir Douglas Haig, *FSR* was designed for the eventuality of a major continental war.[76] As Director of Military Training and then Director of Staff Duties, Haig was one of the key architects of *FSR*. In his final despatch in 1919, he stood by its applicability, noting that 'the principles of command, Staff work and organisation elaborated before the war have stood the test imposed upon them and are sound'. He went on to state that, although 'some modification of existing ideas and practice will be necessary . . . if our principles are sound these will be few and unimportant'.[77] This was a view promoted at the highest levels of command. A May 1917 memorandum reminded each Army that 'the pre-war manuals remain in force and that the instructions issued by General Headquarters [GHQ] are merely amplifications'.[78] By that logic, it is reasonable to assert that *FSR1* was applicable throughout the war because it was intended to be employed in conjunction with other manuals.[79] *FSR1*'s inherent flexibility was both a strength and a weakness. With its mantra of deference to the man on the spot, it encouraged individual initiative, but, conversely, its lack of guidance resulted in a proliferation of different interpretations and tactical methods.

Whilst pre-war discussion of *FSR1* generated considerable heat, with debates occurring both inside and outside the military institution, the regulations remained unchanged throughout the First World War. This

---

[72] LHCMA, Papers of General Sir J. S. M. Shea, 2/5, Draft of Brigadier-General Thompson Capper 'The Doctrine of a "Doctrine"', n.d. (c. 1912), p. 6. Original emphasis.
[73] See Simpson, *Directing Operations*, pp. 18–20.
[74] The French army's revised *Règlement de Manoeuvre d'Infanterie* was published in 1904, whilst the German Army's updated *Felddienstordnung* appeared in 1908.
[75] TNA, WO 279/48, General Staff officers conference, 13–16 January 1913, p. 15.
[76] Strachan, 'Continental Commitment', p. 92.
[77] J. H. Boraston (ed.), *Sir Douglas Haig's Despatches (December 1915 – April 1919)* (London: J. M. Dent, 1919), pp. 343–344.
[78] Australian War Memorial [AWM], AWM25 947/76, Infantry Training – France 1917, Butler to GOCs Armies, 6 May 1917.
[79] Simpson, *Directing Operations*, p. 20.

was not true of *FSR2*, which underwent revision in 1917 in response to 'the overwhelming mass of evidence . . . as to the importance of engineering in war'.[80] Much like Part I, *FSR2* adhered to the need for principles over prescription. The opening chapter highlighted the potential diversity of operational conditions, which made it 'impossible to design . . . a system of organisation applicable, without modification, to every campaign'. However, 'although the strength and composition of the forces . . . must vary . . . the general principles which govern the organisation remain practically the same'.[81] While the 'inherent simplicity' of *FSR2* was a strength, it also led to 'a number of problems' with the plans for administering the army in wartime.[82]

Prior to the outbreak of the Boer War, the only regulations relating to organisation and administration were contained in the obsolete 'Regulations for the Lines of Communication of an army in the field' and in the *King's Regulations*.[83] Given the problems of administration during the Boer War, there was a desire to produce a set of regulations that ensured this debacle would not be repeated.[84] *FSR2* was designed as much to inform individuals of the chain of command as it was to advise on the wartime administration of the army, yet the chain of command and the various responsibilities were inherently problematic.

There was much soul searching in the years leading up to 1914 on administrative responsibility, particularly between the Inspector-General of Communications [IGC] and the Quartermaster-General [QMG] in the field.[85] Various memoranda flew about Whitehall in an attempt to delineate and make sense of this dual responsibility. It was not until the 1914 General Staff conference that the debate came to a head. Major-General Edward Altham, who became IGC to the Mediterranean Expeditionary Force [MEF] in 1915, criticised the administrative arrangements found in *FSR2*, delivering two stinging rebuffs to the conference: first, that there was 'no real strategical *raison d'être*' to *FSR2*'s administrative system, and secondly, that the British army would do well to look to the French army for 'administrative efficiency'. Unsurprisingly, his comments came under fire. One commentator warned the conference that Altham's criticisms and accompanying suggestions 'practically strikes as the root of the *Field Service Regulations* – they would have to be scrapped if his suggestions were adopted'. There was a reluctance to amend *FSR2*

---

[80] See TNA, WO 32/4802, Duties of Engineers-in-Chief and Chief Engineers: Amendments to Field Service Regulations, 1916–1917, p. 2.
[81] General Staff, *Field Service Regulations Part 2* (London: HMSO, 1909), p. 23.
[82] Brown, *British Logistics*, p. 44.
[83] TNA, WO 279/18, General Staff officers conference, 7–10 January 1908, p. 26.
[84] Ibid., p. 27.
[85] TNA, WO 32/4735, Incidence of Administrative Responsibility in the Field, Joint Memorandum, 28 January 1908.

in any meaningful way. Field Marshal Sir John French (CIGS, 1912–1914) remained unconvinced that 'any change in the Regulations is necessary', but diplomatically resolved that the question would receive 'careful consideration'.[86] Such careful consideration was little more than lip service.

As with *FSR1*, there are understandable reasons as to why *FSR2* was not amended in the lead up to the First World War: first, it was difficult to determine how it would work in practice and it was, therefore, desirable to allow for flexibility of interpretation. As it turned out, this was counterproductive in the early years of the First World War. Robertson recalled how he 'was convinced that the system [in *FSR2*] would not work in practice'. Indeed, rather than following *FSR2*'s precepts, Robertson, as the BEF's QMG, 'swept away the regulations'.[87] Secondly, while subject to sustained intellectual interrogation pre-war, administration clearly played second fiddle to operations much to the army's detriment, particularly in the early years of the First World War. While this deficiency was righted in the inter-war period, the army was forced to amend and expand on *FSR2* during the First World War to accommodate the changing scale and nature of conflict.[88] Although debates from 1909 onwards appear to suggest an inflexible mind-set where *FSR2* was concerned, the army's willingness to amend its regulations in time of war suggest an organisation open to change. *FSR2* was no straitjacket; its revisions were adopted in all theatres of operations, but with the appropriate degree of flexibility for each theatre's 'specific arrangements and responsibilities'.[89] Senior officers and generals singled out this flexibility after the war. For Lieutenant-General Sir Travers Clarke, whatever administrative system the army adopted 'had to be extremely flexible'. This system, driven by *FSR2*, was 'tested pretty thoroughly . . . under every possible climatic condition, and . . . was conclusively proved to be wholly sound and strong'. Clarke found support from Major-General Sir Frederick Maurice who believed that it was 'the establishment of a *purely British* system' that resulted in the 'great success' of *FSR2* in time of war.[90]

---

[86] TNA, WO 279/495, General Staff officers conference, 12–15 January 1914, pp. 32, 35, 92–93.

[87] Robertson, *Private to Field Marshal*, p. 200.

[88] For discussion of changes to *FSR* in the inter-war period, see D. French, 'Doctrine and Organisation in the British Army, 1919–1932', *Historical Journal* 44 (2) (2001), pp. 497–515.

[89] TNA, WO 161/41, Letters of Brigadier-General E. M. Paul to Director of Fortifications and Works (War Office), Letter 18, 8 February 1917.

[90] H. S. G. Miles, 'Army Administration', *JRUSI* 68 (429) (1923), pp. 38, 40. Added emphasis.

The British Officer Corps: Influence and Homogeneity

Despite the establishment of the General Staff and the adoption of *FSR*, the prerogative of the individual commander overruled any desire for uniformity, particularly where training and tactics were concerned. This resulted in an individualised and personality-driven approach to problem solving and learning; one that prized 'common sense', whilst shunning stereotyped thinking and prescription. This approach was underpinned by the influence and homogeneity of the officer corps. A number of historians have examined the background and relative uniformity of the Edwardian army officer corps in considerable detail.[91] However, for our purposes, it is sufficient to highlight certain commonalities that existed within the officer corps that shaped its relative uniformity, notably its social background, education, and leisure pursuits.

Regular army officers were drawn from a fairly small section of British society. There was a strong link between the landed classes and the military. One prominent sociologist estimated the proportion of officers from landed classes, namely the aristocracy and the gentry, as 53 per cent in 1830, 50 per cent in 1875, and 41 per cent in 1912.[92] Edwards Spiers largely corroborated these figures that amongst senior officers in 1914, 42 per cent were from the landed classes, 25 per cent from an armed forces background, 6 per cent from the clergy, and 27 per cent from other professions.[93] In hindsight, we can see that the demography of the officer corps broadened in the lead up to the First World War, yet it was still overwhelmingly Anglo-Saxon, Protestant, and upper class.[94] Kinship or marriage served to enhance further the homogeneity of the officer corps. Major (later Lieutenant-General Sir) Hew Fanshawe married the daughter of Field Marshal Sir Evelyn Wood, for example; while a number of officers were brothers-in-law, including Field Marshal Lord Cavan and General Sir Julian Byng, Field Marshal Lord Chetwode and General Sir Noel Birch, and Major-General Sir John Shea and Lieutenant-General Sir Walter Congreve VC.[95]

The educational background of the officer corps reinforced this class consciousness. The bulk of officers came from a very narrow band of schools, namely Eton, Cheltenham, Clifton, Harrow, Marlborough, and

[91] See e.g. G. D. Sheffield, *Leadership in the Trenches: Officer-Man Relations, Morale, and Discipline in the British Army in the Era of the First World War* (Basingstoke: Macmillan, 2000); Robbins, *British Generalship*; Bowman and Connelly, *Edwardian Army*.

[92] P. E. Razzell, 'Social Origins of Officers in the Indian and British Home Army', *British Journal of Sociology* 14 (3) (1963), p. 253.

[93] Spiers, *Late Victorian Army*, p. 94.   [94] Robbins, *British Generalship*, p. 3.

[95] I am grateful to Professor John Bourne for his assistance on this point.

Wellington.[96] As Simon Robbins has shown, of 700 senior commanders and staff officers who served on the Western Front during the First World War, 537 officers (77 per cent) attended public school; of whom 93 (13 per cent) attended Eton.[97] Attendance at the same school formed an important social network for officers. Indeed, some Anglo-Irish officers were sent to English public schools precisely in order to 'establish the social networks they would later need'.[98] During the First World War, the 'old school tie' manifested itself in the numerous school, university, and regimental dinners that took place on all fronts during the war. These dinners, often advertised in the General Routine Orders of each expeditionary force, served to provide extra lubricant for the mechanics of socialisation.[99] Old Etonians throughout the army's theatres celebrated the 'Fourth of June', while Brigadier-General Ernest Craig-Brown, an old boy of Merchiston Castle School, arranged a dinner in August 1918 for over fifty 'old academy' boys in the British Salonika Force [BSF] who had attended Scottish independent schools, such as Fettes, Glenalmond, Loretto, and Merchiston.[100]

The public school system, of which so many officers were a product, aimed to instil certain values within its pupils, such as character, initiative, integrity, and loyalty. These values reflected what it meant to be a gentleman or, perhaps more importantly, an English gentleman in Edwardian Britain. The public school system had, perhaps, the 'largest share in moulding the character' of such a man.[101] However, the term 'gentleman' was not a static concept. Indeed, the idea of a gentleman comprises 'so many values – from behaviour and morals to education, social background, the correct attire and table manners that it would . . . be restrictive to limit it to just one brief, defining sentence'.[102] To be a gentleman meant different things to different people throughout history. In 1714, one commentator remarked that 'the appellation of Gentleman is never to be affixed to a man's circumstances, but to his Behaviour in them'.[103] An 1845 article in *The Spectator* declared that the

---

[96] Bowman and Connelly, *Edwardian Army*, p. 10.

[97] Robbins, *British Generalship*, pp. 205–206.

[98] N. Perry, 'The Irish Landed Class and the British Army, 1850–1950', *War in History* 18 (3) (2011), p. 317.

[99] TNA, WO 123/293, General Routine Orders – Salonika Nos. 297 (15 January 1918), 330 (10 May 1918), and 331 (14 May 1918).

[100] Imperial War Museum [IWM], Papers of Brigadier-General E. Craig-Brown, Con Shelf 1/4, vol. 11, Craig-Brown to wife, 10 August 1918.

[101] P. Parker, *The Old Lie: The Great War and the Public-School Ethos* (London: Constable, 1987), pp. 41–42.

[102] C. Berberich, *The Image of the English Gentleman in Twentieth-Century Literature* (Farnham: Ashgate, 2007), p. 5.

[103] Quoted in Berberich, *English Gentleman*, p. 6.

'English gentleman is that ideal character which all Englishmen aspire to be, or at least to be thought'. After listing the various qualities of the gentleman – physically and morally brave, veracious, educated, humane, and decorous – the author outlined the perception of the gentleman by 'the mob' or the lower classes: they had 'never been long faithful to any leader who was not by education and habits a gentleman'.[104]

For the Edwardian officer corps, to be an officer was to be a gentleman. Some officers, such as Captain Reginald Hawker, an Old Wykehamist, believed one could not simply become a gentleman unless born to it. Remarking on a lecture entitled 'Duties of an Officer', Hawker hoped it was 'addressed to Officers of K[itchener]'s Army who have had *no chance* of learning how to be gentlemen'.[105] Unsurprisingly though, some officers of Kitchener's Army had educational and social backgrounds that were not radically different from those of the pre-war officer class. If a Kitchener Army officer lacked gentlemanly qualities, it might simply have been 'in the sense of not possessing a private income, not sharing the regular's interest in landed pursuits, or not having attended a sufficiently exclusive school'.[106] To be a gentleman did not necessarily confer the full range of professional ability, however. Commenting on the Australian general, Sir Harry Chauvel, Lieutenant-General Sir William Birdwood noted that he was 'a very nice fellow and a gentleman', but lacked 'great character or ability'.[107] Similarly, in a June 1915 letter to the War Office, Major-General Walter Braithwaite (CGS, MEF) remarked that, although the new IGC of the MEF, Major-General Alexander Wallace, was a 'very worthy and charming gentleman', he 'knows nothing whatever about the organisation of the British Army'.[108]

In addition to the 'old school tie' of the public schools, shared attendance at the military colleges, or membership of a regiment played an important role in nurturing desired qualities, as well as fostering links between British officers. Major-General Charles 'Tim' Harington, for example, recalled that 'the great factor of the Staff College were [sic] the firm friendships made there'.[109] For Major-General Oliver Nugent

---

[104] 'The English Gentleman', *The Spectator*, 22 February 1845, p. 22.
[105] National Army Museum [NAM], Papers of Captain R. S. Hawker, 1988-09-86, Diary, 20 January 1916. Original emphasis.
[106] M. Petter, '"Temporary Gentlemen" in the Aftermath of the Great War: Rank, Status and the Ex-Officer Problem', *Historical Journal* 37 (1) (1994), p. 139.
[107] AWM, Papers of Senator Sir George Pearce, 3DRL/2222 2/11, Birdwood to Munro Ferguson, 9 May 1917.
[108] TNA, WO 107/43, Inspector-General of Communications: Letters, Braithwaite to Cowans, 22 June 1915.
[109] Quoted in P. Harris, *The Men Who Planned the War: A Study of the Staff of the British Army on the Western Front, 1914–1918* (Farnham: Ashgate, 2015), p. 34.

(General Officer Commanding [GOC], 36th [Ulster] Division), hardly any of his patrons were Irish: the most important contacts came from his 'operational or regimental links'.[110] General Sir Charles Bonham-Carter's experience also offers a good example of the importance of these links. Following his appointment as head of the Training Directorate at GHQ in October 1917, Bonham-Carter wrote to his sister about his new colleagues:

I know a good number of the men at GHQ so shall be among friends. As a matter of fact of the other three Brig-Gens of the General Staff at GHQ – two, [John] Davidson and [Kenneth] Wigram, were at Sandhurst with me – and Wigram was as you may possibly remember at Winchester with Phil...The Deputy Chief of the G[eneral] S[taff] is [Richard] Butler who was with me at the Staff College...The Chief of the GS is [Launcelot] Kiggell whom I have known since I served with him in the Warwickshire Regiment.[111]

Such connections were also forged through membership of social networks outside the army, proving an important foundation for personal learning networks in time of war. However, these networks also fuelled the social ethos of the army that often ran parallel and occasionally intersected with the army's intellectual ethos. That there was an obvious social ethos within the army should not mark out the organisation as backwards or anti-intellectual. There were officers, notably those in the 'upper class' ranks of the Guards and the cavalry, who may have regarded their time in the army as a social career. However, as we shall see in later chapters, some of those well-heeled individuals who hunted foxes or big game nevertheless proved extremely adept at learning and adapting to the situation that faced them during the First World War.

The pre-war officer corps was dominated by the values of the gentry whose leisure pursuits were largely based around field sports, such as foxhunting, polo, and pigsticking, as well as game shooting.[112] Not only did these pursuits reinforce the educational and social exclusivity of the officer corps, but they also served to strengthen the social bonds between its members. A number of notable senior officers and generals rode with a hunt. Lieutenant-Colonel Richard O'Connor, for example, rode with the North Warwickshire hunt, Haig regularly hunted with the Bicester and Worcestershire hunts, Captain (later Brigadier-General) Richard Howard-Vyse was the huntsman of the Stoke Place Beagles, while Lord

---

[110] Perry, 'Irish Landed Class', p. 330.
[111] Churchill Archives Centre [CAC], Papers of General Sir C. Bonham-Carter, BHCT 2/2, Bonham-Carter to sister, 8 October 1917. 'Phil' refers to Charles Bonham-Carter's older brother, Philip.
[112] Robbins, British Generalship, p. 5.

Cavan was Master of Foxhounds of the Hertfordshire Hunt.[113] Such encounters often added colour to future military relationships. Brigadier-General Webb Gillman (Brigadier-General, General Staff [BGGS], BSF, 1917–1918) recalled an eventful hunting anecdote involving Major-General Frederick Koe (IGC, BSF) and Lieutenant-General Sir George Milne (Commander-in-Chief [CinC], BSF) before the war:

the only time Milne met him [Koe] . . . was some years ago while hunting with the 'United' in Cork, when Koe belted Milne's horse over the nose for shoving its head into his new pink coat. We have pulled Koe's leg and told him that Milne has been looking for him ever since![114]

Much like foxhunting, shooting and pigsticking also provided opportunities to build networks and enhance the social ethos. Game shooting experienced growing popularity in the years leading up to the First World War, increasing at twice the rate of foxhunting. It provided a social nexus within which the old order and the new could interact, as well as those from military and political spheres. Shooting was 'pursued primarily as a means of developing contacts'. One did not attend shooting parties 'for the sake of amusement', but in order 'to hear what is going on'.[115] This kind of sociability governed the eccentric Sir Claude Champion de Crespigny's decision to hold an annual 'South African Picnic' – a shooting party consisting entirely of men who had fought in the Second Boer War.[116]

The increase in driven-game shooting and the perceived emasculation of foxhunting in the late nineteenth century soon led to the view that such sports were artificial, effeminate, and even un-British.[117] Pigsticking and big game hunting, however, were 'considered by many as the ultimate challenge – a complete test of male mettle'.[118] They also, once again, allowed for the development and enhancement of social networks.

---

[113] LHCMA, Papers of General Sir R. O'Connor, 2/2/5, Ms Diary, 18 March 1919; 'Supplement', *Country Life*, 18 October 1913, vi; G. U. Robins, *Lays of the Hertfordshire Hunt and Other Poems* (London: Arthur L. Humphreys, 1916), pp. 103–112.

[114] Royal Artillery Historical Trust [RAHT], Papers of General Sir W. Gillman, MD 1161 4/19, Salonika Diary, 1 August 1916.

[115] J. Martin, 'The Transformation of Lowland Game Shooting in England and Wales in the Twentieth Century: The Neglected Metamorphosis', *IJHS* 29 (8) (2012), pp. 1143, 1147.

[116] C. Champion de Crespigny, *Forty Years of a Sportsman's Life* (London: Mills and Boon, 1910), p. 272.

[117] C. McKenzie, 'The British Big-Game Hunting Tradition, Masculinity and Fraternalism with Particular Reference to the "Shikar Club"', *The Sports Historian* 20 (1) (2000), pp. 74–75.

[118] Mangan and McKenzie, 'Martial Conditioning', p. 1139.

Such bonding often forged relationships that would be valuable in a military context. Francis Grenfell, for instance, recalled taking part in the 1905 Kadir Cup – 'the Derby of the sport of pig-sticking' – where he was reacquainted with Haig and Lieutenant-General Bryan Mahon, and 'made many pals'.[119] Similarly, big game hunting, while often portrayed as a solitary sport, also allowed for the creation of fraternal bonds, as well as the assertion of 'true masculinity'.[120] During his time as a subaltern in India, Field Marshal Lord Alan Brooke regularly hunted big game. His letters to and from various individuals of high political and military standing, requesting information on the best shikaris, transportation, and terrain, attest to the importance of an extensive social network when hunting on the subcontinent.[121]

While these various pursuits constituted an important 'network of sociability' both inside and out of the military, contemporaries were also aware of the martial benefits of field sports.[122] Despite the army's relative unease towards field sports in the late nineteenth century, a 1911 Army Council order highlighted the 'special military value' of hunting.[123] Field sports developed courage, initiative, and risk taking. Foxhunting, for example, seemed to offer the necessary combination of nerve, danger, decision, and an eye for fast movement across country. Lieutenant-Colonel Edwin Alderson's *Pink and Scarlet*, with its subheading 'hunting as a school for soldiering', is an obvious example. In its preface, Alderson declared that 'the hunting man is already a more than half-made soldier'.[124] The very existence of the yeomanry regiments reinforced this. However, such a positive view of field sports was not universal. As Major-General Sir Arthur Lynden-Bell (CGS, Egyptian Expeditionary Force [EEF], 1915–1917) declared in September 1916, 'we have got far too many of the grand old Yeomanry type of commanding officer and fellows who think that because they can hunt a pack of hounds they can command a Yeomanry brigade'.[125]

The shared educational and social background of the officer corps contributed to and was, in turn, shaped by the army's ethos. The

[119] J. Buchan, *Francis and Riversdale Grenfell: A Memoir* (London: Thomas Nelson, 1920), pp. 60–61.
[120] See McKenzie, 'Big-Game Hunting', pp. 70–96.
[121] LHCMA, Private Papers of Field Marshal Viscount Alanbrooke, 1/4, Hunting Journal 1910–1911.
[122] R. W. Hoyle, 'Introduction', in R. W. Hoyle (ed.), *Our Hunting Fathers: Field Sports in England after 1850* (Lancaster: Carnegie, 2007), p. 14.
[123] Riedi and Mason, *Sport and the Military*, pp. 77–78.
[124] E. A. H. Alderson, *Pink and Scarlet* (London: William Heinemann, 1900), vii.
[125] IWM, Papers of Major-General Sir A. L. Lynden-Bell, 90/1/1, Lynden-Bell to Maurice, 19 September 1916.

values instilled within the officer corps reflected the public school ethos, which was in itself an articulation of what it meant to be British; the one fundamentally supported the other. Initiative, devotion to duty, courage, and obedience were touchstones of what it meant to be both an officer and a gentleman. In addition to these characteristics, the relatively small size of the pre-war army helped promote a highly individualised officer corps. The social ethos of the army allowed for the development of networks that would play an important role in the development of learning relationships between individuals and operational theatres.

Although the officer corps was fairly homogeneous in its education and social background, the army produced officers and generals that were capable of promulgating significant change. Their capacity to do so was enhanced by the army's devolution of authority. Unit commanders could on occasion 'flout higher directives, and sometimes even the orders of their own immediate superiors'.[126] The lack of an authoritative doctrine pre-1914 thus also resulted from the 'social and organisational structure of the army and of its officer corps, including the formal and informal power of the regiments, and of prominent generals'.[127] Officers did not take kindly to general directives from above which appeared to limit their freedom of action.[128] Unsurprisingly, for some officers, the General Staff in particular was seen as a challenge to their freedom, leading the Army Council to remark that it was not 'intended to relieve Commanding Officers of their prime responsibility for the efficiency and proficiency of their officers in institutional and professional respects'.[129] This left unit commanders with considerable scope for developing solutions peculiar to their own formations. In 1907, the Duke of Connaught noted that there was a 'go as you please' attitude towards tactics, and a 'tendency to [form] cliques around particular Generals'.[130] These cliques were exemplified by the Wolseley and Roberts Rings, which, while permeable, still proved to be a divisive factor in the politics of the late Victorian army.[131]

The combination of the General Staff, *FSR*, and the free hand granted to the officer limited the uniformity of the army. This diversity encouraged a broad range of different training practices and approaches, some

---

[126] French, *Military Identities*, p. 270.
[127] S. Badsey, *Doctrine and Reform in the British Cavalry 1880–1918* (Aldershot: Ashgate, 2008), p. 4.
[128] Griffith, *Battle Tactics*, p. 26.   [129] Strachan, 'Continental Commitment', p. 90.
[130] Quoted in Jones, *Boer War to World War*, p. 51.
[131] H. Kochanski, *Sir Garnet Wolseley: Victorian Hero* (London: Hambledon Press, 1999), p. 272.

of which were 'manifestly wrong'.[132] Although the General Staff was able to issue seemingly binding injunctions, it had very limited means of enforcing them owing to the army's laissez-faire tendencies. In an effort to address this, the army decided to establish the position of Inspector-General of the Forces [IGF]. The duties of the IGF were straightforward in principle. He was to

> review generally and to report to the Army Council on the practical results of the policy of that Council, and for that purpose to inspect and report upon the training and efficiency of all troops under the control of the Home Government, on the suitability of their armament and equipment, on the condition of fortifications and defences, and generally on the readiness and fitness of the Army for war.[133]

The creation of the IGF led to a system of feedback generation based on lessons learned, inspiring lengthy annual reports on training. However, this system did not necessarily result in increased uniformity. If a particular regimental commander disagreed with accepted practice, the variance would become apparent in the annual inspection of performance in combined training or manoeuvres. The responsibility for the correction of these variances rested with the Army Council, but whether the correction was made or not was the sticking point.[134]

Despite attempts to unify training methods, the nature of the officer corps served to reinforce the primacy of local custom, thwarting the army's attempts to impose and disseminate central guidance. This barrier proved insurmountable in the years leading up to the First World War and proved to be an obstacle throughout the war, too. In 1908, the IGF reported that 'there is not yet sufficient uniformity of system, either in adherence to authorised principles, or in the methods by which these principles are put into practice'.[135] The 1913 'Memorandum on Army Training' noted that 'commanders should endeavour to establish a common school of thought among their subordinates . . . so that all in the formation may be imbued with a common doctrine and be ready

---

132 TNA, WO 27/504, Memorandum on Military Training, 1905, Aldershot Command. See also Bowman and Connelly, *Edwardian Army*, pp. 69–70.

133 Parliamentary Papers [PP], Order in Council Defining the Duties of the Inspector-General of the Forces [Cd. 2252], XLVI, 1905, p. 301.

134 G. Leonard, 'The Limits of Decision Making: Accounting, Budgets, Tactical Efficiency and the Choices of the British General Staff, 1908–1913', paper presented at 13th World Congress for Accounting Historians, Newcastle-upon-Tyne, July 2012, p. 5 [private copy].

135 TNA, WO 163/14, Appendix – Annual Report of the Inspector General of the Forces for 1908, p. 159.

for the closest co-operation'.[136] The IGF also reported in 1913 that some progress had been made towards imbuing a common method in some units. Time was all that was needed to achieve more satisfactory results.[137] Little did they know, this time was fast running out.

A Thinking Army?

Critics of the army's pre-war officer corps have pointed to its anti-intellectual bent, aversion to book learning, and lack of formal doctrine as evidence of its unthinking and insular nature.[138] Indulgence in field sports and the gentrified milieu of these pursuits provides another stick with which to beat the army's leadership. However, this critique imposes unrealistic expectations of intellectual endeavour upon the officer corps as a whole, thereby leading to a misleading impression of academic bankruptcy. Not every officer in the pre-war army was a 'thinking officer'. Yet, there were many who took their profession seriously and devoted considerable attention to its study. While the army railed against prescribed doctrine and stereotyped thinking, it did not object to individual officers debating and writing their own works on tactical or doctrinal matters, often for quite intellectual reasons. These debates often took place outside the army's organisational structure. The production of commercial publications such as Callwell's *Small Wars* (1896), Ernest Swinton's *The Defence of Duffer's Drift* (1904), and Richard Haking's *Company Training* (1913) were matched by the considerable increase in service journals after the Boer War. By 1914, roughly a quarter of the army's regular officers were members of the Royal United Services Institute [RUSI].[139] Individuals such as Ivor Maxse, Haking, and Fuller regularly contributed to debates in service journals. Indeed, Maxse, Reginald Kentish, and other infantry officers were involved in an intense debate in the *RUSI Journal* on the decision to restructure the battalion into four, rather than eight, companies.[140] The *Cavalry Journal* was founded in 1905, providing a forum for intellectual development and discussion. By

---

[136] RAHT, MD 2818, 'Memorandum on Army Training during the Individual Training Period, 1912–13', 11 November 1913, pp. 5–6.

[137] Leonard, 'Limits of Decision Making', pp. 5–6. See also TNA, WO 163/20, Appendix – Annual Report of the Inspector General of the Home Forces for 1913–1914, p. 326.

[138] See Travers, *The Killing Ground*, pp. 38–39.

[139] I am grateful to Dr Andrew Duncan for sharing this information with me. See A. Duncan, 'The Military Education of Junior Officers in the Edwardian Army', Unpublished PhD Thesis, University of Birmingham, 2016.

[140] See F. I. Maxse, 'Battalion Organization', *JRUSI* 56 (1) (1912), pp. 53–86; R. Kentish, 'The Case for the Eight Company Battalion', *JRUSI* 56 (2) (1912), pp. 891–928; H. Wake, 'The Four Company Battalion in Battle', *JRUSI* 59 (2) (1914), pp. 362–377.

1913, the journal's committee reported that 'in most cavalry regiments every officer received the journal'.[141] These debates were not isolated occurrences; they were 'signs of a great intellectual awakening'.[142]

The army was well aware of the potency of service journals as a seedbed for discussion and dissemination of best practice. This led to the establishment of the short-lived *Army Review* in 1911 under the auspices of General William Nicholson (CIGS, 1909–1912).[143] The continental armies had benefitted from a number of such journals for some years.[144] For Nicholson, the *Army Review* provided a public vehicle through which the General Staff's view could be disseminated throughout the army. The aims of the journal centred on the distribution of the latest information on military subjects, inculcating the lessons of history, and encouraging the formulation and expression of individual ideas on matters open to discussion. Undoubtedly aware of the diversity of approach across the army, Nicholson hoped that the *Army Review* would not only encourage 'the discussion of matters of military interest', but that it may also prove conducive 'to the unity of doctrine and the intelligent application of the principles laid down by a superior authority, which are essential to the systematic training in peace and successful action in the field'.[145]

While the service journals and the *Army Review* provided an intellectual and professional outlet for the discussion of military subjects, knowledge derived from experience still tended to reside within individual soldiers or formations. There were clear, practical difficulties in transferring tacit, experiential knowledge into something more tangible. This tendency was raised as a concern at the 1909 General Staff conference. No army, argued Colonel Aylmer Haldane, 'has greater experience of war than our own', yet 'most of the experience gained is stored in the heads of the fortunate ones who have seen much service . . . they have recorded little for the use of those who will come after them'.[146] While it was agreed that a 'precedent book' be implemented for collating hints and tips for staff officers, tactical lessons and experience still failed to influence the army as a whole, serving to widen the different practices

---

[141] Various, 'The "Cavalry Journal" Committee', *The Cavalry Journal* 9 (January 1914), p. 110.
[142] Luvaas, *Education of an Army*, p. 251.
[143] J. Gooch, 'The Creation of the British General Staff, 1904–1914', *JRUSI* 116 (1971), p. 53.
[144] J. Gooch, *The Plans of War: The General Staff and British Military Strategy, c. 1900–1916* (London: Routledge, 1974), pp. 122–123.
[145] Ibid., p. 123.
[146] TNA, WO 279/25, General Staff officers conference, 18–21 January 1909, pp. 59–60.

and tactics employed by individual formations.[147] Lord Roberts's well-known publication *Notes for Guidance in South African Warfare* provides a good example. Issued after he replaced General Sir Redvers Buller as commander of British forces in South Africa, the publication was heavily influenced by Roberts's North West Frontier experience. It supported Hamilton's actions at Elandslaagte with its call for the abandonment of close order formations between fifteen hundred and eighteen hundred yards from the enemy, keeping an extension of between six and eight paces per man, and making maximum use of cover.[148]

Yet, these precepts were not new. They had been hinted at within service journals in the aftermath of the Tirah Expedition.[149] However, the army's limited methods for disseminating knowledge, coupled with its distaste for prescription, meant that these lessons remained within the regiments that served in these campaigns, or were consigned to military journals with limited circulation. In the case of the latter, the army had no mechanism for ensuring these articles were read by its personnel, let alone acted upon. Though an observation on official doctrine, Brian Holden Reid's comment on service publications is apposite in this instance: 'publishing a doctrinal pamphlet or circulating a paper is no more proof of the acceptance of a doctrinal policy than shouting its conclusions from the roof of the old War Office'.[150] As we shall see in later chapters, the army was forced to develop other ways and means of disseminating lessons and experience that catered for the myriad needs of its changing demography.

The British Army's Ethos on the Eve of the First World War

Priding itself on its adaptation and devolved decision-making, the army had a pre-war ethos that was both flexible and highly individualised. The small size of the army and the relative homogeneity of the officer corps made this approach feasible. However, with the industrialised nature of the First World War, the army was forced to expand and transform from a small professional force to a mass citizen army in a very short timeframe. The officer corps alone (including territorial and Special Reserve officers) expanded from 28,060 in 1914 to 164,255 by war's end – an

[147] Moreman, *The Army in India*, p. 36. [148] Jones, *Boer War to World War*, pp. 65–66.
[149] See e.g. A. C. Yate, 'North-West Frontier Warfare', *JRUSI* 42 (248) (1898), p. 1191; W. F. Gatacre, 'A Few Notes on the Characteristic of Hill Fighting in India and the Training of Infantry Necessary for the Same, Possible in England', *JRUSI* 43 (260) (1899), pp. 1065–1086.
[150] B. Holden Reid, *A Doctrinal Perspective 1988–98* (Camberley: SCSI, 1998), p. 14.

increase of nearly 600 per cent.[151] This transformation inevitably had an effect on the army's approach to learning and the sustainability of its pre-war ethos.

Although the army would expand and change during the war, a number of factors existed that would go some way to ensure its ethos continued to animate much of its business. First, there was continuity of command at the highest levels of the army. Certainly, commanders were replaced or changed and those who held senior commands were not always the best men for the job. However, regular army officers continued to dominate the high command.[152] These men were members of an officer corps imbued with the army's ethos and set the tone for those below them. In some instances, these regular officers found themselves in positions where they could influence the training of the various forces. For one general, the need for 'sufficient pre-war personnel capable of imparting instruction' was vital.[153] In this respect, ethos remained the golden thread running through the entire organisation.

Secondly, as we saw earlier, *FSR* remained in force throughout the war. Although some commanders did not find its principles applicable, it was often required reading or, at least, a key text for training schools in each expeditionary force.[154] General Sir Edmund Allenby, as CinC of the EEF, declared that it was 'unnecessary to issue instructions from GHQ as to the Training of Divisions for Offensive Action. The principles in *Field Service Regulations* Part I, and in the various pamphlets, are a sufficient guide and should be read in conjunction with one another'.[155] *FSR* would often be used to integrate newcomer organisations, such as the Australian Imperial Force [AIF], into the army, forming the basic building block of their training schools.

Thirdly, the army developed a series of socialisation methods ranging from regimental affiliations to the attachment of newcomers to long-serving formations. Regarding Kitchener's New Armies, the decision to append the battalions to existing regiments helped instil a sense of tradition and familial association. This not only linked those new battalions to the victories of the past, forging loyalties, but also helped to ensure a continuity of ethos between the regular and the Kitchener Army.[156] For

---

[151] War Office, *Statistics of the Military Effort*, p. 234.

[152] Robbins, *British Generalship*, pp. 210–212.

[153] LHCMA, Shea Papers, 6/4, Lecture on Palestine Campaign, n.d.

[154] See e.g. TNA, WO 95/4946, BSF Infantry School, Course Syllabus, 3 February 1918; AWM, AWM 25 881/34, Course in Staff Duties in 1st Australian Division, Memo, 28 June 1917.

[155] TNA, WO 95/4368, EEF GHQ War Diary, Chief of the General Staff's Conference, 20 August 1917.

[156] Palazzo, *Seeking Victory*, pp. 16–17.

one soldier, the '"halo of the traditions of the old regiment" has been a very great factor in the making of the new units . . . there is much journalistic gush about the "spirit of the New Army"; as if that spirit were something new, and not the legacy handed down by the old regulars'. The Kitchener Army was very much 'modelled on the old; trained on its system, and imbued with its traditions'.[157] The army also used integration methods, including training schools, tactical exercises, and attachments, to instil within newcomers the values of the army. Attachments proved a particularly useful way of integrating newcomers, introducing them to the front line, but also setting an example in terms of discipline, esprit de corps, and soldierly tradition. Through a combination of these means, the ethos of the pre-war army endured and determined much of how the army approached the challenge of the First World War.

Conclusions

Ethos provided a framework within which the army could interpret, develop, and modify its method of waging war. Although there are examples in history where military ethos ossified into an intellectual straitjacket, the same cannot be said of the British army of 1914.[158] Grounded in the cultural values of its parent society, the British army's ethos was able to operate and thrive in the uncertain environment posed by the First World War. However, rather than seeing this pre-war ethos as singular, it can be sub-divided into two strands: social and intellectual. Although there were undoubtedly officers who saw the army as a social career, the two 'ethe' were not always mutually exclusive and, in many cases, intersected. There were plenty of intellectual officers who took their profession seriously, but sought to enhance their social networks for professional and personal reasons. These networks would often provide an important means of transferring knowledge and expertise, underscoring the highly personalised nature of the officer corps.

That is not to say that this two-stranded ethos was problem-free. The emphasis on pragmatism, individual action, and a preference for principles over prescription, caused problems for citizen soldiers who had little or no experience of battle. The army would have to recalibrate its ways and means of learning, pursuing a far more systematic approach to knowledge creation and dissemination to cater for its new found size. That it was able to carry out this recalibration, whilst still stressing the

[157] C. N. W. (pseud.), 'The Making of the New Unit', *JRUSI* 61 (1916), pp. 606–607.
[158] Examples where military ethos has ossified include the Japanese samurai, the Janissaries, and the French Army in the 1930s. See King, 'The Ethos of the Royal Marines', p. 32.

importance of initiative and deference to the man on the spot, speaks to the inherent flexibility of the organisation. Over the course of the war, the army's social composition changed enormously. Yet, in spite of this, its ethos arguably increased in importance, providing an important touchstone in the face of organisational challenges. Whether through the continuing use of *FSR* or by appending Kitchener units to existing regiments, the army sought to imbue newcomers with its characteristic spirit, ensuring they were able to adapt to the changing character of war. The army's ethos and the factors that shaped it provides the basis for any determination of whether a culture of learning flourished within the army after 1914.

2   A Networked Army

'We were slow to adapt our methods', wrote Major-General Arthur McNamara. 'We were slow to appreciate that totally different conditions required a complete change of method . . . In short we showed a tendency to be hide-bound, to try to fight battles by rule of thumb (or pamphlet), and to fail to deal with differing problems on the merits of each'.[1] McNamara's scathing comments to the 1932 Kirke Committee on the Lessons of the Great War make for damning reading. They suggest an army that was inflexible and unimaginative; an army that struggled to learn. As we have seen, on the eve of the First World War, the army possessed and cultivated an ethos that prized individual action and initiative. This ethos was not without its weaknesses, nor was it always intellectually driven, but it was inherently flexible. McNamara's criticisms cut especially deep, casting doubt on the effectiveness of the army's learning process. Were there fundamental problems with how the army adapted during the war? Did the army's ethos enable learning to take place? To answer these questions, it is necessary to move beyond the army's culture and to examine the practical ways in which it learned.

Learning is a normal, if problematic, process in every organisation.[2] For the military, the institutional barriers of speaking truth to power often exacerbated this difficulty. In peacetime, the army is educated to respect the military hierarchy, suggesting an adherence to the status quo and an aversion to risk. In wartime, however, militaries tend to become more fluid. Out of necessity, they have to find ways of mitigating both the friction and fog of war. This may involve developing and, indeed, prioritising different ways of learning. McNamara's criticism of the army's slowness to adapt underestimates the inherent difficulty of organisational learning, particularly in a time of crisis. The complex network of relationships that exist between different agents and different

---

[1] LHCMA, Papers of General Sir W. M. StG. Kirke, 4/4, 'Notes by Major-General Arthur McNamara on Training', May 1932, pp. 1–2.
[2] M. Easterby Smith, 'Disciplines of Organizational Learning: Contributions and Critiques', *Human Relations* 50 (1997), pp. 1085–1113, 1109.

processes complicates learning in any large, dispersed and highly pressured organisation. By unpacking and understanding the ways in which the army learns, it is possible to reflect on the validity of McNamara's criticisms, as well as to interrogate the nature of the institution and some of the problems it encountered in wartime.

Relationship between Organisational and Individual Learning

Before considering the ways in which the army learned, it is important and useful to delineate between individual and organisational learning and to explore what these terms mean in a broader context. Can organisations learn? Is learning an individual or collective function, or is it a combination of the two?

Individual learning is important to an organisation because all organisations are composed of individuals. At every level of the organisation, individuals encounter new ideas, errors, puzzles, and other opportunities for learning. In many respects then, learning takes place inside human minds.[3] Yet, there is an inherent paradox when considering the relationship between individual and organisational learning: organisations can learn independent of any specific individual but not independent of all individuals.[4] Individual learning is, therefore, a necessary but not a sufficient condition for broader, institutional learning. There needs to be a process for transferring that learned by the individual to the wider organisation. For some theorists, organisational learning is that which is reflected in an organisation's collective rules, procedures, and beliefs, rather than simply the sum of each member's learning.[5] Although organisations do not have brains, they do have cognitive systems and 'memories' in the form of protocols and standard operational procedures [SOPs]. Members will leave and leaders will change, but organisations' memories preserve certain behaviours, norms, and values through these systems.

While there is general consensus that learning occurs through and amongst people, the problem lies in the ability to transfer the knowledge and experience acquired at the individual level to the wider organisation. This is known as multi-level learning. Put simply, individuals learn through intuition and interpretation. Once learning has been

[3] H. A. Simon, 'Bounded Rationality and Organizational Learning', *Organization Science* 1 (2) (1991), p. 125.
[4] Kim, 'Link', p. 37.
[5] B. Levitt and J. G. March, 'Organizational Learning', *Annual Review of Sociology* 14 (1988), p. 320; Fiol and Lyles, 'Organizational Learning', p. 804.

interpreted, it can be shared with others and integrated at the group level before it is subsequently institutionalised at the organisational level.[6] Clausewitz expressed similar sentiments when he wrote: 'If in warfare, a certain means turns out to be highly effective, it will be used again; it will be copied by others and become fashionable; and so, backed by experience, it passes into general use and is included in theory'.[7] On paper, the process of learning is simple: the movement of a neatly packaged 'product' – knowledge – from A to B. The reality is quite different. The process is disjointed, complicated, and fragile. It is subject to dead ends and wrong turns. Knowledge itself is sticky, inherently difficult to package, and often resists translation. Organisations face a series of difficult tasks: they have to simultaneously acquire and assimilate this new knowledge, whilst leveraging existing knowledge. They have to try and identify good ideas over bad ones. They also have to negotiate inherent frictions, such as trust, relevance, and motivation (or lack thereof). Underpinning all this is the requirement for an organisational culture that allows for and facilitates learning. It was in this latter area that McNamara thought the army deficient.

A Networked Approach to Learning

How the army learned during the First World War was dictated in part by its ethos, but also by the exigencies of conflict. While some commentators have debated the continuing relevance of military ethos and culture during wartime, it is clear that, for the British army at least, its ethos was vital in shaping its approach to learning.[8] The highly individualised approach that had served it well in the pre-war years, for instance, was not always appropriate given the rapid expansion of the army in the early years of the war. Traditionally, the ways in which the army learned have generally been considered in two categories: formal and informal. However, it is possible to delineate further, adding nuance and complexity to the process. Instead, learning should be viewed as a network, which includes liberal, horizontal, vertical, and external approaches.[9] Rather

[6] This is a simplified version of Mary Crossan's 4I model. See M. Crossan, H. W. Lane, and R. E. White, 'An Organizational Learning Framework: From Intuition to Institution', *Academic Management Review* 24 (3) (1999), p. 522.

[7] C. Clausewitz, *On War*, trans. M. Howard and P. Paret (London: Oxford World Classics, 2007), p. 125.

[8] See Daddis, 'Eating Soup with a Spoon'; P. Porter, *Military Orientalism: Eastern War through Western Eyes* (New York: Columbia University Press, 2009), pp. 5–16.

[9] See R. F. Poell, G. E. Chivers, F. J. Van der Krogt, and D. A. Wildemeersch, 'Learning-Network Theory: Organizing the Dynamic Relationship between Learning and Work', *Management Learning* 13 (1) (2000), pp. 25–49.

than adhering to the simplistic formal-informal binary, viewing the process as networked provides us with a rounded yet granular understanding of how the army learned in war. Learning can only occur in an organisation that is rich in connections and relationships.[10] By highlighting the importance of the relational connections between individuals and between resources, learning can be explored more holistically. For ease of explanation and analysis, it has been necessary to compartmentalise the army's ways of learning into the four approaches of liberal, horizontal, vertical, and external. The reality, however, is far more complex. Generally speaking, all four approaches or networks were employed within the army at once, although certain ones were used more frequently than others at different times and in different places. These networks should not be seen as standalone either: they often intersected, or informed, one another, leading to a hybridity of learning. Indeed, the links between these various ways of learning can be likened to a kaleidoscope: the precise constitution of the interconnections is momentary, but the networked nature of the interconnectedness itself is constant.[11] In short, networks exist and relate to each other, but the ways in which they do so are constantly changing.

The 'liberal' network of learning has parallels with the sort of informal, unstructured learning often associated with individual learning. This approach is self-directed and grounded in contractual relationships between individuals.[12] These individuals are empowered to seek out their own strategies for learning. As Chapter 1 revealed, individualised action and initiative were important aspects of the army's pre-war culture. It is unsurprising then that a liberal approach flourished in the more fluid conditions of wartime. The relative informality of this approach makes it impossible to discern all the different ways that such learning occurred, but there are two primary avenues that can be identified: first, incidental interaction with individuals or resources, and secondly, pre-existing social networks that provide the basis for personal learning networks. In both instances, these unstructured interactions resulted in relatively rapid learning at a lower level.

Incidental interactions – whether through an individual's engagement with a training pamphlet, or a fleeting conversation between two unconnected individuals on a training course – underscores the highly unstructured nature of the liberal approach. It is often the most prevalent form

[10] M. J. Wheatley, 'Can the U.S. Army Become a Learning Organization?', *Journal for Quality and Participation* 17 (2) (1994), pp. 50–55.
[11] A. Lester, 'Imperial Circuits and Networks: Geographies of the British Empire', *History Compass* 4 (1) (2006), p. 134.
[12] Poell et al., 'Learning-Network', p. 36.

of learning, yet its ephemerality and occurrence at the individual level means it is difficult to chart its cumulative effect on the army as a whole. In most instances, such learning remains localised, exercising little influence on the wider institution. Having said that, there are rare documented instances of incidental interactions leading to higher level change and learning. The experience of Major Henry Hemming, BEF GHQ's adviser and coordinator of flash spotting on the Western Front, provides a good example of multi-level learning from individual to organisation. At the outbreak of war, Hemming was a Canadian engineering student, studying in Paris. When war was declared he obtained a commission in the 12th Battalion Duke of Wellington's Regiment. Owing to his previous experience and manifest intelligence, he was appointed to the artillery staff of the 18th (Eastern) Division, which, as he noted in his memoirs, had 'remarkable consequences'. His promotion from a divisional staff officer to GHQ adviser highlights the significance of the liberal approach to learning. According to Hemming, his appointment was due to a spontaneous, fleeting encounter with a staff officer:

I heard a voice outside calling, 'I say, can I come in?...Just wanted to have a look at the jolly old Hun'...and then seeing my alidade he said, 'I say, what's that wonderful gadget? No, don't tell me, I wouldn't understand'. I explained that it was to take bearings on the flashes of the enemy guns...'How perfectly marvellous', he said, and then was gone...Two days after the visit by the Hon. Freddie, I got a note from Brigadier Stone C[ommander] R[oyal] A[rtillery], saying that the 18th Division had been ordered to send an officer to Third Army HQ to attend a course on flash spotting.[13]

This course brought him into contact with Colonel Harold Winterbotham, a regular Royal Engineers [RE] officer, who nurtured Hemming's ideas and career. That initial, incidental exchange between Hemming and 'the Hon. Freddie' proved an important catalyst, which eventually resulted in broader learning and change. Hemming's professional and social network was enhanced and widened by Winterbotham who 'brought down a number of Artillery generals, and senior staff officers' to consider Hemming's flash spotting innovations.[14] His flash and buzzer board soon became an authorised piece of equipment, securing his position as adviser to GHQ.

Along with incidental exchanges, the prevalence of the social network as a facet of this liberal approach cannot be overlooked. Social networks allow individuals to circumvent often unwieldy formal systems,

[13] IWM, Papers of Lieutenant-Colonel H. H. Hemming, PP/MCR/155, Ts memoir, n.d., pp. 33–34.
[14] Ibid., p. 74.

thus reducing the problem of knowledge lag.[15] They allow individuals to discover what they know, share it with colleagues, and, in theory, create new knowledge for the organisation.[16] In many instances, people learn by listening to the experiences of their peers, rather than through documented means. However, knowledge does not simply result from processes or activities; it comes from people and communities of people. For conversations to take place, a connection is required. As we have seen, these connections could be made in a number of ways: marriage, public school, shared attendance at Sandhurst or staff college, previous military service, or through membership of other social groups, such as hunts. Individuals were clearly comfortable using their personal relationships to identify solutions to specific problems. This approach was used both intra- and inter-theatre. Throughout the Gallipoli campaign, for example, Rawlinson was in regular communication with senior officers in the MEF, including Alec Godley, Walter Braithwaite, and Hamilton. The correspondence between these men considered the reasons for success or failure in the different theatres. In a letter to Clive Wigram, Rawlinson wrote that he had

> heard from Braithwaite the other day describing the difficulties of the situation which confronts them – Achi Baba is not dissimilar to many of the fortified strongholds which confront us here so I sent him some of our experiences on the best way to deal with barbed wire and trenches.[17]

While also serving at Gallipoli, Major-General Henry de Beauvoir De Lisle (GOC, 29th Division) kept in close contact with his former staff from the 1st Cavalry Division. Through these contacts, Beauvoir De Lisle was able to disseminate best practice relating to machine gun tactics from the Western Front within his theatre of operations.[18] In a similar fashion, out in Salonika, Brigadier-General Philip Howell (CGS, BSF, 1915–1916) took advantage of his personal relationship with Haig to secure up to date training publications and reports.[19]

While there are obvious strengths to the liberal approach, such as relative speed and relevance, there were also drawbacks, notably the

---

[15] The use of informal networks to circumvent formal knowledge channels does pose greater problems for the organisation through lost knowledge. See O'Toole and Talbot, 'Fighting for Knowledge', pp. 42–67.

[16] T. Davenport and L. Prusak, *Working Knowledge: How Organizations Manage What They Know* (Boston: Harvard Business School, 1998), pp. 90–92.

[17] NAM, Papers of Lord Rawlinson, 5201-22-18, Letterbook 1915–1916, Rawlinson to Wigram, 7 June 1915. I am grateful to Professor Gary Sheffield for bringing this quotation to my attention.

[18] LHCMA, Papers of General Sir I. S. M. Hamilton, 7/1/21, Beauvoir De Lisle to Hamilton, 24 July 1915.

[19] LHCMA, Papers of Brigadier P. Howell, 6/2, Haig to Howell, 21 March 1916.

ephemeral and incidental nature of this form of learning. It is often situational: an individual learns something, but does not write it down or disseminate the solutions, resulting in the loss of innovation or knowledge to the organisation. It can also be opportunistic, of the moment, with an individual acting on their initiative without taking into account the organisation's SOPs.[20] The often random nature of these informal exchanges, particularly with the movement of individuals to new positions or theatres, could lead to organisational forgetting.[21] This loss of knowledge was an acute problem for the army and had yet to be resolved from the years leading up to the war. 'I have seen subjects brought up which have been decided three or four years before', remarked William Nicholson in 1909, 'and yet they are started again because [a] record has not been made'.[22] Failure to capture and disseminate knowledge was clearly nothing new, but, in a mass army, such knowledge loss could proliferate exponentially. Yet even had it wanted to, the army could not prevent these individual exchanges from taking place. To do so would be to deny its own ethos, and undermine the initiative of the officer corps that it had created. There was a recognition that learning and innovation at the coalface could be of wider benefit to the army. Attempts were made to try and capture these lessons and experiences both formally and informally. Howell, for example, asked that subordinate commanders write down their experiences for the common good of the BSF. Their reports should be 'thoroughly well circulated' and 'when they have all had their say, a meeting of all . . . to discuss definite points, which will have cropped up, would be extremely useful'.[23] Though well intentioned, the sheer amount and diversity of experiences and ideas meant that such measures only scratched the surface.

While similar in many respects to the liberal approach, 'horizontal' learning generally takes place at the group level. Although the individual plays an important role in the movement of knowledge, the lessons or experiences that are shared are often anonymous; there is little claim of ownership. As such, relationships are generally more egalitarian in nature and, in some cases, are strengthened by homophily – or certain similarities – between groups.[24] Robert Foley has shown how this approach occurred within the German Army of the First World War.

[20] Kim, 'Link', p. 46.   [21] Catignani, 'Coping with Knowledge', p. 3.
[22] TNA, WO 279/25, General Staff officers conference, 18–21 January 1909, p. 61.
[23] LHCMA, Howell Papers, 6/2, Howell to Fuller, 3 May 1916.
[24] Recent research by Nina Kollars et al. has examined aspects of both homogeneous and heterogeneous horizontal learning using 'communities of practice' theory. See N. A. Kollars, R. R. Muller, and A. Santora, 'Learning to Fight and Fighting to Learn: Practitioners and the Role of Unit Publications in VIII Fighter Command 1943–1944', *Journal of Strategic Studies* 39 (7) (2016), pp. 1044–1067.

While Foley provides compelling evidence to support the German predilection for this kind of learning, there is a question mark over how horizontal the process actually was. As with the German Army, horizontal learning took place at all levels in the British army. It occurred in the front line, behind the line, during reliefs, or across formation boundaries. In many respects, it was just as ubiquitous as the liberal approach, and could be just as incidental. It was self-directed – the impetus for the development of new ideas came from the commanders and staffs of units without necessarily waiting for direction from above.[25] Of course, there were instances where units required a degree of prompting from senior command to take note of key developments or experiences. This does not necessarily undermine the process of horizontal learning, but rather it rightly forces us to position this approach within a broader network, further attesting to the mosaic-like nature of learning.

There are a number of factors within the army that enabled horizontal learning to take place. One of these was the army's ethos. Formations were encouraged to innovate and learn within broader institutional parameters. This applied to all levels of command. Staffs and commanders at Army level, for example, often exchanged best practice on a push and pull basis up and down the front line. 'Tim' Harington (Major-General, General Staff [MGGS], Second Army) provided his counterpart in Fourth Army, Major-General Archibald Montgomery, with a number of pamphlets relating to Second Army's 1917 operations, as well as details on the role of the 'Army Centre' at the battle of Messines. Harington's accompanying note detailed further suggestions, including potential improvements on existing practice.[26] Montgomery also pulled in knowledge through horizontal means. A letter from First Army's machine gun officer, Colonel George Lindsay, indirectly highlights Montgomery's concerns over machine gun deficiencies in Fourth Army. Lindsay provided Montgomery with recommendations for increasing the size of the Machine Gun Corps (MGC). His recommendations were based on the Canadian Corps's machine gun policy from which 'a good deal of 1st Army policy was taken'.[27] In many respects, the dialogue between Lindsay and Montgomery spoke to the need for a broader, force-wide approach that transcended the horizontal sharing of best practice. The aim was 'a definite policy' that could be disseminated institutionally.

---

[25] Foley, 'Horizontal', pp. 802–803.
[26] LHCMA, Papers of Field Marshal Sir A. A. Montgomery-Massingberd, 7/35, Harington to Montgomery, 6 July 1917.
[27] LHCMA, Montgomery-Massingberd Papers, 7/38, Lindsay to Montgomery, 18 June 1918.

Instances of horizontal learning at the operational and tactical level were abundant across all theatres of operations, suggesting a culture that facilitated rather than hindered this approach. We need to be mindful, of course, that, as with liberal learning, it was incredibly difficult for the army to control such exchanges. In many instances, horizontal learning was built into the fundamentals of an army at war, particularly in the reliefs procedure. During the 229th Brigade's relief of the 230th Brigade in July 1918, for instance, it handed over a number of papers containing 'files from 61st Division, including... action in case of attack... raids, signalling, artillery, trench mortars', along with other administrative aspects.[28] This form of learning ensured that localised knowledge was retained and passed on to incoming formations.

A second factor that facilitated horizontal learning was homophily – the idea that 'similarity breeds connection'.[29] Sources of homophily include shared class, culture, race, and geographical proximity. Similar occupations can also influence the adoption of innovations as we have seen with Montgomery and Harington. However, one of the most potent sources can be linked to national identity, particularly for Dominion and Irish formations. National pride often coloured perceptions of other forces and units. Writing in February 1915, one Australian lieutenant bemoaned the fact that

the Australians get the credit of any wrongdoing here. The New Zealanders (who are no class and will never be soldiers)... cannot do anything wrong. Every New Zealander always takes every opportunity to put the dirt into us... We can beat them in every department of the game.[30]

An officer in the 6th Royal Dublin Fusiliers displayed a similar degree of national fervour. Having recently had an 'uppish' draft of Norfolk Regiment officers attached to his battalion, Drury seethed when he 'overheard a few remarks about their "hard luck"' in being attached to an Irish Regiment. 'By the Lord', he declared, 'I'll make them have sense'.[31]

Naturally, not all nations displayed the same degree of zeal, nor were they all so blinkered to the faults and idiosyncrasies of their own forces. Yet, it is clear that homophily was important to horizontal learning. The

---

[28] TNA, WO 95/3153, 230th Brigade War Diary, 'List of Papers Handed Over to 229th Infantry Brigade', 24 July 1918.

[29] M. McPherson, L. Smith-Lovin, and J. M. Cook, 'Birds of a Feather: Homophily in Social Networks', *Annual Review of Sociology* 27 (2001), p. 415.

[30] AWM, Papers of Lieutenant G. L. Makin, 1 DRL/0473, Makin to parents, 25 February 1915.

[31] NAM, Papers of Captain N. Drury, 7607-69, vol. 2. Serbia and Salonika, diary entry, 18 October 1915.

staff of the 2nd Australian Division, for example, shared recent expertise on brigade tactics with its counterparts in the newly constituted 4th Australian Division in June 1916.[32] A further example can be found at corps level, involving the Australians and Canadians, again in 1916. This example is particularly interesting as it was predicated on the interpersonal relationship between the two BGGS who had both been to staff college together. Sent to relieve the Canadian Corps in the Ypres sector, I Australian and New Zealand Army Corps's [ANZAC] BGGS, Brigadier-General Cyril Brudenell White, handed over a sheaf of papers to his counterpart, Brigadier-General Percy Radcliffe. Within this sheaf of papers were 'some useful notes by one of our best brigade commanders . . . his orders for certain operations . . . some training orders by the same brigade . . . [and] a sample of divisional orders, which are the best available, although they go into a great amount of detail'.[33] Copies of these documents were passed down to all Canadian divisions. The Canadians reciprocated in kind, furnishing the I ANZAC with copies of maps and schemes for the sector to be taken over.[34] While one would expect relieving forces to provide relevant information and advice to the other, this exchange went above and beyond what was standard practice. Similar interactions were commonplace throughout the war. Shared national identity facilitated by proximity to one another in the front line, for example, allowed for the exchange of practical knowledge between 'old comrades' the 2nd Royal Munster Fusiliers (50th Division) and the 5th Connaught Rangers (66th Division) on the tactics and disposition of the German Army in mid-October 1918.[35] These two formations had also served together as part of the 10th (Irish) Division out in Salonika and Palestine, adding another layer to their relationship.

In Foley's discussion of horizontal learning, it was the lack of rigid, top-down interference that allowed for the rapid exchange of knowledge and experience between formations. However, even Foley acknowledges the role that higher command played in encouraging horizontal learning. While not necessarily interventionist in nature, higher command was vital in creating an environment for learning from experience. Unsurprisingly, some commanders were better at this than others. Despite his mediocre performance on the Western Front as GOC 21st Division,

[32] AWM, Papers of General Sir J. Monash, 3DRL/2316 3/41, 'Report on Minor Enterprise', Jackson to Monash, 21 June 1916.
[33] Quoted in K. Radley, *We Lead Others Follow: First Canadian Division 1914–1918* (St Catherines, ON: Vanwell, 2006), p. 90.
[34] R. Stevenson, *To Win the Battle: The 1st Australian Division in the Great War, 1914–1918* (Melbourne, VIC: Cambridge University Press, 2013), pp. 157–158.
[35] NAM, 7603-69-1, Papers relating to Royal Munster Fusiliers, 'The End of the Great War – 1918', 31 November 1970.

Major-General George Forestier-Walker adopted a far more consultative approach when appointed to command the 27th Division in Salonika in December 1916. One of his first decisions upon taking command was to inaugurate weekly conferences. These would allow for 'discussing questions of general interest at a time when everybody concerned was present', whilst also giving commanders and staff officers an opportunity of getting to know each other. This provided a solid bedrock for the horizontal sharing of ideas and knowledge. Forestier-Walker acted as a facilitator. He insisted on circulating 'all . . . schemes received from Inf[antry] B[riga]des or 16th Corps', as 'an interchange of ideas would be interesting and perhaps lead to further ideas'. In addition to this, he believed that 'for perfect co-operation . . . all should know what their neighbours are doing and how they did it'. Brigade commanders were actively encouraged to 'visit one another's defence lines', as a 'great deal of information can always be obtained by such visits'.[36]

In some cases, senior command had to be more direct. Out in Italy, the 69th Brigade's adoption of a Western Front style defence in depth method in December 1917, for example, drew considerable praise from Lord Cavan as GOC XIV Corps. In a note to his divisions, Cavan wrote how 'everyone can learn' from the 69th Brigade and that its work was 'in advance of anything that is being carried out at the moment'. He requested 'all units of the Corps to study, and where possible to initiate, the system which is to be seen in this Brigade sector'. The 7th Division acted on Cavan's request, despatching officers to visit the 69th Brigade's defensive system in January 1918.[37] Though more direct in his approach, Cavan, like Forestier-Walker, acted as a facilitator, encouraging formations to look to their neighbours for best practice and innovation. It is clear then that, rather than working in silos, formations were encouraged to learn from one another and adopt methods where appropriate.

Unlike the ephemeral, unstructured nature of liberal learning or the often informal, group-driven horizontal approach, vertical learning is largely centralised and often top-down in nature.[38] Vertical learning is directive, an activity that is orientated to improving certain tasks. On the surface, this approach appears to lend itself well to the hierarchical nature of the military organisation, particularly with the formal relationships that existed between different command levels. Aspects of this vertical approach were certainly apparent within the army. Military

[36] TNA, WO 95/4878, 27th Division GS War Diary, Divisional Conference Proceedings, January–April 1917.
[37] TNA, WO 95/4237, 69th Brigade War Diary, Memo from XIV Corps, 27 December 1917.
[38] Poell et al., 'Learning-Network', p. 36.

pamphlets and instructional manuals, for example, were produced by GHQ and pushed down to lower levels of command. Even though these manuals advocated a principle-based approach, they were written and codified at the top of the organisation.

Given the army's pre-war aversion to top-down interference and prescription, this vertical approach caused some problems. For regular officers who had been schooled in *FSR* and imbued with the ethos of initiative and individual action, such an approach was unwelcome and often difficult to enforce. One divisional commander remarked in July 1916 that it was difficult to order subordinates to 'hold a particular place, in a particular way with limits to the number of men he employs, *without the justifiable reproof of interference in details*'.[39] This degree of micromanagement clashed with the central tenets of *FSR*. However, in many respects, the army had little choice but to embrace a more structured, often top-down approach to learning, given its changing demographic from 1915 onwards. Commanders like General Sir Hubert Gough (GOC, Fifth Army), for instance, felt they needed to be more prescriptive than *FSR* allowed since their subordinate commanders and troops were inexperienced.[40] Some commanders recognised and, indeed, welcomed the benefits of more top-down involvement. Reflecting on his division's experience on the Somme, Major-General Sir Ivor Maxse remarked that 'inexperienced armies cannot be fed on "general principles" only. They require definite methods . . . we should from time to time issue papers . . . and these papers should indicate *methods* of carrying out accepted principles'.[41] Major-General Tom Bridges (GOC, 19th Division) was broadly in agreement, noting that, while the 'spirit of the men' was excellent, his troops 'labour under the disadvantage of being of unsporting habits and lacking those soldier instincts which generations of military service alone can supply'.[42]

The musings of Maxse and Bridges underscored some of the problems associated with the pre-war ethos and the army's traditional approach to learning. Significantly, their ruminations did not simply disappear into the ether. They constituted part of a vertical – 'deep dive' – learning process initiated by General Sir Henry Rawlinson (GOC, Fourth Army) and his MGGS, Montgomery. Throughout the Somme campaign, Montgomery requested specific feedback from corps level down on the

---

[39] LHCMA, Montgomery-Massingberd Papers, 7/3, Furse to Montgomery, 26 July 1916. Added emphasis.

[40] Simpson, *Directing Operations*, pp. 41–42.

[41] LHCMA, Montgomery-Massingberd Papers, 7/4, Maxse to Montgomery, 26 November 1916. Original emphasis.

[42] LHCMA, Montgomery-Massingberd Papers, 7/3, Bridges to Montgomery, 9 September 1916.

lessons identified from recent fighting. Montgomery was well known for his interest in training, and sought to inculcate a culture of learning within the Fourth Army. Best practice from its battalions was often highlighted and rapidly disseminated in pamphlet form. An account of the capture of Zenith trench on 2 November 1916 by two battalions from the 17th (Northern) Division, for example, was produced as a pamphlet in less than a week for Army-wide dissemination. The actions of these two battalions demonstrated 'initiative shewn by Battalion and Company commanders, the good leading by officers, and the fine fighting spirit shewn by all ranks'.[43]

Yet such a culture of learning required a degree of speaking truth to power. Although Maxse included an apologia on the 'freedom' of his remarks to Montgomery, he felt empowered to raise his concerns as there was an 'obvious desire to get at the real truth' and a wish 'to obtain the ideas of Divisional commanders'.[44] Rawlinson and Montgomery's aim was to ensure that such vital experience was not lost, but instead retained and codified for future use, particularly for new divisions rotating into the Fourth Army. Such an aim required an environment that allowed for constructive criticism. The consultative feedback system bore fruit with the production of *SS119 Preliminary Notes on the Tactical Lessons of Recent Operations*. Endorsed by GHQ and published by its operations branch, this manual had a force-wide influence. It proved a successful example of senior commanders actively reaching down to the tactical level, resulting in the production and dissemination of a manual based on bottom-up lessons and experiences, crafted into a coherent whole. The conversation did not stop there either: divisional commanders were also invited to comment on *SS119*, suggesting amendments or areas for improvement as part of an ongoing process.

SS119 is just one example of the broader approach to pamphlet creation during the war.[45] The Stationery Service [SS] pamphlets were usually written and disseminated by GHQ, but were often the product of other ways of learning. *SS143 The Training of Platoons for Offensive Action*, for example, was largely based on French army tactics, highlighting the importance of external input to this process.[46] *SS148 Forward*

[43] Fourth Army, *Attack on Zenith Trench, 2 November 1916* (1916).
[44] LHCMA, Montgomery-Massingberd Papers, 7/3, Maxse to Montgomery, 31 July 1916.
[45] For the army's doctrine writing process, see J. Beach, 'Issued by the General Staff: Doctrine Writing at British GHQ, 1917–1918', *War in History* 19 (4) (2012), pp. 464, 491.
[46] A. Geddes, 'Major-General Arthur Solly-Flood, GHQ and Tactical Training in the BEF, 1916–1918', Unpublished MA Dissertation, University of Birmingham, 2007, pp. 27–35; LHCMA, Montgomery-Massingberd Papers, 7/4, Shea to Montgomery, 28 November 1916.

Inter-communication in Battle, on the other hand, was the product of a four day 'Staff and Signal Conference'. The outcomes of this conference were written up in four days, most likely by some of the participants, and the pamphlet then published within two weeks.[47] Pamphlets were not static either; they were fluid documents, sensitive to the demands of war, and subject to revision. The organic nature of these documents was encapsulated in the mundanely titled *SS177 Instructions on Wiring*. While stating the need for standardisation of method, the pamphlet advocated modification of existing practice. Crucially, however, it acknowledged the importance of bottom-up learning and its symbiotic relationship with top-down approaches:

If in any unit a better type or drill is discovered, the fact should be reported. The new method will then be thoroughly tested under GHQ arrangements, and if found more satisfactory will be adopted officially in place of the old one, and all units and training schools will be informed.[48]

A number of pamphlets were revised based on experiences from the front line, such as *SS135 The Training of Divisions for Offensive Action, SS143*, and *SS148*, which was subsumed into *SS191 Inter-communication in the Field*. The particular challenges associated with *SS148* and its eventual modification sheds light upon the deep-seated concerns that still existed around doctrine and its potentially prescriptive nature. Although an 'immense advance' on what had come before, *SS148* was 'by no means ideal'. Its principal failing was 'a certain rigidity in the advocacy of particular methods' and a 'tendency towards dogma'. As a result, little to no play was given to the 'imagination of the individual signal officer'.[49] Even in the penultimate year of the war, the army was still trying to unpick the knotty issue of standardisation versus flexibility. While responding to bottom-up experiences, *SS191* addressed this recurring tension through 'the adoption of a more tentative attitude'. It advocated a 'general uniform system' that set broad parameters within which units and individuals could adapt.[50] Such an approach harked back to recommendations made during the 1909 General Staff conference, which called for

---

[47] Beach, 'General Staff', p. 470; R. E. Priestley, *Work of the RE in the European War, 1914–19: The Signal Service (France)* (reprint, Uckfield: Naval & Military Press, 2006 [1921]), pp. 180–181.

[48] General Staff, *SS177 Instructions on Wiring* (1917), p. 5. A similar, contemporary example can be found in the UK Ministry of Defence's GEMS scheme. This scheme is open to all Ministry of Defence civilian and Armed Forces personnel and ex-employees. Staff are encouraged to contribute original, constructive ideas for improving efficiency and organisation anywhere within Defence.

[49] Priestley, *Signal Service*, pp. 181–182, 217.

[50] General Staff, *SS191 Inter-communication in the Field* (1917), pp. 27–28.

uniformity of approach through a 'general, broad-minded system'.[51] The circumstances may have changed, but the response was still the same.

While some aspects of vertical, top-down intervention were welcomed, others were not. One only needs to look at the experience of the Inspectorate of Training to discern some of the problems associated with perceptions of vertical learning. Though the army was a hierarchical and inherently deferential organisation, there was a dislike of prescription in all forms. In many ways then, the establishment of the Inspectorate was a gamble for the army. Once more, the continuing potency of the army's ethos was pit against the changing needs and demography of the 1918 army.

Established in July 1918 under the command of Ivor Maxse, the Inspectorate of Training was designed to relieve pressure on the existing Training Directorate at GHQ. According to senior officers, despite the existence of this directorate, the training carried out on the Western Front was 'neither perfectly coordinative nor altogether evenly distributed'.[52] While the Inspectorate had 'no executive functions', it would 'advise and assist in the preparation and revision of training manuals, instructions and syllabuses of training for issue by the General Staff at GHQ', and in the 'supervision and control of training establishments'.[53] Its rationale was carefully worded to reassure subordinate commanders that they should expect minimal interference. Maxse himself noted that 'we inspect and help and advise – through the local commanders on the spot. We are not to command but we expect to *stimulate those who do*'.[54] Despite this clear statement of intent, grumbles about Maxse reverberated around the BEF and soon reached Major-General Guy Dawnay at GHQ: 'gossip is arising in formations that you are going to train their troops. We must stop this'.[55]

Although there is evidence to support the distrust felt by senior officers, the Inspectorate found encouragement from a number of prominent, regular officers, including Aylmer Hunter-Weston, William Heneker, and Cameron Shute. The latter was effusive in his support: 'you may rely upon me to carry out your principles entirely. What is the use in selecting a man for a job who has proved himself the best

---

[51] TNA, WO 279/25, General Staff officers conference, 18–21 January 1909, p. 61.

[52] LHCMA, Montgomery-Massingberd Papers, 7/32, Dawnay to Montgomery, 31 October 1918.

[53] IWM, Papers of General Sir F. I. Maxse, 69/53/13 File 56, Haig to War Office, 16 June 1918.

[54] J. Baynes, *Far from a Donkey: The Life of General Sir Ivor Maxse* (London: Brassey's, 1995), p. 210. Original emphasis.

[55] IWM, Maxse Papers, PP/MCR/C42/53–58, Dawnay to Maxse, 9 September 1918.

exponent of it, and then other commanders make up other ideas'.[56] While perceptions of the Inspectorate were not always positive, it is clear that attempts had been made to align its ethos with that of the wider army. Maxse understood this need completely. In a letter to Basil Liddell Hart written in 1928, Maxse advised him '*never* tell your audience that you are going to explain a *new* idea to them. Say you are putting "old ideas, other people's ideas into a new form only"'.[57] The Inspectorate's advisory, rather than executive, function demonstrated an understanding of the army's ethos and its distrust of prescription. Emphasis on the Inspectorate's 'teach the teacher' schemes, for example, was a deliberate attempt to move away from accusations that it was dictatorial in its approach. Hunter-Weston encapsulated the Inspectorate's proposed approach perfectly:

Teaching the officers and N[on] C[ommissioned] O[fficer]s and teaching them how to teach, is of even greater importance than teaching the men, and half the time, and more than half the thought, of Battalion and higher commanders must be devoted to teaching the teachers.[58]

Much like Montgomery's collation of experience following the Somme, Maxse was keen to highlight and disseminate best practice where it occurred. Through his assistant inspectors of training [AIT], it was possible to 'watch the battles on the spot' and identify tactical innovations on the ground. One of the AITs recalled observing the 9th (Scottish) Division attacking in late 1918 using blobs or 'Maxse formations'. The AIT was 'taking notes and . . . produced a report which Maxse was extremely pleased with and gave him the picture of the adoption of his tactics'. The Inspectorate compiled these reports into pamphlets which were then circulated to infantry brigadiers for their views.[59]

Both GHQ and the Inspectorate made it clear that they wanted to hear from individuals on how training and tactics could be improved. This was not lip service. In a letter to Major-General Sir Herbert Uniacke, Deputy Inspector of Training, one brigade major in the Royal Artillery wrote that 'Guy [Dawnay] has told me that you are asking for a few of our "experiences" with single guns and mobile T[rench] M[ortars]'.[60] Both Maxse's and Uniacke's papers contain numerous

---

[56] IWM, Maxse Papers, PP/MCR/C42/60, Shute to Maxse, 30 August 1918.

[57] LHCMA, Papers of Captain B. Liddell Hart, 7/1920/28, Maxse to Liddell Hart, 4 February 1921. Original emphasis.

[58] IWM, Maxse Papers, PP/MCR/C42/53–58, Hunter-Weston to Maxse, 12 August 1918.

[59] Liddle Collection, University of Leeds [LC], Papers of Sir J. F. Evetts, Liddle/WW1/GS/0533, Tape 588, July 1979.

[60] RAHT, Papers of General Sir H. Uniacke, MD 1160/1/4, Unknown Brigade Major RA to Uniacke, 30 September 1918.

letters from brigade command upwards which outlined what they believed to be the 'needs and requirements out in France'. The proposal submitted by the 46th (North Midland) Division's Brigadier-General, Royal Artillery [BGRA] on the close support role of artillery sections in open warfare, for instance, was deemed by Maxse to be 'an admirable report – which might well be epitomised and issued to our inspectoring staff'.[61] The pamphlets that the Inspectorate produced were 'founded upon a comprehensive, if anonymous, body of experience'. They were not the 'product of a single pen nor even of the Training Staff alone'.[62] They were essentially illustrations of the army's official manuals that showcased best practice drawn from the front line, presenting it in an easily digestible manner for soldiers and officers with different levels of experience. This 'bubble up' process extended to senior officers and generals who were also encouraged and, more importantly, were willing to write to the Inspectorate suggesting material for future publications. Brudenell White suggested two future pamphlets, one focusing on 'how brigade commanders coordinate and influence training', and another that showed how to '*think out* training programmes'.[63] General Sir Charles Fergusson advocated a back to basics approach, requesting 'little schemes for teaching advanced guards, outposts etc on the principles of company walks, i.e. by lecturing and demonstration'.[64]

The signing of the Armistice certainly curtailed the work of the Inspectorate. While its raison d'être was clearly disseminated through conferences, the dedicated personnel attached to Army headquarters, and its training leaflets, it lacked the luxury of time. Though shaped by, and responsive to, the army's ethos, its reach was not ubiquitous. Maxse frequently complained that commanders ignored the advice from GHQ, suggesting that the Inspectorate faced challenges with little time to overcome them. The vertical approach to learning embodied by the Inspectorate was necessary yet problematic. The sheer size of the army and the varying degrees of competence and experience within the organisation demanded a more structured, often top-down approach. For higher command, imbued with an ethos of pragmatism and flexibility, the ability to rationalise this vertical approach relied on a responsive organisational culture that could tolerate such a departure from learning as usual.

The final network of learning relates to that which originates from outside the organisation. For the British army, 'external' learning was

[61] Ibid., Memo, BGRA 46th Division to HQ RA IX Corps, 29 October 1918.
[62] RAHT, Uniacke Papers, MD 1160/3, *Training Leaflets* (1919).
[63] IWM, Maxse Papers, PP/MCR/C42 File 58, White to Maxse, 31 August 1918. Original emphasis.
[64] IWM, Maxse Papers, PP/MCR/C42 File 60, Fergusson to Maxse, 31 August 1918.

harnessed through three primary means: enemies, allies, and external – often civilian – experts. These external inputs acted as important triggers or catalysts and usually challenged existing practice. Indeed, the intervention of these external actors played an important role in the continual dynamic of learning. Where its enemies were concerned, the army had to respond constantly, trying to remain one step ahead in the innovation game. The external influence of adversaries often resulted in shocks to the system, requiring the modification of existing tactics, techniques, and procedures. This modification worked both ways, with Germany and the Central Powers augmenting or overhauling their own ways and means. Where Britain's allies were concerned, the tensions associated with differing national and organisational cultures came into play. As we shall see in later chapters, the British were not always amenable to learning the lessons of their allies. At times, there was obvious scepticism, bordering on arrogance, but there were instances at lower levels and in certain branches, such as artillery survey and airpower, where a fruitful, two-way exchange of knowledge and experience occurred.

For all belligerents engaged in this total war, external expertise was exploited for the good of the nation and the military. In the British case, civilian expertise was used in a number of different ways – through learned societies, as troubleshooters and consultants, or as commissioned officers embedded in various branches of the military. There were obvious strengths to using external experts. They were not bound to the same extent by the hierarchical structures or cultural taboos that often limited the scope of action experienced by members of the military.[65] In some cases, these external experts brought clarity and a desire for action, often applying necessary pressure to implement decisions. Naturally, there were concordant drawbacks to external input. A number of social and organisational barriers had to be surmounted, including institutional memory of earlier failures, organisational regulations and procedures that limited the ability to try new approaches, and the fear of losing something of value, such as position or authority.[66] The experience of Sydney businessman, Robert Anderson, reveals both the advantages and drawbacks associated with external agents. Appointed by Sir George Pearce, the Australian Minister for Defence, Anderson was tasked with

---

[65] A. Berthoin Andal and C. Krebsbach-Gnath, 'Consultants as Agents of Organizational Learning: The Importance of Marginalia', in M. Dierkes, A. Berthoin Andal, J. Child, and I. Nonaka (eds), *Handbook of Organizational Learning and Knowledge* (Oxford: Oxford University Press, 2001), p. 477.

[66] A. C. Lewis and M. Grosser, 'The Change Game: An Experiential Exercise Demonstrating Barriers to Change', *Journal of Management Education* 36 (5) (2012), p. 671.

implementing root and branch reform of business practices at AIF Head-quarters in London. Pearce's confidence was well placed. Within two months of his arrival, Anderson had negotiated a complete financial readjustment with the War Office. Instead of attempting to account for every item of clothing, arms, and equipment supplied to AIF troops, a fixed rate per head was agreed upon. Such was the success of this scheme that the Canadian High Commissioner wished to emulate it for the Canadian Expeditionary Force's [CEF] own administration.[67] Ander-son's business acumen, drive, and no-nonsense attitude were invaluable. Yet his abrasive, straightforward personality proved a problem.

Impatient by nature and aggressive when thwarted, Anderson did little to endear himself to his military counterparts. For him, 'military business is the same as any other business – it is a matter of organisation'.[68] His appointment was an uncomfortable fit in many ways. Desirous to carry out his role in civilian garb and 'not to be interfered with', Anderson was informed that 'circumstances here were such that a man in mufti would have no position of authority'.[69] Appointed as a colonel and put in mil-itary uniform to facilitate his acceptance and authority, Anderson kept 'pegging away' until he gradually felt 'the atmosphere of suspicion clear-ing away'.[70] However, his short, sharp dealings with professional soldiers were not something that rank and uniform could smooth over. Ander-son distrusted regular officers who he believed closed ranks against out-siders, particularly civilians, irrespective of their abilities or talents. Cor-respondence between regular AIF officers suggested that Anderson was an annoyance to be tolerated, one remarking how: 'the only saving clause about him is that he does not seem to stay in the same job very long, and if the war lasts long enough, he will have left the Defence Department before you and I get back'.[71] Despite 'playing the game', Anderson's atti-tude and limited interpersonal skills thus made him unsuitable as com-mandant at AIF Headquarters. He was replaced by a career officer in March 1917 and subsequently returned to Australia. While Anderson was able to fulfil his original brief, his experience as an external agent highlights the often emotional response to knowledge and best practice

---

[67] C. E. W. Bean, *The Official History of Australia in the War of 1914–1918: The Australian Imperial Force in France, 1916*, III (12 vols, Sydney, NSW: Angus and Robertson, 1941), p. 173; AWM, Papers of Brigadier-General R. M. Anderson, PR83/020, Anderson to Trumble, 30 November 1916.

[68] British Library [BL], Papers of Lord Birdwood, MSS Eur D686/77, Anderson to Bird-wood, 26 March 1917.

[69] AWM, Anderson Papers, PR83/020, Anderson to Trumble, 29 March 1916.

[70] BL, Birdwood Papers, MSS Eur D686/77, Anderson to Birdwood, 26 March 1917.

[71] National Library of Australia [NLA], Papers of General Sir C. B. B. White, MS 5172 2.3/40, Chauvel to White, 15 August 1917.

from outside the military organisation. Fear, frustration, and suspicion were constantly at play, proving a salutary reminder of the potency of human feeling to the process of learning.

While the external inputs of civilians, enemies, and allies sometimes occurred in isolation, there were some instances where they intersected. The German use of gas, for example, acted as a catalyst in both the British and French armies leading them to exploit further civilian expertise – particularly in chemistry and meteorology – for the development of offensive and defensive chemical warfare. For the British, the German gas attack on 22 April 1915 resulted in the mobilisation of highly skilled external expertise. Within four days of the attack, Bernard Mouat Jones, an assistant professor at Imperial College, was commissioned into the RE and ordered by GHQ to organise a 'small emergency laboratory at St. Omer'. Initially conceived as an extraordinary measure, this central laboratory soon provided broader scientific advice to all branches of the army, often acting as a clearing house for information on 'consulting experts at home'.[72] Back at the War Office, liaison was established with the Royal Society's chemical subcommittee, which formed part of a larger war committee designed to offer advice to the government and military on scientific matters. Through this subcommittee, expertise for chemical weapons research was rapidly established. On the Western Front, things also moved quickly. There was an increase in fellows and associates of the Institute of Chemistry out in France, rising from 178 to 215 between February and April 1915.[73] A little over a month after the initial German gas attack, Colonel Charles Foulkes, a regular RE officer, had been appointed Gas Adviser to GHQ and given 'practically a free hand' to organise and train the gas troops which eventually became the Special Brigade.[74] By February 1916, the chemical warfare service had its own distinct command structure with representation from Army down to division. Chemical expertise was sought at all levels. This demand led the War Office to call on all universities and colleges 'asking for lists of students or graduates' who were known chemists already serving or were willing to do so. For those already in uniform, instructions were 'sent to the COs of their units, transferring them without question since they were designated "chemists"'.[75] The

---

[72] LHCMA, Papers of Major-General Sir C. H. Foulkes, 6/37, History of the Central Laboratory, n.d.

[73] R. Macleod, 'The Chemists Go to War: The Mobilization of Civilian Chemists and the British War Effort, 1914–1918', *Annals of Science* 50 (5) (1993), p. 459.

[74] LHCMA, Foulkes Papers, 6/61, Draft Chapter for History of RE, n.d.

[75] TNA, WO 162/6, History of the Directorate of Organisation, n.d. (c. 1919), p. 89; IWM, Papers of M. S. Fox, 76/49/1, Ts Memoir, n.d., Chapter 1.

army's response to this external shock was relatively rapid, combining a mixture of ad hoc and formalised means to respond to this new type of warfare.

The British army was not unique in this respect. The French army had developed similar capabilities to the Special Brigade with its *compagnies Z*. These units were 450 men strong with attached medical personnel and, by early 1916, included a specialist meteorology section.[76] The companies had been developed in direct response to an external threat, drawing on external expertise to enhance their capabilities. While the meteorological component to these units was welcome, it was not without its problems. On the outbreak of war, the French War Ministry did not have its own meteorological service, relying instead on the civilian Bureau Central Météorologique [BCM] before the eventual establishment of the military-run Bureau Météorologique du Ministère de la Guerre in late 1915.[77] While the BCM provided high level forecasting, the German gas attack near Fouquescourt on 21 February 1916 revealed deficiencies in the meteorological education of the *compagnies Z*. The shock of Fouquescourt coupled with the efficacy of German meteorology resulted in the French embarking on a systematic meteorology training programme for artillerymen, airmen, and the *compagnies Z*. Led by members of the BCM, this 'massive' training programme focused on the analysis and drafting of meteorological telegrams, the reading of forecast maps, and the identification of weather phenomenon. The British clearly did not have a monopoly on rapid adaptation in war. All belligerents were trying to find ways to cope with an incredibly complex battlefield.

External learning – perhaps more than any of the other networks – highlights the three-dimensional nature of organisational learning. The army did not exist in a vacuum. It was engaged in a life or death struggle, which required it to manage, shape, and facilitate a complex learning process. The influence of external agents shows learning to have been an interpersonal process. Some of these agents sat outside the army or were only briefly part of it, such as Anderson, but they played a significant role in shaping what and how the army learned. Attitudes towards these external agents demonstrated the highly individualised nature of the army. Though bound by a shared ethos, the army was still an organisation made up of individuals with their own motivations, ideals, and

---

[76] Service Géographique de l'Armée [SGA], *Rapport sur les Travaux Exécutés du 1er Aout 1914 au 31 Decembre 1919: Historique du Service Géographique de l'Armée pendant la Guerre* (Paris: Imprimerie du Service Géographique de l'Armée, 1936), p. 201.

[77] S. Di Manno, '"Hier sur tous les fronts … Demain sur tous les mondes" Mobilisation météorologique et reconfigurations disciplinaires, militaires et aéronautiques durant la Première Guerre mondiale', *Cahiers d'histoire. Revue d'histoire critique* 127 (2015).

agency. Rather than ignoring this friction, it should be regarded as an interrelated factor in the process of learning, not as a distinct or independent element. As one serving officer remarked, 'jealousies, differences in opinion, want of co-ordination, want of exact system laid down on paper would generally, I think, have been fatal amongst other nations, but it worked with us, on the whole . . . because every officer was doing his best to help the work along'.[78]

A Learning Kaleidoscope?

Having detailed the various networks discretely, it is now worth returning to the kaleidoscope analogy outlined earlier in the chapter; the idea that the network of learning is constant, but the precise nature of the connections is ever changing and often fleeting in nature. There was not a standard approach to learning nor was there a definitive formula. As we have seen, innovations and lessons were identified and acted upon in different ways. Depending on the type of knowledge or expertise involved, different means of learning played a greater or lesser role. With Hemming and flash spotting, we can see a liberal-vertical network in play. Initially engaged in liberal learning, Hemming's experiments with flash spotting, through encounters with more senior individuals in the command chain, were pushed up and out across the wider expeditionary force. The 69th Brigade's defence in depth arrangement can be seen as a vertical-horizontal network, with Cavan identifying this best practice and encouraging neighbouring formations to adopt it. Some learning involved the intersection of multiple networks. The development of *SS143*, for example, involved external, horizontal, and vertical networks. In short, the various networks fit together in different ways. However, it is clear that without engaging with a vertical network, often driven by senior leaders, front line innovation would remain local (or at unit level), rather than leading to improved operational performance.[79] In the anarchical environment of war, a coordinated system was required to ensure that lessons and knowledge were identified, selected, supported, and disseminated.

How learning is diffused is dependent on the size, extent, and degree of coupling of the various networks involved. However, it also relies on the importance of different members' roles and position. While it is relatively easy to identify the relationships between these networks, how

---

[78] C. Close, 'British Survey on the Western Front: Discussion', *Geographical Journal* 53 (4) (1919), p. 272.

[79] For a contemporary take on this, see Foley et al., 'Transformation in Contact'; O'Toole and Talbot, 'Fighting for Knowledge'.

they work in practice is more troublesome to pin down. One way of exploring this is by considering the roles that certain members play as nodes between groups. For our purposes, these nodes are individuals who actively stimulate, facilitate, and coordinate the exchange of knowledge and learning, forming part of a broader leadership constellation. Using their own personal and professional connections, they build up effective working relationships with others in different parts of the organisation, which enhances trust and provides legitimacy. Positioned across the wider organisation, their job description is less important than the personal characteristics that they display.

Three particular roles can be discerned within this constellation, reaching from the men in the field to those at the top of the army.[80] First, you have experts – individuals who have certain expertise or knowledge that sets them apart from their peers. We can place Henry Hemming and his sound ranging counterpart, Lawrence Bragg, in this field. This expertise could be put down on paper, but in many cases it was intuitive and tacit. Secondly, you have entrepreneurs. These individuals were not necessarily innovative in their own right, but they were able to lead a project to a successful conclusion, often in the face of organisational resistance. In modern terms, these individuals can be seen as facilitators. Guy Dawnay, for example, was an entrepreneur as seen through his promotion of the Inspectorate of Training. For Dawnay, the Inspectorate was 'one of his biggest works', and so he actively laid the groundwork, smoothing over as many problems as possible beforehand. This not only increased its legitimacy within the army, but it also indicated that Maxse and his team had support and buy-in from senior decision makers. Before the Inspectorate's establishment, Dawnay held a luncheon for all the MGGS of the Armies where 'they got all their grumbles off which was a great thing'. Even after the launch of the Inspectorate, Dawnay's work was far from over. Writing to his wife three days after its establishment, he recalled how he had been 'round to half a dozen divisional and corps HQ, and had lots of talk about whether GHQ could do more to help and if we were going the right way about it'. He also 'consulted commanders [as] to their views on various points. They all like this and it does good'.[81]

Like Dawnay, Harold Winterbotham also proved to be an important entrepreneur for new artillery survey techniques. An 'experienced sapper surveyor', Winterbotham supported and pushed forward the ideas of

---

[80] These three roles are derived from Michel Goya's discussion of drivers of innovation. See Goya, *La Chair*, pp. 204–207.

[81] IWM, Papers of Major-General G. P. Dawnay, 69/21/3, Dawnay to wife, 16 June 1918 and 12 July 1918.

key officers such as Hemming and Bragg, whilst receiving the backing of senior generals such as Haig, Rawlinson, and Allenby. Winterbotham was well connected both inside and outside the army. He had plied his trade in the colonial survey section before the First World War, bringing a wealth of experience and civilian connections to his wartime role. Inside the army, he cultivated influence and connections with generals at Army level and above. In 1914, it was Rawlinson, supported by Major-General Arthur Holland (CRA, 8th Division) who had requested that Winterbotham bring 'a small Ranging Section to France'.[82] The original records for this section are annotated with a brief pencil scrawl: 'Asked for by Rawlinson – Trained on Salisbury Plain and embarked with 8th Division'.[83] When in Allenby's Third Army, which was deemed 'something of a haven for men with new technical ideas', Winterbotham was well supported in his survey endeavours by both Army commander and the Army's new Major-General, Royal Artillery [MGRA], who fortunately proved to be the very same Arthur Holland.[84] Winterbotham capitalised on his own experience and influence, pressing for further investigation into the French experiments with sound ranging, and had soon 'persuaded the army authorities to set up an experimental section'.[85] Winterbotham did not seek to stifle innovation. Instead, he sought to circulate it. Upon his appointment to GHQ, Hemming had asked Winterbotham what he wanted him to do: 'Make all the flash spotting groups as good as the best one, and now get on with it'.[86] Such was his legacy that Major-General Sir Henry Tudor, the innovative commander of the 9th (Scottish) Division, remembered the name of only one survey officer during the war: Winterbotham.[87]

The third and final role in the constellation was that of 'leader'. Usually holding general officer rank, these individuals had to simultaneously lead operations as well as manage adaptation. They could be seen as the 'benevolent protectors' of the innovators.[88] Nowadays, they might be seen as project champions, fostering adaptation by 'creating a

[82] R. Macleod, 'Sight and Sound on the Western Front: Surveyors, Scientists, and the "Battlefield Laboratory", 1915–1918', *War and Society* 18 (1) (2000), p. 32.

[83] TNA, WO 181/527, 'Survey on the Western Front', preliminary report by H. Winterbotham, 20 December 1918, p. 9.

[84] S. Marble, *British Artillery on the Western Front: The Infantry Cannot Do with a Gun Less* (Farnham: Ashgate, 2013), p. 119.

[85] A. M. Glazer and P. Thomson (eds), *Crystal Clear: The Autobiographies of Sir Lawrence and Lady Bragg* (Oxford: Oxford University Press, 2015), p. 88.

[86] IWM, Hemming Papers, PP/MCR/155, Ts Memoir, p. 97.

[87] RAHT, Papers of Major-General Sir H. H. Tudor, MD 1167, Ts Memoir, August 1917, p. 32.

[88] Goya, *La Chair*, p. 417.

coherent vision and encouraging purposive action'.[89] Their prestige and support was often the vital precondition for an innovation to succeed. This reflects Rosen's ideas on the role of visionary senior military figures who, with their own strategies for innovation, create promotion pathways for their subordinates.[90] These high-ranking figures used their legitimacy and position within the organisation to protect these mid-level officers, enabling them to innovate. While it was important to cultivate a coherent vision, these figures also needed to create the space and environment to enable individual innovators to address challenges. Tudor, for example, highlighted the important role that Major-General Sir William Furse played in the development of smoke barrages. Before his appointment as Major-General of the Ordnance, Furse was Tudor's commanding officer in the 9th Division. An artilleryman and fellow advocate of smoke, Furse was deemed a 'considerable technologist and innovator'.[91] Tudor benefitted from Furse's patronage, support, and his willingness to 'send to us ... many badly needed weapons ... such was the result of appointing a man of vision and energy, who knew from personal experience what was wanted at the front, to such a vital post'.[92] Within this 'leader' role, we can also place Cavan for his support in spreading the 69th Brigade's defensive arrangements, as well as Edmund Allenby for supporting Winterbotham's efforts with artillery survey. Similarities can also be seen within the French army. As commander of the French First Army, General Auguste Dubail actively observed and encouraged tactical innovations, supporting individuals such as Colonel Fetter in his development of a prototype flamethrower in October 1914. Likewise, senior generals, such as Phillipe Pétain and Joseph Joffre lent their support to Colonel Estienne's idea for the tank in 1915.[93]

Without a supportive culture, encompassing both structure and leadership, ideas and knowledge will remain fixed or undeveloped. Individual, unconnected initiatives from lower levels will remain just that. Pétain had remarked in 1915 that the war had engendered a 'lack of curiosity and mental laziness' in combatants, that new equipment and ideas were only known by those who had developed them, that what was learned from operations was 'little shared' with those who did not take part.[94]

[89] Harkness and Hunzeker, 'Military Maladaptation', p. 783.
[90] See Rosen, *Winning the Next War*, p. 127.
[91] J. P. Harris, *Men, Ideas, and Tanks: British Military Thought and Armoured Forces, 1903–1939* (Manchester: Manchester University Press, 1995), p. 131.
[92] RAHT, Tudor Papers, MD 1167, Ts Memoir, n.d., entry for 31 December 1916.
[93] Goya, *La Chair*, pp. 206–207; T. Gale, *The French Army's Tank Force and Armoured Warfare in the Great War: The Artillerie Spéciale* (London: Routledge, 2013), pp. 19–20, 22.
[94] Quoted in Goya, *La Chair*, p. 225.

Learning and innovation needed the support of leaders like Allenby and Cavan who were prepared to support and foster this process. It also needed facilitators, officers like Dawnay and Winterbotham, to smooth over organisational resistance. These individuals did not always act in the same way. Dawnay, for example, was not the 'go to' entrepreneur for all types of learning. These roles were often situational, and could be filled by different individuals at different times. In short, successful change was reliant on a network of individuals at all levels of the organisation to aid its adoption. Yet, the unavoidable corollary of the importance of these individuals was the inherently unpredictable nature of the learning process.

Conclusions

Learning is a problematic process. In wartime, difficulties snowball. The ways in which the army learned were diffuse and multifarious. How it learned at the beginning of the war was not necessarily how it did so at war's end. As an initially small organisation, it is unsurprising that a liberal-horizontal approach was more common in the army of 1914. Yet, the expansion of the army, its changing demographic, and its increasing global commitments necessitated a change in tack. It is unhelpful to state that the army simply learned, or that it learned in one way or another. Out of necessity, it had to develop a broad approach. This approach involved vertical intervention when necessary. Viewing learning as a network provides us with a far more holistic yet granular understanding of this process. It reveals the interconnectedness of different types of learning, whether formal or informal, individual or organisational, bottom-up or top-down. It also forces us to take note of the blockages and the constraints that existed within the network. While the existence of a wide-ranging leadership constellation could surmount or lessen the impact of these constraints, they remain unavoidable characteristics, which require integration into analyses of the learning process.

McNamara's post-war demolition of army learning was not entirely fair. Mechanisms were in place for the rapid movement of knowledge and expertise, facilitated in part by the army's ethos, but also necessitated by the exigencies of war. However, no learning process is perfect, particularly in organisations composed of millions of individuals. Despite both ad hoc and institutional attempts, it was impossible for the army to capture all lessons and experiences. Its sheer size meant that interactions took place continuously, resulting in many different networks and strands of learning. The development of a more coordinated approach could, where possible, rationalise and regulate this process. However, the perfect diffusion of individual learning to the wider organisation simply did not, and cannot, exist. Barriers – both necessary and unintended – got in the way, often exacerbated by the anarchical environment of war. Irrespective of time and place, individuals used the best means at their disposal to obtain the ends that they desired. The institutional environment in which these individuals operated goes some way towards explaining this behaviour. In this respect, we can see how important an organisation's ethos is to the shape and evolution of learning. The very nature of human choice and behaviour adds another layer to the complexity of coordinating learning. For the army, coordination was, therefore, sought through a general system within which individuals and groups could develop their own solutions. Rather than wholly pursuing a top-down, vertical approach, spontaneity – often unavoidable in time of war – was factored into this system. As with the ways of learning, the methods through which knowledge and expertise were diffused and acted upon were also subject to the same degree of flexibility. It is to those means that we shall now turn.

3 Disseminating Learning

The creation, storage, and transfer of knowledge is a key support for innovation and learning. The army had to ensure that its constituent parts, from entire expeditionary forces down to the newly arrived subaltern in the front line, were aware of the latest trends in military practice taking place not only in theatre, but also around the globe. Such a requirement demanded the holistic use of diverse learning methods: institutional and individual, systematic and incidental, printed and pictorial, oral and visual. The war's global reach and increasing complexity forced the army to grapple with increased bureaucracy when recording and disseminating learning. However, owing to the proximity of the enemy and the inability to disengage fully from the battlefield, heuristic or 'on the job' means were just as necessary as more explicit ones. For effective learning to take place, the army needed to blend a variety of different means, catering for different competencies and styles of learning. These methods were not static. They were deployed at different times and at varying frequencies to suit different tasks and purposes. Identifying and mapping out these methods tells us much about the complex, shifting nature of learning in the army, and provides a useful basis for the different forms of learning explored in Part II.[1]

Publications

One of the most ubiquitous and bureaucratic forms of disseminating learning was through the medium of military pamphlets. Although this is the first study to address the full range of the army's methods for learning, the writing and production of pamphlets, notably the SS series, has been the subject of a number of detailed investigations. The first

---

[1] Some of these ideas were explored in A. Fox-Godden, 'Beyond the Western Front: The Practice of Inter-Theatre Learning in the British Army, 1914–1918', *War in History* 23 (2) (2016), pp. 190–209.

SS pamphlet, *SS23 Preliminary Deductions, for Instruction, from Recent Engagements* was issued in November 1915. Prior to this, publications were printed by the War Office's Central Distribution Section [CDS]. The earliest known CDS pamphlet, *CDS1 Notes on Field Defences*, was published in December 1914. The CDS series was largely concerned with local tactical matters and technical adaptations, but it also published translated documents from French and German forces. The CDS and SS pamphlets covered a myriad of topics, ranging from the training and employment of bombers, the training of platoons, intercommunication, to lessons drawn from specific operations.

While it is not proposed to detail the specifics of pamphlet production here, it is still instructive to provide a brief overview of the initial stages of the process. Although there was provision for a printing depot in the field as part of the BEF's mobilisation plans, the initial production of military publications was the responsibility of the War Office's CDS. Once printed, these CDS publications were despatched to France for distribution via the Army Printing and Stationery Service [APSS], located in the field. Although the APSS began printing its own material at the beginning of 1915, it was not until late 1915 that this material gained the 'SS' prefix. To cope with the demands of a growing army, the APSS in France expanded to accommodate the influx of requests for general stationery and publications. The APSS also received direct requests from the GHQs of the subsidiary theatres who desired the latest Western Front publications.

Initially, these ad hoc requests were met by the APSS or, in some cases, the War Office. However, the practice became unworkable. Following a request for recent SS pamphlets by the Mesopotamia and Salonika theatres in February 1917, British headquarters in France instructed the APSS to issue three copies of all publications forthwith to the commanders of forces in 'Egypt, Salonica, Mesopotamia [and] ... India'.[2] Further copies of these pamphlets were to be produced locally or requested from the War Office directly. The RE initiated a similar practice from 1916 onwards for the distribution of its own notes and publications. Five hundred copies of each publication were sent to the War Office for issue to home units and the various expeditionary forces.[3]

---

[2] TNA, WO 95/4189, DAPSS War Diary, 14 February 1917. Instructions for the formal dissemination of SS pamphlets to the British Force in Italy were agreed on 13 January 1918.

[3] G. H. Addison, *The Work of the Royal Engineers in the European War, 1914–19: The Organization of Engineer Intelligence and Information* (Uckfield: Naval and Military Press, 2006 [1926]), p. 81.

The army's decision to standardise the distribution of SS pamphlets marked the transition from 'pulled' transfer – where theatres requested pamphlets which would be of use to them – to 'pushed' transfer – where all publications were sent out to the various theatres, irrespective of need or relevance. This decision ran counter to the army's pre-war practice. The pushed transfer of publications aimed to reach as many individuals as possible. However, this decision did not represent a complete departure from its ethos. It still remained up to each expeditionary force to judge whether or not to circulate the material upon receipt. There was flexibility within the military organisation, allowing for independent learning to suit the needs of the subsidiary theatres. Indeed, the growth of these theatres led to the establishment of individual base supply depots; one of whose functions was fulfilling a force's printing needs. This not only allowed the various expeditionary forces to meet their own general stationery demands, but it also allowed them to publish their own pamphlets, based on their experience in theatre. Examples of this include the Italian Expeditionary Force's [IEF] *SS652 I.E.F. Traffic Orders* and a local publication on 'Hill Training', as well as the EEF's *Notes on the Employment of Lewis Guns in the Desert*.

In addition to the SS series, there were 'unofficial' pamphlets along with formal, branch-specific ones. Unofficial or privately published pamphlets were not unique to the First World War army as seen with Callwell, Haking, and Swinton's pre-war volumes. A number of pamphlets that were not endorsed by GHQ proliferated during the war. Maxse's *Hints on Training*, published during his time as GOC XVIII Corps, was just one such example, yet it had considerable reach beyond both the corps and the Western Front itself. Major-General Sir Archibald Macdonnell (GOC, 1st Canadian Division) wrote 'I will never forget the way I pounced upon and devoured your *Hints on Training* and how eagerly my Brigadiers and Battalion commanders followed it up'.[4] The publication was also used by formations in Italy: the proceedings of the 23rd Division's conference on 1 February 1918 record that 'Battalions to reorganize their sections and platoons on a permanent basis. The instructions on training by Lt-Gen Maxse, commanding 18th Corps . . . will be carried out'.[5] Further endorsement from Italy came from Major-General Herbert Shoubridge. In June 1918, Shoubridge, GOC 7th Division and one of Maxse's former brigadiers in the 18th Division, wrote that

---

[4] IWM, Maxse Papers, PP/MCR/C42/60, Macdonnell to Maxse, 1 February 1919.
[5] TNA, WO 95/4229, 23rd Division GS War Diary, Divisional conference proceedings, 1 February 1918.

Hints on Training are most popular and I am getting many applications from company commanders for more copies. My prestige as to training has gone from 1000 to 0 as they now realise more fully where I learnt most of the things I have tried to teach them!![6]

Maxse's *Hints* were republished a number of times throughout 1918 and influenced many of the Inspectorate of Training's leaflets. Its reach and influence across formations and theatres demonstrates the liberal-horizontal network in action.

Branch- and formation-specific pamphlets such as the RE's *Mining Notes* also acted as an important means for collecting and disseminating specific knowledge. Prior to their production, tunnelling companies had rendered reports to the division under which they were working. These were then forwarded up the command chain to GHQ. Unsurprisingly, this took time with such reports often lingering on some commanders' desks. By the time the information was communicated vertically, it was likely to be out of date. The production of *Mining Notes* sought to mitigate these delays, taking advantage of the newly streamlined mining command structure. The *Notes* offered a timely and systematic way of codifying incidental exchanges, capturing low level experiences, and disseminating these both vertically and horizontally.[7] Tunnelling companies were encouraged to forward new techniques or operational experiences to their Controller of Mines at Army HQ level. These would then be passed directly to the Inspector of Mines at GHQ where they would be codified and disseminated back down to all companies. Issued frequently, sometimes every four to seven days, *Mining Notes* contained front line experiences as well as the results of experiments from the various Army mine schools. *Mining Notes No. 1*, for example, outlined the 178th Company's experience of 'enemy methods in chalk ascertained by listening', which had been forwarded to GHQ by Third Army's Controller of Mines.[8] Some of the notes, including *No. 73* and *No. 86*, illustrated the transfer of technology and knowledge between Dominion and allied forces. *Mining Notes No. 73* was dedicated to experiments involving the Calyx or 'Wombat' boring machine which had been 'brought over by the Australian mining companies'.[9] Designed by Captain Stanley Hunter, an Australian civilian mining engineer, the 'Wombat' boring machine was widely adopted across the British army owing to its ability to bore vertically and horizontally. Where necessary,

---

[6] IWM, Maxse Papers, PP/MCR/C42/44, Shoubridge to Maxse, 21 June 1918.
[7] For a Second World War example of this, see Kollars et al., 'Learning to Fight', notably pp. 1054–1059.
[8] TNA, WO 158/130, *Mining Notes No. 1*, 20 February 1916.
[9] Ibid., *Mining Notes No. 73*, 21 October 1916.

the notes also incorporated schematics and sketches of new devices and techniques that allowed for ease of understanding and reproduction by other companies.

As a learning method, military pamphlets were important for a number of reasons. First, they were a form of explicit knowledge. In organisational learning terms, they are a 'people-to-documents' method. They represent the formal process by which information is extracted from an individual or unit, made independent, and reused for various purposes. This particular approach, known as 'codification', gives individuals access to organised knowledge without having to go direct to the originator.[10] Furthermore, the distillation of tacit knowledge, often from a variety of contributors, into a portable format allows for ease of transfer not only between different sites, but also different situations. James Edmonds, for example, recalled giving American engineer officers a number of pamphlets as part of their attachment to GHQ as learners, while Brigadier Ernest Craig-Brown promised a brother officer a series of SS pamphlets on 'the latest ideas in infantry work so that he could bring himself up to date'.[11] This enabled the accumulated experience of assorted British and Dominion forces, gathered over the past three years, to be transferred quickly, easily, and in a reproducible manner.

Secondly, pamphlets provided a way of codifying and distributing best practice without needing to revamp wholesale *FSR* or branch-specific manuals. As we have seen, although *FSR* offered guidance, it militated against commonality of method. While this approach was acceptable in a small war, or in a small army, the lack of common tactics, techniques, and procedures served to increase the possibility of friction in a large-scale conflict when command had to be exercised at the Army level. Initiative and individual action were still held up as the norm, yet the army could not expect its citizen soldiers to display the same level of initiative as a battle hardened regular. As one pamphlet highlighted,

officers and troops generally do not now possess that military knowledge arising from a long and high state of training which enables them to act promptly on sound lines in unexpected situations. They have become accustomed to deliberate action based on precise and detailed orders.

10   M. T. Hansen, N. Nohria, and T. Tierney, 'What's Your Strategy for Managing Knowledge', *Harvard Business Review* 77 (2) (1999), p. 2; R. Cowan and D. Foray, 'The Economics of Codification and the Diffusion of Knowledge', *Industrial and Corporate Change* 6 (3) (1997), p. 597.
11   LHCMA, Papers of Brigadier-General Sir J. E. Edmonds, 3/12, Memoirs, Chap 28, p. 18; IWM, Craig-Brown Papers, 92/23/1, Diary, 29 March 1918.

Officers and men in action will usually do what they have been practised to do or have been told to do in certain situations.[12]

This level of naiveté required the army to adapt its learning methods in order to accommodate less experienced troops, while still remaining true to its common character. The high command, therefore, saw the publication of these pamphlets as 'amplifications' of the army's pre-war manuals, produced to 'meet the varying requirements' of the war.[13] As such, they were designed to be read in conjunction with existing manuals like *FSR*.

Thirdly, the pamphlets were constantly evolving in terms of content and presentation to reflect the changing learning needs of their readership. While primarily a printed method of dissemination, where appropriate, they often included pictorial representations of the principles under consideration. Research into text processing has shown how pictures serve as 'text adjuncts'.[14] In the army's pamphlets, both organisational and interpretational pictures were used to aid understanding. In the case of the former, organisational pictures provide a structural framework for the text, such as an illustrated map, whereas interpretational pictures help to clarify difficult text. While this may seem a rather trivial distinction, the increasing use of pictorial aids throughout the war, particularly in pamphlets designed for junior officers, speaks to the army's awareness of the changing needs of its personnel. As Charles Bonham-Carter had accurately observed in 1914, 'men require picture books as much as children, when they are to learn something of which they know nothing previously'.[15]

The pre-war manuals had been of little help in this respect. *FSR* did not include any pictorial aids, while the *Field Service Pocket Book* (1913) included only a few general, organisational illustrations, such as schematics of the ammunition supply for a division and the supply service for an army of four divisions. *Infantry Training* (1914), on the other hand, included some representational diagrams relating to saluting, trailing arms from the order, and fixing bayonets. One privately printed manual, tellingly entitled *Key to Infantry Training 1914*, decried

[12] General Staff, *SS109 Training of Divisions for Offensive Action*, 1916, Clause 9.
[13] AWM, AWM25 947/76, Infantry Training France 1917, O.B./165, 8 May 1917.
[14] R. N. Carney and J. R. Levin, 'Pictorial Illustrations *Still* Improve Students' Learning from Text', *Educational Psychology Review* 14 (1) (2002), p. 7; J. R. Levin, 'On Functions of Pictures in Prose', in F. J. Pirozzolo and M. C. Wittrock (eds), *Neuropsychological and Cognitive Processes in Reading* (New York: Academic Press, 1981), pp. 203–228.
[15] C. Bonham-Carter, 'Suggestions to Instructors of Recruits', *Army Review* 7 (1) (1914), p. 126.

that 'the new "Infantry Training 1914" differs so much from the previous text-book, that I found it necessary to draw rough sketches of each movement (owing to the scarcity of plates) before the movement could be understood'.[16] At the 1913 General Staff conference, concerns were raised over the lack of useful pictorial aids with one officer remarking that 'in the Infantry Drill Book of the date when I joined there were actually diagrams of an advanced guard on a road, or a plain etc. . . . The young officer of today has no such aids to knowledge'.[17] It is little surprise that with the influx of citizen soldiers the army had to consider other ways of enhancing the knowledge found within its pamphlets. By the final year of the war, a marked shift towards the use of pictorial aids had taken place. Revised in 1918 as *Platoon Training*, *SS143* contained a number of detailed field sketches accompanied by pared back graphic interpretations to illustrate various platoon tactics and training exercises. These pamphlets were supported by the later efforts of the Inspectorate of Training with its production of highly illustrative leaflets that clarified 'in "ocular" form the existing official manuals'.[18]

While pamphlets were designed to capture new innovations and operational best practice in a more accessible format, they were not viewed positively by all concerned. Brigadier-General John Lamont (CRA, 8th Division), for example, referred to the pamphlets as 'BUMF'.[19] For some, the sheer number of pamphlets simply added to the fog of war. Recalling preparations for the second battle of Gaza, one soldier in the 5th Battalion Highland Light Infantry recalled that 'pamphlets on the attack, written for trench warfare in France, were liberally issued . . . One's brain became terribly confused'.[20] For others, it was felt that pamphlets could lead soldiers down the dangerous road of doctrine-dogma-indoctrination, as we saw with *SS148*. Retrospective commentary from contributors to the Kirke Report on the Lessons of the Great War suggested that the army's use of pamphlets had fundamentally undermined the ability and willingness of officers to show initiative. In his testimony, the ever critical McNamara argued that:

---

[16] A. H. Sandford, *Key to Infantry Training 1914* (Melbourne, VIC: Critchley Parker, 1915), p. 3.

[17] TNA, WO 279/48, General Staff officers conference, 13–16 January 1913, p. 15.

[18] RAHT, Uniacke Papers, MD 1160/3, *Training Leaflets* (1919).

[19] RAHT, Uniacke Papers, MD 1160/1, Papers on Training, Lamont to Uniacke, n.d. (c. September–October 1918).

[20] F. L. Morrison, *The Fifth Battalion Highland Light Infantry in the War, 1914–18* (Glasgow: MacLehose, Jackson, 1921), p. 147.

Fed on innumerable pamphlets on war lessons, all concerned accepted them as the last, and only, word on war, but were apt to mis-apply them under altered conditions ... solutions to all problems are rapidly becoming almost standardised, the quality, quantity and action of the enemy often getting scant attention ... At conferences lessons are rubbed home by quotations from manuals and pamphlets, and as enemy methods and action are constant, the officer is apt to get an impression that there is a stereotyped right answer, and that he is ignorant, or unfortunate when he gives the wrong one.[21]

The use (and abuse) of pamphlets provided a stick with which post-war commentators could, unfairly, beat the army and its inability to adapt. For McNamara, the plethora of pamphlets was clearly at odds with, and undermined, the army's ethos. This is unfair. These pamphlets were produced and intended to be used in sympathy with the army's pre-war ethos, but became increasingly necessary in a mass citizen army. While the bureaucratisation of knowledge was far from popular both at the time and after, the army, out of necessity, recalibrated its learning style, embracing a more standardised approach to reflect the needs of its personnel. It is important to note that, within the pamphlets, there was built-in latitude for interpretation which formations and individuals could take advantage of as their experience and expertise increased.

Training Schools

While the military pamphlet embodied the codification and portability of knowledge, tacit knowledge was still required in order to interpret the information found within these documents. Furthermore, the pamphlet was still an inherently 'sticky' document, which often raised concerns around the relevance and applicability of the information contained within. The simple dissemination of a pamphlet was no guarantee that it would be acted on either. No soldier was ever expected to read every training pamphlet, nor did the army have the means to enforce this.[22] Sometimes the problem was one of interpretation: documents could be read in different ways, no matter how carefully written. The training school system offered one method of calibrating interpretation. While training schools were often used as a means of providing respite

---

[21] LHCMA, Kirke Papers, 4/4, 'Notes by Major-General Arthur McNamara on Training', May 1932, pp. 1–2.

[22] This was not just a problem within the British army. As one British artillery officer wrote when attached to the Italian army in 1917, 'leaflets are of little value as they are not read by half of the rank and file'. See TNA, CAB 25/22, Impressions of Lt-Col C. N. Buzzard, October–December 1917.

for fatigued officers and men, they also proved to be an active and evolving site for learning. The training school represented a nexus between the institutional and the individual. Established and mandated by the army, it was a formal site where doctrine was taught and demonstrated. However, it also provided a space for the exchange of ideas between individuals.

Before considering the role that schools played in the dissemination and creation of knowledge, it is worth outlining the development of the training school system on and beyond the Western Front, including the creation of the wartime staff schools. Prior to the creation of the Training Directorate in January 1917, the establishment of training schools was left to the initiative of individual commanders. By the winter of 1916–1917, there were numerous schools at Army, corps, and divisional levels, but, in a manner reminiscent of the pre-war army, little uniformity existed as to how these schools were run or the methods taught. Owing to GHQ's limited involvement at this point, individual commanders and their staff took it upon themselves to determine the course content and how it was to be delivered. After its establishment, the Training Directorate offered a way of enforcing uniformity of doctrine, as well as standardising the teaching of that doctrine. Bonham-Carter recalled his position as being 'in charge of the Schools of Instruction directly under GHQ', visiting divisions, and 'learning their experiences in order to keep everyone up to date with any tactical development that takes place by sending round pamphlets'.[23] This task had similarities with that of the pre-war IGF in that it involved 'ensuring that similar principles and methods of training' were adopted throughout the army.[24]

The publication of *SS152 Instructions for the Training of the British Armies in France* encapsulated this drive for uniformity. Published as a provisional document in June 1917, *SS152* set out the army's 'general policy of training', and the system it would use to ensure 'uniformity of doctrine'.[25] The policy of training in France was based upon two beliefs: first, that, much like the pre-war army, the responsibility for the training and efficiency of all officers and men in a unit belonged to the commanding officer; and secondly, that special instructors were to be trained at dedicated schools to assist them in that task. Its publication led to a complete overhaul and standardisation of the schools system within the BEF. A reduction of the number of schools limited the scope for

[23] CAC, Bonham-Carter Papers, BCHT 2/2, Bonham-Carter to sister, 8 October 1917.
[24] CAC, Bonham-Carter Papers, BHCT 9/2, Autobiography, n.d., p. 14.
[25] A slightly revised version of *SS152* was published in January 1918.

divergent training school creeds. This made the system more manageable. Corps schools were placed on an even footing, providing training for platoon commanders and NCOs, while divisional schools were abolished. Training at the tactical level continued, but in the form of 'classes of instruction'.[26]

To complement the newly standardised school system, *SS152* was highly prescriptive regarding the syllabus for each school, including the number of students in each cohort and the types of publications to be used.[27] Instructors were also expected to keep up to date with the latest developments through refresher courses and visits to the front line.[28] However, *SS152* attempted to perform two conflicting roles simultaneously: to help disseminate common doctrine, and to preserve the independent responsibility of divisions and their units for training their men.[29] In essence, it was promoting both obedience and initiative, hampering its effects. While *SS152* constituted a coherent attempt to standardise training, it was not followed religiously. There continued to be a diversity of approach, highlighting the army's continuing unwillingness to adhere to prescription.

That said, the reach of *SS152* extended beyond the Western Front, and provided the basis for schools in the subsidiary theatres. As with the Western Front, it was employed with a certain degree of flexibility to suit the conditions found in each theatre with both the EEF and BSF, in particular, interpreting the recommended syllabi as they saw fit.[30] In the case of the latter, the BSF Lewis and Vickers gun school decided to eliminate some aspects from *SS152*'s prescribed syllabus, notably revolver training and 'warfare of highly organised defences'.[31] In the force's infantry school, the core pamphlets mirrored those used in France, including *SS135*, *SS143*, and *SS185 Assault Training*, yet responsibility was placed on the local commandant and his instructors to ensure that the course was relevant to conditions in Salonika.[32] Again, this process of adaptation served to highlight *SS152*'s conflict of purpose, but also suggested that the centre (the Western Front, in this context) was positively delegating responsibility to the periphery – a theme that we will pick up on in the next chapter.

[26] Geddes, 'Solly-Flood', pp. 19–20.   [27] Ibid., p. 21.
[28] GHQ, *SS152 Instructions for the Training of the British Armies in France*, 1917, pp. 14–15.
[29] Boff, *Winning and Losing*, p. 59.
[30] TNA, WO 95/4946, BSF Lewis and Vickers Gun School War Diary, 24 June 1918; TNA, WO 95/4368, EEF GHQ War Diary, Memo to GOCs XX, XXI and DMC, 16 October 1917.
[31] TNA, WO 95/4946, BSF Lewis and Vickers Gun School War Diary, 24 June 1918.
[32] Ibid., BSF Infantry School War Diary, Appendix 7, 3 February 1918.

The establishment and manning of these tactical training schools was vital, yet so too was the development of a parallel system of staff officer training both on and beyond the Western Front. Staff training not only offers a snapshot of the army's flexibility in time of war, but also highlights the trial and error nature of learning. It thus merits exploring in detail. At the outbreak of war, the two peacetime staff colleges at Camberley and Quetta were closed. This proved to be a grave mistake. The closure of these schools denied the army a formal solution to the growing requirement for staff officers to administer a rapidly expanded army. The shortage of trained officers against the sheer scale of the war was a 'situation for which no precedent existed'.[33]

With no move to reverse the decision to close the two colleges immediately forthcoming, the army initially adopted an ad hoc approach to meet its staff needs. This approach was evident both on and beyond the Western Front. In the BEF, a staff learner system was instituted within the first few months of the war. This system saw regimental officers attached to headquarters from brigade up to Army level, providing these officers with their first step on the staff ladder.[34] Alongside this learner scheme, certain enterprising formations took it upon themselves to devise their own courses for 'instruction in staff duties'.[35] The 1st Division's course for junior officers, for example, took place in mid-1915. This course lasted four weeks with approximately fifteen attendees, representing almost every unit in the division. One officer in the 1/5th Battalion King's Own Royal Lancaster Regiment recalled his initiation into the

mysteries of staff organisation from GHQ downwards. We learnt to appreciate the logic of its division into two main branches, the 'General Staff' proper whose concern is to help the High Command devise and execute designs for the enemy's discomfort and defeat, and the 'A' and 'Q' branches whose function is to assure the supply of manpower and the other commodities needed to carry out the purposes of the campaign. After about a week spent in absorbing this necessary foundation we went on to consider problems of a practical nature, such as moving a brigade from one part of the front to another without blocking necessary supply lines … The second fortnight was spent in a series of attachments: to

---

[33] J. Hussey, 'The Deaths of Qualified Staff Officers in the Great War: "A Generation Missing"?', *Journal of the Society for Army Historical Research* 75 (1997), p. 254.

[34] Harris, *The Men Who Planned the War*, p. 105.

[35] A. Fox-Godden, '"Hopeless Inefficiency?" The Transformation and Operational Performance of Brigade Staff, 1916–1918', in M. LoCicero, R. Mahoney, and S. Mitchell (eds), *A Military Transformed? Adaptation and Innovation in the British Military, 1792–1945* (Solihull: Helion, 2014), p. 144.

Brigade Headquarters, to a battery of the Divisional artillery and to Divisional Headquarters itself.[36]

Having previously relied on either the BEF or the War Office for staff officers, from early 1916 onwards both the BSF and EEF set up their own respective staff learner schemes. The need for such schemes was urgent: in March 1916, Philip Howell drew attention to the 'rapidly decreasing' proportion of BSF staff officers with staff college or specialist training. The BSF invited its corps to 'submit programmes showing arrangements made ... to improve divisional staffs and by divisions to improve brigade staffs'.[37] A suitable attachment scheme was agreed upon in the BSF whereby 'young' staff officers, namely those who were currently serving as adjutants, staff captains, General Staff Officer 3rd Grade [GSO3], or brigade majors, were attached to the staffs of corps or at Army level. While these young staff officers were attached to higher headquarters, regimental officers would 'act in their places', thus allowing them to 'learn the elementary work by really having to do it'.[38] The EEF formally instituted its own version of the learner system in August 1916. While acknowledging that such a system had existed in a 'general way', EEF GHQ ordered that 'active steps should be taken to ensure that it is done in a systematic way'. Its formalised policy was to allow adjutants and 'good squadron, battery and company officers' to 'understudy junior staff appointments on brigade or divisional headquarters'.[39] The remaining junior staff officers at brigade and divisional level were then encouraged to understudy higher staff positions.

While the learner system offered a useful form of 'on the job' learning, which endured until the end of the war, it had considerable weaknesses. It lacked uniformity; each formation had their own way of doing things. Once again, the army was forced to balance the independent responsibility of forces and formations alongside the more pressing need for uniformity. In the BEF, these forays into uniformity emerged after the battle of Loos with GHQ's decision to trial a staff school under the command of Lieutenant-Colonel John Burnett-Stuart at St. Omer in December 1915. The school had the backing of Robertson and boasted a range of senior officers from GHQ as guest lecturers, including Brigadier-General Frederick Maurice and Major Sidney Clive.[40] However, Burnett-Stuart,

---

[36] IWM, Papers of Major T. C. Owtram, 83/17/1, Ts memoir, n.d., p. 15.
[37] TNA, WO 106/1347, Correspondence between BSF and CIGS, Howell to GOC XII Corps, 1 March 1916.
[38] LHCMA, Howell Papers, 9/6/50A, Howell to XII and XVI Corps, 19 March 1916.
[39] AWM, AWM4 1/6/14, EEF GHQ War Diary, Lynden-Bell to GOCs, 15 August 1916.
[40] Harris, *The Men Who Planned the War*, p. 107.

desperate to return to the front line, was a reluctant commandant, and refused to run more than one course.[41]

It was not until November 1916 that the BEF established regular staff schools, initially located at Hesdin, catering for junior and senior appointments.[42] These represented the first institutional attempt to standardise staff training. In a letter to his father, Bonham-Carter, the first commandant of the senior staff school, outlined GHQ's approach:

I am to be in charge of a school for the instruction of officers who have not had previous staff training before the war but who have been holding junior positions on the Staff, and who are considered likely to become fitted for more important work. This school, which has been given the high sounding name of the Senior Staff School is to take two or three courses for 20 men each, lasting about six weeks. There is also a Junior Staff School which is to train promising regimental soldiers for junior staff appointments.[43]

Both the senior and junior staff schools offered a highly condensed version of the two year pre-war course at the staff college. Students were exposed to aspects of all three branches of staff work. The syllabus for the first course, based on Bonham-Carter's perception of 'the probable course of next year's campaign', gave students an insight into the 'duties of the staff in the attack and during marches', as well as the army's management and supply. Students were taken to visit an undisclosed base on the British coast where they saw 'a bakery where bread for 240,000 men is baked every day', and a 'supply store containing enough food to provide for the whole of London for a couple of days'.[44]

The BEF's staff schools at Hesdin provided the template for the EEF's own staff school in Cairo. The Mena House staff school opened in January 1917 for the 'instruction of promising officers in staff work', established 'on the Staff College lines as obtains in France'.[45] Planned as a short term venture, the War Office had sanctioned the establishment of the Mena House school for five months.[46] During that time, three courses were run, each with an intake of between thirty and forty students. Interestingly, on the first two courses, BSF students made up half

[41] LHCMA, Papers of General Sir J. T. Burnett-Stuart, 6/1/7, Unpublished memoir, n.d., p. 76. Paul Harris suggests that one further course was run at St. Omer under a different commandant.
[42] TNA, WO 256/15, Summary of Schools for Training for the BEF during Winter 1916–1917, n.d., p. 1.
[43] CAC, Bonham-Carter Papers, BCHT 2/1, Bonham-Carter to his father, 24 October 1916.
[44] Ibid., Bonham-Carter to his father, 19 November 1916.
[45] TNA, WO 161/42, Brigadier-General E. M. Paul to Director of Fortifications and Works (War Office), Letter 19, 10 April 1917.
[46] IWM, Lynden-Bell Papers, 90/1/1, Lynden-Bell to Maurice, 10 January 1917.

of the intake, whereas the third course consisted of forty EEF candidates. In his capacity as the EEF's CGS, Arthur Lynden-Bell had an influential role in the conception and running of the course. At the end of each course, he interviewed each student individually to determine whether they would make a 'valuable addition to our stock of young staff officers'.[47]

To ensure the school ran efficiently and effectively, Mena House required experienced instructors. As a result, three regular officers, all with experience of staff duties, were despatched from the Western Front to administer proceedings. Of these three officers, two had been instructors in staff duties in the UK. Like the Hesdin schools, Mena House exposed its students to all three branches of staff work. Brigadier-General Ernest Paul, the EEF's Director of Works, gave a lecture to the second course in March 1917 on 'engineer work at the Base and Lines of Communication', which was garnered during his service at Gallipoli, Salonika, and Egypt. One of his colleagues also gave a lecture to the second course on the subject of the employment of divisional RE and army troops companies drawn from personal experience.[48]

Both the Hesdin schools and Mena House closed in March and June 1917, respectively. Approximately two hundred students passed through the senior and junior schools at Hesdin, while one hundred students completed Mena House. In lieu of a formal school, both the BEF and the EEF resorted to GHQ-mandated attachments schemes in order to provide a pool of trained staff officers after this point.[49] Formations in the BEF were also given latitude to offer their own short courses during this period. The 1st Australian Division, for example, ran a six day course in staff duties in July 1917. This course focused primarily on lower level General Staff duties, and included the writing of orders, preparation of plans, and the ideal qualities of a staff officer.[50]

On 1 October 1917, the senior and junior staff schools reopened at Cambridge University. Like its predecessor, the function of the senior staff school was to train officers for the duties of GSO1, Assistant Adjutant-General [AAG], Assistant Quartermaster-General [AQMG], and Assistant Adjutant and Quartermaster-General [AA&QMG]. Similarly, the junior staff school was to fit officers for lower level positions

---

[47] Ibid., Lynden-Bell to Maurice, 20 May 1917.
[48] TNA, WO 161/42, Brigadier-General E. M. Paul to Director of Fortifications and Works (War Office), Letter 19, 10 April 1917.
[49] AWM, AWM25 889/1, Instructions with reference to training of staff officers, Harington to GOC II ANZAC, 30 July 1917.
[50] AWM, AWM25 881/34, Course in staff duties at Baizieux, Memo, 1st Australian Division to Brigades, 28 June 1917.

such as GSO2, Deputy AAG, Deputy AQMG, Deputy AA&QMG, and brigade major.[51] The Cambridge courses were longer than those at Hesdin, running for two and a half months, but worked to a similar curriculum. To encourage close working, candidates were organised into syndicates, their work based on actual operational orders from Armies or corps in France. Such an arrangement placed learning into an operational context, rather than an invented theoretical scenario.[52] Major Alan Brooke attended the senior staff school in early 1918 and recalled both the diversity and intensity of instruction. Writing to his mother, Brooke noted that 'the main difficulty is to raise our power of absorbing knowledge sufficiently to soak all the knowledge available without mixing it up'.[53] During the first month of the course, Brooke had listened to 'close on 70 lectures and done 20 schemes'. Much like Hesdin, the Cambridge schools exposed students to all three branches of staff work with trips to ordnance and remount establishments, while lectures were given on the Labour Directorate, interior economy, transport, reconnaissance, bombardments, and open warfare.[54] The Cambridge establishment also extended its offer of training to candidates in the subsidiary theatres from late 1917 onwards. In January 1918, the EEF was allotted three places on the senior course and four places on the junior course.[55] For both the BSF and the EEF, this was a welcome offer given the closure of Mena House. The extension of centralised staff training to the various expeditionary forces allowed those future staff officers to meet and converse with fellow candidates from the Western Front.

What we see with the development of wartime staff training is a learning process in microcosm. There was a clear process of trial and error at play with the establishment of attachment schemes, temporary centrally-run schools, and courses run by formations, before the eventual establishment of the Cambridge schools. There were two constants throughout this development. First, the, by now familiar, tension between uniformity of training and operational pressure. Secondly, attachments or 'shadowing' schemes were in constant use throughout. There was a clear recognition of, and support for, learning on the job. While lectures and schemes were important requirements, attachments facilitated the transfer of tacit knowledge from those with experience to those without.

---

[51] AWM, AWM25 937/29, Training of staff officers: junior and senior staff schools, 1917–18, Butler to GOC Second Army, 17 August 1917.

[52] Fox-Godden, '"Hopeless Inefficiency"?', p. 146.

[53] LHCMA, Alanbrooke Papers, 2/1/11, Brooke to his mother, 13 January 1918.

[54] LHCMA, Alanbrooke Papers, 3/6, Notes from Senior Staff School, Cambridge, 1918, n.d.

[55] TNA, WO 95/4369, EEF GHQ War Diary, 14 January 1918. The BSF and IEF were also offered places on the two staff courses.

Although they each had their own distinct functions, training schools were an important space for learning in three ways. First, as mentioned previously, the schools helped unlock and subsequently reinforce doctrine through lecturing, demonstration, and conferences. The three approaches catered for a variety of different learning styles, including visual and auditory learning. Training schools from across the army's theatres employed this three-pronged approach. The syllabus of the EEF's senior officers' course, for example, clearly stated that 'all theory will be followed by demonstration and practical work as far as local facilities admit'.[56] While lecturing represented a very traditional form of imparting knowledge, demonstration offered a way of 'teaching by sight'. As Bonham-Carter noted, 'doctrines can be spread quicker by the demonstration method than by any other'.[57] The eventual establishment of demonstration platoons and, under the Inspectorate of Training, 'travelling' companies, attests to the importance of practical demonstration, showing how to apply 'principles of tactics in the best way under various conditions'.[58] Demonstration also had a place beyond the training school, and was used extensively as a learning tool by formations as part of unit or collective training.

Secondly, schools were often sites of innovation in their own right. Experiments with different tactics and military methods by participants could end up contributing to institutional doctrine.[59] Material for *Mining Notes* and the RE's *Field Work Notes*, for example, was partly obtained through experiments conducted at GHQ, the RE Training School at Rouen, the Army mine schools, and schools back in the UK.[60] Similarly, the Machine Gun School at Camiers maintained a 'progressive policy' where 'any idea that might assist in the development of the uses of the machine gun was thoroughly probed and tried, and if proved to be good no stone was left unturned to secure its introduction'.[61]

More often than not, schools facilitated lower level tactical innovation, drawing on the experience of students to enable formation and force (group level), rather than institutional, learning. The commandant at the EEF's senior officers' course, for example, was called on to 'inform General Headquarters on any points, which may come to his notice, commonly practised in units which differ from official manuals or

[56] AWM, AWM25 877/12, Senior Officers' Course, Heliopolis – Organisation, n.d.
[57] LHCMA, Alanbrooke Papers, 3/6, Notes from Senior Staff School, Cambridge, 1918, n.d.
[58] CAC, Bonham-Carter Papers, BHCT 9/2, Autobiography, n.d., p. 7.
[59] See Beach, 'General Staff', pp. 470–471.   [60] Addison, *Engineer Intelligence*, p. 81.
[61] J. H. Luxford, *With the Machine Gunners in France and Palestine* (London: Whitcombe and Tombes, 1923), p. 34.

pamphlets'. These tactical reports would be forwarded on to the force's corps commanders 'for their information'.[62] Knowledge and innovations gathered at the school had a wider reach through the practice of cascade training or 'teach the teacher' schemes.[63] Major-General John Monash, for example, wrote that to keep up the supply of trained instructors in the 3rd Australian Division, 'selected officers and NCOs do courses of from one to three weeks... and are then returned to their units to continue the training of the junior personnel'; while Brigadier-General Herbert Gordon (GOC, 70th Brigade) decided to deliver a lecture to his men on his 'recent course with the French at Verona'.[64] Gordon's approach was recommended by SS152, which advised that 'lectures should be given on matters of interest by Officers recently returned from Schools, by Staff Officers and outside Lecturers when procurable'.[65]

Thirdly, and related to the previous point, schools provided a space for the incidental exchange of ideas between individual students, enabled by the conferences and smoking meetings that often followed the day's session. The object of the first RE school of instruction at Le Parcq in 1916, for example, was to 'enable officers from different parts of the line to exchange their experiences and methods, to their mutual advantage'. The second RE school, which started at Blendecques in December 1917, built on the exchange principles espoused at Le Parcq. However, unlike Le Parcq, officers at Blendecques 'came to know each other much better and consequently more discussion took place'.[66] This forum for discussion was not simply reserved for attendees on the course. In connection with the school, several conferences of divisional commanders RE [CRE] were held under the presidency of an Army Chief Engineer. The encouragement of 'free discussion' afforded 'an invaluable opportunity for exchange of ideas'.[67] Similarly, at the Cambridge staff schools, evenings were spent socialising, allowing candidates to discuss their own experiences and methods. This interaction resulted in 'smartening friction', encouraging individuals to learn from colleagues via discussion and debate.[68] Indeed, time spent circulating amongst new people and in different locations, whether that was a new branch or expeditionary force, enhanced individual networks and made links that were of enduring utility to the process of learning.

---

[62] TNA, WO 95/4368, EEF GHQ War Diary, Dawnay to corps commanders, 16 October 1917.
[63] This was also practiced extensively in the German Army. See Foley, 'Dumb Donkeys', p. 290.
[64] AWM, Monash Papers, 3DRL/2316 1/1, Monash to wife, 11 January 1917; TNA, WO 95/4239, 70th Brigade War Diary, 4 March 1918.
[65] GHQ, SS152, pp. 8–9.   [66] Addison, Schools, pp. 354–355.
[67] Ibid., p. 357.   [68] Harris, The Men Who Planned the War, p. 34.

Secondments and Attachments

The importance of the individual to the learning process of the army cannot be overlooked. People-centred methods formed a central part of this process.[69] This aligned with the army's ethos, its amateur tradition, and the continuing importance of personalities. Research into corporate workplace learning has revealed that nearly two-thirds of work-related information comes from face-to-face meetings, mentoring, and apprenticeships.[70] As we have seen with the staff schools, secondment and attachment opportunities within the army played a key role in the acquisition and dissemination of knowledge between individuals, but also between theatres and allies.

The army's policy for secondments and exchanges was multi-faceted. In order to influence or share current knowledge with allies, for example, the War Office established formal military missions, such as the Baker mission to the US and Brigadier-General Charles Delmé-Radcliffe's mission to Italy.[71] To understand the situation facing the army's expeditionary forces, the War Office deployed a number of liaison officers for attachment at the various GHQs. Liaison between the War Office and the Salonika front was established as early as 1916.[72] The initiative of the BSF's proactive chief of staff, Philip Howell, may well have hastened this decision. Writing to his wife in February 1916, Howell lamented how the BSF was 'hopelessly out of touch with the W[ar] O[ffice]', and that he was going to '*write* this week and urge that we send someone home every fortnight or so; and that they in turn send someone here'.[73] Lieutenant-Colonel Kenneth Barge, a liaison officer to the BSF, was instructed to 'keep the War Office acquainted with the situation on the Macedonian front, particularly the British sector, and with the needs of the British Forces at Salonika'.[74] Barge was expected to gather information relating to 'details of defence, method of holding the line, and system of reliefs' along with supply and transport considerations. Later, in October 1918,

---

[69] Foley, 'Dumb Donkeys', pp. 291–296.
[70] See W. Swap, D. Leonard, M. Shields, and L. Abrams, 'Using Mentoring and Storytelling to Transfer Knowledge in the Workplace', *Journal of Management Information Systems* 18 (2001), pp. 95–114.
[71] For a fuller consideration of military missions, see E. Greenhalgh, 'The Viviani-Joffre Mission to the United States, April-May 1917: A Reassessment', *French Historical Studies* 35 (4) (2012), pp. 627–659; Greenhalgh, *Victory through Coalition: Britain and France during the First World War* (Cambridge: Cambridge University Press, 2005), pp. 75–101.
[72] TNA, WO 106/1347, Correspondence between BSF and CIGS, Report on Administrative Control of Salonika Army by Egypt by Lieutenant-Colonel C. C. M. Maynard, n.d. (c. September 1916).
[73] LHCMA, Howell Papers, 6/1, Howell to wife, 9 February 1916. Original emphasis.
[74] Ibid., P. de B. Radcliffe to Barge, 1 June 1918.

a liaison officer called Major Denniston was escorted round the Salonika front 'to see and learn as much as he can of this Force and I have asked him to make notes of everything that strikes him as being something which he has not known of, or realised'.[75]

In July 1917, Robertson appointed a liaison officer between the War Office and the EEF: Lieutenant-Colonel Archibald Wavell. Explaining his motives to Allenby, Robertson was at pains to stress that Wavell is 'in no way a spy', but rather he was appointed 'to help you and to help me'.[76] Much like the liaison officers to Salonika, Wavell was entrusted by the EEF to act as a petitioner to the War Office. After one of Wavell's first visits, Lieutenant-General Sir Philip Chetwode believed him to be 'considerably impressed by the magnitude of the business and I hope that all he has seen and what you will tell him result in his impressing on the CIGS that we must have certain things if we are to attain certain results'.[77] By establishing this system of liaison officers, the War Office had the eyes and ears to appreciate the many difficulties facing the different expeditionary forces, both tactically and administratively. The system also provided the means of sharing information and knowledge.

Along with these high level appointments, forces and formations established less formal attachments. These attachments operated in two ways: first, they could be used as a way of enabling units to gain knowledge, particularly for the purposes of acclimatisation. Cadres of individuals were often attached to units or formations to facilitate their acclimatisation to a new front or part of the line.[78] At Gallipoli, Lieutenant-General Sir William Birdwood referred to 'shepherding' the men from the 54th (East Anglian) Division who were attached to Australian formations. In a letter to Hamilton, he spoke of 'putting them into the trenches platoon by platoon mixed up with the old Brigades, who I find doing as you would say "father to mother" to them'.[79] The attachment of inexperienced individuals provided a useful form of kinaesthetic, or 'hands on', learning, which could then be disseminated further through cascade training within sub-units. In some cases, the attachment scheme did not go quite to plan. One officer recalled his company going

[75] TNA, WO 106/1347, Correspondence between BSF and CIGS, Cory to Radcliffe, 5 October 1918.
[76] LHCMA, Robertson Papers, 8/1/62, Robertson to Allenby, 4 July 1917.
[77] IWM, Papers of Lieutenant-Colonel V. M. Fergusson, PP/MCR/111, Chetwode to Lynden-Bell, 30 July 1917.
[78] For a fuller exposition of this, see A. Fox, '"Thomas Cook's Tourists": The Challenges and Benefits of Inter-Theatre Service in the British Army of the First World War', *Journal of Historical Geography* (Published Online 10 July 2017. DOI: 10.1016/j.jhg.2017.06.012).
[79] LHCMA, Hamilton Papers, 7/1/16, Birdwood to Hamilton, 9 September 1915.

into the line with a regular battalion of Munster Fusiliers: 'they were good to us, taught us the rudiments of our trade and took good care to steal our rum ration'.[80]

Secondly, attachments could be used as a way of imparting knowledge. Requests for suitable instructors for training schools are an obvious example, but the same can also be said for staff officers or those individuals with specialist knowledge.[81] Rawlinson, for example, temporarily attached two highly skilled staff officers to the GOC 51st (Highland) Division owing to continuous reports of unsatisfactory staff work. These two, handpicked officers were to 'answer questions and help him formulate . . . plans properly', as well as helping with the framing of divisional orders.[82] More broadly, the army actively promoted a 'mentoring' scheme for its Dominion forces, ensuring that they had access to high quality staff officers for effective command and administration arrangements.[83] However, sometimes requests for experienced individuals were far more localised. Upon arriving at Gallipoli, Lieutenant-Colonel Sir Henry Darlington, commander of the 1/5th Battalion Manchester Regiment, requested for 'someone to be attached to give us the tips about trench warfare'. A regular officer from the Munster Regiment, who 'was all through the landings here', was duly attached to Darlington's battalion, imparting his experience to this new formation.[84]

Dialogue

The personalised nature of the secondment and attachment system highlights the importance of 'learning by doing' in a structured manner. However, as we saw in the previous chapter, it was often through incidental, informal interactions between individuals that knowledge and best practice could be exchanged in the most rapid manner. Dialogue between individuals served a dual purpose: it acted as both a way and a means for learning. Owing to the availability of source material, historians have tended to focus on explicit means of learning, such as pamphlets and, to a lesser extent, training schools. As a result, the impact of

---

[80] LHCMA, Papers of Major W. G. Wallace, Ts memoir, 1935, p. 30.
[81] TNA, WO 95/4371, EEF GHQ War Diary, Telegram, War Office to EEF GHQ, 17 September 1918.
[82] CAC, Papers of Field Marshal Lord Rawlinson, RWLN 1/3, Diary entry, 11 June 1915.
[83] See D. Delaney, 'Army Apostles: Imperial Officers on Loan and the Standardization of the Canadian, Australian, and New Zealand Armies, 1904–1914', *War in History* 23 (2) (2016), pp. 169–189; Delaney, 'Mentoring the Canadian Corps: Imperial Officers and the Canadian Expeditionary Force, 1914–1918', *Journal of Military History* 77 (3) (2013), pp. 931–953.
[84] LHCMA, Papers of Lieutenant-Colonel Sir H. Darlington, 1/1, Darlington to wife, 22 June 1915.

informal, lateral relationships has been overlooked, or simply dismissed as gossip. It is true that, much of the time, these interactions were more about acquiring information and exchanging pleasantries than necessarily sharing best practice. Yet this does not make them any less important, particularly as sharing gossip allowed for the regulation, control, and strengthening of existing social networks. This was particularly true for those officers and men based in the subsidiary theatres and thus on the periphery of army bureaucracy. For example, when CinC EEF, General Sir Archibald Murray wrote to Godley thanking him for his letter in November 1916 because 'as usual, it gives me a certain amount of army gossip which is always of interest to us out here'.[85] Lieutenant-Colonel Alexander Weston Jarvis, commander of the 1/3rd County of London Yeomanry stationed at the Suez Canal defences, was pleased to note that 'people are very good about writing to me, and I get a host of letters every week, with first hand information both from home and abroad'.[86] Weston Jarvis was a well-connected individual, receiving letters from Rawlinson (his commander in the Boer War) and, upon his eventual return to the Western Front, from Philip Chetwode, too. Like Weston Jarvis, Lieutenant-General Sir Stanley Maude was also keen to keep in touch with Western Front developments during his time as CinC of Indian Expeditionary Force 'D' out in Mesopotamia. Writing to his family, Maude noted that he was 'getting a good many letters now ... from the War Office, and from Army, Corps and Divisional Commanders in France and Egypt'. This ensured that he was kept 'posted with what is going on there'.[87]

Far from preventing opportunities for dialogue, the army tolerated and, in some cases, facilitated these discussions. The organisation of conferences following training courses proved to be one method of encouraging dialogue. Another was through the army's continuing exploitation of concepts such as 'clubbability' and the 'old school tie', which still held currency in Edwardian society. We can see this through the establishment of officers' and social clubs in the UK and abroad, such as the King George and Queen Mary Clubs and the AIF's War Chest Club in London.[88] Although the clubs were primarily established

[85] LHCMA, Papers of General Sir A. Godley, 3/193, Murray to Godley, 14 December 1916.
[86] NAM, Papers of Lieutenant-Colonel A. Weston Jarvis, 1999/03/43, Weston Jarvis to sister, 27 February 1916.
[87] A. Syk (ed.), *The Military Papers of Lieutenant-General Frederick Stanley Maude, 1914–1917* (Stroud: The History Press, 2012), p. 149.
[88] See S. Cozzi, '"When You're a Long, Long Way from Home": The Establishment of Canadian-Only Social Clubs for CEF Soldiers in London, 1915–1919', *Canadian Military History* 20 (2011), pp. 45–60; AWM, AWM25 1007/5, Correspondence relating to

for rest and relaxation, they served another purpose for the army who used them as an information clearing house, posting communications and orders from the front on their bulletin boards.[89] At a local level, in theatre, officers' clubs were seen as 'a medium for social discourse', but also, as Monash suggested when recommending the establishment of a club for the 4th Australian Division, for the 'receiving and posting of war and other news and bulletins of interest'.[90] Coupled with their role as clearing houses, serendipitous meetings and conversations in these clubs provided a further avenue for the informal dissemination of knowledge.[91] This was recognised by Godley who thought it useful for Australian and New Zealand divisions in the II ANZAC to subscribe to the Bailleul officers' club: 'Bailleul is rather the natural centre to which everybody in this part of the world gravitates . . . they would find it a good thing to have a place to go to, to meet fellows of other Divisions'.[92] In short, the army's social ethos was harnessed for the good of its intellectual development.

Throughout the course of the war, the army used a multitude of methods for recording and disseminating learning. Some of these were simply refinements of those used pre-war, while others were developed to meet the demands of the conflict. The army's use of different dissemination modes represents a 'learning curve' in and of itself – an ongoing process of trial and error depending on the situation at hand. That it deployed a variety of methods at different rates and at different times speaks of an institution that recognised the importance, but also the complexity, of learning. In modern parlance, the army can be seen as employing aspects of both codified and personalised knowledge management strategies. In the case of the former, the production of pamphlets provided important 'scaffolding' necessary for the creation of a formalised knowledge base. On the other hand, the army also employed methods more in line with a personalised strategy of learning. Through its use of training schools and conferences, it provided both a physical and intellectual space to facilitate discussion and the exchange of ideas between personnel. Furthermore, as a result of the army's highly personalised culture, individuals were able to exchange knowledge by making use of existing social networks. Organisational culture is one of the most significant challenges to effective knowledge management. The army was willing and able to recalibrate and rebalance its approach from the highly individualised

formation of AIF and War Chest Club, London, Anderson to Mrs Samuel, 14 August 1916.
[89] Cozzi, 'Long, Long Way', p. 46.
[90] AWM, Monash Papers, 3DRL/2316 3/38, Monash to OCs Brigades, n.d. (c. March–May 1916).
[91] DiBella, 'Learning Organization?', p. 120.
[92] AWM, Monash Papers, 3DRL/2316 3/43, Godley to Russell, 3 November 1916.

attitude that typified its pre-war experience to one that embraced the bureaucratic trappings of modern war.

For an institution that prided itself on adaptation and devolved decision-making, the army embraced the need for more bureaucratic methods very early on in the war, producing its first formal publications in late 1914. While there were those who criticised the use of pamphlets, it was both important and necessary to codify information in an accessible format. There were obvious barriers that prevented the continuation of a highly individualised learning process that typified the army's pre-war experiences. These barriers largely related to the increasingly civilian demographic of the army, and its multiple commitments across the globe. Formal, systematic methods, such as publications and training schools, became essential when attempting to integrate both combat formations and national contingents into the army. While the pamphlets themselves were cast in the same mould as *FSR* with their focus on principles, they became far more user friendly to those without military experience through the inclusion of pictorial examples and changes in style. Furthermore, as the war progressed, attempts were made to allow more latitude for interpretation within these pamphlets, suggesting a greater confidence in the citizen soldier and a reaffirmation of the army's pre-war culture.[93]

While training schools were used from the outset, it took until early 1917 for the eventual standardisation of the school system. That it took a relatively long time to standardise speaks, again, to some of the tensions that emerged when the army recalibrated its approach towards learning: enforcing uniformity while preserving the independent training responsibility of formations, and encouraging free discussion while attempting tactical standardisation. These organisational tensions were further underscored by the continuing use and relevance of people-centred methods. Both secondments and attachments were systematic in their use and intended outcome. Incidental exchanges between individuals, however, proved to be an unregulated constant throughout the war. Connections, patronage, and networking were important aspects of the army's culture. Who individuals knew had a significant impact on what they came to know.[94] The real problem though was the knowledge that fell between the cracks, occurring outside the army's institutional processes. The army tried to harness the knowledge found within these

[93] LHCMA, Alanbrooke Papers, 3/6, Notes from Senior Staff School, Cambridge, 1918, n.d.

[94] R. Cross, A. Parker, L. Prusak, and S. P. Borgatti, 'Knowing What We Know: Supporting Knowledge Creation and Sharing in Social Networks', *Organizational Dynamics* 30 (2) (2001), p. 100.

individual exchanges through conferences and discussions after training schools: it recognised that such knowledge was important. However, the ad hoc occurrence of these exchanges was far more difficult to capture and codify.

Conclusions

Put simply, learning is determined by an organisation's formal learning systems. However, it is also influenced by the pervasiveness of informal learning within which individuals can interpret and make sense of their experiences and share new operational knowledge through social interaction.[95] The army certainly recognised these realities. The various methods it used were mutually supportive, suggesting that the army had a heightened awareness of the relationship between the sharing of knowledge and the promotion of learning and innovation. Culturally, the army was flexible enough to allow for the incorporation and use of new, more bureaucratic methods, but with this recalibration came seemingly conflicting tensions that pitted the need for uniformity against the continuing importance of initiative and individual action. While, superficially, these tensions were problematic, they also tell us much about the elasticity of the army's culture, which managed to bind forces, formations, and individuals together, whilst simultaneously allowing them to adapt and adjust. This elasticity would prove to be fundamental to the maintenance of the army's culture of learning, particularly when it sought to learn from its own experiences fighting alongside allies and across the globe. As we move into Part II of the book, we will see that such experiences were not without their difficulties. Whether learning from its different expeditionary forces, its allies, its civilians, or through the integration of newcomers, the army had to navigate culture clashes, scepticism, wilful parochialism, and the inherent tensions associated with a flexible ethos as it tried to learn in a dangerously competitive environment.

[95] Catignani, 'Coping with Knowledge', pp. 30–31.

Part II

Learning in Practice

4   Inter-Theatre

Writing in 1921 for the *Army Quarterly*, a soldier using the pseudonym 'H.B.R.' theatrically recalled his experience in one of the subsidiary theatres:

These minor theatres were not very reputable places of entertainment, and failed consequently to attract the best kind of public. But later on – after perhaps two or three years – they had learned some lessons in the presentation of the drama; the influence of the Principal Theatre was, I believe, responsible for many improvements. The performances certainly became more legitimate, more conventional; the art of stage-management had, in many cases, been thoroughly mastered, and starred names, even, appeared upon the bills.[1]

Though somewhat tongue in cheek, the quotation contains a kernel of truth regarding the relationship between the Western Front and the subsidiary theatres. For this soldier, the Western Front, as the 'Principal Theatre', was responsible for increased legitimacy and conventionality in the 'minor theatres'. He was not a lone voice in this respect. Other contemporaries expressed similar opinions about the unequal relationship between the Western Front and the other theatres. Even to this day, the Western Front is seen almost exclusively as the site of British army learning in the First World War. Perceptions of the relationship between the Western Front and the subsidiary theatres can be usefully understood with reference to the traditional view of the centre-periphery concept from imperial history. For the purposes of this chapter, the Western Front can be perceived as the centre, and the subsidiary theatres as the periphery. In imperial history, this traditional, now largely defunct, view sees the relationship between centre and periphery as decidedly one-way. Put simply, the centre informed the periphery, but the periphery did not exert the same level of return influence on the centre.

Just as organisational learning theory has embraced a networked view of learning, so too has imperial history considered a 'networked'

---

[1] H.B.R. (pseud.), 'A Memory of a Side-Show', *Army Quarterly* 3 (1) (1921), p. 77.

approach to Empire, highlighting the multiplicities of centres and peripheries that existed.[2] This approach offers a model that can be appropriated to understand and interrogate the links that existed between the army's operational theatres. Superficially, these links, or networks, can be considered in terms of the physical movement of people and things, the relationship between them, and the infrastructure that facilitated their movement.[3] However, this physical movement also allowed for the movement of knowledge and ideas through some of the methods highlighted in the previous chapter. For our purposes, the key take away is that it is no longer useful or appropriate to consider learning as a purely Western Front concern. To do so underplays the complexity associated with military learning, and also leads to an incomplete understanding of the tensions that existed within the army as an institution.

The army's ability and its desire to learn from its different expeditionary forces was subject to constraints or frictions. Some of these related to questions of relevance based on the climate or terrain in theatre. Others were organisational in nature with snobbery and scepticism coming to the fore. It is difficult to conceive of learning without confronting and engaging with the ways in which it was constrained, regulated, or limited by certain frictions.[4] While the Western Front exerted its dominance in tactical and doctrinal matters, the process of learning was by no means a one-way street. Lessons were shared from periphery to centre, as well as between peripheral theatres. Travelling between different locations reveals to us the constant and complex interchange of ideas that typified military learning

'A Complex Mesh of Networks'

To understand how inter-theatre learning took place, it is necessary first to foreground the interactions between the various operational theatres.

---

[2] See e.g. T. Ballantyne, *Between Colonialism and Diaspora: Sikh Cultural Formations in an Imperial World* (Durham, NC: Duke University Press, 2006); Ballantyne, *Orientalism and Race: Aryanism in the British Empire* (London: Palgrave Macmillan, 2001); C. Bridge and K. Fedorowich, 'Mapping the British World', *Journal of Commonwealth and Imperial History* 31 (2) (2003), pp. 1–15; Z. Laidlaw, *Colonial Connections, 1815–45: Patronage, the Information Revolution and Colonial Government* (Manchester: Manchester University Press, 2005).

[3] T. Cresswell, 'Mobilities II', *Progress in Human Geography* 36 (5) (2012), p. 651.

[4] Scholarship associated with the 'new mobilities paradigm' provides a useful way of viewing friction and 'bordering practices'. See T. Richardson, 'Borders and Mobilities: Introduction', *Mobilities* 8 (1) (2013), pp. 1–2.

In this respect, Tony Ballantyne's 'web metaphor' is useful in helping conceptualise features of this relationship. A web captures 'the ways in which . . . institutions and structures connected disparate points in space into a complex mesh of networks'.[5] It also takes into account the horizontal linkages between different physical sites, such as ports and cities. While each expeditionary force had its own commander-in-chief and infrastructure, it was the War Office at Whitehall that ran Britain's military theatres. There was a distinct theatre 'pecking order' in terms of matériel and manpower. As the principal theatre of operations, the Western Front ranked top. It was not unusual for senior generals in France and Flanders to make calls on the other theatres for resources and expertise. In June 1916, for example, Launcelot Kiggell (CGS, BEF, 1915–1917) pleaded with Robertson for additional artillery officers from the subsidiary theatres. In Kiggell's eyes, 'we are "up against it" here in a way that they are not and can never be in those countries. Even if it is necessary to retain divisions there, it is surely better that they should make the best of raw material in officers rather than we should have to do so'.[6] Similarly, Birdwood, as GOC AIF, was able to 'call upon light horse officers . . . to fill staff appointments' in his force on the Western Front, much to the chagrin of Allenby.[7] While the Western Front may have been the principal theatre, it too was often constrained by events overseas. Artillery supply shortages were experienced at both Neuve Chapelle and Festubert, for example, as a result of concurrent operations at Gallipoli.

The priority after the Western Front was Egypt. Proximity to the Suez Canal enhanced its strategic significance. It also proved a key nodal point, acting as a feeder for both Mediterranean and Middle Eastern theatres, including Aden, Gallipoli, Mesopotamia, and Salonika. While it had a parent relationship to a number of these fronts, it remained simultaneously peripheral in its relationship to the Western Front.[8] Egypt provided more than just matériel to theatres under its administrative control, yet it was primarily through this oversight that important networks were developed. The need to coordinate local resources and minimise shipping demands necessitated a much closer relationship with Palestine and Mesopotamia in particular. From

---

[5] Ballantyne, *Orientalism*, pp. 14–15.

[6] LHCMA, Papers of Lieutenant-General Sir L. E. Kiggell, 4/19, Kiggell to Robertson, 3 June 1916.

[7] AWM, Pearce Papers, 3DRL/2222 3/3, Birdwood to Pearce, 14 July 1916.

[8] Lester, 'Imperial Circuits', p. 133.

mid-1916 onwards, 'a network of links' developed between Egypt, Palestine, India, and Mesopotamia as agricultural resources and labourers moved between theatres. These horizontal connections expanded on 'long-standing intra-regional linkages'.[9]

While the existing links between maritime communities in the Gulf and those in the broader Indian Ocean were enhanced, this was not so in the case of the relationship between Egypt and Salonika. The relationship between the two theatres was a fraught one, particularly where supply was concerned. Initially supplied by the Levant Base until early 1916, Salonika was dependent on Egypt – formally and informally – for much of its supply. The correspondence that exists between Ernest Paul and Major-General Sir George Scott-Moncrieff (Director of Fortifications and Works [DFW], War Office) contains a litany of complaints about the 'insistent and somewhat ill-tempered' demands of the Salonika theatre.[10] The tipping point came in the middle of July 1916 where 'the almost daily demands from Salonika for Engineer Stores' were 'so considerable and unexpected'. This demand led to Paul visiting the BSF to 'confer with the Army Commander' so that a 'complete and cordial understanding might be arrived at'.[11] Where the BSF was concerned, however, it perceived itself to be the injured party. As early as February 1916, Howell outlined the difficulties of operating under Egypt's control, stating that 'a system which worked very well in France, of a GHQ at St Omer controlling several A[rmy] HQs situated within an hour's motor drive or within 15 seconds on a telephone will not work out here. An Army Commander must have greater administrative freedom when 1,000 miles away: not, as is the case now, less'. Furthermore, Howell argued, 'it is impossible now . . . to keep GOC Egypt so thoroughly au fait with the situation here as to enable him to pass judgement on our administrative wants'.[12]

While complaints from both parties appeared rather parochial, there was some sympathy for the BSF from outside observers. In a letter to his wife, Commodore Roger Keyes acerbically remarked how 'there are 115 generals in Cairo – no wonder we are the laughing stock of the continental armies! And the HQ of the Salonika Army is in Egypt. Everything goes via Egypt nearly – adding 1,000 miles and 4 or 5 days extra

---

[9] K. C. Ulrichsen, *The Logistics and Politics of the British Campaigns in the Middle East, 1914–22* (London: Palgrave Macmillan, 2011), pp. 74, 82–83.
[10] TNA, WO 161/43, Correspondence between Brigadier-General E. M. Paul and DWF WO, Letter 20, 10 May 1917.
[11] TNA, WO 161/36, Correspondence between Brigadier-General E. M. Paul and DWF WO, Letter 14A, 10 September 1916.
[12] LHCMA, Howell Papers, 6/2, Howell to Keyes, 4 February 1916.

submarine risk'.[13] Lieutenant-Colonel Charles Maynard, one of the War Office's liaison officers, also thought the BSF hard done by, and raised concerns over the operational impact of Egypt's control. In his report on the administrative control of the BSF by Egypt, Maynard commented that

> although Egypt has nominally no control over operations in Salonika, yet in practice, by with-holding [sic] stores and equipment... Egypt may force the GOC Salonika Army to modify his plans of action [...] cases have already arisen when Egypt has queried the demands put forward by General Milne to meet his calculated requirements for operations in the field. A case in point is gun ammunition. Salonika worked out very carefully the total number of rounds per gun which it considered necessary to maintain within the Salonika theatre... Egypt thought the number excessive and wanted a reduction.[14]

Salonika was formally removed from the administrative control of Egypt in late September 1916. It is unclear whether Maynard's report played any part in this move. The BSF's new chief of staff, Webb Gillman, rejoiced at the 'divorce' from Egypt, playfully remarking that 'when mother and stepdaughter feed out of the same dish mother often turns out a hungry person!'[15] Gillman's remark clearly highlights the unequal relationship between Egypt and Salonika, whilst also suggesting that, as a 'stepdaughter', the Salonika theatre had been unwanted from the outset. Going forward, there was to be 'mutual cooperation' between Paul and Brigadier-General Hubert Livingstone (Chief Engineer, BSF). However, much to Paul's exasperation, while Salonika formally indented on the War Office for its stores, it often turned to Egypt for certain requests. It was not long before he had cause to remark, again, that 'Salonika are a continual thorn in our sides as the demands never seem to cease'.[16]

While Ballantyne's web metaphor reveals the important connections, both vertical and horizontal between sites, there is also an important duality to this metaphor: webs are inherently fragile. Important threads can be broken and structural nodes destroyed.[17] Sources of strength

---

[13] P. G. Halpern (ed.), *The Keyes Papers: Selections from the Private and Official Correspondence of Admiral of the Fleet Baron Keyes of Zeebrugge, Vol. 1, 1914–1918* (London: Navy Records Society, 1972), p. 334.

[14] TNA, WO 106/1347, Correspondence between BSF and CIGS, 'Administrative Control of Salonika Army by Egypt' n.d. (c. September 1916), pp. 2–3.

[15] RAHT, Gillman Papers, 1161/4/19, Salonika Diary, 23 September 1916.

[16] TNA, WO 161/62, Personal letters and narratives (General E. M. Paul), Paul to Scott-Moncrieff, 3 April 1917.

[17] For an early discussion of this in relation to the military, see P. M. Kennedy, 'Imperial Cable Communications and Strategy, 1870–1914', *English Historical Review* 86 (341) (1971), pp. 728–752.

often result in inherent weaknesses. The infrastructure that connected the army's disparate theatres of operations, providing them with manpower, matériel, and the means to share knowledge, was vulnerable. Despite their occasional veneer of permanence, stability, and ubiquity, infrastructure networks are 'precarious achievements'. They are, in effect, 'processes that have to be worked toward', requiring 'constant support and maintenance'. Furthermore, infrastructures are more than just ships, railways, and rolling stock working together collectively; they are, instead, complex assemblages bringing together all manner of human, non-human, and natural agents into a multitude of continuous connections across a geographic space.[18]

Britain's theatres were primarily connected through a network of ports and sea lanes. With the increasing U-Boat menace, these lanes were under threat. British, French, and Italian shipping losses in the Mediterranean escalated to a peak of 113 ships and 248,018 tons of cargo between October and December 1916.[19] For Mesopotamia, the situation was so grave that drafts were temporarily diverted to the Cape route. The vulnerability of knowledge and expertise in transit was also at risk – the drowning of Lord Kitchener on HMS *Hampshire* in June 1916, for instance, provides an obvious example. In the Mediterranean, the SS *Ivernia* was sunk on 1 January 1917, carrying two instructors in staff duties, who had been personally requested to run the new Mena House staff school.[20] Though both survived the torpedo attack, their misfortune at sea delayed the opening of the school. Similarly, there were fears in August 1917 over the safety of a high-ranking staff officer, bound for Palestine on SS *Saxon*, which was also under threat from a U-Boat.[21]

The increasing vulnerability of the sea lanes required the development of an alternative infrastructure: the 1,460 mile long Cherbourg-Taranto overland route. Writing to Haig, Lord Derby provided a neat rationale for its establishment. 'Whatever views we may severally hold as to the campaigns in those places', he wrote, 'the shipping problem is so acute that we cannot afford to delay the institution of this service'. Derby went on: 'The various theatres of war are not easily separated. It is a part of the French transportation problem if the forces in Egypt and Salonika have to be maintained overland. Similarly, rails for Egypt or

[18] S. Graham, 'When Infrastructures Fail', in S. Graham (ed.), *Disrupted Cities: When Infrastructures Fail* (London: Routledge, 2010), pp. 9–11.
[19] K. C. Ulrichsen, *The First World War in the Middle East* (London: Hurst, 2014), p. 44.
[20] IWM, Lynden-Bell Papers, 90/1/1, Lynden-Bell to Maurice, 10 January 1917.
[21] TNA, WO 106/718, Correspondence between War Office and Egypt, Lynden-Bell to Maurice, 26 August 1917. The staff officer in question was Brigadier-General Sir Richard Howard-Vyse.

barges for Mesopotamia, are all part and parcel of your transportation question'.[22] Feasibility studies into the overland route were entrusted to Sir Guy Calthrop, General Manager of the London and North Western Railway. Consisting of railway, naval, and army personnel, Calthrop's delegation left for Italy on 14 January 1917, reporting promptly on 7 February that there was 'no great difficulty' in the establishment of such a route.[23] Despite some initial delays, the mission was ultimately successful with the first passenger train leaving Cherbourg on 28 June 1917 and the first goods train on 7 August.[24] The establishment of the Taranto route reveals how Britain's operational theatres, so often treated as distinct, were in fact part of larger networks that were intrinsically connected.

The Taranto route proved an important means of mitigating shipping losses, but it too was a fragile network containing vulnerabilities that could rapidly become choke points. In late 1917, the service was suspended due to Italian reversals at Caporetto, and briefly repurposed for the movement of troops from the Western Front to the Italian theatre. Prior to its closure, 380 deadweight tons of stores per day were carried over the Taranto route to Salonika and Egypt. However, during the period after the route reopened, this had reduced to an average of 184 deadweight tons per day.[25] While this reduction was not of immediate concern, it served to highlight the 'serious complications' that would ensue if the Taranto route was interrupted by enemy action. If the route was compromised, increasing forces in Salonika, Egypt, Palestine and Mesopotamia would 'become an impossibility'.[26] The route connected almost all of Britain's major military theatres from mid-1917, saving shipping and enabling officers and men from the Middle East to go on home leave, but it was still vulnerable. The route's strength in connecting the peripheral theatres with the centre was its biggest weakness: disruption had a cumulative effect across the system.

Centre to Periphery

Despite the susceptibility of these networks, they provided the means through which lessons and experience from the Western Front could

---

[22] LHCMA, Kiggell Papers, 4/97, Derby to Haig, 3 April 1917.
[23] TNA, CAB 24/7/11, Proposed overland supply route to Salonica, Calthrop report, 7 February 1917.
[24] TNA, CAB 24/23/55, Memo on Cherbourg-Taranto route, Derby to Cabinet, 17 August 1917, p. 261.
[25] TNA, CAB 25/62, Taranto Route: Effect of closure on operations east of Italy, Report from General Nash to Supreme War Council, 30 January 1918, p. 6.
[26] Ibid., Nash to Wilson, 24 January 1918, p. 2.

make their way to the other theatres. They facilitated the movement of new technologies, publications, and personnel. Indeed, one of the most potent methods of disseminating Western Front knowledge to other forces was through the movement of individuals, particularly those of high rank or influence. These individuals often acted as knowledge conduits, propagating knowledge between various formations and theatres. High-ranking generals or officers, for example, could be sent to the subsidiary theatres for a number of reasons. They could form part of a 'stiffening' party, such as General Sir Herbert Plumer who was despatched to the Italian front in late 1917 until January 1918. However, in some instances, the subsidiary theatres were seen as the province of those who had been 'stellenbosched'.[27] Henry Tudor suspected that Allenby's appointment to command the EEF came as a result of his being '"degommed"; presumably for going on in that foolish way after the victory of the 9 April'.[28] As we shall see, the prospect of being sent to the subsidiary theatres was not one that all commanders relished.

There was certainly an appetite and, in some cases, a preference within peripheral theatres for commanders and officers with Western Front experience. At Gallipoli, for example, Hamilton was desirous of men like the successful artillery commander, Brigadier-General Hugh Simpson-Baikie. In a letter to Lieutenant-General Sir James Wolfe Murray (CIGS, 1914–1915) in April 1915, Hamilton wrote:

I think you were in the room when Lord K[itchener] said I was to have Simpson-Baikie, a very thoughtful capable officer with recent French experience as Artillery Commander. Lord K said he was far too good for liaison officer which was what he was doing at the moment...I, as you know, have got Fuller...he has not that recent knowledge of artillery work in France which I should have thought quite indispensable to a newly constituted force such as this.[29]

Although Hamilton secured Simpson-Baikie for the 29th Division under his command, he was not always so fortunate in his requests for officers with 'French experience'. Writing to Kitchener in June 1915, Hamilton requested a new corps commander. The two men he suggested were Julian Byng and Rawlinson, as 'both possess the requisite qualities and seniority; the latter does not seem very happy where he is, and the former would have more scope than a Cavalry Corps can give him in France'.[30]

[27] If an officer was stellenbosched, degommé, or degommed, it meant they had been sacked or removed from their position.
[28] RAHT, Tudor Papers, MD1167, Ts memoir, n.d., p. 23.
[29] LHCMA, Hamilton Papers, 7/1/11, Hamilton to Wolfe Murray, 7 April 1915.
[30] LHCMA, Hamilton Papers, 7/2/4, Hamilton to Kitchener, 15 June 1915.

Though Byng eventually commanded a corps in the MEF, Kitchener initially declined Hamilton's request. He felt that Sir John French could not spare the services of these two generals and that the Western Front must take priority. This was not unusual. Writing to the wife of an officer seeking service in the MEF, Hamilton warned her that

the people in Flanders resent the idea of our drawing in any way upon their officers. So at least I understand. Anyway, the War Office have told us that we must not ask for any officers whose regiments are serving in France or Flanders, or who are themselves in either of those countries.[31]

Within Hamilton's response can be detected the implicit suggestion that Western Front experience was clearly valued, but was often deemed too precious to be squandered on the subsidiary theatres.

This predilection for 'French experience' was apparent throughout the chain of command. In a letter to Hunter-Weston, Beauvoir De Lisle expressed frustration at not being able to find a suitable officer locally to appoint to GSO3 in the 29th Division. Beauvoir De Lisle's preference would have been to transfer a proven staff officer from the BEF. He had even gone to the effort of compiling a list of favoured officers in order of merit:

1. Capt H. Tomkinson, Royal Dragoons, Provost Marshal 1st Cav Div BEF;
2. Capt C. Heydeman, 2 Dragoon Guards (Speaks French like a Frenchman also German) 1st Cav Bde BEF;
3. Capt R. Benson, 9th Lancers, 2nd Cav Bde, BEF. Now in England wounded;
4. Capt Bullock-Marsham, 19th Hussars, Staff Captain, 9th Cav Bde BEF.[32]

Unfortunately, Hamilton's military secretary wrote that 'it is little use applying for anyone now actually employed in France'.[33]

These explicit requests were not unique to Gallipoli nor were they limited to the first few years of the war. Similar appeals for those with Western Front experience litter the war diaries and personal papers of senior officers across all of the army's operational theatres. Some requests were simply wishful thinking and were denied for political reasons.[34] Others were more successful. Generally speaking, it was far

---

[31] LHCMA, Hamilton Papers, 7/1/5, Hamilton to Mrs Katty Lloyd, 26 June 1915.
[32] LHCMA, Hamilton Papers, 7/1/24, De Lisle to Hunter-Weston, 3 July 1915.
[33] Ibid., Pollen to Hunter-Weston, 5 July 1915.
[34] Lynden-Bell's desire for 'some really good brigadiers from France for the Australian brigades', for example, was a political impossibility. See TNA, WO 106/718, Correspondence between War Office and Egypt, Lynden-Bell to Maurice, 27 July 1917.

easier for theatres to request instructors or short term attachments to address immediate skills needs than the permanent transfer of key individuals. Schools in the subsidiary theatres wanted instructors with 'recent experience in France', as well as those familiar with the latest literature from schools in Britain. In addition to the two torpedoed staff instructors for the Mena House school, the EEF also requested 'two regular officers with recent experience in France' to run the senior officers' course at Heliopolis.[35] Brigadier-General Geoffrey Salmond (GOC, Middle East Brigade, Royal Flying Corps [RFC]) called for the attachment of a GSO1 to help him 'keep in touch with progress at home and in France', but also to help 'coordinate methods of training out here with those at home'. For Salmond, the current lack of expertise meant that it was 'not possible to keep abreast of improvements in France...and this affects operations'.[36] The BSF was just as keen as its Egyptian counterpart. In Salonika, a regular regimental sergeant-major was brought over from France to act as 'Sergeant of Training' at the force's infantry school, while two assistant instructors and three sergeant instructors were sent from the Machine Gun Training Centre at Grantham to run the Lewis and Vickers gun school.[37]

Not content to wait for knowledge to be sent to them, some forces sent officers on short term attachments to the Western Front to seek out best practice for themselves. George Milne, for example, was very hands on in this respect, sanctioning two detachments to the Western Front in 1917 to unearth practical lessons relating to training and artillery, respectively. The first detachment saw Brigadier-General Webb Gillman sent to the Western Front in early July 1917. He 'went round all the training schools in General [Sir Arthur] Holland's 1st Corps and picked up a lot of tips as regards modern developments of training'.[38] Upon his return to Salonika later that month, Gillman carried out a form of cascade training; he went 'round the various fronts and explained what I had learnt in France as to the system of training'. In a letter to his wife, he noted how busy he was 'explaining to our corps and division commanders the innovations and good points I noticed...and shall get things going on the newer lines'.[39] Gillman's visit had a tangible effect, leading to the establishment of the new Army Infantry School in Salonika in late 1917.

[35] TNA, WO 95/4367, EEF GHQ War Diary, 8 May 1917.
[36] Ibid., Salmond to War Office, 8 March 1917.
[37] TNA, WO 95/4946, BSF Infantry School War Diary, 10 January 1918; TNA, WO 95/4946, BSF Lewis and Vickers Gun School War Diary, 26 June 1918.
[38] RAHT, Gillman Papers, MD1161 4/19, Salonika Diary, 9–10 July 1917.
[39] RAHT, Gillman Papers, MD1161, 4/20, Gillman to wife, 23 July 1917.

Milne's second detachment saw a number of senior artillery officers attached to formations on the Western Front to 'study modern artillery methods' in mid-July 1917. This party included the force's MGRA and XII Corps's BGRA. The report they provided on their return highlighted key differences between Salonika and France, particularly where matériel was concerned: 'the difference between here and there is in masses of guns. In France for an attack you require a gun for every 8 yards of front... Here we have one gun for every 200 yards. There they have a 18 pounder field gun barrage which allots 15 yards to a gun; here there is one 18 pounder for every 600 yards of front'.[40] Yet despite these differences, Milne's decision to sanction this detachment led to the appointment of a counter-battery staff officer [CBSO] in the BSF's XII Corps to 'carry out counter battery work as employed in France'.[41]

Interestingly, while the BSF belatedly adopted a CBSO in September 1917, the EEF appeared not to adopt this particular Western Front innovation, revealing, once again, the non-unitary approach to lessons learned. The EEF's experimentation with counter-battery work was rather more improvised in nature. Prior to July 1917, no corps artillery headquarters had existed in Egypt or Palestine. When Allenby arrived in theatre, he formed improvised Heavy Artillery Groups to perform this command function in his corps.[42] Of course, attempts had been made to align existing practice in Palestine with guidance emanating from the Western Front before Allenby's arrival. In May 1917, Major-General Sydenham Smith, the EEF's MGRA, issued two pages of accompanying notes when he disseminated *Artillery Notes No. 3: Counter-Battery Work*, and *Artillery Notes No. 4: Artillery in Offensive Operations*, published in March and February 1917, respectively. Smith noted that the two artillery pamphlets applied to 'conditions of trench warfare such as appertain in France... we must therefore be careful to adapt the principles to the nature of such defences as confront us from time to time'.[43] Smith sought to adapt the counter-battery command structure found in the pamphlets to that in his force, but did not go so far as to advocate a CBSO. Part of this decision must have come down to the obvious differences in supply, disposition, and opposing forces. Indeed, Smith's final comment was telling: 'these notes have been formulated on the assumption that the opposing forces are almost within assaulting distance of

[40] RAHT, Gillman Papers, MD1161 4/19, Salonika Diary, 5 August 1917.
[41] TNA, WO 95/4757, BSF GHQ War Diary, Memo to GOC XII Corps, 29 August 1917.
[42] Erickson, *Ottoman Army*, p. 105.
[43] TNA, WO 95/4367, EEF GHQ War Diary, 'Notes by MGRA', 4 May 1917.

each other, and that the amount of artillery is very much greater in proportion to the front, than we can ever expect to be able to employ'.[44]

The scale and intensity of warfare in France and Flanders produced a wealth of men and officers with considerable experience that was held in high regard beyond the Western Front. An obvious example of this can be seen in Allenby's move from France to Palestine in July 1917. Before his departure for Palestine, Allenby supposedly broke down in front of Byng, his successor as commander of Third Army. Allenby was 'desolate' at being moved to Palestine and saw it as a punishment for his failings as commander of Third Army during the battle of Arras.[45] In spite of this, his presence in Palestine contributed to an increase in morale and a greater dissemination of Western Front practice throughout the EEF. Although the appointment of commanders and senior officers was both systematic and bureaucratic in nature, the subsequent impact of that commander was highly individual.[46]

As the newly appointed CinC of a largely demoralised force, Allenby had little difficulty impressing his Western Front experiences and ways of working on to the EEF. Post-war reminiscences wax lyrical about Allenby's effect on the force. One officer credited him with bringing about a 'miraculous change' in atmosphere, while another wrote how Allenby 'inspired his troops with confidence and affection'.[47] Contemporary accounts from the time also suggest that his impact was almost instantaneous. No doubt familiar with Allenby's explosive reputation in France, Lynden-Bell was surprised at his sensitivity towards his force:

General Allenby has been generous enough to issue a most complimentary order to the Force regarding what he saw during his visit to the front. I must say it is a most unusual thing to do, because one knows so well that most generals when they take over command proceed to say everything is so damn rotten so as to be able to improve it later themselves ... we have received the most unstinting praise from the new Chief which everyone most thoroughly appreciates.[48]

Within six weeks of taking up his appointment, Allenby tailored his force to mirror the formations he had commanded in France. He deconstructed Murray's ad hoc, mixed forces of infantry and cavalry divisions, and created conventional headquarters – two infantry corps (XX and XXI) and a cavalry corps (the Desert Mounted Corps [DMC]). This

44 Ibid.   45 M. Hughes (ed.), *Allenby in Palestine* (Stroud: Sutton, 2004), p. 7.
46 Beach, 'General Staff', p. 467.
47 LHCMA, Papers of Brigadier-General F. A. S. Clarke, 1/4, Ts Memoir, 1968, p. 1; TNA, CAB 45/80, Official History Correspondence: Palestine, Wigan to Historical Section, 3 January 1930.
48 IWM, Lynden-Bell Papers, 90/1/1, Lynden-Bell to Maurice, 11 July 1917.

enabled contemporary British doctrine as had evolved in France to take root in the Middle East.[49] He also demonstrated a willingness to trial innovative technologies that had proved their worth in France. Less than a month into the job, Allenby wrote to Robertson requesting gas equipment and personnel. Gas had been used to great effect by Third Army in the opening stages of the battle of Arras in April 1917, and Allenby was certain that gas 'ought to be of great use opposite Gaza, and possibly elsewhere'.[50] While gas was rarely used in EEF operations, there was an enormous increase in chemical capabilities in Palestine following Allenby's appointment, along with the broader adoption of Western Front firing patterns.[51]

Along with the promulgation of Western Front methods, Allenby, like Hamilton, actively sought 'young and vigorous' officers with 'French experience' to fill key positions in the EEF. Major-General Louis Bols was one of the first of these 'French' officers. Bols had served as Allenby's chief of staff in Third Army, and replaced Lynden-Bell as the EEF's CGS in September 1917. According to Allenby, Lynden-Bell had 'for some weeks past not been up to the mark . . . the strain of prolonged service in the East has told on him'.[52] It is unclear whether Allenby requested Bols, or whether Robertson manoeuvred behind the scenes to effect the transfer. Either way, the appointment was viewed positively. T. E. Lawrence's pen portrait of Bols revealed him to be a 'little, quick, brave, pleasant man; a tactical soldier, perhaps, but principally an admirable and effaced foil to Allenby, who used to relax himself on Bols'.[53]

Along with Bols, Allenby requested by name two senior staff officers from France as BGGS for the newly created DMC and XX Corps: Brigadier-Generals Sir Richard Howard-Vyse and William Bartholomew, respectively. Howard-Vyse was a known quantity to Allenby, having served as brigade major to the 5th Cavalry Brigade, which formed part of the Cavalry Corps – a formation Allenby had commanded from late 1914 to May 1915. It was felt that the DMC's Australian commander, Harry Chauvel, required a 'first-class cavalry soldier' with 'lots of push'. In Allenby's mind, there was no one better to support Chauvel than Howard-Vyse – 'the best staff officer in the British

[49] Erickson, *Ottoman Army*, p. 105.
[50] LHCMA, Robertson Papers, 8/1/68, Allenby to Robertson, 8 August 1917.
[51] Y. Sheffy, 'Chemical Warfare and the Palestine Campaign, 1916–1918', *Journal of Military History* 73 (3) (2009), p. 827.
[52] TNA, WO 106/718, Correspondence between War Office and Egypt, Allenby to Robertson, 12 September 1917.
[53] T. E. Lawrence, *Seven Pillars of Wisdom* (reprint, London: Book Club Associates, 1974 [1922]), p. 392.

army'.[54] The appointment was rather unpopular in the EEF, reflecting scepticism and a natural uncertainty when faced with change. Existing commanders, including Chetwode (GOC, XX Corps) and Lieutenant-General Sir Edward Bulfin (GOC, XXI Corps), questioned the decision to bring in newcomers 'to undertake an operation where local knowledge and local experience of the country are a great asset'.[55] Chauvel understood his new BGGS to be 'very ugly, wears an eyeglass and goes by the name of "Wombat"'.[56] However, as later chapters will show, the relationship between Chauvel and Howard-Vyse developed into a highly successful and productive one.

Chetwode, on the other hand, was uncommonly praiseworthy of the talents of his new BGGS, Bartholomew, particularly in preparation for the attack on Beersheba in October 1917. Chetwode recalled how the plan was 'entirely worked out by him for me and the complications were so great in moving four divisions by night over an absolutely road-less country without water, timing and coordinating the arrival of the 74th and 60th Divisions to make the attack, with the encircling movement of the Desert Corps Cavalry, that my heart nearly failed me'.[57] Bartholomew had experience of planning operations on the Western Front as GSO1, 4th Division before moving to work under Frederick Maurice at the War Office where he was responsible for the Palestine theatre. His combined operational and strategic experience was worthy of Chetwode's respect. The relationship between Chetwode and Bartholomew was both a successful and close one. Upon the latter's appointment to a staff position at EEF GHQ in April 1918, Chetwode commented on their 'unforgettable experience together', and that 'throughout the nine months you have been with me, your clear head, grasp of detail, tactical knowledge, and your advice and support has been of more value to me than I can ever properly acknowledge'.[58] Their personal and professional relationship continued well into the 1930s with Bartholomew's appointment as Chetwode's CGS during the latter's tenure as CinC India.

Allenby was not naïve. He recognised that his staffing decisions would elicit a heated response and were likely to 'cause a little soreness', but he

---

[54] Quoted in Badsey, *Doctrine and Reform*, p. 286.

[55] IWM, Fergusson Papers, PP/MCR/111, Chetwode to Assistant Military Secretary, 6 August 1917.

[56] AWM, Papers of General Sir H. Chauvel, PR00535 4/10, Chauvel to wife, 29 August 1917.

[57] TNA, CAB 45/78, Official History Correspondence: Palestine, Chetwode to Mac-Munn, 17 May 1926.

[58] LHCMA, Papers of General Sir W. H. Bartholomew, 1, Chetwode to Bartholomew, 25 April 1918.

felt that 'a little new blood . . . will do good. There is some slight tendency to put forward the local article as being the only one worth considering. Changes are always uncomfortable; but I am being firm'.[59] By virtue of his position as CinC, Allenby was able to select the best man for the job. This was particularly important where staff officers were concerned. An inadequate supply of trained staff officers was a problem in all theatres. The frequency and intensity of operations on the Western Front provided staff officers with considerable experience in operational planning and execution. This experience was vital in theatres where operations were necessarily complex, but often infrequent in nature. By bringing in Western Front staff officers, Allenby ensured that commanders with combat experience in Palestine were supported by staff that had cut their teeth in high tempo operations.

The movement of commanders and officers from the Western Front to the subsidiary theatres could be incredibly successful, resulting in positive change. Leadership turnover facilitates adaptation, disrupts institutional memory, and exposes units to new practices and approaches, particularly if, as with Allenby, they had different backgrounds or experiences to their predecessors.[60] One of the reasons for Allenby's success is that he enacted change that, for the most part, went with the organisational grain, rather than against it. He appreciated the fragility of the force he had inherited, and was aware of its social and cultural mores. By moving his headquarters from Cairo to Khan Yunis – just behind the front line at Gaza – carrying out a series of tours around front line troops, and accurately reading the state of morale, Allenby presented himself as a commander able and willing to shoulder the responsibility of managing both his new force and operations in a new theatre.

There was, of course, a down side to personnel changes in the form of organisational 'stickiness' and 'not invented here' syndrome. On occasion, the appointment of new commanders from the Western Front proved problematic and friction was common. Following his appointment as GOC IX Corps at Gallipoli, for example, Byng was criticised by Hamilton for his adherence to Western Front principles:

Byng now declares he must have lots and lots of ammunition. All these fellows from France come here with this idea. Byng would like to have four days' successive bombardment for an hour, and then attack, and speaks of one high explosive shell per yard as if they were shells we could pick up on the sea shore.[61]

---

[59] LHCMA, Robertson Papers, 8/1/68, Allenby to Robertson, 8 August 1917.
[60] Harkness and Hunzeker, 'Military Maladaptation', p. 782.
[61] LHCMA, Hamilton Papers, 7/1/6, Hamilton to Kitchener, 21 September 1915.

For some commanders arriving from France, it took time for them to cut their operational coats according to their cloth.

In the case of Byng and, as we shall see later, with the administrative setup in each theatre, the relevance of their experience proved key. It governed the decision to adopt – or, indeed, ignore – a number of the doctrinal pamphlets and operational lessons emanating from the Western Front. The difference in conditions between the Western Front and the other theatres, and the dangers of 'trenchmindedness' were key concerns to senior officers. In his post-war lecture to the staff college on the Gallipoli and Palestine campaigns, Guy Dawnay warned of

the well marked tendency to apply the lessons of experience indiscriminately and to run to extremes ... but in a theatre ... in which no colossal artillery could be brought up or maintained for a position of warfare, the application of some of the methods of the main theatre of war was not very clearly apparent.[62]

Redolent of pre-war arguments, the Kirke Report highlighted the 'dangers of applying conclusions from one set of operations to others entirely different'.[63] Such concerns were not reserved for the post-war wash up, however. One officer derisively remarked on Gallipoli's 'slavish imitation' of the Western Front with its mania for rest camps, bomb schools, and training camps: 'was it in a fine spirit of official irony, or on the *lucus a non lucendo* principle' that Gallipoli required these 'sorts of luxuries'?[64] Some concerns were more serious in tone. Though an advocate of Western Front expertise, Hamilton bemoaned the fact that senior officers have been 'saturated with pamphlets and instructions about trench warfare, and their one idea is to sit down and dig an enormous hole to hide themselves in'.[65] Similarly, while actively endorsing recent SS pamphlets to BSF formations, Gillman cautioned against cramping the initiative of commanders and curbing the offensive spirit of the troops.[66]

On the whole, the pamphlets and operational lessons that emerged from the Western Front were generally well received. There was a clear appetite for these lessons and innovations in the subsidiary theatres. Underpinning that was a recognition of the importance of interoperability between the army's various forces. For formations to be able to integrate and work together, they needed a certain degree of uniformity

[62] IWM, Dawnay Papers, 69/21/1, Staff College Lecture, n.d., pp. 19–20.
[63] LHCMA, Kirke Papers, 4/11, Lessons from the Great War: Gallipoli, September 1932, p. 21.
[64] Morrison, *Fifth Battalion*, p. 33. *Lucus a non lucendo* is a non sequitur, and translates as '[it is] a grove because it is not light'.
[65] LHCMA, Hamilton Papers, 7/1/6, Hamilton to Kitchener, 11 August 1915.
[66] TNA, WO 95/4756, BSF GHQ War Diary, Gillman to GOCs XII and XVI Corps, 6 July 1916.

of structure and training. This was clearly understood by both the BSF and EEF. Howell informed the BSF's formations that it was impossible to 'define the kind of operations in which the troops here may next be involved. We must therefore prepare for *both* of the two most probable types of warfare (a) offensive operations in Macedonia and (b) return to trench work in France'.[67] The EEF went one step further, and established a specialist school at El Arish for 'practical instruction in trench warfare' to complement its training in semi-mobile operations.[68] The school syllabus was focused around key Western Front pamphlets, and was regularly inspected to ensure that it was providing up to date instruction in cooperation between infantry, machine guns, and artillery, and the siting of machine guns in trenches.[69] As formations were liable to be transferred between theatres at short notice, this constant state of operational readiness and preparedness was essential.

Balancing the uniformity associated with interoperability against the army's adaptable approach to learning created ongoing tensions that could only ever be partially mitigated rather than fully resolved. Individual formations were encouraged to innovate. They could select what appealed to them, or what they thought they needed. They were not expected to adopt Western Front practice, and were welcome to adapt it if deemed appropriate. The decision to adapt lessons suggests that, despite its move towards more bureaucratic methods for knowledge dissemination, the army still encouraged a pragmatic approach to learning. Of course, some pamphlets were broad enough to cover most operational requirements, such as *SS135*, which often provided the foundation for infantry training in the subsidiary theatres. The BSF's infantry school, for example, listed *SS135* as required reading for officers undertaking the course, while corps and divisional commanders' conferences in the IEF referenced the same pamphlet for the purposes of patrolling and hill warfare.[70]

With tactical publications such as *SS143*, a highly individualised approach to interpretation and adaptation can be seen. The pamphlet, published in February 1917, codified tactical best practice from the Somme, and represented a 'vital milestone in tactics'.[71] It advocated the reorganisation of platoons into four highly specialised sections of

[67] Ibid., Howell to GOCs XII and XVI Corps, 26 February 1916. Original emphasis.
[68] TNA, WO 95/4367, EEF GHQ War Diary, 12 June 1917.
[69] TNA, WO 95/4368, EEF GHQ War Diary, 15 August 1917.
[70] TNA, WO 95/4946, BSF Infantry School War Diary, 'Instruction for "first hour"', 3 February 1918; TNA, WO 95/4229, 23rd Division GS War Diary, Corps commander's conference, 24 March 1918.
[71] Ramsey, *Command and Cohesion*, p. 33.

riflemen, grenadiers, rifle grenadiers, and Lewis gunners. However, for the EEF's 74th Division, this new structure was deemed incompatible with the conditions it faced in theatre. During its training period in August 1917, the division reorganised its platoons as per *SS143*, but swapped out the rifle grenade section for a sniper section.[72] The 60th Division, in contrast, believed that the platoon system was 'absolutely correct', but later experience at Beersheba in November 1917 revealed that adaptations were required where grenadiers and rifle grenadiers were concerned.[73] Though both served in the same corps (XX Corps), these two divisions had very different views on how *SS143* should be interpreted. A similar example can be found within the I Indian Corps in Mesopotamia. While the corps believed the new platoon structure to be 'the best', there were concerns that *SS143*'s 'normal form of attack' would be used 'too rigidly... regardless of the prevailing conditions'. While evidently striving for interoperability, I Indian Corps was clearly mindful of the differences between Mesopotamia and the Western Front in terms of geography, supply, and the nature of its opposition. It encouraged its divisions to be flexible when interpreting the pamphlet's guidance, advising that 'distances between lines or waves of attack must be varied according to the conditions of each attack'.[74] For the subsidiary theatres, pamphlets were seen as a collection of principles, rather than prescription, reinforcing pre-war attitudes towards doctrine.

Whereas operational lessons and tactical best practice could be adapted or modified for use beyond the Western Front, this was not uniformly true for administration, which proved itself to be highly context-specific. While those responsible for supply and transport kept their finger on the Western Front pulse, there was a certain reluctance when it came to importing that theatre's best practice. Much like the tactical lessons, it came down to relevance, as well as inherent differences in infrastructure and terrain. While campaigning in hostile territory was not unique to the Middle Eastern theatres, the fighting on the Western Front occurred within an industrialised context. By contrast, the difficulties of conducting an industrialised war in the ecological conditions of the Middle East magnified the logistical complexity of supply and transport arrangements. With a reliance on man and animal power, there was

---

[72] C. H. Dudley Ward, *The 74th (Yeomanry) Division in Syria and France* (London, 1922), p. 67.
[73] TNA, WO 95/4660, 60th Division GS War Diary, Memorandum on Lessons Learned, 13 November 1917.
[74] TNA, WO 95/5053, I Indian Corps GS War Diary, Memo to 3rd and 7th Divisions, 25 August 1917.

an 'awkward synthesis' between tradition and modernity in the largely hostile and pre-industrial desert terrain of the Middle East.[75]

Indeed, some of the administrative friction experienced beyond the Western Front came down to the failure to consider local conditions and the over-application of 'French' methods. This friction was particularly acute in December 1915 in the Mediterranean theatres. With the evacuation of the Gallipoli peninsula and the simultaneous opening of the Salonika theatre, resources were stretched and tensions were high. In a letter to the War Office, Major-General Frederick Koe, then Director of Supply and Transport [DST] to the MEF, commented on the work of Brigadier-General Reginald Ford who worked on the MEF Lines of Communication. Though 'an extremely able man', Ford suffered under 'the disadvantage of not having been up here and . . . does not realise the conditions'. His method for the advanced supply of rations – 'obviously the result of his experience in France' – was incompatible with the conditions faced by the MEF. Ford's decision to undertake automatic supply was predicated on the complex logistical infrastructure as found on the Western Front. However, this infrastructure simply did not exist in the MEF in late 1915. Koe rightly complained that if automatic supply were to be used, the result would be a 'harbour full of ships which [I] could not get unloaded'. Ford's natural reference point was the Western Front, but he implemented his method with little understanding of the complexities facing the Mediterranean theatre.[76] Not only do Koe's frustrations underscore the administrative differences between the Western Front and the Mediterranean, but they also highlight the tensions that existed between the centre and the man on the spot. Two days after his exchange with the War Office, Koe took to his directorate's war diary to note his increasing frustration with the situation in the Mediterranean: 'it takes two months (instead of 24 hours in France) to get supplies from home. This seems to be forgotten, even by the War Office at home, who sometimes evince surprise that we cannot produce *anything* that anybody asks for at a moment's notice'.[77]

Koe's concerns with Ford's approach clearly highlight the difficulties of applying Western Front practice under markedly different local conditions. That is not to say that efforts were not made to learn and apply these lessons. Koe, in particular, was in regular contact with the War Office, seeking out the latest innovations. However, he was often disappointed when attempting to implement them. Writing to the War Office

---

[75] Ulrichsen, *Logistics and Politics*, pp. 44, 138.
[76] TNA, WO 107/22, DST MEF to War Office, 1 December 1915.
[77] TNA, WO 95/4269, DST MEF War Diary, 3 December 1915. Original emphasis.

in October 1915, Koe thanked the DST for his notes on clearing houses, but regretfully informed him that 'the case out here as compared with France is so different that they are not so helpful as I hoped they would be'. Part of this difference came down to infrastructure. In France, discrepancies in supply appeared to be a case of 'tracking missing railway truck of supplies'. However, in the Mediterranean theatre, Koe remarked ruefully, 'it is a case of tracking a missing lighter load of supplies, which never again materialise because they . . . are under the waves'.[78]

Unsurprisingly, this question of relevance was not limited to the Mediterranean theatre in 1915. It was a recurrent issue in different theatres at different points of the war. Prior to the Beersheba operations in October 1917, for example, Chetwode consulted Rawlinson, a fellow Old Etonian, over the difficulties of water supply in the Palestine theatre. The reply from Rawlinson was sensible enough: 'Why don't you do as I've done in my Army Area here? I've got nearly twenty miles of pipe lines laid down'. Chetwode noted, doubtless with a sense of satisfaction, how 'I must tell him . . . we've already got one hundred and fifty miles of pipe line'.[79] As with Koe, Chetwode was desirous to glean useful principles from the Western Front, using his own personal network to do so. In this case, however, the ecological and infrastructure differences between the two theatres proved to be insurmountable, necessitating a more adaptable approach.

A further source of administrative friction concerned the interrelated issue of conceit and scepticism – a recurrent problem in the army's experience of learning. In the subsidiary theatres, this scepticism was fuelled by the perceived lack of initiative engendered by service on the Western Front. Out in Salonika, the Deputy DST, Colonel Philip Scott, was forthright in his opinion on the matter, declaring that 'nothing adds more to one's trials and temper than the remark – often heard – "We always did so and so in France"!!! Macedonia is not France, and Salonika does not compare with the combined advantages of Havre, Boulogne, Calais, with their short sea distances from the fount of all good things'. For Scott, good infrastructure and proximity to Britain dulled the wits of those working in supply and transport on the Western Front: 'Personally I think a training in France is apt to destroy initiative, but Macedonia will soon demand its pound of flesh'.[80] R. H. Beadon, the official historian

[78] TNA, WO 107/22, Director of Supply and Transport, MEF to War Office, 6 October 1915.
[79] G. E. Badcock, *A History of the Transport Services of the Egyptian Expeditionary Force, 1916–1917–1918* (London: Hugh Rees, 1925), p. 313.
[80] TNA, WO 161/20, DST Salonika to DST WO, Scott to DST WO, 11 January 1916.

of the Army Service Corps [ASC], took a similar view when considering the lot of those supply and transport officers in the Italian theatre. The hurried despatch of an expeditionary force to Italy necessitated the rapid development of a transport system to support it. This was partly achieved by the direct recruitment of British subjects in Italy, but also by transferring available men and officers from France. The transportation infrastructure in Italy 'followed the lines of the organisation of the BEF in France'.[81] Yet despite this similarity the systems proved very different, not least in terms of scale. For Beadon, the experience of Italy had a 'useful and salutary effect' on these individuals, as it required them to 'improvise and adapt for a widely differing set of circumstances'. Their experiences on the Western Front, where they had been 'small cogs in a vast machine', were little more than 'matters of routine'. Administration on the Western Front was seen to be 'highly organised and perfected, with unlimited resources at its disposal and near its bases of supply, operated . . . surely and inexorably under static conditions'.[82]

The Western Front exerted considerable influence over the subsidiary theatres: they were deluged with the latest literature and innovation from what undoubtedly represented the 'centre' of British military activity in an organisational sense. Yet the approach of each theatre was far from consistent and was governed by the perennial issue of relevance. Some pamphlets were used in unadulterated form as 'official text books'; others were subject to heavy revision and interpretation. For some commanders, the operational lessons of the Western Front led to 'trench-mindedness'. Godley, for example, believed the failure at Sari Bair in August 1915 was due to 'training in trench warfare which had given them all the idea that directly they came under shrapnel or shell fire of any kind, they must at once dig in'.[83] For others, Western Front principles were not followed closely enough.[84] In short, there was no one size fits all approach. What the subsidiary theatres were able to learn from the Western Front tells us as much about the problems associated with information overload, as it does about the non-unitary nature of learning in each theatre.

---

[81] Institution of Royal Engineers, *History of the Corps of Royal Engineers*, V (London: Longman's, 1952), pp. 691–692. The medical system in Italy was also modelled on that found in the BEF, although it was subject to modifications and adaptation in theatre. See G. N. Stephens, 'The Medical Work of the Italian Expeditionary Force', *JRUSI* 64 (1919), pp. 647–659.

[82] R. H. Beadon, *R.A.S.C.: History of Supply and Transport in the British Army*, II (2 vols, Cambridge: Cambridge University Press, 1931), p. 350.

[83] NAM, Rawlinson Papers, 2011-11-18, Godley to Rawlinson, 17 October 1915.

[84] TNA, WO 95/4757, BSF GHQ War Diary, Memo to GOC XII Corps, 19 May 1917.

Periphery-Centre

The primacy of the Western Front, both in contemporary thought and in scholarship, often obscures the reverse flow of lessons learned that emanated from the subsidiary theatres. The influence of the periphery upon the Western Front is certainly more difficult to discern, and it is perhaps unsurprising that minor theatres were unable to exert the same level of return influence on the centre. There are some parallels here with the pre-war army. As we saw in Chapter 1, although there was discussion around 'colonial tactics', they had little appreciable impact on official training. Furthermore, there were concerns that such tactics would not hold water against a continental enemy. Similar concerns coloured the BEF's view of innovations and best practice emerging from the subsidiary theatres. If, as Kiggell suggested, these theatres were not 'up against it' in the same way as the Western Front, then what possible benefit could the BEF derive from their experiences?

It is both unfair and incorrect to assume that the army could learn nothing from its global commitments, but where tactical and operational best practice was concerned there was a degree of scepticism. For commanders, staff officers, and formations moving from the subsidiary theatres back to the Western Front, their experience was not always viewed positively by BEF high command. When the first formations arrived on the Western Front from Gallipoli, eyebrows were raised over their fighting quality. In July 1916, Haig commented on the poor performance of Hunter-Weston's VIII Corps, noting that 'the majority of his officers are amateurs in hard fighting and some think they know much more than they do of this kind of warfare, simply because they had been at Gallipoli'.[85] Such dismissive attitudes towards extra-European experience continued throughout the war. In an anecdotal account of the German spring offensive of 1918, James Edmonds, the British official historian, recalled how 'information of the GHQ policy became essential', but he could 'learn nothing' from Lieutenant-General Sir Herbert Lawrence (CGS, BEF, 1917–1918) or Guy Dawnay, as both were 'Palestrinians [sic] and not used to fighting Germans. They seemed terror stricken'.[86] Similar attitudes can be detected in the German Army. From 1916 onwards, the Western Front was viewed as the principal

---

[85] TNA, WO 256/10, Ts Diaries of Field Marshal Sir Douglas Haig, 29 June 1916.
[86] LHCMA, Edmonds Papers, 3/14, Memoirs, Chapter 30, pp. 621–622. There is no corroboratory evidence to support Edmonds's assertion. Paul Harris has taken issue with Edmonds's casual dismissal of Lawrence's experience in Egypt and Palestine. See P. Harris, 'Soldier Banker: Lieutenant-General Sir Herbert Lawrence as the BEF's Chief of Staff in 1918', *Journal of the Society for Army Historical Research* 90 (361) (2012), pp. 44–67.

theatre of operations. The experience of those officers and men with service in the East was not always viewed favourably. Some of Erich Ludendorff's views on tactics – a product of his experience in the East – did not find a welcome audience on the Western Front. Crown Prince Rupprecht, for instance, thought that because of Ludendorff's experience in the East, he underestimated the difficultly of conducting an offensive in the west. In particular, he did not realise the difficulty of bringing up the second wave of divisions close enough to maintain the attack when the first wave stalled.[87]

For the so-called 'malaria replacements' – those formations that were transferred from the EEF to the Western Front to bolster the BEF during the German spring offensive – their experience of semi-mobile operations was not always viewed positively. These formations' experiences of transitioning to the Western Front, whilst endeavouring to disseminate their own tactical best practice, is a neat example of the ways in which knowledge and ideas can become 'stuck' and forced to wait for a receptive audience.[88] One officer in the 52nd (Lowland) Division wrote how 'the authorities in France, I imagine, were wholly confident that troops coming from Palestine were bound to be deficient in the most elementary military knowledge'.[89] Sergeant Charles Jones, an NCO in the 2/15th Battalion London Regiment, bitterly recalled his formation's first encounter with a Western Front general during a training exercise in which his battalion was to 'advance across a piece of open country'. For Jones, the exercise gave his unit the opportunity to showcase their experience of mobile operations: 'we thought we could show these trench-bound soldiers a thing or two'. However, the general's response was far from complimentary:

'What the hell do you mean by lining up like this? Where are your sections? What's the sergeant think he's doing in the rear?' And so it flowed on, in would-be strong language that seemed mild to us, while we 'looked at each other with a wild surmise'. Sections! An arrangement which corresponded to no known need of warfare, except where specialists were concerned. We had tried out the 'sections' method years before and found it wanting . . . We marched home with an uneasy feeling that the powers that be, although they now wished the troops trained in open-order warfare, had forgotten the elements of it themselves . . . Our new commanders did not find our methods to their taste; in fact they probably considered us inefficient. It is not surprising that the feeling was reciprocated.[90]

---

[87] I am grateful to Dr Tony Cowan for sharing these details with me.
[88] Cresswell, 'Mobilities II', p. 651.
[89] IWM, Papers of Major W. R. Kermack, PP/MCR/214, Memoir, n.d.
[90] LHCMA, Papers of Sergeant C. F. Jones, 2, Unpublished memoir, n.d., pp. 351–352.

The situation encountered by the 'malaria replacements' is notable for two reasons: first, as shown by Jones's account, they had experience of semi-mobile operations, which was of increasing importance to the BEF, but was not always well received. There were exceptions to this negativity, however. The 14th Battalion The Black Watch (Royal Highlanders), part of the 74th Division, was asked to give 'an exhibition of the attack in open warfare, for the edification of the Canadians who were in the neighbourhood', offering an example of horizontal learning in action.[91] The mixed response to the new arrivals highlights the unevenness in attitude and approach to experience gained overseas. Secondly, the systematic dissemination of Western Front literature had long formed the bedrock of their training while in Palestine. They had also undergone intensive pre-deployment training prior to their departure for France, focusing on anti-gas measures in particular. In theory, this training aimed to prepare formations for the Western Front as well as legitimise their experience, but, in practice, it did very little to mitigate the initial difficulties and prejudices they faced. In short, the difficulties experienced by these formations highlight the friction and stickiness associated with the movement of knowledge and its subsequent application to situations beyond its theatre of origin.

In fact, successful operational performance did more to legitimise these formations than pre-deployment training. Formation loyalty notwithstanding, there are examples in private papers of officers and men from the 'malaria replacements' that revealed high levels of initiative, and instances of tactical adaptation based on their experience in Palestine. In an account of his battalion's operations near Messines in late 1918, Jones, for example, recalled how 'the formation in fashion at the moment demanded one section out in front as a screen'. However, as a result of his battalion's previous experience in Palestine, it was decided to dispense with the screen as 'it served no useful purpose'.[92] Similarly, during the Pursuit to the Selle in October 1918, an officer in the 6th Royal Dublin Fusiliers complained how

we have been getting too far out in front of the general line, as the other troops don't know anything about running a moving battle and they feel lost if they get the least gap between sections and platoons. Our men on the other hand are quite happy with a couple of hundred yards between sections of machine guns and give each other cross fire along their front to help them forward, as a matter of course.[93]

91 D. D. Ogilvie, *The Fife and Forfar Yeomanry and 14th (F. & F. Yeomanry) Battalion The Royal Highlanders 1914–1919* (London: John Murray, 1921), pp. 120–121.
92 LHCMA, Jones Papers, 2, p. 375.
93 NAM, Drury Papers, 7607-69, France Diary, 12 October 1918, p. 26.

According to its unit historian, the 14th Battalion The Black Watch's performance on the Western Front drew praise from neighbouring formations. Upon seeing the 'broken spur' at Faustine Quarry in September 1918, an Australian officer asked if it was the badge of the 74th Division: "'Well", he added, "we call you 'Allenby's harriers', because you're the only division we can't keep up with". Coming from an Australian that was "some" praise'.[94] These accounts reveal much about how these individuals from peripheral theatres viewed their own tactical experience and prowess, yet with a limited corresponding paper trail it is difficult to assess how these tactics were perceived, or whether they were adopted (or adapted) by neighbouring formations.

Given the primacy of the Western Front and scepticism towards the other theatres, it is easy to dwell on dismissive attitudes towards best practice coming from the army's periphery. There were instances, however, where tactical, technological, and doctrinal best practice in the subsidiary theatres had a discernible, positive effect on the Western Front. This was not limited to the British either. Both German and French forces imported relevant lessons and experience from their own subsidiary theatres. Colonel Georg Bruchmüller's methods for controlling fire support, which had been developed on the Eastern Front were used, albeit with some initial scepticism, in the west.[95] The German official history also suggested that the victory at Caporetto had made an important contribution to the 'final and to some extent decisive signposts' to the manual 'The Attack in Trench Warfare', which was used to train the assault divisions in preparation for the German spring offensive.[96] In the French army, the Bureau des calculs – an office coordinating the work of astronomers, physicists, and university professors to help develop sophisticated calculation methods for heavy artillery fire plans – developed a method of mountain shooting on the Italian front that was later employed in Salonika and on the Western Front.[97] Where the British were concerned, the tempo of operations in the subsidiary theatres often allowed individuals and formations to obtain experience without the same level of risk faced in France and Flanders. This was particularly true for the practice of sniping. Heralded as the army's first

---

[94] Ogilvie, *The Fife and Forfar Yeomanry*, pp. 144–145.
[95] For further discussion of this, see D. T. Zabecki, *The German 1918 Offensives: A Case Study in the Operational Level of War* (London: Routledge, 2006); Zabecki, *Steel Wind: Colonel Georg Bruchmüller and the Birth of Modern Artillery* (Westport, CT: Praeger, 1994).
[96] Reichsarchiv, *Der Weltkrieg 1914 bis 1918: Die Kriegführung an der Westfront im Jahre 1918*, XIV (14 vols, Berlin: E. S. Mittler, 1944), p. 46.
[97] Y. Roussel, 'L'Histoire d'une Politique des Inventions', *Cahiers pour l'Histoire du CNRS* 3 (1989), pp. 46–47; SGA, *Historique*, p. 148.

sniper unit, the 1/1st and 1/2nd Battalions Lovat Scouts (who subsequently amalgamated to become the 10th (Lovat's Scouts) Battalion
Cameron Highlanders in September 1916) saw service in Gallipoli and
Salonika before returning to the Western Front in mid-1918. Its experience of sniping in the subsidiary theatres proved exceedingly useful
when it returned to France. As a result of wounds or illness, some
members of the Lovat Scouts returned to France early, and were subsequently attached to Major Hesketh Hesketh-Prichard's First Army
sniping school at Linghem.[98] These highly experienced officers and
men were trained to become instructors and observers. Formed into
nine, twenty-strong groups, they were subsequently attached to various
Armies on the Western Front, thus enabling them to pass on their experience to new candidates.[99] Similarly, upon the return of the 10th Battalion Cameron Highlanders from Salonika in mid-1918, efforts were
made to capitalise on their 'exceedingly useful' experience. Once again,
this was done through the attachment of groups of men and officers
to various corps in the BEF, notably IX, XIII, and XV corps, to act
as observers, signallers, and glassmen during the final Hundred Days
offensive.[100]

In addition to practical, hard won experience, doctrinal pamphlets,
reports, and experiments from the subsidiary theatres, particularly Palestine, also found their way back to France and the UK. While those
at home and on the Western Front viewed the subsidiary theatres as
outposts and, in some cases, as rather cushy billets, attempts were still
made by the War Office to capture experiences and experiments for use
both during and after the war. In 1917, for example, both the EEF
and BSF were asked by the War Office to report on the workings of
Vickers, Lewis, and Hotchkiss guns in theatre.[101] It is likely that their
reports – with the various positives and negatives of each gun – found
their way into later publications such as *Infantry Machine Gun Company
Training*, and *SS192 The Employment of Machine Guns*. The EEF also
produced a number of pamphlets centrally, based on its experience in
theatre. 'Unofficial' corps and divisional publications ran alongside this
centrally mandated literature, such as the 53rd (Welsh) Division's SS
pamphlet-inspired *Notes on Recent Operations – Artillery in Defence*. While

[98] M. Pegler, *Sniping in the Great War* (Barnsley: Pen and Sword, 2008), pp. 129–131.
[99] H. V. Hesketh-Prichard, *Sniping in France 1914–18* (London: Hutchinson, 1920),
      pp. 127–129.
[100] TNA, WO 95/4049/10, 10th Cameron Highlanders War Diary, 19 September, 13 and
      18 October, and 1 November 1918.
[101] TNA, WO 95/4368, EEF GHQ War Diary, 27 November 1917; TNA, WO 95/4946,
      BSF Army Lewis Gun School War Diary, 1 October 1917.

these may have 'lacked the formality' of the BEF's tactical manuals, they brought '"user-friendly" tactical information on current fighting methods to an eager audience'.[102] Though not aligned with the SS pamphlets' distinct brand, the EEF's publications still required sanction from the War Office, particularly if wider circulation was envisaged.

A number of the EEF's pamphlets were sent to the War Office for consumption by formations on the Western Front and in training schools in the UK. While acknowledging the usual caveats associated with the reading and reception of pamphlets, the EEF's decision to send its own publications back to London and the Western Front sheds some light on the cross-theatre learning networks that existed during the war. In January 1918, for example, the EEF sent its pamphlets *Notes on the Employment of Hotchkiss Automatic Rifles during Recent Operations* and *Mounted Action of 17th Machine Gun Squadron at El Mughar* to the War Office, the Cavalry Machine Gun Training Centre at Uckfield, and the Machine Gun Training Centre at Grantham. In return, the EEF asked for 'any information you have regarding Hotchkiss Guns in connection with the recent fighting in France'.[103] A report on the EEF's experiments with tanks also found its way to the War Office in February 1918 as it was felt that this 'might be of interest to the Headquarters, Tank Corps' on the Western Front; while in September of the same year, 120 copies of *Action of 6th Mounted Brigade at El Mughar* were forwarded to the Director of Staff Duties [DSD] for 'instructional purposes'.[104] It was thought this latter pamphlet had immediate relevance to the situation facing the BEF on the Western Front. The 'remarks' at the end of the pamphlet deemed the action a 'good example of what can be affected by mounted troops, moving rapidly in extended formation', as well as highlighting the importance of personal reconnaissance, and the role of machine guns in open warfare.[105]

As with information flows from the centre, the question of relevance – along with the perceived value of lessons and experience derived from the subsidiary theatres – dominated the reverse influence. The smaller scale and the slower tempo of operations in the subsidiary theatres led to questions around the usefulness of lessons derived from them when applied

[102] Erickson, *Ottoman Army*, p. 128.
[103] TNA, WO 95/4369, EEF GHQ War Diary, Memo to War Office, Uckfield, and Grantham, 14 January 1918.
[104] Ibid., Memo to War Office, 19 February 1918; TNA, WO 95/4371, EEF GHQ War Diary, Memo to War Office, 16 September 1918.
[105] EEF, *Action of 6th Mounted Brigade at El Mughar* (Cairo: Government Press, 1918), p. 6.

to the high tempo, industrialised warfare on the Western Front. Formations returning to the Western Front, often with useful, transferable experience of semi-mobile operations, were viewed with scepticism; their efficiency and effectiveness called into question. With attempts made to push experiments, experiences, and lessons back to the principal theatre, it is not difficult to see striking similarities with the pre-war army with the marginalisation of 'colonial' lessons and tactics.

Periphery-Periphery

While it is tempting to focus on the to and fro between the centre and the periphery, it is also necessary to acknowledge the lateral or horizontal networks that connected the subsidiary theatres. The networks were complex and uneven. The higher command in each area tended to cluster together for a variety of reasons, including administrative ties (Egypt and Salonika), ecological similarities (Palestine and Mesopotamia), or through relative geographic proximity (Aden, Mesopotamia, Palestine). However, some theatres, namely Italy, sat apart from this network, relying on the Western Front for its supply and expertise needs.[106] While Milne advocated for an 'interchange of officers between Salonica and the French and Italian fronts', there is little evidence to suggest that these exchanges took place.[107] Indeed, as far as learning was concerned, the Italian theatre was very much an extension of the Western Front. Its transport and medical services were modelled on the Western Front, and all of its formations had served in France and Flanders.[108] As later chapters will show, the IEF actively adopted extant Western Front practice, but with local adaptation.

Where possible, though, there was a certain degree of self-sufficiency within the subsidiary theatres, particularly those in the Near and Middle East, such as Egypt, Palestine, Mesopotamia, Aden, and Salonika. While these theatres were saturated with literature and experiences from the Western Front, they often turned to each other for immediate expertise and supply needs. The Egypt and Palestine theatres proved to be an important hub in this respect. Their administrative networks provided the foundation for the sharing of knowledge and expertise. It was far easier, for example, for the BSF to request experienced personnel

---

[106] For an example of this, see TNA, WO 95/4203, DST IEF Transport Branch War Diary, 30 November 1917.

[107] TNA, WO 106/1347, Correspondence between BSF and CIGS, Seventh tour of Lt-Col E. A. Plunkett, 6 December 1917–17 January 1918.

[108] Stephens, 'The Medical Work', pp. 647–648.

from the EEF than to petition the War Office.[109] The scale, infrastructure, and tempo of operations in both Egypt and Palestine provided a fertile ground for experimentation and innovation, a reality which was acknowledged by other theatres. As well as sending reports and pamphlets back to the Western Front and the UK, the EEF also disseminated knowledge to neighbouring forces: copies of *Action of 6th Mounted Brigade at El Mughar*, for example, were sent unsolicited to Mesopotamia and India for information and instruction purposes.[110] It is little surprise that EEF GHQ also received requests for information from forces nearby. In late 1917, GOC Aden Field Force requested any 'papers dealing with armoured cars and tanks'. GHQ obliged by sending reports compiled by the EEF's Tank Corps and the DMC, along with a report it had submitted to the War Office outlining its recent experiments with tanks.[111]

The Egypt and Palestine theatres also drew in key lessons and innovations from other subsidiary theatres. Localised innovations such as 'wire' roads, first used during the landings at Gallipoli, were trialled in the Egyptian theatre in February 1916. Explicitly based on 'RE experience at Helles', the use of wire roads was rolled out across the EEF after the capture of Romani in August 1916.[112] In his regular letters to Scott-Moncrieff, Paul noted how the rabbit wire netting was found to be 'quite effective and reduces fatigue'.[113] By 1918, close to one thousand miles of wire roads had been laid across the desert. The success of these wire roads also reached a broader audience with Colonel John Douglas-Scott-Montagu, an adviser on mechanical transport services to the Indian government, asking for 'particulars of our wire roads ... and other applications of wire netting'.[114] Modifications to existing technology, such as the BSF's device for enabling the night firing of Lewis guns, were forwarded to the EEF to ascertain whether they could be of practical use. The EEF took transfer technology seriously and, in this instance, requested that the XXI Corps conduct experiments in the field to determine this device's use with the Hotchkiss machine gun.[115] The BSF also provided the EEF with tactical suggestions, notably on trench raiding. The lower operational tempo in Salonika necessitated an

---

[109] See TNA, WO 95/4395, DST EEF War Diary, 20 March 1916.
[110] TNA, WO 95/4371, EEF GHQ War Diary, 16 September 1918.
[111] TNA, WO 95/4368, EEF GHQ War Diary, 25 October 1917.
[112] TNA, WO 161/62, Personal letters and narratives (Brig-Gen E. M. Paul), Paul to Edmonds, n.d. (c.1928–29).
[113] TNA, WO 161/40, Paul to DFW WO, Letter 17, 19 December 1916.
[114] TNA, WO 161/52, Paul to DFW WO, Letter 29, 23 May 1918.
[115] TNA, WO 95/4369, EEF GHQ War Diary, MGGS EEF to GOC XXI Corps, 22 March 1918.

increase in raiding as it was thought it kept up 'the pecker of the troops', as well as testing and sharpening infantry skills, leading to the accumulation of a wealth of experience at the tactical level.[116] A number of these raids were rather involved, with engineers cutting wire with Bangalore torpedoes, demolishing machine gun emplacements, and sometimes bridging streams.[117] Best practice was rapidly accumulated, and deemed worthy of distribution beyond the original theatre of operations. As with pamphlets from the Western Front, the EEF acknowledged the best practice received from Salonika and used it to supplement its own pamphlet *Notes on Trench Raids*. It sent this pamphlet out to its infantry corps with the 'particulars' of two trench raids from Salonika.[118]

Frictions still existed between theatres. Just as those on the Western Front viewed troops from Palestine with scepticism, similar attitudes were expressed when troops were circulated between the subsidiary theatres. This was particularly true for troops from Salonika and Mesopotamia. There was a perception that formations arriving from Salonika had 'little fighting experience' and a belief, in some quarters, that their fighting value was 'greatly reduced' as a result.[119] One former officer in the 54th (East Anglian) Division recalled how his unit was 'kept in the line so long as General Allenby insisted that... those from Salonica were in need of intensive training in open warfare. His view was that the old divisions did not need any special training'.[120] The arrival in Egypt of the 60th Division was greeted with some dismay as it was believed to be 'only... a fully trained trench warfare division'.[121] With the arrival from Mesopotamia of the 7th (Meerut) and 3rd (Lahore) Divisions, concerns were raised in the EEF around the proficiency of the divisions' junior officers even though the majority had served on the Western Front.[122] While such attitudes were governed by operational requirements and expediency, they also spoke to the broader politics of identity that existed within each expeditionary force.

[116] LHCMA, Hamilton Papers, 7/1/16, Hamilton to Birdwood, 14 June 1915; M. Connelly, *Steady the Buffs! A Regiment, a Region, and the Great War* (Oxford: Oxford University Press, 2006), p. 91.
[117] Institution of Royal Engineers, *History of the Corps of Royal Engineers*, VI (London: Longman's, 1952), p. 137.
[118] TNA, WO 95/4367, EEF GHQ War Diary, 16 June 1917.
[119] TNA, WO 106/1347, Situation at the front and in Salonika, First tour of Lt-Col K. Barge, 3 June–5 July 1918.
[120] LHCMA, Clarke Papers, 1/4, Ts memoir, 1968, p. 8.
[121] IWM, Papers of Field Marshal Lord Chetwode, PP/MCR/C1, Chetwode to Lynden-Bell, 22 July 1917.
[122] TNA, WO 95/4481, XX Corps GS War Diary, Wavell to Shea, 6 June 1918.

Conclusions

It was difficult enough for forces to make sense of their own experiences let alone having to process and interpret those from other theatres. Efforts were made, however, to learn from these multiple experiences whether through letters to friends, pamphlets, training schools, or secondments. An examination of the interactions between theatres showcases the multiple layers of learning occurring across multiple sites. Rather than seeing this as a purely Western Front concern, then, or as a one-way transmission, the circulation of knowledge and expertise should be seen as part of a network involving multiple participants. Sometimes knowledge was understood or interpreted in different ways by different individuals or groups, and put to use in ways not originally intended.[123]

With its numerous actors and sites, this network of learning could be interrupted by a number of different constraints and frictions. These difficulties regulated, channelled, and limited the movement of knowledge and experience, and can be viewed in four ways. First, there was friction relating to the relative stability or, in some cases, instability of the infrastructure networks that connected theatres. Without the vital web of transport links, letters, publications, personnel, and matériel remained spatially fixed and unable to exert broader influence. Secondly, resistance resulted from the geographical, ecological, and administrative differences that characterised each theatre. Knowledge – whether in the form of individuals or pamphlets – could arrive in theatre, but that did not necessarily equate to its successful employment. Whether it was the question of automatic supply in Gallipoli, the utility of rifle grenades in Palestine, or the use of semi-mobile desert tactics on the Western Front, conditions in theatre governed the relevance and applicability of this incoming knowledge. In this respect, a lack of adaptation was not always necessarily a bad thing. Thirdly, and related to the previous point, there were frictions associated with the intangible, cultural differences that existed within each force, reinforced by the explicit hierarchy of the operational theatres. This highly subjective pecking order resulted in scepticism towards some knowledge and individuals based on variables such as service history, nationality, or, where formations were concerned, whether they were regular, Territorial, or New Army. While individuals like Allenby were able to negotiate these tensions successfully, others were not so fortunate. The different ways of working inherent to each theatre were to be ignored at a newcomer's peril. Finally, and common across all theatres, there were difficulties related to the army's culture

---

[123] Burke, *Encyclopédie to Wikipedia*, pp. 86–87.

of initiative and pragmatism versus the irresistible need for a system of uniformity: was it possible to encourage standardisation whilst allowing for ad hocism? Should initiative be sacrificed for the sake of uniformity? The army attempted to deal with these tensions by encouraging formations and individuals to innovate within institutional parameters. Western Front expertise and innovations, for example, were greeted cordially, but not imbibed unthinkingly. Initiative and flexibility were prioritised, but often with messy and uneven results, suggesting that there could be limits to the usefulness of initiative. Learning was a process determined by major friction. As subsequent chapters will show, this was not limited to how the army learned from its own experiences. It dominated how it learned from its allies and its own civilians.

5   Allies

Lack of firmness in command is the main weakness of the British, at all levels of the hierarchy. They do not demand the strict execution of the orders they give. Much calmness and methodical action, in general a great deal of common sense, but not the slightest sign of decisiveness... Efforts are made to leave them as much initiative as possible. This concern for their initiative derives, no doubt, from an exaggerated respect for individuality.

– General Pierre des Vallières, in E. Greenhalgh, *Liaison*

General Pierre des Vallières was unimpressed with the British army's tendency towards initiative and individuality. As head of the French Military Mission to GHQ, he was afforded a unique insight into the inner workings of the BEF and it is clear that he did not always like what he saw. Vallières's comments emphasise some of the tensions that we have seen around the usefulness of initiative. They also reveal fundamental differences in approach between allied armies.

Like Britain, France had operational commitments beyond the Western Front. With troops deployed to Salonika, Palestine, and Italy, the French were forced to work closely with their British ally in Europe and the Middle East. These encounters created opportunities for learning, but such possibilities were underpinned by suspicion. In the early years of the war in particular, the thin veneer of cooperation and unity concealed 'a rotting structure underneath'.[1] For some historians, it was only through ad hoc encounters, informality, and the actions of motivated individuals that cooperation and learning took place between allies. Was there a desire within the British army to learn from its closest ally? Was such a process more successful beyond the Western Front, or did long-standing tensions thwart this relationship throughout the war?

---

[1] J. Krause, *Early Trench Tactics in the French Army: The Second Battle of Artois, May–June 1915* (Farnham: Ashgate, 2013), p. 142.

Perfidious Albion?

Discussion of the extent to which the British army learned from its French counterpart requires a brief sketch of the relationship between the two nations that had been more often enemies and rivals than allies. While it is not necessary to go into detail, it is worth highlighting some touchstones of this relationship.[2] First of all, we cannot overlook the British desire to maintain insularity in the years immediately preceding the outbreak of war. This mind-set is evident in parliamentary discussions on the Channel Tunnel project in 1913 and early 1914. As one MP remarked, 'of all the mischievous ideas ever brought forward in this country one of the most mischievous was the idea of the Channel Tunnel – a vague, sentimental idea, which would have the effect of destroying the greatest protection that this country has, namely, the sea which surrounds her shores – a protection given her by Nature'.[3] Britain's island nation status was a key pillar of her national identity. It set her apart from her continental neighbours. As we saw in Chapter 1, by contrasting itself with other nations, Britain was able to define both itself and its identity. As an 'island race', the British perceived that they had developed the free, manly qualities associated with maritime nations as contrasted to the despotic, militaristic traditions of land-based continental nations.[4] British insularity was further reinforced by its perceived uniqueness in a geostrategic sense, which influenced its methods of war. Suggestions that the British army look to its French neighbour for 'administrative efficiency' or doctrinal cues were habitually greeted with widespread derision. Naturally, there were some exceptions to this rule. While commandant of the staff college, Brigadier-General Henry Wilson's close relationship with Ferdinand Foch, his counterpart at the École Supérieure de Guerre resulted in the adoption of 'Allez, Allez' exercises at Camberley from 1909 onwards.

Beyond geography and identity, there were practical differences between the two nations that would lead to problems during the First World War. The lack of shared language was an obvious difficulty. Of the 488 French Army officers promoted to the rank of general between 1889 and the opening months of the war, only 106 (21 per cent) had a language qualification in English compared to the 347 (71 per cent)

[2] Anglo-French relations have been covered in detail by W. J. Philpott, *Anglo-French Relations and Strategy on the Western Front* (London: Palgrave Macmillan, 1996); Greenhalgh, *Victory*.
[3] *Hansard*, 'Civil Services and Revenue Departs Estimates, 1913–14', House of Commons debate, 29 May 1913, vol. 53 c457.
[4] K. Kumar, 'English and French National Identity: Comparisons and Contrasts', *Nations and Nationalism* 12 (3) (2006), p. 416.

that had a similar qualification in German.[5] Anecdotes relating to Field Marshal Sir John French's excruciating attempts to communicate with counterparts like General Charles Lanrezac serve to highlight a broader point around problems of understanding.[6] Even Haig, who was able to speak French fairly well, was often unable to 'seize all the *nuances*' leading to problems of interpretation.[7] As well as obvious cultural and language differences, there were practical disparities not least of which was each nation's system of measurement. The difference between metric and imperial is easy to overlook, but it affected cooperation in a number of ways. Joint creeping barrages, for instance, required the French to factor in a time delay to allow for the shorter British measurements to catch up, while two measurement grids were often needed for interpreting maps.[8]

Throughout the First World War and across different theatres of operations, these difficulties and tensions ebbed and flowed. Personality clashes were common, while polite – and sometimes impolite – disagreements occurred over command and relative spheres of influence, particularly in the subsidiary theatres. The Salonika theatre was a point of contention between Britain and France. A War Cabinet minute from December 1916 makes the British point of view abundantly clear: 'Salonica is one long story of the British Government acting against its better judgement in the interest of the other Allies'.[9] Political tensions aggravated relations in theatres. The rapport between George Milne and the French commander, Maurice Sarrail, was strained at best. While Sarrail and Bryan Mahon, Milne's predecessor, had enjoyed an amicable relationship, Sarrail was, in Milne's eyes, 'conceited, excitable, ambitious, impetuous and unscrupulous'.[10] Not known to mince his words,

---

[5] Quoted in Greenhalgh, *Victory*, p. 9.

[6] W. Philpott, 'Gone Fishing? Sir John French's Meeting with General Lanrezac, 17 August 1914', *Journal of the Society for Army Historical Research* 84 (2006), pp. 254–259; F. Heimberger, 'Fighting Together: Language Issues in the Military Coordination of First World War Allied Coalition Warfare', in H. Footitt and M. Kelly (eds), *Languages at War: Policies and Practices of Language Contacts in Conflict* (Basingstoke: Palgrave Macmillan, 2012), pp. 47–57; Heimberger, 'Of Go-Betweens and Gatekeepers: Considering Disciplinary Biases in Interpreting History through Exemplary Metaphors', in B. Fischer and M. Nisbeth Jensen (eds), *Translations and the Reconfiguration of Power Relations: Revisiting Role and Context of Translation and Interpreting* (Vienna: LIT, 2012), pp. 21–34.

[7] Greenhalgh, *Liaison*, p. 102. Original emphasis.

[8] Greenhalgh, *Victory*, pp. 4–5; SGA, *Historique*, pp. 140–141.

[9] TNA, CAB 37/162/17, War Cabinet: 21st Meeting, 26 December 1916, Appendix IV, p. 8.

[10] Quoted in D. French, *The Strategy of the Lloyd George Coalition 1916–1918* (Oxford: Clarendon Press, 1995), p. 98.

Robertson labelled Sarrail a 'wrong "un"' with 'too much of the politician about him'.[11] Howell remarked in February 1916, 'we are directly under the French and should have to obey orders without question and without necessarily knowing the reason why (Sarrail is anything but confiding)'. With the BSF operationally under Sarrail but administratively under GOC Egypt, politics loomed 'much larger' and were 'terribly involved'.[12] In Palestine, Allenby respected the demeanour and soldiering abilities of Colonel de Piépape, commander of the French detachment, but voiced frustration at the constant tension between British military authority in the Middle East and the French zone of interest in Syria. As with Salonika, politics loomed large. Writing to Allenby in July 1918, General Sir Henry Wilson, the new CIGS, warned that any potential extension of British administration into Syria in the Levant 'would be liable to serious misconstruction both in France and in Syria'.[13]

Inter-Allied Learning and the 'Scientific' Aspects of Warfare

Extant political and strategic tensions invariably coloured the relationship between the two allies. One historian has suggested that the greatest degree of cooperation occurred between civilians, rather than between those operating in the military or political spheres; that, for the most part, collaboration and the appetite for learning from the other's experience was predicated on informal relationships between individuals.[14] From a learning perspective, cooperation in the civilian sphere can certainly be seen in the sharing of knowledge relating to the more scientific aspects of warfare, such as airpower, communications, and artillery survey. In the realm of scientific and civilian expertise, some British officers and generals thought the French had much to teach the army. One brigadier in Salonika wrote that 'the French have elbowed us out considerably. It is a real object lesson to me to watch their work. They have the enormous advantage of having civilianly [sic] trained specialists to draw on'.[15] Initial forays into learning between allies were predicated on close interpersonal relationships – sometimes grounded in pre-war partnerships. If deemed useful, the lessons and technology resulting from these

[11] LHCMA, Robertson Papers, 4/4/11, Robertson to Mahon, 6 March 1916.
[12] LHCMA, Howell Papers, Howell to Keyes, 4 February 1916.
[13] TNA, WO 33/960, Telegrams: Egypt, Wilson to Allenby, 25 July 1918.
[14] Greenhalgh, *Victory*, p. 283.
[15] TNA, WO 107/43, Inspector-General of Communications: Letters, Cowans to Altham, 13 November 1915.

exchanges were subsequently incorporated within the broader institution. In keeping with the army's networked approach to learning, the transformation from interpersonal to institutional required the input of entrepreneurs and leaders who could smooth over any frictions.

While efforts had been made pre-war to observe and learn from French airpower developments, it was the close wartime relationship between Brigadier-General Hugh Trenchard and his French counterpart, Colonel Paul du Peuty, that played an important role in the shaping of the RFC's emerging doctrine.[16] The French contribution to the development of British military aviation is critical, but has often been overlooked. In the autumn of 1915, Trenchard and du Peuty met to coordinate the French Tenth Army's air activity with that of adjacent RFC units. Matters of 'real substance' were addressed at this meeting, and the fundamental principles that governed the employment of aircraft in war were distilled. The two men talked, argued, and thrashed out policy. The result was the concept of the strategic offensive – a fundamental component of the RFC's doctrine.[17] Central to this relationship was the role of Maurice Baring, Trenchard's liaison officer. Neither Trenchard nor du Peuty was fluent in each other's language, requiring Baring to act as both translator and mediator between the two men. When the French Tenth Army moved to support operations at Verdun in March 1916, a network of liaison officers was established between du Peuty and Trenchard.[18] One of the French liaison officers, La Ferrière, was particularly well regarded. Baring commented on his 'invaluable' services and that he 'did almost more than anyone to bring about good feeling between the French and English services'.[19] Through du Peuty and the other attached liaison officers, the RFC received a stream of operational data and reports. Criticisms that the British did not learn lessons from the French experience at Verdun do not hold water where airpower was concerned. The valuable lessons that emerged from the French experience at Verdun were incorporated into the RFC's planning for the battle of the Somme. Indeed, du Peuty's findings 'anticipated to a remarkable degree the offensive tactics that Trenchard was to pursue relentlessly

[16] For further details on French influence on the RFC / RAF, see P. Dye, *The Bridge to Airpower: Logistics Support for Royal Flying Corps Operations on the Western Front, 1914–18* (Annapolis, MD: Naval Institute Press, 2015); Dye, 'France and the Development of British Military Aviation', *Air Power Review* 12 (1) (2009), pp. 1–13.
[17] Dye, 'Military Aviation', p. 8.
[18] J. Pugh, *The Royal Flying Corps, the Western Front, and the Control of the Air, 1914–1918* (London: Routledge, 2017), pp. 52–53. I am thankful to Dr James Pugh for sharing with me an advanced copy of this work.
[19] M. Baring, *Flying Corps Headquarters 1914–1918* (London: William Blackwood, 1968), p. 129.

for the remainder of the war'.[20] While the RFC did not embrace these lessons to the detriment of its own pre-Somme experiences, there was a clear synergy between French experience at Verdun and the RFC's own experiences on the Western Front.

Of course, one effective working relationship between two individuals does not a learning process make. Yet, this was not an isolated incident. Similar exchanges occurred throughout the army at various levels and on various fronts. The importance of interpersonal relationships and liaison underpinned a number of 'scientific' lessons that the British learned from the French. In August 1915, for instance, information was received through a liaison officer that the French were successfully experimenting with listening posts to overhear German conversations. Seven days later, the First Army's Officer Commanding [OC] Signals visited the post to examine the installation. The product of 'the fertile brain of a French infantry private who had been an electrician by profession', this apparatus proved to be the forerunner of the listening set, which would grow in prominence as the war progressed.[21] In January 1916, the first two examples of the French signal service's 'IT' listening set were installed on the British front at Vermelles. Though not widely used, they served to revolutionise 'current ideas of overhearing'.[22] On the eve of the Somme campaign, the relationship between the French and British signal services was further strengthened by the appointment of a dedicated liaison officer at GHQ whose duty was to visit units and research departments in the BEF as well as the French and Belgian armies in order to keep 'the Director of Signals informed of everything in signal practice and intention that was new and likely to be useful'. This officer was able to collect and disseminate the most practical ideas through *Signal Notes* and memoranda – a similar, concurrent development to that found in the army's tunnelling companies.[23]

Like communications, artillery developments, particularly those relating to survey, showcase an effective Anglo-French lessons learned partnership where, once again, we see an important synergy between the experiences of the two nations. While both independently developed their own gunnery and survey methods, a post-war consideration in the *Revue d'Artillerie* concluded that British methods were similar to and, in some cases, in advance of those employed by the French.[24] In his post-war memoir, Brooke, for example, recalled an important encounter with

[20] S. F. Wise, *Canadian Airmen and the First World War: The Official History of the Royal Canadian Air Force* (Toronto, ON: University of Toronto Press, 1980), p. 361.
[21] Priestley, *Signal Service*, pp. 101–102.   [22] Ibid., p. 107.   [23] Ibid., p. 168.
[24] Anon., 'Évolution des Methods de Tir des Artilleries Alliées Pendant la Guerre', *Revue D'Artillerie* 87 (January–June 1921), p. 544.

Major Pierre Héring – an artillery expert and French liaison officer to the Fourth Army. Brooke escorted Héring around the 18th Division's front, finding him 'most interesting to talk to and learned a great deal from him'. Of particular note was a recent form of French artillery support, which involved

one 75m gun to each 10 to 15 metres of front, and kept up a continuous rate of fire of some 4 rounds per gun per minute, increasing the range by increments of 50 metres at periods corresponding with the predicted rate of advance of the infantry. This was nothing more nor less than the inception of the 'Creeping or Rolling Barrage' which became so famous and so universal.[25]

Brooke recalled discussing this approach 'extensively' with the 18th Division's CRA, Brigadier-General Casimir van Straubenzee, who bought into the idea and agreed to apply it in future operations. With the support of senior generals, Brooke was empowered to build on this French lesson through the development of his colour-coded barrage maps. Maxse, though initially unclear as to how the barrage would work in practice, backed the expertise of his artillery commanders and was vindicated by the success of his division's creeping barrage on 1 July 1916.

Developments in sound ranging, artillery observation, and aerial photography were similarly grounded in an effective, collaborative relationship between Britain and France. However, this relationship was not without friction or suspicion. The French use of sound ranging had attracted the attention of individual British officers in early 1915, and eventually led to a deputation of RE officers evaluating French methods, and included experts on artillery, electricity, and topography.[26] Led by Harold Winterbotham, the committee reported favourably on the French use of the Bull-Weiss system, but apathy and opposition by some senior figures at BEF GHQ initially stymied attempts to trial French equipment and methods. It was through the combined efforts of Winterbotham and Lieutenant-Colonel Ewen Jack, head of GHQ's topographical section, that GHQ's opposition was assuaged and an experimental Bull set purchased from the Institut Marey in Paris.[27] To understand how the set worked in practice, two officer-scientists – Harold Robinson and Lawrence Bragg (the 1915 Nobel Laureate in Physics) – were sent to a section in the French Seventh Army in the Vosges for three weeks of instruction. In October 1915, after picking up the Bull set in Paris,

[25] LHCMA, Alanbrooke Papers, 5/2/13, 'Notes on My Life', 1954, p. 52. I am grateful to Dr Doug Delaney for drawing my attention to this reference.
[26] W. Van der Koot, 'Lawrence's Bragg's Role in the Development of Sound-Ranging in World War 1', *Notes and Records of the Royal Society* 59 (2005), p. 274.
[27] E. M. Jack, 'Survey in France during the War', *Royal Engineers' Journal* [hereafter *REJ*] 30 (1) (1919), pp. 21–22.

Bragg and Robinson were then sent up to the Fifth Army sector in Belgium where they started operations. It was at this point that we begin to see that synergy between French and British experience. Building on initial French experiments, Bragg and his sound ranging sections experimented with air currents and gun reports to great effect. For Bragg, the reason such a rapid development occurred with this technology was rapid cooperation, low level initiative, and proximity to the front line. They were empowered to experiment: 'we gave each section a mechanic with tools and a small lathe, so that it could try out gadgets on the spot. We arranged a meeting of heads of sections about every two months, when experiences were exchanged and new devices described'.[28]

Further localised learning relationships sprang up both on and beyond the Western Front. In January 1915, for example, the staff of the Second Army near Cassell frequently sent a number of liaison officers to the nearby French Groupe de Canevas de Tir [GCT]. Established by the Service Géographique d'Armée [SGA], the GCTs were specialised units that surveyed the terrain and updated maps used by the French army through aerial reconnaissance, sound ranging, flash spotting, and other methods. A number of 'trainee officers' were also sent to this particular GCT to study French operations and familiarise themselves with French methods.[29] Further cooperative work occurred between British and French forces in Belgium with complementary aerial photography and artillery mapping. In the case of the latter, the GCT created the artillery map of the Ypres salient to serve both armies. Owing to the different systems of measurement in place, it published the artillery map with both a British and French grid. From June 1915, British batteries at the southernmost junction with the French Tenth Army were provided with battery boards or 'planchettes' by that army's GCT. A graphic interpretation of the ranges, bearing, and aiming points of artillery, the planchette spread in popularity, leading the British to develop their own variation of this battery board.[30] In line with closer working between the RFC and the Aéronautique Militaire, there was more formalised cross-pollination with British officers attending the French Sixth Army's photographic interpretation school at Boves. This school was one of many inter-allied courses set up from October 1916 onwards. With one course per army group, the courses were designed to provide special instruction for officers responsible for the analysis of aerial photography.[31] Up and down the Western Front, the British and French forces were learning

[28] Glazer and Thomson, *Crystal Clear*, pp. 91–99.   [29] SGA, *Historique*, p. 140.
[30] TNA, WO 181/527, 'Survey on the Western Front', pp. 19–21.
[31] SGA, *Historique*, p. 67.

from one another. This learning was not limited to a single army, stretch of front, or time period. It was an ongoing, reciprocal process. In some instances, learning was predicated on a close interpersonal relationship between individuals, facilitated by liaison officers. However, many of these opportunities were horizontal and localised in nature, often occurring at the junction between British and French formations.

Away from the high tempo, densely populated Western Front, we see high levels of cooperation and similarly close relationships developing between British and French surveyors, particularly in Salonika and Italy. The non-unitary nature of learning comes to the fore once again in these subsidiary theatres with different methods and types of organisation facilitating the transfer of knowledge. The British topographical section in Salonika worked well with both its French and Serbian counterparts. In agreement with the French commander of the Service Topographique de l'Armée d'Orient, the British and Serbian sections adopted the scale and battery boards of their French counterparts.[32] A similar degree of cooperation was evident in Italy. To 'ensure close collaboration' with the French before the IEF's departure to Italy, Winterbotham was despatched to the SGA in Paris to consult over maps of the new theatre. Though the French maps of Italy were 'coarse and much inferior' to those of the Italians, the French had 'overprinted upon them a coordinate system of a suitable project'. This system of reference was adopted for British use. Cooperation was extended and enhanced in theatre. The RE official historian was moved to note how, on the Italian front, 'British and French units were able to exchange locations on the same system of reference, as they were never able to do in France'.[33] A series of training schools were also developed for the sharing of knowledge and expertise. In March 1918, for instance, the Force Françaises en Italie's [FFI] GCT developed a course specifically for *officiers orienteurs*. These officers were specially trained subalterns who aided in the interpretation of survey data for artillery groups and batteries. Located at Albaredo, the course's organisation and syllabus was similar to the French school at Vendôme on the Western Front. Between March and May 1918, forty-five French officers were trained alongside a number of British and Italian officers.[34] While this collaborative course worked well on the Italian front, British attempts to introduce *officiers orienteurs* on the Western Front foundered. A British topographical officer recalled how

[32] Ibid., p. 157.   [33] Institution of Royal Engineers, *History*, V, pp. 685–686.
[34] Ministère de la Guerre, *Les Armées Françaises dans la Grande Guerre*, Tome VI, vol. 1, Annex vol. 1 (Paris: Imprimerie Nationale, 1932), p. 479 [hereafter *AFGG* 6/1, followed by page or annex number]; SGA, *Historique*, pp. 58–59, 147.

the principle in use in the French army, of having a specially trained subaltern in each brigade and in each super heavy battery as an 'officier orienteur' was tried but failed miserably. We are of a different temperament from the French. Few British gunner majors will listen to advice from a subaltern even if he is an expert in his subject.[35]

In this instance, the appetite and empowerment to learn from French experience was evident, but the cultural differences between the two forces frustrated attempts to implement French best practice. It also highlights, once again, the different attitudes and approaches to learning within the army's respective theatres of operations.

In a lecture to the Royal Geographical Society [RGS] after the war, Winterbotham recalled the 'very close and cordial co-operation which existed between the Geographical Staffs of the various Allied Armies'. He also spoke warmly of General Robert Bourgeois, the long-serving director of the SGA, who 'we all regard[ed] ... as an elder brother, and with more affection than that relationship necessarily implies'. Winterbotham went further: 'It was immaterial, too, whether it were a French, American, Italian, or Belgian mapping unit that one visited, *one found throughout not acquaintances but friends, and a helpfulness which was rather astonishing*, that augurs well for the future of any international geodetic association'.[36] Where the more 'scientific' aspects of war were concerned, the pre-war language of internationalism still seemed to permeate the relationship between allies.[37] In the years preceding the war, there was an explosion of international associations, scientific conferences, and increased scientific and intellectual cooperation.[38] Through numerous international conferences before the war, senior figures in both the RGS and the General Staff's Geographical Section were well acquainted with French counterparts such as Bourgeois.[39] This pre-existing network of interpersonal relationships and a culture of transnational collaboration

---

[35] TNA, WO 181/528, Lieutenant-Colonel F. J. Salmon, 'Survey Work on the Western Front', *Transactions of the Engineering Association of Ceylon* (1920), pp. 34–35.

[36] H. S. L. Winterbotham, 'British Survey on the Western Front', *The Geographical Journal* 53 (4) (1919), p. 271. Added emphasis.

[37] Aspects of this scientific internationalism leached into the early interwar years. See e.g. V. Prott, 'Tying Up the Loose Ends of National Self-Determination: British, French and American Experts in Peace Planning, 1917–1919', *Historical Journal* 57 (3) (2014), pp. 734, 738–742.

[38] F. J. Lambert, 'Internationalisme Scientifique et Révolution Quantique: Les Premieres Conseils Solvay', *Revue Germanique Internationale* 12 (2010), pp. 159, 170; A. Rasmussen, 'Tournant, Inflexions, Ruptures: Le Moment Internationaliste', *Mil Neuf Cent. Revue d'Histoire Intellectuelle* 19 (1) (2001), p. 35.

[39] M. Heffernan, 'Geography, Cartography and Military Intelligence: The Royal Geographical Society and the First World War', *Transactions of the Institute of British Geographers* 21 (3) (1996), pp. 508–509.

provided a solid base for effective cooperation during the war. While there was certainly some friction and cries of exceptionalism, Britain and France sought to learn from one another's wartime scientific developments. National institutions, such as the Ordnance Survey, the Meteorological Office, and their allied equivalents, collaborated with one another at the highest levels.[40] This collaboration trickled down to the battlefield itself. The German use of gas, for example, resulted in close working between the British army's initially ad hoc central laboratory at St. Omer and its French counterpart, the Laboratoire Municipal in Paris. With the increasing regularity of gas attacks, frequent exchanges and 'direct communication' between the two laboratories led to increased levels of liaison and cooperation which proved to be of 'great mutual advantage'.[41]

In some instances, French scientific lessons and experiences had an institutional impact, such as artillery sound ranging and RFC doctrine. On the other hand, many of these learning opportunities were localised in terms of branch or theatre, leading to incremental adjustments. This did not, however, make them any less valuable to the army. Whether small-scale or institutional in nature, the common thread was the importance of individuals and the relationships that existed between them. These relationships could be fairly incidental as with Brooke and Héring, or they could be long standing such as that between Bourgeois, Winterbotham, and Jack. While we can detect a 'spirit of internationalism', particularly in the relations between learned societies or scientific laboratories, the overriding motivation was a desire for proven experience whether in the form of technology or ideas.

Tactical Developments and the Tabula Rasa

The sharing of scientific and technical knowledge highlights just one aspect of a successful learning relationship between the two nations. Where tactical developments were concerned, however, there is little consensus amongst historians as to whether the British were able, or indeed willing, to learn from French tactical developments. One historian suggests that, prior to the Somme offensive, there was little '*formal* transmission of French documents or tactical lessons', and that such exchanges – when they did occur – were largely informal in nature.[42]

---

[40] H. G. Lyon, 'Meteorology during and after the War', *Monthly Weather Review* 42 (2) (1919), p. 81.

[41] LHCMA, Foulkes Papers, 6/37, 'History of the Central Laboratory', n.d.; C. Moureu, 'La Chimie et La Guerre: Science et Avenir', *La Revue d'Infanterie* 340 (58) (1921), pp. 192–193.

[42] Greenhalgh, *Victory*, p. 63.

There is some truth to this statement. As GSO1 to the 13th Division in early 1915, Webb Gillman noted that part of his division's preparatory training for the Western Front involved 'certain details from our attack at Neuve Chapelle, and some of the French attacks'.[43] This information was not part of the CDS or SS series of pamphlets, suggesting a more informal exchange. However, from June 1915, the army was formally distributing French lessons learned and best practice. Translated from French, *CDS23 Preliminary Deductions for Instructions from Recent Engagements* and *CDS24 Object and Conditions of Combined Offensive Action* represent the first formal dissemination of French methods within the British army.[44] These publications were followed up later in the year with *CDS333 A Study of the Attack in the Present Phase of War: Impressions and Reflection of a Company Commander* – a translation of Captain André Laffargue's famous pamphlet. Of course, the simple act of distribution was no guarantee that it would be read let alone favourably received. What it does show, however, is that there was a formal dissemination process of Allied literature in place by mid-1915, which was continually supplemented by an incidental and informal exchange of information. As we have seen, such unstructured interactions were an important aspect of the army's learning experience. A failure to acknowledge this reality is to ignore a vital part of both military and organisational learning.

The end of the Somme campaign resulted in much soul searching and introspection within the British army, as well as an acknowledgement that they could usefully learn from the French. The BEF in particular sought to make sense of its experiences and modify them where appropriate. In addition to internal reflection such as Montgomery's 'deep dive' for best practice during the Somme, some officers and generals were minded to visit the various French armies to observe and report on their experiences. At first, these visits were likely ad hoc in nature, involving a variety of individuals from different Armies. In November 1916, for example, Major-General John Shea (GOC, 30th Division) of the Fourth Army and three fellow generals from the Third Army visited the French Fourth Army near Châlons.[45] He was 'very very greatly impressed' by everything he saw and meant 'as far as possible, always of course with certain modifications to suit our circumstances, to train

---

[43] RAHT, Gillman Papers, MD1161/2/11, Gallipoli Diary, 11 January–14 June 1915.

[44] I am thankful to Christopher Henderson for this detail as well as his painstaking work in the compilation of an accurate list of CDS and SS pamphlets.

[45] The three other individuals were Brigadier-General Lord Loch (BGGS, VI Corps); Brigadier-General Arthur Solly-Flood (Commandant, Third Army School); and Lieutenant-Colonel Charles Grant (GSO1, 12th (Eastern) Division).

my people on the same lines'. As far as he was concerned, there was
'no reason' why the British army should not adopt the French scheme
of training.[46] Shea's report on tactical training and platoon development
had an appreciable effect on Fourth Army with Rawlinson and Montgomery declaring that the platoon will be the 'fighting unit', and that
the weapons at its disposal will be 'rifle and bayonet, grenade and rifle
grenade, and . . . the Lewis gun as well'.[47]

Further visits were conducted throughout the winter of 1916. Between
5 and 8 January 1917, a substantial party of twenty officers and generals
ranging in rank from major-general to major visited the French Second
Army at Verdun. Organised by GHQ, this delegation was made up of
individuals from First, Third, and Fifth Armies, and included Major-
Generals Arthur Currie (GOC, 1st Canadian Division), Herbert Uniacke (MGRA, Fifth Army), and Cameron Shute (GOC, 63rd [Royal
Naval] Division), as well as John Burnett-Stuart and Brooke. While the
visit was primarily concerned with training and infantry tactics, around
two-thirds of the delegates were gunners.[48] Brooke detailed the visit in
his memoir, recollecting how

we were taken to Army HQ, Corps HQ, Divisional and Brigade HQ, and
explained in detail all the plans for the attacks which had proved so successful.
We were taken over the ground and under experts explained all the dispositions
and the results of the attacks . . . The whole trip was intensely interesting.[49]

The visit to the French Second Army had a profound effect on the delegates, particularly Currie who produced his 'Notes on French attacks
north-east of Verdun in October and December 1916' for Julian Byng
(GOC, Canadian Corps) on 23 January 1917.[50] Amongst other things,
Currie's report drew attention to the French army's elastic doctrine, con-
demned linear tactics, and stressed the importance of devolved command. A formal report was produced for wider dissemination.[51] While
some aspects of the GHQ report were more guarded, particularly on

[46] LHCMA, Montgomery-Massingberd Papers, 7/4, Shea to Montgomery, 28 November
1916.
[47] LHCMA, Montgomery-Massingberd Papers, 7/34, Montgomery to GOC corps, 12
December 1916.
[48] Simkins, *Somme to Victory*, p. 48
[49] LHCMA, Alanbrooke Papers, 5/2/13, 'Notes on My Life', 1954, p. 58.
[50] M. O. Humphries, '"Old Wine in New Bottles": A Comparison of British and Canadian
Preparations for the Battle of Arras', in G. Hayes, A. Iarocci, and M. Bechtold (eds),
Vimy Ridge: A Canadian Reassessment (Waterloo, ON: Wilfrid Laurier University Press,
2007), p. 67.
[51] The report is both unsigned and undated. However, Simon Robbins suggests that GHQ
prepared the report. See S. Robbins, *British Generalship during the Great War: The Military Career of Sir Henry Horne (1861–1929)* (Farnham: Ashgate, 2010), p. 159.

staff work and the types of tactics used, there were obvious similarities with Currie's report. GHQ highlighted the 'considerable latitude' given to French formations along with their tendency 'to attack with greater elboe-room [*sic*] than we allow'. Greater latitude allowed for elasticity and manoeuvre.[52] In the French approach, GHQ caught a glimpse of the basis of the British army's own training before the war:

The basis of the French infantry training is well-known; it consists in the perfecting of the platoon as a self-reliant and self-sufficient unit of battle... The success of such a system depends rather on a meticulous attention to details of organisation and the development of the initiative of Company, Platoon, Section and Squad leaders, rather than on any fixed formation or procedure. It is necessary for us to revive our own training on these lines.[53]

The various visits to the French army were fundamental to the development of both *SS143* and *SS144 The Normal Formation for the Attack*, which were published in the first few months of 1917. There is no need here to go into the various debates surrounding the production of these pamphlets; these have been covered extensively elsewhere.[54] However, it is important to note that the development of specialised platoon tactics was not solely a result of British exposure to French experience. The 9th (Scottish) Division and various Canadian divisions had been actively experimenting with new platoon tactics both during and immediately after the Somme campaign independent of French developments.[55] But, as with the RFC, there was a clear cooperation between British and French practice; the latter was certainly a catalyst, providing the much-needed impetus for changes to tactics and training.

Perhaps more important than the publication of *SS143* and *SS144* was the opportunity for introspection provided by examining how another army faced the challenges of the Western Front. Observing and making sense of French practice acted as a mirror, allowing the British army to reflect on its own strengths and weaknesses. The French experience, particularly at Verdun, was a tabula rasa upon which the British army projected its own conceptions of warfare.[56] While validating the army's pre-war approach to tactics, training, and initiative, these visits also revealed the inadequacies of an individual-driven approach to warfare. During

---

[52] LHCMA, Montgomery-Massingberd Papers, 7/34, 'Notes on a Party of British Officers to Verdun, January 5th – 8th 1917', n.d., p. 1.
[53] Ibid.
[54] See e.g. Geddes, 'Solly-Flood'; Humphries, 'Old Wine'; Griffith, *Battle Tactics*, pp. 56–57, 77–79.
[55] Humphries, 'Old Wine', pp. 67–69; LHCMA, Papers of Major-General J. F. C. Fuller, 1/1/32, n.d.
[56] Humphries, 'Old Wine', p. 73.

his own visit to French schools at Mailly and Châlons in late January 1917, Montgomery pointed out the benefits of 'uniformity in the training of troops' with 'general direction from above'. This regularity was not designed to be restrictive: sufficient elasticity was granted to subordinate commanders 'to prevent any chance of the drill or organisation becoming too stereotyped or elastic'.[57] The French had seemingly resolved a problem that the British had been grappling with since 1909. Impressed by what he had seen, it is little wonder that Montgomery advocated for the 'necessity for a training branch at GHQ', uniformity in drill, and 'some form of standard drill attack formations ... as a guide to subordinate commanders'.[58] Employing his usual consultative approach, Montgomery circulated his findings amongst Fourth Army's corps and divisional commanders. Lord Cavan (GOC, XIV Corps) endorsed Montgomery's propositions, reinforcing the need for an 'authoritative book of instructions', and that no time should be lost in drawing up 'Instructions for the Training of a Platoon for Offensive Action'.[59] Montgomery's cover note to Lieutenant-General Sir Richard Butler, the BEF's deputy CGS, implored GHQ to lay down some 'definite organisation':

Principles were all very well before the War when you had a lot of experienced officers who could be relied upon to use their own intelligence; but as you know, the situation is entirely different now. In the present conditions an officer is very likely to be taught one thing in his battalion, another thing in his divisional school, another thing in the Army school and, if he is transferred to another battalion, something quite different there, and in the end he does not know where to begin or what to do.[60]

Montgomery did not see uniformity of method and flexibility as mutually exclusive. Key to him was the establishment of clear foundations upon which formations could build and innovate as they saw fit and as the situation demanded. Without such foundations, the army was forcing its units to make bricks without straw.

The army's observation of French practice and its general introspection over the winter of 1916–1917 raises three important points. First, that the British took French experience and tactical developments seriously. Representatives from almost all the British Armies visited a number of French formations at various locations on the Western Front. Third Army was particularly active in this respect, but it was not alone. Fourth Army was determined to ensure that parties of officers desirous

[57] LHCMA, Montgomery-Massingberd Papers, 7/34, 'Report on a Visit to the French Training Camp at Mailly and the Army School at Chalons', pp. 1–2.
[58] Ibid., p. 11.   [59] Ibid., Cavan to Montgomery, 30 January 1917.
[60] Ibid., Montgomery to Butler, 27 January 1917.

of seeing the 'various forms of training' in the French army were encouraged and facilitated where possible.[61] Of course, tensions, friction, and snobbery were unavoidable when attempting to learn from an allied power. The process was not perfect. Relevant experience was ignored or discounted. However, the appetite for lessons was certainly apparent at the operational level and below.

Secondly, the process of observation and critique enabled British self-reflection. Critical reflection of another's methods and approaches shapes existing knowledge and can facilitate learning. By observing French practice, British commanders were forced to grapple with the strengths and weaknesses of their own organisation through comparison. For some, French methods simply reaffirmed the status quo, but for others they underlined both marginal and fundamental challenges. A lengthy report from an Australian field artillery officer after his two week visit to the French Tenth Army in January 1917 reflected on various artillery matters, including battery tactics, barrage fire, destruction of wire, and communication methods. While the officer noted that 'the French methods are much the same as our own', he believed that 'we have something to learn from them', particularly where wire cutting was concerned: 'the French system is almost mathematical in its certainty'.[62] Following his visit to French Fifth Army in February 1917, Brigadier-General Louis Vaughan (BGGS, XV Corps) noted how the French methods endorsed the formations found in *SS144*, but also revealed that British fire and manoeuvre required further improvement.[63] Observation rarely led to the slaughter of sacred cows, but it could result in the refinement of, or incremental changes to, existing practice.

Finally and related to the previous point, there were renewed calls by senior British officers for an increasingly standardised approach to learning, particularly where tactics were concerned. This proved difficult for a whole host of reasons as mentioned previously, particularly as top down, vertical intervention was not always popular. Cavan's January 1917 letter to Montgomery captures this dilemma perfectly:

There is always a reluctance in the mind of an old soldier to depart from the teaching of the textbook on which he was brought up. The sole obstacle to the instant adoption of a uniform organisation of the platoon for attack is the sentence in *I[nfantry] T[raining]* Chapter IX . . .

[61] Ibid., Training conference notes, 21 February 1917.
[62] AWM, AWM27 305/8, Notes on the Xth Army Artillery Course, 17–31 January 1917, pp. 6, 13.
[63] AWM, Papers of General Sir C. B. B. White, 3DRL/1400 4/7, Brigadier-General L. R. Vaughan, 'Note on a Visit to Fifth French Army, 15–19 February 1917', 2 March 1917.

'It is impossible as well as highly undesirable to lay down a fixed and unvarying system of battle formations'

Circumstances have now changed ... In my opinion, therefore, any authoritative book of instructions for the training of the platoon is not only necessary and urgent but would be mostly heartily welcomed by every commander to whom I have spoken.[64]

What we see with Montgomery, Shea, and Cavan amongst others is a step change in the thinking and attitudes of senior regular officers and generals. They clearly demonstrated intellectual flexibility and considerable bravery in recognising that, despite the importance of initiative and individual action, some standardisation was necessary even if, on the surface, this undermined the army's ethos. Observing the French brought to mind the halcyon days of pre-war training – of effective fire and manoeuvre, of self-sufficiency and self-reliance. This rose-tinted view clearly overlooked some of the problems that had dogged the army in the years leading up to 1914. Some attendees at the 1913 General Staff conference, for instance, had criticised the army for failing to provide a 'definite foundation' for young officers, that it was desirable to offer something 'more authoritative and up to date'.[65] Now, in the midst of the First World War, these problems were far more acute: they required a definite answer. Yet, despite initial good intentions, difference of method persisted throughout the war. This dilemma was akin to a scratched record; the army kept skipping back and revisiting this same problem over again. Writing to Montgomery in October 1918, Dawnay bemoaned the state of British training anew: 'I am constantly being told by divisions moving from corps to corps and army to army that they are taught differently – different doctrine and different methods – as they move from one command to another'.[66] Dawnay's remarks were almost a verbatim copy of Montgomery's own criticisms of January 1917. Indeed, despite the establishment of the Inspectorate of Training in July 1917 and the production of more authoritative publications, the army's continuing aversion to top-down, vertical intervention won out. Here we see, once again, both the strengths and weaknesses of the army's ethos of flexibility coming to the fore: initiative was prioritised, but sometimes at the expense of uniformity of effort.

---

[64] LHCMA, Montgomery-Massingberd Papers, 7/34, Cavan to Montgomery, 30 January 1917, p. 1.

[65] TNA, WO 279/48, General Staff officers conference, 13–16 January 1913, p. 15.

[66] LHCMA, Montgomery-Massingberd Papers, 7/32, Dawnay to Montgomery, 31 October 1918.

Learning in a Collaborative Context

Whilst Anglo-French relations on the Western Front were often fraught, there were instances of cooperation and joint working where other mutual allies were concerned. Admittedly, the two allies' relationship with the US was not always plain sailing. The two separate and, for the most part, competitive missions to the US in April 1917 suggested that issues of national pride were getting in the way of coordination. As Colonel Edward House remarked, 'distrust lies close beneath the surface, and a little difference between them would bring it from under cover'.[67] When it came to training the newly arrived American formations, there were inherent problems associated with the 'simultaneous teaching of British, French and American methods'.[68]

While difficulties persisted with the US, the opportunity for reciprocity of experience between France and Britain was enhanced by having to work with their Italian ally from 1917 onwards. Both nations treated their mutual ally with a degree of snobbery: aspersions were regularly cast on Italy's 'stomach' (or lack thereof) for fighting and war, leading to questions around the competency of her soldiering.[69] Both contemporaries and modern scholars highlight the important role played by Britain and French forces in influencing the learning process of the Italian forces. As the Duke of Aosta remarked to Cavan in January 1919, 'without the presence of you and your troops . . . there would have been no Vittorio Veneto'.[70] While there were understandable frictions, this broadly collaborative approach to learning encouraged, as far as possible, dialogue and cooperation between forces. Drawing on past experiences and existing knowledge, the three forces could help one another address certain challenges through a variety of means, including demonstration and discussion-based practices.

It would be easy to view learning in this context as one-way rather than collaborative, but this was not the case. The British and French formations that had been sent to Italy had all served on the Western Front; it was their only common point of reference. The geographic and climactic differences between that front and the Italian front were stark. Newly

---

[67] Greenhalgh, 'Viviani', pp. 640–641, 650.

[68] TNA, WO 106/499A, General Reports on Operations from British Military Mission, Final Report of the 3rd Course of the American Staff College, 11 September 1918.

[69] For an alternative view on morale and the combat effectiveness of the Italian army, see V. Wilcox, *Morale and the Italian Army during the First World War* (Cambridge: Cambridge University Press, 2016), and J. Gooch, *The Italian Army and the First World War* (Cambridge: Cambridge University Press, 2014).

[70] Gooch, *Italian Army*, p. 297.

arrived formations required the expertise of their ally to help them acclimatise and adapt to this new theatre. This expertise was harnessed for seemingly trivial problems, such as the loan of tractors and advice on driving motor transport on steep mountain roads.[71] British units were also attached to Italian formations in order to acclimatise to the very different conditions found in the mountains and plains of Italy. The 23rd Division sent 'parties of 1 officer and 40 OR' from two of its brigades for attachment to Italian units.[72] This attachment scheme served two purposes: first, the XIV Corps (in which the 23rd Division served) was due to relieve the Italian I Corps and this was, therefore, standard practice when conducting a relief. Secondly, as the 23rd Division was new to the area, it gave it the opportunity to familiarise itself with the line to be held. To ensure that the reliefs went smoothly, the Italian 70th Division left one officer and two NCOs at each unit headquarters for twenty-four hours after relief.[73] The XI Corps had a similar experience when it relieved the Italian VIII Corps in late January 1918. The departing Italians 'left numerous English-speaking officers both in the front line and with the headquarters of formations to assist us... They left steel helmets for the sentries to prevent the enemy from discovering that British troops were in the line'.[74] The important role that Italian forces played in this acclimatisation process was recognised by XI Corps commander, Lieutenant-General Sir Richard Haking, in a letter to the commander of the Italian XX Corps: 'you have enabled us to learn a great deal regarding the method of conducting mountain warfare which was new to us, and we hope to profit by what you have shown us'.[75]

Naturally, working closely with Italian formations during relief afforded the British a chance to observe their ally close up. Soon enough, questions and concerns were raised about the nature of the Italian defensive system. Following the relief of the Italian I Corps, the 23rd Division, for 'greater convenience', adopted the Italian defence plan, but it soon began to 'reorganise the defence in accordance with principles... adopted in France'.[76] One artillery officer in the 48th (South Midland) Division questioned the wisdom of the Italian single line defence. After a series of reconnaissances with his colonel, the

---

[71] M. Young, *Army Service Corps 1902–1918* (Barnsley: Leo Cooper, 2000), pp. 151–152.
[72] TNA, WO 95/4229, 23rd Division GS War Diary, 28 November 1917. The XI Corps carried out a similar practice in December 1917–January 1918.
[73] Ibid., Divisional Order 12, 1 December 1917.
[74] TNA, WO 95/4211, XI Corps GS War Diary, Memo (GS 1080/4), 29 January 1918.
[75] Ibid., Haking to Vittorio, 23 January 1918.
[76] H. R. Sandilands, *The 23rd Division 1914–1919* (London: William Blackwood, 1925), p. 224.

officer in question deemed the system to be 'not altogether sound'. As the Italian trench system ran along the crests of the hills, there was considerable dead ground in which 'the enemy could form up unseen in the valley, move up, and then rush the trenches in a short assault giving the defence no chance'.[77] French commanders similarly remarked on these defensive inadequacies. General Émile Fayolle, the FFI's CinC, commented on the lack of depth in the Italian defence and how the front lines were packed with troops.[78]

For the British and French, the Italian defensive arrangements were just the tip of the iceberg. In one of his reports to the CIGS, Plumer highlighted a number of areas where additional improvements were needed: staff work was 'so theoretical that they do not understand practical difficulties of their orders', and the infantry 'lack training and have not much confidence in their officers'.[79] Fayolle provided his own litany of tactical deficiencies. The Italians, however, were capable of self-criticism, particularly their new CinC, General Armando Diaz, who was aware of these shortfalls and was taking his own steps to remedy the situation. Yet both the French and British saw their role as educating and revitalising the Italian army, which was not always popular.[80] Mindful of the need for sensitivity, the two forces, where possible, imparted knowledge and experience through a variety of familiar means, including publications, personnel, demonstration, and schools. This multi-faceted approach not only highlights the numerous means for sharing knowledge, but also the importance of recognising and responding to different organisational cultures.

British publications, for example, were issued 'in large numbers' to Italian formations. By January 1918, Italian officers began to ask for 'copies of notes and suggestions...and have asked us for any Notes or Hints on Training'.[81] In addition to this, the Italians embarked on their own international exchanges, seeking out German best practice, including a British translation of a document by Ludendorff. From May 1918, the Italians began publishing a regular series of bulletins on British and French operations on the Western Front along with translations of captured German and Austro-Hungarian documents. One Italian general returned from Versailles with a '"treasury" of practical knowledge

[77] NAM, Papers of Colonel R. Macleod, 8112–9, 'An Artillery Officer in the First World War', n.d., p. 193; TNA, CAB 24/32/18, Memorandum: Italian situation, Cavan to War Office, 10 November 1917.
[78] Gooch, *Italian Army*, pp. 266–267.
[79] TNA, WO 106/810, Report by General Plumer on the Condition of the Italian Army, 20 January 1918.
[80] Gooch, *Italian Army*, p. 251.
[81] TNA, CAB 24/39/94, Report on Italian situation, 13 January 1918.

and new theories of war' that he had learned from the 'defenders of the Somme'.[82] Much like British forces in the subsidiary theatres, there was an obvious appetite for Western Front knowledge and experience in the Italian army.

Exchanges of personnel were also employed as a form of collaborative learning. Within weeks of its arrival, the IEF sent a number of British officers to the Italian front lines. Lieutenant-Colonel C. N. Buzzard, a British artillery officer, recalled how he 'arranged that every day an officer from one of our batteries... should visit the front line with an interpreter'. This arrangement was in response to the strained relationship between the Italian infantry and artillery. Buzzard recalled how this British intervention was 'so much appreciated' by the Italians who have 'done so much for us in this line'.[83] The British also sent staff officers to the Italian front to advise on administrative issues, and to familiarise Italian troops with the presence of senior officers. Plumer noted that the Italian 'higher commanders and staffs were not sufficiently in touch with the conditions in front and that there was not sufficient sympathy between the front and rear authorities'. He thought that the presence of British officers would encourage Italian officers to visit the front line more often. These exchange officers could act as catalysts, facilitating the sharing of knowledge and best practice. These visits allowed officers to discuss matters with the Italians, 'throwing out suggestions' relating to defences, machine gun arrangements, wiring, and reliefs.[84]

While these more informal attachments were perceived, by the British at least, to be successful, problems arose when attempts were made to attach formally British and French officers to Italian headquarters. It was felt by both the IEF and FFI that the quickest way of establishing similar procedures within the Italian staff was through centrally arranged secondments. The initial plan was to send British and French officers to lecture at the Italian staff college under the guise of an 'exchange of ideas'. To lessen suspicion, it was suggested that Italian officers might lecture to allied officers; an *Alpini* officer or engineer might, for example, give a lecture on mountain warfare. The eventual approach taken was more sensitive with a plan for the reciprocal attachment of officers to allied headquarters.[85] It was felt that such an interchange might make the arrangement more palatable. However, this was easier said than done with continued resistance from the *comando supremo*. Indeed, it was not

[82] Gooch, *Italian Army*, pp. 284–285.

[83] TNA, CAB 25/22, Impressions of Lieutenant-Colonel C. N. Buzzard, October–November 1917.

[84] TNA, CAB 24/39/94, Report on Italian situation, 13 January 1918.

[85] *AFGG* 6/1 Appendix 219, Foch to Fayolle, 28 December 1917, pp. 396–397.

until April 1918 that Italian high command authorised twelve majors to complete an attachment at headquarters in the FFI.[86] As one British officer remarked, it was 'difficult, tactfully, to dictate to an Allied nation measures for the improvement of their forces'.[87]

Practical demonstration proved to be a less intrusive way of sharing knowledge and experience with the Italians. Not long after their arrival in Italy, both the IEF and FFI began to carefully reorganise the defences in their sectors to reflect their experience of defence in depth on the Western Front. To mitigate the inadequacies encountered in Italian preparations, the IEF organised its defences 'very carefully so as to bring prominently to notice the value of a defence in depth . . . and folly of depending on single defensive lines into which all men, machine-guns etc are crowded'. Where the IEF was concerned, this was a deliberate attempt to lead by example. A letter from Foch to Diaz suggests that the FFI was employing a similar approach, its defensive arrangements characterised by embankments and natural obstacles connected by sections of trench and supported by machine guns.[88] The adoption of modified Western Front methods by the FFI had practical results as demonstrated by the French 47th Division's assault on Mont Tomba on 30 December 1917. Drawing on the lessons of Verdun and La Malmaison, such as careful artillery preparation and effective artillery-infantry liaison, the Austrian division opposite was pushed back eighteen hundred metres, leaving behind five hundred dead and fifteen hundred prisoners. In contrast, the French division suffered 54 killed and 205 wounded.[89]

Frequent visits by Italian officers resulted in this modified Western Front practice finding its way back to their higher command. Italian front lines were soon 'being thinned and they have taken up our system of the employment of machine-guns'.[90] This new, allied-inspired approach to defence was crystallised in a manifesto by Diaz, which highlighted the problems of 'putting too many men in the front line'. According to Plumer, it was clear that the Italians were now 'paying attention to defence in depth . . . and are certainly improving'.[91] One British liaison officer observed in May 1918 that the Italian Fifth Army seemed 'to be inspired with the right spirit and to understand the principles of

---

[86] *AFGG* 6/1, pp. 199–120.

[87] TNA, CAB 25/22, Impressions of Lieutenant-Colonel C. N. Buzzard, October–November 1917.

[88] *AFGG* 6/1 Appendix 85, Foch to Diaz, 18 November 1917, p. 152.

[89] E. Greenhalgh, *The French Army and the First World War* (Cambridge: Cambridge University Press, 2014), p. 264.

[90] TNA, CAB 24/39/94, Report on Italian situation, 13 January 1918.

[91] TNA, CAB 24/37/69, Letter on the Italian Situation, 2 January 1918.

defence... The machine gun emplacements seemed to be in the right place'.[92]

One of the most successful methods for inter-allied learning came about through the establishment of training schools. This cooperative method allowed for the exchange of best practice between all three allies, and was advocated at a very early stage. From as early as November 1917, the FFI was keen to establish training centres similar to those on the Western Front. Fayolle believed that establishing these training centres would not only benefit French units, but would also allow for Italian officers to 'take advantage of our teaching and our methods'.[93] This collaborative approach was soon extended to the British. In December 1917, Foch encouraged Fayolle to liaise closely with both Diaz and Plumer for the development of similar training centres in both Italian and British forces. Furthermore, he was keen that 'close liaison' and exchange of officers at the various schools should take place to ensure that 'each army benefits from the other two'.[94]

Both the IEF and FFI established their training schools around the same time in January 1918. Around fourteen FFI schools were in operation in the Lake Garda-Verona region. These facilities could accommodate around 120 Italian soldiers with the possibility of increasing this number based on demand. Similarly, British officers were also able to attend French schools with an allowance of fifteen officers per course. In a show of reciprocity, twelve French officers were posted to British schools. The IEF's schools were grouped in a comparatively small area around Padua so that they could be 'easily visited by the Italians'. Like the FFI, the IEF had 'asked the Italians to send officers – as many as they like up to 100'. Despite the belief that shared attendance at schools would have a 'beneficial effect', there was reluctance at first with Plumer remarking that 'I hope the Italians would have accepted the offer... but they are very sensitive... any attempt at pressure is fatal'.[95] By February 1918, the Italian force was sending its officers to British schools, although a British liaison officer remarked that, even in May 1918, the Italians still did not take up all the vacancies allotted to them.[96] Another British officer was slightly more optimistic in his outlook, believing that this inter-allied approach led to a 'constant interchange of ideas' between

---

[92] P. Robinson (ed.), *The Letters of Major General Price Davies VC, CB, CMG, DSO* (Stroud: The History Press, 2013), p. 201.
[93] *AFGG* 6/1 Appendix 126: Fayolle to Duchene, 28 November 1917, pp. 218–219.
[94] *AFGG* 6/1 Appendix 219: Foch to Fayolle, 28 December 1917, pp. 396–397.
[95] LHCMA, Robertson Papers, 8/3/47, Plumer to Robertson, 21 January 1918.
[96] Robinson, *Price Davies*, p. 201.

the three forces.[97] This interchange was facilitated by the visits of senior Italian and French officers who would live at the schools to witness demonstrations.[98] The German Army employed a similar inter-allied approach. Schools set up on the Western Front in early 1917 sought to train commanders in the latest defensive doctrine. In late March 1917, a number of German officers from the Eastern Front, along with seven Austro-Hungarian and four Turkish officers took advantage of this valuable opportunity.[99]

While these schools provided a useful way of bringing the Italian forces up to speed, they also acted as a forum for inter-allied learning, particularly between the British and French. Richard O'Connor detailed his experience at a French training school in January 1918 where he shared a villa with a French 'captain of cavalry, and two Chasseurs Lieut[enant]s'.[100] The structure of the course was comparable to that found in British army courses: in the morning, there were one or two hours of lectures by the commandant, and the afternoon spent in practical demonstration. These demonstrations included the company in attack, the employment of machine guns, and the battalion in attack. Course content was not limited to the Italian front either; examples of experience on the Western Front were also covered, such as the precepts of defence in depth and a narrative account of the French XXI Corps's action at La Malmaison in October 1917. O'Connor confessed that the French language was difficult to follow at first, but he found the course both useful and satisfying, remarking on the 'sad farewell' he bid his French counterparts. The course commandant was a 'very good lecturer' and 'comprised everything which a commanding officer and a gentleman should know'. O'Connor's comments were borne out by a March 1918 report on the situation of FFI, which suggested that the French schools were held in high regard by the allies.[101]

Schools were also places for experimentation and demonstration with new or existing technology. While the British trench mortar school at Teolo delivered the usual inter-allied courses, it also became a forum for the demonstration of modified mortars, attracting interest beyond the IEF. In March 1918, for instance, the 6" Newton trench mortar, which had been modified for use in mountain warfare, was tested. The demonstrations were conducted to an audience of French mid-level officers as

[97] IWM, Papers of Lieutenant-General A. N. Floyer-Acland, 12635, Memoirs, n.d., p. 74.
[98] Robinson, *Price Davies*, p. 208.
[99] I am grateful to Dr Tony Cowan for bringing this to my attention.
[100] LHCMA, O'Connor Papers, 2/2/4, Ms Diary, 28 January–16 February 1918.
[101] *AFGG* 6/1 Appendix 467: Report on the FFI, 16 March 1918, p. 1100.

well as Italian and French brigadiers.[102] One British attendee spoke of the 'expression of gratitude and thanks' received from the international representatives.[103] In August 1918, the school experimented with a new mobile mortar to around one hundred visitors, including representatives from the British, Italian, French, and American forces.[104] The commandant recognised the potential value of these mobile mortars beyond the Italian front. Perhaps too late to have any appreciable impact, the commandant and six ORs from the 48th Division nevertheless entrained for the Western Front with 'sample mobile mortar equipment' in tow for demonstration.

It is clear that the British and French had a significant part to play in enhancing the combat effectiveness of their Italian ally. However, it is important that we do not ascribe all the successful changes to allied intervention. Diaz was well aware of the difficulties facing his force and was implementing measures independent of Britain and France. Inter-allied cooperation was not without its frictions either. The Anglo-French contingent recognised that working with the Italians, sharing expertise with them, had to be done 'quietly and patiently'.[105] While the Italian force was willing to learn, it was 'proud and sensitive' and would not respond well to 'any appearance of superiority or of imparting instruction'.[106] Both the IEF and FFI, while expressing consternation and frustration to their home governments, treated the Italian force with a certain degree of understanding, prioritising illustration and demonstration as the favoured methods for knowledge sharing. The two forces soon enough remarked on some of the lessons that the Italians had picked up from its close liaison. A French report noted the establishment of a counter-battery office in the Italian First Army, which was similar to the French Service des renseignements de l'artillerie. It also highlighted similarities of method in the use of gas shells and in some elements of operational planning.[107] French infantry tactics also proved influential. By September 1918, new Italian regulations for attack by divisions were issued. The method prescribed was a 'series of articulated attacks coordinated rapidly', which resembled French regulations from December 1917.[108] A post-war consideration of artillery development highlighted the importance of the French Tenth Army's artillery course

---

[102] TNA, WO 95/4206, Trench Mortar School War Diary, 22 March 1918 and 17 May 1918.
[103] Robinson, *Price Davies*, pp. 211, 213.
[104] TNA, WO 95/4206, Trench Mortar School War Diary, 26 August 1918.
[105] TNA, CAB 24/38/56, Italian Situation, Plumer to Robertson, 7 January 1918.
[106] TNA, CAB 24/39/94, Report on Italian situation, 13 January 1918.
[107] *AFGG* 6/1 Appendix 467: Report on FFI, 16 March 1918.
[108] Gooch, *Italian Army*, p. 285.

for the disseminating of methods to the Italians. While remarking on certain similarities, the article pointed to the extremely centralised nature of Italian artillery intelligence.[109] If managed in a sensitive manner, with due attention paid to organisational and cultural differences, knowledge sharing between allies could bear fruit.

Of course, we must not lose sight of the fact that both the IEF and FFI were importing Western Front practice and experience – albeit modified – to this theatre. Having fought in the locality for longer, Italian formations were ultimately best placed to decide which methods to adopt and which to discard. Accounts, both official and confidential, from the French and British view the process of knowledge sharing in a positive light, yet this is only half the story. There was undoubtedly resentment and frustration at perceived allied interference, underscored by broader concerns that the allies were fighting to obtain colonies and territorial concessions.[110] Both British and French forces were also required to adapt their own methods to suit the new conditions on the Italian front. However, the close proximity of the allies and the slower operational tempo encouraged close cooperation between these two forces. This cooperation created a fertile environment for the sharing of knowledge and expertise.

Conclusions

Let us return to Vallières's observation of initiative in the British army. The lack of firmness and 'exaggerated respective' for individuality that Vallières saw as weaknesses were cornerstones of the army's ethos. Yet, as an outsider looking in, Vallières could see some of the inherent problems with an individual-driven approach. These were problems that the British grappled with long before the First World War and would continue to remain unresolved by its end. Cooperating with the French, in particular, threw those problems into even sharper relief.

The army's relationship with its allies was at times fraught, and there is ample evidence to suggest that this was an area of weakness in the 'learning process'. The notion that learning only occurred through ad hoc encounters and informality, operating on a 'needs must' basis, is true up to a point. Attempts were made to establish a formal basis for learning, however, and these did yield fruit. From mid-1915, there was a formal process for the dissemination of French doctrine and best practice

---

[109] Anon., 'Évolution des Methods de Tir', pp. 548–549.
[110] TNA, CAB 25/22, Impressions of Lieutenant-Colonel C. N. Buzzard, October–November 1917.

through the CDS series, yet there was little chance of this formal process overriding incidental and horizontal methods of learning.

Although there are obvious examples where French experience and knowledge had a wide-ranging, institutional impact, it was usually more successful at the local level whether through ad hoc interactions between individuals, long-standing relationships, or proximity in the front line. Collaborative learning was common in the more scientific aspects of war, but also beyond the Western Front. In the case of the latter, the operational tempo was much slower and the rotation of formations less frequent. This enabled formations to get to know each other more intimately. Resources were less plentiful, which also encouraged the sharing of assets and expertise. Fundamental to inter-allied learning, more generally, were individuals and the relationships between them. Liaison officers, for example, played an important nodal role within this network of learning. They acted as a vital link, facilitating cooperation and communication between various groups and individuals. Men such as Baring, La Ferrière, and Héring were important and often acted as catalysts, kick-starting initial conversations or helping propel specific innovations further up the chain of command.

Attempts at learning were often unsuccessful, undermined by tensions at the political and strategic level, yet the British army encouraged a permissive environment that enabled individuals to visit and consult with the French and Italians. By observing French practice or taking part in collaborative training schools, individuals came face-to-face with some of the weaknesses of their own formations. Others were perceptive enough to recognise these shortcomings, others displayed a wilful obstinacy bordering on arrogance. Some individuals saw what they wanted to see, reinforcing Vallières's observation of the inviolability of individual action in the British army.

6   Civilian Expertise

Writing in 1918, the American journalist Isaac Marcosson remarked that 'war has become a business'. Focusing on the British army in particular, Marcosson considered that, as a whole, it was

in many respects the most amazing business institution that I have yet seen [. . .] Britain's way had been the scientific way. She has made the business of war the prelude to an orderly, efficient and constructive peace [. . .] In no Allied country have business talents been so completed commandeered as in England.[1]

The army's decision and, more importantly, its self-awareness in seeking out these 'business talents', particularly those from the realms of transport and engineering, highlighted the multi-faceted and flexible nature of its learning network. The introduction of these transferrable occupational skills allowed civilian ideas and values to influence the army. To use Goya's terms, these 'emigrants' played an important role in 'fertilising' units in and behind the front line. They did not have the same preconceptions as professional soldiers; yet like army officers, they were also used to managing individuals, making decisions, and assuming responsibilities.[2] In some instances, they moved within similar socio-economic spheres through membership of the same clubs, or attendance at the same schools. The importance of civilian expertise to the British army is usually considered through the work of transport gurus, such as Eric Geddes, or through the efforts of scientists.[3] However, learning from civilian expertise was not limited to such isolated examples nor was it purely operational in focus: it was the second lieutenant with a background in the textile trade working for the Royal Army Clothing Department; the female clerks handwriting details on card indexes used

---

[1] I. F. Marcosson, *The Business of War* (London: The Bodley Head, 1918), pp. 208–209.
[2] Goya, *La Chair*, pp. 203–204.
[3] See Brown, *British Logistics*; K. Grieves, *Sir Eric Geddes: Business and Government in War and Peace* (Manchester: Manchester University Press, 1989); R. Macleod, 'The Chemists Go to War'; Macleod, 'Sight and Sound'.

across the army; or the director of the Geological Survey of Egypt troubleshooting the EEF's water pipeline. Civilian expertise was ubiquitous. With this in mind, this chapter seeks to answer three questions: what links existed between the military and civilian spheres to provide the army with access to civilian expertise? How important was this expertise to the army's learning process? What does it reveal about the existence of a culture of learning within the army?

Civil-Military Relations Pre-War

To understand the nature and effectiveness of the army's relationship with civilian expertise, it is necessary to examine the state of affairs as they existed before 1914. The permeability of the military and civilian spheres was not purely a wartime phenomenon. It was well established before the First World War. Such a relationship was founded on the bond between army and civilian advisory bodies, including learned societies, as well as the establishment of civilian-influenced training courses, and the secondment of military officers to the Egyptian army or government departments in the Crown colonies.

Learned societies, particularly those relevant to the engineering profession, represented a key knowledge repository for the army. The Institution of Civil Engineers [ICE], for example, considered the passing of engineering knowledge between peers of paramount importance.[4] Members of the ICE often gave lectures at the School of Military Engineering at Chatham, or provided articles for the *Royal Engineers' Journal* or the *RUSI Journal*. RE officers of all ranks reciprocated in kind, giving lectures at the Institution's headquarters in London. In 1913, for instance, Captain Crofton Sankey delivered a paper on bridging operations conducted under military conditions. He prefaced his talk with the following:

The Author would not have ventured to submit this Paper to the Institution of Civil Engineers had he not thought that it might be acceptable in view of the close connection of The Institution with the Special Reserve Officer Corps of Royal Engineers.[5]

Sankey's paper generated considerable discussion from both the civil engineers and senior RE officers in attendance. Scott-Moncrieff, an

---

[4] W. Linssen and P. Raymaekers, 'Engineering Institutions and Networking in Nineteenth-Century Belgium and Britain', *Proceedings of Institution of Civil Engineers* [hereafter *PICE*] 166 (EH1) (2013), pp. 25–35.

[5] C. E. P. Sankey, 'Bridging-Operations Conducted under Military Conditions', *PICE* 192 (1913), p. 77.

associate member of the ICE with a diverse career in civil and military engineering, declared that it was 'impossible for him to say how much the engineering branch of the Army owed to The Institution', and that 'there was hardly a volume of its Proceedings in which there was not some valuable instruction bearing upon their [RE] daily work'. Similarly, Sir John Griffith, a civil engineer and member of the ICE, noted that 'his own experience had taught him that civil engineers had a great deal to learn from their Royal Engineer brethren'.[6] There was a tacit acknowledgement that the two branches, although distinct, were closely bound together.

Armed forces membership of the ICE was limited, yet a small number of associate members and student members had been granted a commission in the Special Reserve in 1908. Officers commissioned into the Special Reserve had to be recommended to the Army Council by the ICE, or by the professor of engineering at any British university. This process ensured that a highly qualified reserve of officers was available to the RE, and added another layer to the army's long-standing relationship with the ICE. While acknowledging the need for highly qualified 'civils', the army also recognised the importance of imperial assignments and took measures to circulate individuals across the Empire in anticipation of deployment overseas. Evidence from the War Office's 1908 Committee on the Provision of Officers recommended that

in the case of junior officers of the Royal Engineer Special Reserve who have the opportunity of taking up civil posts, especially abroad, as much latitude as possible should be allowed in exempting them from annual training, if such civil work be of a nature calculated to render them more fit for the discharge of their military duties.[7]

Given the specialised nature of their field, a number of these Special Reserve officers were already employed in civil posts within the colonies, working in Public Works Departments [PWD] or on colonial railways.[8] On the outbreak of war, there were approximately seventy members of the ICE in the Special Reserve, thirty-four of whom were in the Royal Reserve of Engineers.[9] This figure represented a very small percentage of both ICE (less than 1 per cent) and Royal Reserve of Engineers

[6] Various, 'Discussion. Bridging-Operations Conducted under Military Conditions', *PICE* 192 (1913), pp. 132–133.

[7] TNA, WO 33/2985, Fourth Report on the Commission of the Provision of Officers, Clause 12 (g), 12 March 1908.

[8] TNA, ZLIB 21/237, Institution of Civil Engineers, Charter, Supplemental Charters, By-Laws and List of Members (London: ICE, 1914), pp. 58–329.

[9] Various, 'Discussion. The Work of the Royal Engineers in the Great War', *PICE* 210 (1920), p. 85; TNA, ZLIB 21/237, pp. 58–329.

(2.7 per cent) membership.[10] However, comments on the impact these officers had during the war suggested they were punching well above their weight. With a wealth of experience to bring to their commissions, one senior general remarked that it would not have been possible for 'the war to have been carried to a successful conclusion if the Royal Engineers had not had the assistance of these gentlemen, many of them of the highest eminence in their profession'.[11]

Yet the relationship between the ICE and the military was multi-layered and went back far further than the Special Reserve. The Institution had been the driving force behind the establishment of the Engineering and Railway Staff Corps [ERSC] in 1865. Formed amidst the French invasion scares of the 1860s, the ERSC was the brainchild of Charles Manby, secretary to the ICE, and constituted for 'the purpose of directing the application of skilled labour; and of railway transport to the purposes of national defence, and for preparing, in time of peace, a system of which such duties should be conducted'.[12] The corps consisted of officers only, its membership drawn from civil engineers and contractors, as well as officers of railway and dock companies. However, only 'civil engineers of standing and experience, who have directed the construction of the chief railways and other important works of the country, and the General Managers of the leading lines of railway, and of the leading Commercial Docks' were eligible for the rank of lieutenant-colonel in the ERSC.[13]

An elite organisation, the ERSC comprised some of the leading engineers of the time. On the outbreak of war in 1914, it totalled sixty members.[14] In many respects, it was one of the first expert advisory bodies to the British and, later, the Australian armed forces.[15] In theory, these bodies would be consulted by their country's respective governments. However, in practice, their members were usually consulted in their individual capacities. The primary object of the British ERSC was to 'afford to the Government information on subjects connected with the Railway Transport of Troops'.[16] It is, therefore, unsurprising

---

[10] TNA, WO 114/108, Special Reserve Establishment and Strength, 1 July 1914.
[11] Various, 'Discussion. The Work of the Royal Engineers in the Great War', *PICE* 210 (1920), p. 88.
[12] E. A. Pratt, *British Railways and the Great War* (London: Selwyn and Blount, 1921), pp. 5–6.
[13] TNA, RAIL 1014/17/1, Rules of the Engineer and Railway Staff Corps, 17 November 1908.
[14] TNA, WO 114/114, Territorial Force: Establishment and Strengths, 1908–1914.
[15] For details on the Australian ERSC, see G. H. Knibbs, *Official Year Book of the Commonwealth of Australia 1901–1911, No. 5* (Melbourne, VIC: McCarron, Bird, 1912), pp. 1094–1095.
[16] Institution of Royal Engineers, *History*, V, p. 124.

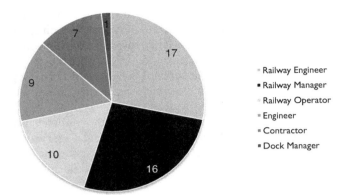

Figure 6.1 Engineering and Railway Staff Corps membership by occupation on the outbreak of war. From C. E. C. Townsend, *All Rank and No File: A History of the Engineer and Railway Staff Corps RE, 1865–1965* (London: The Engineer and Railway Staff Corps, RE (TAVR), 1969), pp. 94–96.

that the ERSC counted individuals such as Sir William Forbes (General Manager, London, Brighton and South Coast Railways), Eric Geddes (Deputy General Manager, North Eastern Railways), and Sir Sam Fay (General Manager, Great Central Railways) amongst its members (Figure 6.1).

Following the enactment of the 1907 Territorial and Reserve Forces Act, the ERSC became an official part of the Territorial Force and remains so to this day.[17] It provided a direct link between the ICE and the army, yet some of its pre-war members saw its role as far from the expert resource that it is regarded as today. Sam Fay recalled that, although the ERSC was 'established for the purpose of rendering expert assistance in time of war', its regular function was 'that of having dinner, with members of the War Office staff as guests'.[18] Though the ERSC could be dismissed as a mere luncheon club, the guest list of the 1913 dinner suggests otherwise. It emphasises the perceived importance of the ERSC to the military, as well as the importance of social links between the two spheres.[19] The military guests at the dinner included Sir John French; Sir Charles Douglas (CIGS in August 1914); Sir John Cowans; Sir Horatio Yorke (Chief Inspector of Railways); and Osborne Mance

[17] M. Stancombe, 'The Staff Corps: A Civilian Resource for the Military', *PICE* 157 (5) (2004), pp. 22–26.
[18] S. Fay, *The War Office at War* (London: Hutchinson, 1937), p. 39.
[19] Phillips, 'Managing Armageddon', p. 45.

(a staff captain who acted as liaison between the army and the railway companies prior to August 1914).[20] Fay was quick to acknowledge the ERSC's wartime role: 'all its members in one form or another rendered service to the State throughout the great struggle'.[21] The role of some ERSC members, particularly railway managers, was most notable during Britain's mobilisation process. As far as they were concerned, their part in mobilisation was simply the 'practical outcome of... peace-time preparations'.[22]

Some of the railway members of the ERSC were also members of the Railway Executive Committee [REC]. Established by the government in 1912, the REC consisted entirely of the railway industry's leading general managers.[23] Its role was to contribute to the establishment of a mobilisation scheme for time of war, to act as a forum for the dissemination of ideas, and to act as a conduit for information between the railways and the War Office. Its most significant contribution would be the production of the 'secret timetable' that guided the BEF's mobilisation in August 1914.[24] Upon mobilisation, it was expected to

co-ordinate the railway transport requirements in connection with the mobilisation of the naval and military forces... to ensure the transit of war material and the maintenance of food supplies of the civil population; to apportion the traffic... and to arrange programmes with a view to avoiding any clashing of interests.[25]

With the establishment of both the ERSC and the REC, civilian engineering and transport professions had been engaged in a mutually beneficial, cooperative process with the military for over half a century. Of course, this relationship was not limited to Britain. France demonstrated similar tendencies. Scientists and military men developed 'cozy relations' during the Third Republic long before 1914. Journals such as the *Revue Scientifique* carried articles in the 1880s directly related to military issues. Scientists taught at schools under the Ministry of War, and were on admissions committees for specialist schools such as the École d'application d'artillerie navale. The exchange was two way: army officers were sometimes granted permission to publish in academic journals

[20] Ibid.; Townsend, *All Rank*, p. 42.
[21] Fay, *War Office*, p. 39.   [22] Pratt, *British Railways*, p. 114.
[23] In 1914, the members of the REC were Herbert Walker (London and South Western Railway), Sir Sam Fay (Great Central Railway), Donald Matheson (Caledonian Railway), Francis Dent (South Eastern and Chatham Railway), Frank Potter (Great Western Railway), Sir Robert Turnbull (London and North Western Railway), John Aspinall (Lancashire and Yorkshire Railway), Sir Guy Granet (Midland Railway), Sir Alexander Butterworth (North Eastern Railway), Charles Dent (Great Northern Railway), and Sir William Forbes (London, Brighton and South Coast Railway).
[24] Phillips, 'Managing Armageddon', p. 47.   [25] Pratt, *British Railways*, p. 42.

and send notes to the Académie des sciences.[26] Formal civil-military committees were also established, such as the 1894 committee on inventions for the army and navy. This committee included six civilians alongside six army and four navy committee members. These civilians were usually drawn from university faculty or commercial businesses, and were often members of L'Institut de France – a French learned society, which incorporated the five Académies. On 11 August 1914, the commission was expanded to forty-six members, twenty of whom were members of the Académie des sciences, including Georges Claude and Gustave Eiffel.[27] Unlike Britain and France, the pre-war German officer corps was, generally speaking, 'poorly trained in scientific and economic matters'. However, at the outbreak of war, we see the belated establishment of the Raw Materials Section (Kriegsrohstoffabteilung) at the War Ministry, which represented the coming together of the military and major industrialists, headed up by AEG's Walther Rathenau and supported by Wichard von Moellendorff – a disciple of Taylorism and scientific management.[28]

Through these learned societies, and bodies such as the ERSC and the REC, the government and the British military had ready access to civilian experts with 'experience of coherent large scale organisation'.[29] However, they recognised that soldiers, particularly those in the technical branches of the army, could derive further benefits from training in, and exposure to, civilian skills. This took place in a number of fora from lectures to formal courses. Indeed, when commandant of the staff college in 1905, Henry Rawlinson invited Julian Corbett to lecture on naval strategy, requesting that he examine 'the Function of the Army in relation to gaining command of the sea, and in bringing war with a Continental Power to a successful conclusion'.[30] Where more formal courses were concerned, one of the best known examples was the London School of Economics [LSE] 'Course for the Training of Officers for the Higher Appointments in the Administrative Staff of the Army'. The brainchild of Richard Haldane, Sir Halford Mackinder, and Edward Ward, the course was geared to produce 'a thinking school of officers who desire

---

[26] H. W. Paul, *From Knowledge to Power: The Rise of the Scientific Empire in France, 1860–1939* (Cambridge: Cambridge University Press, 1985), p. 320.

[27] Roussel, 'L'Histoire', pp. 25, 36.

[28] G. D. Feldman, *Army, Industry, and Labor in Germany, 1914–1918* (Princeton, NJ: Princeton University Press, 1966), pp. 35, 45–47.

[29] K. Grieves, 'The Transportation Mission to GHQ', in Bond et al., *Look to Your Front*, p. 65.

[30] A. D. Lambert, 'Sir Julian Corbett, Naval History, and the Development of Sea Power Theory', in N. A. M. Rodger, J. Ross Dancy, B. Darnell, and E. Wilson (eds), *Strategy and the Sea: Essays in Honour of John B. Hattendorff* (Woodbridge: Boydell, 2016), p. 193.

to see the full efficiency which comes from new organisation'.[31] In his address to the first cohort in 1907, Mackinder believed that it was advisable for officers to make themselves businessmen:

We here can only put before you the ordinary civilian methods. Business men, you must remember, are not merely business men, but bankers, or brokers, or merchants. What you have to form is another special kind of business man, the soldier... You may at a time come into contact, as many of you did in South Africa, with a civilian population characterized by deeply engrained business prejudices and methods of its own, and it will be of the utmost importance to you to know civilian business.[32]

The course sought to draw on the lessons of previous campaigns, such as the Boer War, which had demonstrated the 'need for specialised administrative officers whose training should include financial, commercial and legal qualifications'.[33] The syllabus included subjects such as accounting and business methods, statistics, and railway management in war and peace. Leading authorities from academia and commerce delivered these subjects, including Graham Wallas, the noted Fabian, who lectured on public administration, and Wilfred Tetley Stephenson, a former member of North Eastern Railway, who ran the module on railway management and organisation.[34]

Conscious efforts were made to ensure that the material taught to army officers was both current and relevant. By 1910, it was felt that some modules had 'less immediate practical bearing'. Accordingly, modules relating to banking, statistics, public administration, and geography were omitted, while lectures on 'business organisation' were introduced instead.[35] Indeed, for Richard Haldane, the LSE course was the means – albeit experimental at first – of 'getting the army on "a sound business footing"'.[36] These particular lectures were concerned with manufacturing industries, the organisation of a commercial office, legal restrictions on industry, and the impact of government departments, such as the Boards of Trade and Agriculture. To complement these formal modules, 'observation visits' were also arranged. These visits included

[31] W. Funnell, 'National Efficiency, Military Accounting and the Business of War', *Critical Perspectives on Accounting* 17 (2006), p. 728.
[32] PP, Army. Report of the advisory board, London School of Economics, on the first course at the London School of Economics, January to July, 1907, Appendix C, p. 11 [Cd. 3696].
[33] Funnell, 'National Efficiency', p. 734.
[34] P. Grant, *Philanthropy and Voluntary Action in the First World War: Mobilizing Charity* (London: Routledge, 2014), p. 71.
[35] PP, Army. Report on the fourth course at the LSE, October 1909 to March 1910, p. 3 [Cd.5213].
[36] Funnell, 'National Efficiency', p. 735.

the offices of *The Times* newspaper, Great Western Railway Works, the London Omnibus Works, and Lloyd's of London.[37] Mackinder established 'smoking meetings', which took place once a week in the evening. The guest speakers at these meetings were often businessmen. Such an arrangement enabled officers to 'accumulate the experience of practical men' in a highly social setting.[38] This echoed the club culture of the time and chimed with the army's own social ethos, and its belief in the importance of socialising as a way of gathering and disseminating knowledge.

The LSE course was unique in its conception. However, its reach was limited with only 245 officers completing the course between January 1907 and March 1914. The majority of these officers were captains (67 per cent). Although the infantry and other corps were represented, ASC officers made up the largest share of the overall intake (eighty-five officers). A number of these ASC officers would go on to hold significant appointments during the war, including Lieutenant-Colonel Oscar Striedinger (Class of 1909 and DST BSF, 1915); his successor as DST BSF, Colonel Philip Scott (Class of 1909); and Brigadier-General Wilfred Swabey (Class of 1908 and DST IEF, 1917–1918). The willingness of the War Office and the Army Council to work with an institution like the LSE speaks to the importance of rounding out the education of the officer corps.

In addition to the LSE course, other civilian-influenced training courses were developed in partnership with Midland Railway and HM Dockyard, Chatham. These courses aimed to equip officers with experience of civilian railway work. The importance of railways at home and abroad was well known to the military. Their development had coincided with the creation of accountancy in its modern sense with the rise of companies such as Deloitte, and Price, Holyhead and Waterhouse.[39] They also proved crucial to the development of industrialisation in nineteenth-century Britain, converting engineering from the profession of a handful of talented individuals into a large and diverse organisation covering a wide range of skills.[40] The Midland Railway's 'Course of Instruction in Mechanical Engineering', for instance, gave RE officers who had decided to specialise in railways a 'thorough, practical knowledge of machine design, the fitting, erection and repair of machinery,

---

[37] Ibid., p. 737.   [38] Sloan, 'Haldane's Mackindergarten', p. 335.
[39] T. R. Gourvish, 'The Rise of the Professions', in T. R. Gourvish and A. O'Day (eds), *Later Victorian Britain 1867–1900* (Basingstoke: Macmillan, 1988), p. 31.
[40] R. A. Buchanan, 'Engineers and Government in Nineteenth-Century Britain', in R. Macleod (ed.), *Government and Expertise: Specialists, Administrators and Professionals, 1860–1919* (Cambridge: Cambridge University Press, 1988), p. 43.

and the care and working of boilers'.[41] Established in 1894, the course was intensive: a year in length with nine months spent in the railway shops and three months in the drawing rooms. Officers were to conform to the working patterns of Midland Railway and were actively encouraged to put in extra hours so as to 'be of real assistance to the men with whom they are working, and to win their confidence'.[42] In this respect, RE officers were given a real taste of work in a civilian firm and a first-hand appreciation of civilian man management. Brigadier-General Ralph Micklem undertook the Midland Railway course as a young subaltern in September 1904. After spending a fortnight at Brecon working a single line, he then spent 'two or three months in London on goods working, then to Derby, where I did a month as a fireman, and then to various other places on Civil Engineering jobs'. Although Micklem found the year enjoyable, he confessed that he did not think he had 'learnt a great deal'. Whether this is true or not, Micklem's post-course career saw him seconded to the Egyptian army where he worked with the Sudan Military Railways [SMR], surveying for new lines, and he was later appointed Resident Engineer at Port Sudan. On the outbreak of war, Micklem was serving as assistant to the General Manager of the Atbara-Port Sudan railway. As a trained railway officer, Micklem's wartime service was largely spent in the Movements Directorate at the War Office where he was responsible for 'all the railway arrangements in connection with Home Defence'.[43] Indeed, his experience with Midland Railway had clearly not hampered what was a successful military career.

For officers in the army's technical branches, the courses provided up to date knowledge on civil and mechanical engineering practice. To deploy this knowledge, the army recognised that a number of its officers, particularly those in the RE, could be usefully seconded to the Egyptian army or to government departments, including PWDs, across the Empire.[44] From the mid-1890s onwards, the British government devised a series of development programmes to promote the economies of its

---

[41] The Midland Railway Company course ran from 1894 to 1904 and ceased following the establishment of the Woolmer Instructional Military Railway (later known as Longmoor Military Railway) in 1905. It also provided the template for a similar course run in conjunction with HM Dockyard Chatham.

[42] TNA, WO 32/6164, Instructions for Officers joining the Midland Railway Company's Course of Instruction in Mechanical Engineering, 24 August 1894, p. 1.

[43] IWM, Papers of Brigadier-General R. Micklem, 87/8/1, Memoir, n.d., p. 3, 7. Micklem also served as an assistant to Brigadier-General H. O. Mance who had pre-war service working on the Kimberley Line during the Boer War as Director of Railways and Armoured Trains, along with a period (1908–1911) on the Baro-Kano railway in Nigeria.

[44] See TNA, WO 106/6372, Memorandum on the service of British Officers in the Egyptian Army, 1 March 1906.

Crown colonies.[45] As Secretary of State for the Colonies, Joseph Chamberlain established these schemes which required the issue of colonial loans and engineering contractors.[46] The secondment of military engineers was not a new, nineteenth-century development; it was woven into the fabric of colonial administration. British military engineers, drawn mainly from the RE, had been seconded to the army of the East India Company since the eighteenth century. This trend continued after Crown rule in 1858, with RE officers making up a high proportion of military engineers seconded to the Indian Army.[47]

The experience of engineering in the imperial sphere acted as a social lever for British engineering elites. The Empire provided 'a path to affluence and wealth as well as to high positions in accredited institutions'.[48] Such experience also applied to the RE. Although imperial engineering did not bring about the same wealth and affluence, it often led to influential positions within the military. The experience of imperial civil engineering was highly prized. In his evidence to the 1919 Rawlinson Committee on Engineer Organisation, Major-General Alain Joly de Lotbinière, formerly Chief Engineer to the Australian Corps, suggested that

RE Officers who had a considerable experience of foreign service were as a rule far more useful in the field than those who had spent their service in the British Isles ... An RE officer who has had no engineering experience ... cannot for a moment be compared with a 'free lance' engineer, who has had training *on large works such as construction of Railways, bridges, docks, water supplies etc, in various parts of the world. These are the men who on active service one selects for important undertakings.*[49]

Before joining the RE, Joly de Lotbinière had served as a journeyman fitter in various US and Canadian railway shops. His decision to pursue mechanical engineering allowed him to gain 'practical knowledge and experience' and to familiarise himself with 'the details of railway work'.[50] He also had extensive experience of civil engineering in India: on the

[45] D. Sunderland, 'The Department System of Railway Construction in British West Africa, 1895–1906', *Journal of Transport History* 23 (2) (2002), p. 87.

[46] R. M. Kesner, 'Builders of Empire: The Role of the Crown Agents in Imperial Development, 1880–1914', *Journal of Imperial and Commonwealth History* 5 (3) (1977), p. 316.

[47] J. Black, 'A More Vigorous Prosecution of Public Works: The Reforms of the Indian Public Works Department', *Accounting History* 6 (2) (2001), p. 95.

[48] C. Andersen, *British Engineers in Africa, 1875–1914* (London: Pickering and Chatto, 2011), p. 166.

[49] TNA, WO 32/11379, Papers relating to Rawlinson Committee, Memo, 'Notes for DFW as Regards Future Training of Royal Engineers', 15 January 1919, pp. 1–2. Added emphasis.

[50] A. C. Joly de Lotbinière, 'Obituary: Major-General Sir Philip Twining', *REJ* 31 (4) (1920), p. 220.

Table 6.1 *Pre-War Background of Officers Serving as Directorate Heads in the Transportation Directorate*

Directorate	Officer	Pre-war occupation
Director of Railways	Colonel William Waghorn RE	Deputy Manager, North Western State Railway, India
Director of Light Railways and Roads	Brigadier-General Philip Twining RE	Indian Railways
Director of Traffic	Brigadier-General Henry Freeland RE	Traffic Superintendent, North Western State Railway, India
Director of Docks	Brigadier-General Ralph Wedgewood	Passenger Manager, North Eastern Railways, UK
Director of Inland Water Transport	Brigadier-General Gerald Holland RIM	Marine Superintendent, London and North Western Railways, UK

Note: Information drawn from TNA, WO 32/11379, Rawlinson Committee, Twining to MGO, 8 January 1919.

outbreak of war, he was Engineer-in-Chief to the Bengal PWD.[51] His evidence to the Rawlinson Committee was supported by Major-General Sir Philip Twining (DFW, 1918–1920) who had worked alongside Joly de Lotbinière as a journeyman. Twining went on to serve in India with the Bombay Sappers and Miners, and was involved in surveying the railway through the Khyber Pass. His work on this survey led to his subsequent involvement on the Uganda Railway. Commenting on the future training of the RE, Twining recalled that, during the First World War, the army was 'largely . . . dependent upon India and the British railways for the heads of the Transportation Directorate. Such British Royal Engineers as there were employed in Transportation were all of very junior rank'.[52] This assertion is borne out by a schematic provided by Twining to the Rawlinson Committee, summarised in Table 6.1, which clearly shows the desirability of civilian transport experts, or military personnel who had experience of working on civilian railway lines.

The Scramble for Africa also resulted in a number of secondments for RE officers desiring experience of survey, expedition, and railway work. Much of the surveying, construction, and operation of the railways, particularly in Africa, had been under the direction of RE officers.

[51] TNA, WO 32/11379, Rawlinson Committee, Twining to Master General of the Ordnance [MGO], 17 January 1919. Joly de Lotbinière's pre-war appointments brought him into contact with Lieutenant-General Sir William Birdwood who selected him as Chief Engineer, Australian Corps.
[52] TNA, WO 32/11379, Rawlinson Committee, Twining to MGO, 8 January 1919.

The opportunity to work on railways in the Crown colonies brought RE officers into contact with civilian counterparts, while simultaneously enhancing the former's opportunity for higher appointment. Secondments to the Egyptian army, for instance, provided an opportunity for such experience. Percy Girouard was one such secondee. Graduating from the Royal Military College, Kingston in 1886, Girouard worked for two years on the engineering staff of the Canadian Pacific Railway before accepting a commission in the RE in 1888.[53] Seconded to the Egyptian army in 1896, he served as director of the SMR during Kitchener's invasion of the Sudan. His construction of the railway bypassing the Nile cataracts made possible Kitchener's victory over the Mahdi's forces at Omdurman, solving some of the supply problems that had beset British operations in the region. His railway skills were so highly regarded that he became director of the South African Railways during the Boer War. Girouard compiled his experiences and lessons of that war into a multivolume work. These tomes were deemed an invaluable educational tool for military officers and highlighted, inter alia, the importance of 'the presence of experienced civilian railway engineers', and to what extent 'Military Control [of railways] is necessary and at what point it becomes harmful'.[54] Although Girouard left the military in 1907, he was hailed as 'the greatest authority in the British Empire upon the use of railways in war'.[55]

Like Girouard, Sir George Macauley, who later rendered considerable service to both Murray and Allenby as General Manager of the Egyptian State Railways [ESR], was an RE officer transferred to the Egyptian army in 1896. Initially appointed Chief Engineer of the SMR, Macauley also took part in the 1897 Sudan expedition and Kitchener's subsequent expedition in 1898. After resigning his commission, Macauley served as General Manager of the SMR (1898–1906) before transferring to the ESR.[56] Other notable individuals seconded to the Egyptian army included Brigadier-General Henri Joly de Lotbinière (a contemporary of Girouard and Macauley, and relation to Alain) who was employed

[53] John Flint, 'Girouard, Sir (Édouard) Percy Cranwill (1867–1932)', *Oxford Dictionary of National Biography*, Oxford University Press, 2004; online edn, May 2006, www.oxforddnb.com/view/article/33415. All biographical details are taken from this source unless otherwise noted.

[54] Anon., 'Review of *Detailed History of the Railways in the South African War, 1899–1902*', *REJ* 2 (1) (1905), pp. 134–135.

[55] A. H. M. Kirke-Green, 'Canada in Africa: Sir Percy Girouard, Neglected Colonial Governor', *African Affairs* 83 (331) (1984), p. 237.

[56] NAM, Papers of Sir George Macauley, 8008-72, Allenby to Curzon, 30 August 1922.

by the Survey Department of the Egyptian government in 1906.[57] He served as one of Girouard's staff officers during the Boer War before rising to become Chief Engineer to the XVIII Corps during the First World War. State railways and PWDs proved an important nexus for military, civilian, and government professionals to work together and share expertise. Within these 'laboratories of modernity', the seeds of future civil-military relations germinated.

Civil-Military Relations during the First World War

Building on this strong pre-war relationship, the existing formal ties between the civilian and military spheres were exploited and developed by the army during the First World War in a number of ways. The army's expansion led to a considerable change in the balance of civil-military relations. For Haig, the fundamental principle was to

employ men on the same work in war as they are accustomed to do in peace. Acting on this principle I have got Geddes at the head of all railways and transportation, with the best practical civil and military engineers under him... To put soldiers who have no practical experience of these matters into such positions merely because they are generals and colonels, must result in utter failure.[58]

Where the new Transportation Directorate was concerned, Lord Northcliffe – a vocal supporter of 'experts' – remarked that 'we have brought to France a considerable portion of industrial England'.[59] Although civilian experts dominated the top levels of the Transportation Directorate, and despite the intimate cooperation experience between civil-military spheres pre-war, it is impossible to disregard the suspicion felt by some senior military figures. Both General Sir John Cowans (QMG to the Forces, 1912–1919) and Lieutenant-General Sir William Marshall (CinC, Indian Expeditionary Force 'D', 1917–1918) expressed reservations over the use of civilian expertise, particularly when these experts took over traditionally military appointments. Cowans, for instance, viewed the appointment of Andrew Weir as Surveyor-General of Supply 'unfavourably'; while Marshall, a prominent sceptic of civilian experts, recalled how there were 'altogether too many conferences and

---

[57] TNA, FO 371/168/100, Employment of Major Joly de Lotbinière in Egyptian Government, 21 September 1906.
[58] TNA, WO 256/13, Haig Diaries, 27 October 1916.
[59] Quoted in Grieves, 'Transportation Mission', p. 68.

commissions and, I may add, too many so-called "super-men" during the war'.[60] Lieutenant-General Sir Frederick Clayton (IGC, BEF) expressed similar remarks in his rejoinder to the 1916 Royden Commission. This commission, led by Sir Thomas Royden, chairman of the Cunard shipping line, was established for the purpose of investigating delayed shipping at French ports used to supply the British army. Having advised the War Office in 1912 on the potential problems of disembarking the BEF upon the European mainland, Royden was used to working with military personnel.[61] However, Clayton declared that

it is impossible for the ordinary business civilian to understand [what are] the conditions under which we have to work and that it is a mistake to allow them to interfere with an Army business that most of us have studied all our lives [...] for that reason we should not allow in future any civilian Commission to come out here and criticize our work.[62]

While these incidents seem to bear out the traditional view of the military as a closed shop, averse to civilian intervention and change, we have seen similar instances of scepticism towards knowledge and best practice emanating from different parts of the army itself, as well as from allies. Though the 'not invented here' phenomenon is clearly acute here, instances of inertia were not limited to civilian involvement, nor were they a uniquely British problem. Similar examples can be found in the French army, which, for instance, did not universally welcome the involvement of French scientists Pierre Weiss and Aimé Cotton in the development of sound ranging. Having secured the support of senior military figures in Paris, Weiss and Cotton tested their system on the Western Front between January and February 1915. Results were encouraging with hopes for extensive use of the system. However, the actions of Chief Naval Engineer Ludovic Driencourt stymied their efforts. Driencourt was in charge of the newly instituted sound ranging service (Service de repérage). He was also working on a rival system – the Telegraphe Militare.[63] Although, by July 1915, the Cotton-Weiss system was running to general satisfaction on the front, it was still considered an experimental device by the French military administration. Furthermore, the information collected by the Cotton-Weiss devices was

[60] D. Chapman-Huston and O. Rutter, *General Sir John Cowans GCB GCMG: The Quartermaster-General of the Great War*, II (2 vols, London: Hutchinson, 1924), pp. 199–200; W. R. Marshall, *Memories of Four Fronts* (London: Ernest Benn, 1929), p. 294.

[61] C. Phillips, 'Henry Wilson and the Role of Civil-Military Cooperation during the Planning of British Mobilisation for War, 1910–1914', *Ex Historia* 5 (2013), pp. 125–126.

[62] Modern Records Centre, University of Warwick [MRC], Papers of Sir W. Guy Granet, MSS.191/3/3/14-24, Response to Royden Commission, 30 July 1917.

[63] SGA, *Historique*, p. 37.

not being systematically transmitted to the gunners, whilst favourable reports written by artillery officers never reached the government minister concerned.[64]

External Expertise

While there was systemic and circumstantial scepticism, there was generally a successful civil-military partnership where British supply and transportation was concerned. There were teething problems, but this coordination had a positive effect across all theatres. Indeed, the army's increasing employment of civilian expertise was demonstrated by the organisation of several high level transport missions, which primarily drew on non-military personnel. While the first mission, an investigation into British and French transportation networks on the Western Front in October 1914, was largely unsuccessful, subsequent attempts were more fruitful. The report from this first mission, carried out by Percy Girouard at the request of Lord Kitchener, challenged the status quo and highlighted the overlapping duties and general inefficiencies within the existing transport system.[65] Indeed, his findings supported the pre-war criticisms by Edward Altham outlined in Chapter 1: that the army should abandon the structure laid out in *FSR2* and align with the French system instead. Unsurprisingly, his recommendations were not well received. Major-General Sir Frederick Robb, former IGC in France, was fairly restrained. For him, Girouard's proposal was 'nothing new'. Cowans, however, was far more critical:

In my opinion it would have been better if Sir P. Girouard had restricted himself to what he was told to do. He has far exceeded his instructions. He was not told to produce a scheme for uprooting organisations deliberately laid down after deep deliberation . . . The Regulations have been issued and acted upon and it is no time in the middle of a campaign to tinker with them.[66]

According to Cowans's biographers, Girouard's report 'appears to have been shelved'.[67]

The second transport mission, again to the Western Front, was carried out by Eric Geddes. His detachment in August 1916 included individuals such as Philip Nash, formerly of the Great Northern Railway and the East Indian Railways; George Beharrell, formerly Assistant Goods

---

[64] Roussel, 'L'Histoire', pp. 37–38.
[65] TNA, WO 32/5144, Girouard Report – Report upon railway transport arrangements of the British army on the Continent.
[66] Ibid., Memo by Lt-Gen Sir J. S. Cowans, 27 October 1914.
[67] Chapman-Huston and Rutter, *Cowans*, II, p. 229.

Manager and Commercial Agent to the North Eastern Railway; Osborne Mance, then Assistant Director Railway Transport at the War Office; and Major-General Henry Freeland. Interestingly, both Mance and Freeland were 'uncomfortable' about their membership of a civilian mission designed to scrutinise existing procedures.[68] Geddes fared little better than Girouard at first. His initial encounters with BEF senior command reveal instances of individual inertia. Upon reading the proposal for a transport investigation, Lieutenant-General Sir John Maxwell noted that

it is not stated why the time has arrived to strengthen the transport arrangements of the BEF. So far as the work in France is concerned these arrangements have worked perfectly smoothly and efficiently: 1. In the ports; 2. On the railways and canals; 3. On the roads.[69]

For Geddes, such a response was to be expected. He was aware that

officers who are responsible for the work out there will say – 'Has the Army ever wanted for anything in these last two years of fighting?' My answer to that is that if the Army has not wanted for anything, it is because it has been a stationary Army . . . In the only place where we have made an advance, and not one involving great mileage, the road repair and the capacity of the roads are both matters of anxiety.[70]

Geddes's initial reception at GHQ was 'chilly', while Haig recorded in his diary that Geddes was 'afraid that the Inspector General of Communications resents his visit!'[71] Unsurprisingly, the abolition of the IGC post and Geddes's subsequent appointment as both Director-General of Military Railways at the War Office and Director-General of Transportation [DGT] on the Western Front were met with 'fierce opposition'. Lloyd George was accused of having 'fluttered the military dovecotes' with this 'unconventional appointment', while Brigadier-General the Honourable Richard Stuart-Wortley and Maxwell threatened to resign from their positions.[72] Yet Haig's confidence in Geddes was 'unshakeable'. He was able to convince Maxwell that Geddes had not 'been sent out by . . . Lloyd George to take over the duties which I had assigned to him [Maxwell]'.[73] Maxwell was happy with Haig's assurances, instructing his directors to cease their criticisms. It was this support from the very top of the army that paved the way for Geddes's success.

[68] Grieves, 'Transport Mission', p. 66.
[69] Quoted in Phillips, 'Managing Armageddon', p. 191.
[70] MRC, Granet Papers, MSS.191/3/3/4-13, Geddes to Lloyd George, 15 September 1916, p. 6.
[71] Grieves, *Geddes*, p. 29; TNA, WO 256/12, Haig Diaries, 24 August 1916.
[72] Grieves, *Geddes*, pp. 30–31.   [73] TNA, WO 256/13, Haig Diaries, 30 October 1916.

Initial responses to both Girouard's and Geddes's reports suggest personal rather than organisational inertia. However, to focus on these individual responses overlooks the wider context, namely that Britain was the junior partner in the coalition at this point. Moreover, the army's demands and needs changed over time. The decision to shelve much of Girouard's report lay in the fact that many of his recommendations assumed that the stalemate of winter 1914 was an anomaly. Although some generals expected a long war, there was little impetus to overhaul existing procedures when they appeared to be functioning reasonably well.

Subsequent transport missions did not encounter the same kind of obstructionism. Following Geddes's mission, the Army Council outlined plans for a 'complete survey of the requirements of the various theatres of war for transportation material . . . made by experts . . . in consultation with the General Officers Commanding-in-Chief'.[74] Sir Francis Dent, General Manager of the South Eastern and Chatham Railway and a member of the REC, led the transport mission to Salonika and Egypt in late 1916. Modelled on Geddes's mission and supported by a series of 'technical experts', Dent's investigation would similarly examine rail, light railway, road, docks, wharves, and inland waterways.[75] The mission led to positive change within the BSF, particularly where coordination and cooperation at the ports was concerned. A number of technical officers were sent out from the UK to facilitate improved discharge, clearance, and loading at the ports; one such individual was J. B. Parkhouse, the Warrington district goods manager of the London and North Western Railway, who was commissioned as a lieutenant-colonel and appointed Director of Docks for the BSF.[76]

A follow-up mission to the Egypt and Palestine theatres took place in June 1917 led by John W. Stewart and supported by William McLellan, a consulting engineer and a former colleague of Geddes in the Ministry of Munitions.[77] Stewart himself was a Canadian railway magnate who had helped build the Pacific Great Eastern and Canadian Northern railways before the war. Given a military rank and initially tasked with reorganising light railways on the Western Front, Stewart was soon promoted to Deputy DGT and despatched to Egypt. His mission was also

---

[74] TNA, MT 23/677/9, Mission of Sir Francis Dent to Egypt and Salonika, Secretary WO to CiCs Egypt and Salonika, 24 October 1916.

[75] MRC, Granet Papers, MSS.191/3/3/127, Memorandum on Transport Facilities in the Various Theatres of War, 28 October 1916, pp. 22, 27.

[76] TNA, ZPER 9/32, Unknown, 'Railways and the Salonica Campaign', *The Railway Gazette* (September 1920), p. 111.

[77] L. S. Simpson, 'Railway Operating in France', *Journal of the Institution of Locomotive Engineers* 12 (1922), p. 711.

predicated on the success of Geddes's reorganisation. In a letter to Murray, Robertson offered a glowing recommendation of Stewart and his mission:

Six months ago the railways in France were in a bad way. Today they are splendid, and this is due entirely to the fine railway work put in by people like Stewart. It is extraordinary what improvements can be made and how greatly the capacity of the line can be increased by men who really understand the job... Hear what Stewart and his people have to say and back them for all they are worth. I am sure you will be pleased afterwards. At any rate this was Haig's experience, and this is why I am sending Stewart to you.[78]

Stewart was able to draw both upon his civilian expertise and the experience of military transport he had gained as Director of Light Railways and as a Deputy DGT, thereby combining the freshness of external ideas with the institutional credibility of previous involvement with the military. One of his recommendations advised that, if further construction was required, the 'policy adopted in France should be applied to Egypt'. This would require the provision of suitable equipment and a plant for 'modern railway construction'.[79] On the whole, though, Stewart endorsed the EEF's supply and transport arrangements. In fact, a junior member of the mission remarked on the ingenuity of certain innovations, such as the organisation of labour and the use of a turntable to transport railway vehicles across the Suez Canal.[80] Lynden-Bell crowed a little too loudly when he remarked that 'Stewart, the railway expert... had reported in the very highest terms on our railway... and says he has nothing whatever to suggest and that the railway is a wonderful organisation'.[81]

Conducted on similar lines to Stewart's mission, Major-General Henry Freeland's investigation in Mesopotamia in November 1917 raised a number of fundamental questions around the suitability of transport arrangements, notably the disconnect between India and the authorities in theatre.[82] Robertson requested Freeland personally in a letter to Haig:

[78] IWM, Papers of General Sir A. Murray, 79/43/3/6, Robertson to Murray, 12 May 1917.
[79] TNA, WO 106/720, Stewart (Railway) Commission, Précis of Report, July 1917, p. 4.
[80] Simpson, 'Railway Operating', pp. 712–713.
[81] IWM, Chetwode Papers, PP/MCR/C1, Lynden-Bell to Chetwode, 7 June 1917.
[82] TNA, WO 32/5209, Report of Commission appointed by Government of India to investigate Railway and River Transport Administration in Mesopotamia [hereafter Freeland Mission], Mance to Fay, 15 May 1918.

We must have a man of some kind from you as no one else knows the question, and there is a certain amount of opposition in Mesopotamia and India against tackling the transportation question and introducing something like the system which has been found to work so admirably with you in France'.[83]

Robertson used Geddes's success as an exemplar when broaching the mission with Stanley Maude, noting that 'Haig is more than pleased with the way the transport department has overcome what seemed insuperable differences and has established quite a wonderful organisation'.[84] If Maude had reservations, he did not reveal them. Instead, he welcomed Freeland's appointment admitting that 'good as our communications are considering the local conditions there is no doubt that they can be still further improved and developed, and obviously the more this is done on sound lines and with expert advice the better for the future of the Force'.[85]

A career soldier, Freeland was well suited to his role as inspector. Pre-war, he had worked on the Indian railways where he had come into contact with Geddes. He also had considerable experience of transport on the Western Front. It was his experience of the latter that led him to recommend the amalgamation of the Mesopotamian transportation services under a single authority.[86] This would reduce the pressure on the IGC, while providing a single technical head for all transport matters. Freeland's recommendations were well founded and influenced by more general best practice gathered from the Western Front. They also found support from the Director of Roads and Railways at the War Office who agreed that 'a technical organisation' should be established to streamline the transport situation.[87] However, there was resistance to the appointment of a DGT by William Marshall and the QMG, India.[88] According to Lynden-Bell, then Deputy CIGS at the War Office, 'the DGT idea has been blown upon from France, and Haig says if he had his time again he would not have tried it'.[89] Ultimately, in spite of initial opposition, a DGT was established in Mesopotamia. Freeland was appointed to the Indian Railway Board in support to help reorganise transport issues at the very top of the Indian Army. This appointment earned him

[83] LHCMA, Robertson Papers, 7/7/55, Robertson to Haig, 3 October 1917.
[84] LHCMA, Robertson Papers, 4/4, Robertson to Maude, 3 October 1917.
[85] LHCMA, Robertson Papers, 7/5/73, Maude to Robertson, 6 October 1917.
[86] TNA, MUN 4/6517, Report on work and future development of Basra and of the river and railway communication in Mesopotamia, April 1918, pp. 22–23.
[87] TNA, WO 32/5209, Freeland Mission, Mance to Fay, 15 May 1918.
[88] W. R. Marshall, *Memories of Four Fronts* (London: Ernest Benn, 1929), p. 294.
[89] Fay, *War Office*, p. 162.

'the gratitude of the army' as a result of his 'zealous and unremitting efforts in developing the capacity of the railways in respect of military requirements'.[90]

These predominantly civilian-led transport missions tell us a great deal about the army and its relationship with external expertise. Unsurprisingly, and in line with other case studies, there was no one size fits all approach. With the exception of Freeland's mission, civilian experts led the rest. Some of these experts held military rank, but Dent, for instance, did not. All missions contained a mixture of civilian and military personnel. This collaborative process offered a way of enhancing the legitimacy of the mission. Yet, as we saw with Geddes's mission, not all military members were comfortable scrutinising existing procedures. Indeed, despite these efforts at cohesion, there was still explicit and tacit resistance whether through Maxwell's threats to resign, or Lynden-Bell's comments on military proficiency. Although a former RE officer himself, Girouard misjudged his audience in 1914. His report cut deep, going against the organisational grain. Other missions were more successful: not because they pandered to those in higher command, but because they spoke to commanders in their own language, backed up with considerable professional experience. Robertson himself admitted to a shift in temperament where these experts were concerned, observing that 'we here in the War Office at first regarded with suspicion the setting up of these transportation people, but one and all of us have found that we were wrong'.[91]

Local Civilian Expertise

While the strategic transport missions required high level expertise from both inside and outside the military institution, the army also made use of expertise linked to local state apparatus. Both the MEF and EEF made use of local knowledge for the construction and maintenance of canal defences, piers, and railways. For the EEF, these particular issues required the extensive use of the Egyptian and Cyprus Public Works Departments, the Cairo Water Company, and the ESR. There was a 'necessary dependence' on the existing civil machinery, coupled with the need to mobilise all available resources, both matériel and personnel, for the prosecution of war.[92]

---

[90] *London Gazette*, Issue 31823, 12 March 1920, p. 3271.
[91] LHCMA, Robertson Papers, 8/1, Robertson to Monro, 10 December 1917.
[92] IWM, Murray Papers, 79/48/3, Official Papers 1915–1916, 'Memorandum on Martial Law in Egypt', 26 November 1916.

Due to local conditions and low prioritisation of resources, the increased permeability between the military and civilian spheres was especially vital to the army's war effort in the east. This was notable with the construction of the Suez Canal defences in early 1916. As Murray remarked, the existing engineering staff of the British Force in Egypt was 'inadequate' to deal with the execution of extensive works relating to the defence of the Suez Canal.[93] The army, therefore, called upon the Egyptian PWD to 'provide a special staff to organise and carry out the work'.[94] The PWD's 'intimate cooperation' with the army made 'an accurate definition of the separate spheres of each almost impossible' to discern.[95] Sir Murdoch Macdonald, under secretary of the Egyptian PWD, was appointed Deputy Director of Works [DDW], with the rank of colonel in December 1915. Owing to the shortage of RE personnel at that time, Macdonald's staff consisted of seconded PWD officers and civil engineers who were given local and temporary commissions. In all, seventy-eight technical and clerical members of the Egyptian PWD took part in the work on the canal defences.[96]

Prior to his appointment, Macdonald had also provided informal consultancy to the MEF, notably over the proposed development of a stone pier at Mudros in September 1915. Paul, then DDW Helles, remarked on the 'friendly advice' given by Macdonald and his colleagues in this respect, but his later comments underscored the perceived ignorance of civil engineers when faced with military problems:

He [Macdonald] did not go over to Helles, Anzac, or Suvla, and *it is just as well that civilians do not venture to these shell-swept places*... what he saw at Mudros, and what we were able to tell him, undoubtedly opened his eyes, and those of his friends, so that they, as Civil Engineers, can fully appreciate (*which I am sure they never did before*) the enormous obstacles and great difficulties that we have to overcome in this Campaign.[97]

Although Paul expressed certain reservations towards the civil engineering profession as a whole, Macdonald proved his worth during his time as DDW, highlighting the usefulness of local expertise, particularly the 'ability to make the best use of contractors and the absence of financial

[93] IWM, Murray Papers, 79/48/2, 'Campaign in Egypt 1916: Report of Engineering Works', pp. 2–3.
[94] TNA, WO 161/65, Report on Water Supply to the Army in Egypt and Palestine, n.d, pp. 8–9.
[95] E. H. Lloyd, 'Work in Connection with the Suez Canal Defences in 1916, which was undertaken by the Egyptian Ministry of Public Works Officials for and in Conjunction with the Royal Engineers', *PICE* 207 (1919), p. 350.
[96] Lloyd, 'Suez Canal Defences', p. 373.
[97] TNA, WO 161/62, Personal letters and narratives (General E. M. Paul), Narrative, Dardanelles, July–November 1915, p. 23. Added emphasis.

restrictions'.[98] In June 1916, responsibility for the Canal road and water supply system was eventually taken over by RE staff. Macdonald withdrew from the work associated with the Suez Canal zone, relinquishing his position as DDW. Despite this, he continued to provide advice and consultancy to the EEF under both Murray and Allenby.

Local expertise was also harnessed for the construction of the desert railway. The assistance rendered by the ESR was the most important prop of the logistical network in both Egypt and Palestine.[99] As early as 1914, the ESR was asked to act as 'general agent and storekeepers' for the railways in the Mediterranean theatre of war. This initial role expanded in December 1915 following Macauley's appointment to Director of Railway Transport with the rank of colonel. Macauley's dual appointment secured coordination between the civilian and military organisations. With his previous membership of the RE and his work on civilian railways, Macauley had the necessary experience and legitimacy to oversee railway construction in the desert. During the entire Egypt and Palestine campaign, 627 miles of standard gauge track were laid and eighty-six stations built under the direction of Macauley and the ESR.[100] It is little wonder that the British official history lauded him as 'having provided a network of lines as efficient as those in the European theatres'.[101] Both Murray and Allenby singled his work out for praise. The former wrote how, 'in spite of endless difficulties, owing to heavy sand and lack of water', Macauley and the ESR 'maintained ... a rate of advance which was not far behind that of the fighting troops'.[102] In a letter to Lord Curzon, Allenby wrote that Macauley 'speedily proved that the responsibilities which had been entrusted to him by the War Office had not been misplaced', and that he 'proved himself more than equal to the task'.[103]

Such praise was not universal, however. Given his existing reservations towards civilian expertise, Paul believed Macauley's dual role to have been 'the cause of much trouble'. He argued that 'the Works Directorate was seriously handicapped at not infrequent intervals through the Manager of the ESR', and that 'increased military efficiency would have resulted had Egyptian State Railways been confined to transport of

[98] Institution of Royal Engineers, *History*, VI, pp. 175–176.
[99] Ulrichsen, *Logistics and Politics*, p. 59.
[100] Institution of Royal Engineers, *History*, VI, p. 410.
[101] C. Falls, *Official History of the Great War: Military Operations, Egypt & Palestine*, II (2 vols, London: HMSO, 1930), p. 439.
[102] A. J. Murray, *Sir Archibald Murray's Despatches June 1916–June 1917* (London: J. M. Dent, 1920), p. 122.
[103] NAM, Macauley Papers, 8008-72, Allenby to Curzon, 30 August 1922.

Military Stores'.[104] Paul's concerns highlighted an important, but often overlooked concern: change was not always positive. While Murray and Allenby lauded Macauley's work from their position at GHQ, it was not plain sailing for Paul who had to work with Macauley and the ESR on a daily basis. For him, there were obvious limits to civilian involvement. A similar example can be found in the unsympathetic attitude of Ralph Wedgwood, a senior manager with the North Eastern Railway and the BEF's Director of Docks 1916–1919, to the Labour Corps. Wedgwood had spent his professional life within a company dedicated to implementing the most modern organisational methods available in the pursuit of efficiency. Content to run the docks directorate as his 'personal' fiefdom, Wedgwood's attitude towards the methods of the Labour Corps was disdainful.[105] Civilians were not just innocents abroad, and their expertise was by no means a cure-all.

Combining Local and External Expertise

There were instances where the army was able to blend both local and external expertise to considerable effect. For advice and practical help on water supply, the army subsumed local experts and elements of the local state apparatus into the military. This was easier to do in theatres such as Egypt and Palestine with nearby surveys and PWDs. However, like the high level transport missions, the army also requested further independent expertise, drawing on consultants, academics, and learned societies to examine and troubleshoot its water supply work.

One of the earliest requests for expert advice on water came from the Western Front. In April 1915, Major-General William Liddell (DDW, BEF) wrote to the War Office requesting a geologist to advise on water supply. This request resulted in the appointment of Lieutenant William King as a geologist to the BEF's Engineer-in-Chief. A geologist with the Geological Survey of Great Britain, King had volunteered on the outbreak of war and was commissioned into the 7th Battalion Royal Welch Fusiliers.[106] Upon receiving Liddell's request, King proceeded overseas in June 1915.[107] At the time of King's appointment to the BEF, the

---

[104] TNA, WO 161/60, Letter No. 36 from the Director of Works (General E. M. Paul), 'Memoranda on Engineer Stores', February 1919, p. 142.

[105] Phillips, 'Managing Armageddon', pp. 246–247, 258, 261.

[106] E. P. F. Rose, 'Groundwater as a Military Resource: Pioneering British Military Well Boring and Hydrogeology in World War 1', in E. P. F. Rose and J. D. Mather (eds), *Military Aspects of Hydrogeology: Geological Society Special Publication 362* (London: Geological Society, 2012), pp. 53–54.

[107] W. B. R. King, 'Geological Work on the Western Front', *The Geographical Journal* 54 (4) (1919), p. 201.

MEF had also requested a water supply expert to work with its engineers at Gallipoli. The War Office despatched Arthur Beeby Thompson – a 'water engineer of considerable experience' – who provided advice to the army from 1915 to 1919.[108] Upon his arrival at Gallipoli, Beeby Thompson noted that the problems of water supply occurred because 'little or nothing is known of the geology or hydrography'.[109] Recounting his experience on the peninsula, Beeby Thompson noted that hand-worked tools had been considered adequate when drilling for water and that 'no REs had been trained in the working of mechanical drilling plants of modern design'.[110] Unlike King, Beeby Thompson did not possess a military rank. It was felt that his status as a 'consultant civilian engineer' would give greater weight to his recommendations.[111] His lack of military rank did not appear to impact on his suggestions either. In a letter to the War Office, Alain Joly de Lotbinière (Director of Works, MEF) wrote that 'the water supply at Imbros is in a very fair condition', and that 'Mr Beeby Thompson . . . has every hope that . . . ample water supply will be obtained from deep wells at Imbros'.[112] Following the evacuation from Gallipoli, Beeby Thompson's expertise was secured by the BSF from January 1916 onwards where, once again, he was employed as an engineer without military rank, working directly to Brigadier-General Hubert Livingstone (Chief Engineer, BSF).

Water supply was a considerable problem for the EEF, too. In November 1915, Dr William Hume, the director of the Geological Survey of Egypt based in Cairo, was placed 'at the disposal of the military authorities' where he offered continuous advice to the force between 1915 and 1917.[113] Boreholes were unsuccessfully sunk, which necessitated the use of Nile water and involved 'elaborate works' to remove impurities and parasites. The Cairo and Alexandria Waterworks Companies and the Suez Canal Company proved instrumental in this respect.[114] Both

---

[108] Rose, 'Groundwater', pp. 57–59. In addition to Beeby Thompson, the Geological Survey of Great Britain also despatched three of its members for 'geological work in Gallipoli'.

[109] Quoted in Rose, 'Groundwater', pp. 57–59.

[110] A. Beeby Thompson, *Emergency Water Supplies* (London: Crosby Lockwood, 1924), p. 110.

[111] C. Falls, *History of the Great War: Military Operations, Macedonia*, I (2 vols, London: HMSO, 1933), p. 286.

[112] TNA, WO 161/32, Paul to DFW WO, Joly de Lotbinière to DFW, 29 August 1915.

[113] TNA, WO 161/67, Notes Regarding Water Supply in the Gaza and Wadi El Ghuzze Area by W. F. Hume, Hume to Wright, n.d. (c. July 1917).

[114] Institution of Royal Engineers, *The Work of the Royal Engineers in the European War, 1914–19: Egypt and Palestine – Water-Supply* (Chatham: W&J Mackay, 1921), pp. 46–47.

Murray and Paul highlighted the 'invaluable service' and 'expert advice' of these two companies.[115]

While local expertise and apparatus was useful to a point, the EEF was desirous of a second opinion on its infrastructural work. Following Murray's request for a technical expert of a 'very high standard' to check the quality of the recently constructed pipeline, the War Office despatched Edward Sandeman to Egypt in November 1916.[116] A member of the ICE and an associate professor of water supply and irrigation at the University of Manchester, Sandeman had designed and constructed supply works for local authorities, water boards, and companies throughout Britain. His appointment underscores how the civilian and military spheres could and, more importantly, did cross-fertilise. Sandeman's report on the desert pipeline was largely favourable, noting that the work was 'well carried out' and that, given the rapidity of its construction, the results were 'admirable'. His recommendations on the examination of the effect of salt on the steel pipes and improvements to the intakes were taken seriously. Correspondence between GHQ EEF and its Engineer-in-Chief show that Sandeman's recommendations were put into effect as early as December 1916.[117] Like Beeby Thompson, neither Hume nor Sandeman held military rank. Instead, they remained in advisory appointments, offering information and assistance that was communicated at a high level.

As with the transport missions, a flexible approach to the use of local and external experts was adopted, dictated by the different conditions in each theatre. On the Western Front, where the tempo of operations was high, it was deemed necessary for King to serve in uniform with military rank at GHQ. However, at Gallipoli and Salonika, where infrastructure was less developed and conditions more arduous, the adviser was embedded within the engineering branch at GHQ without military rank. In Palestine, where the hostile, desert terrain exacerbated infrastructure problems, both Hume and Sandeman provided advice to GHQ when required, but they were not embedded within the military organisation.[118]

---

[115] IWM, Murray Papers, 79/48/2, 'Campaign in Egypt 1916: Report of Engineering Works', p. 5; TNA, WO 161/36, Letter No. 14A and supplement from the Director of Works (General E. M. Paul), August–September 1916.

[116] TNA, WO 161/65, Report on Water Supply to the Army in Egypt and Palestine, 1914–1918, n.d., p. 11.

[117] TNA, WO 158/608, Engineer-in-Chief: Water supply on the Eastern Front: Report by Mr. Sandeman, December 1916.

[118] Rose, 'Groundwater', p. 70.

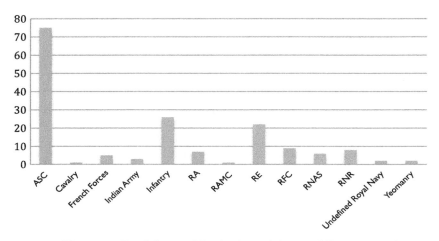

Figure 6.2 Breakdown of Institution of Automobile Engineers' serving membership by corps. From Unknown, 'Roll of Honour', *PIAE* 9 (1914), pp. 537–540.

Internal Civilian Expertise

Though considerable use was made of external civilian expertise, the army also had at its disposal a wealth of skilled civilians who had rushed to the colours on the outbreak of war. A significant number of learned society members, for instance, volunteered for military service. By December 1914, 167 members of the Institution of Automobile Engineers [IAE] were serving in the army or navy.[119] This represented just over 18 per cent of its total membership.[120] Its president-elect, president, and immediate past president were all appointed to senior positions within the ASC's Motor Transport branch.[121] Of this number, 44 per cent had volunteered or held pre-war Territorial appointments within the ASC, suggesting that, for this learned society, civilian roles could be easily mapped across to military equivalents (see Figure 6.2).

Through its Conjoint Board of Scientific Societies, the Royal Society published a list of 'scientific and technical men on active service' in August 1915. It revealed that 904 eminent scientific men were serving in the army by August 1915 (see Figure 6.3). Of this number, 230 men were serving in the RE with electrical engineers making up 57 per cent of

---

[119] Unknown, 'Annual Report and Accounts', *Proceedings of the Institution of Automobile Engineers* [*PIAE*] 9 (1915), p. 520.
[120] Total membership of IAE on 10 March 1915 totalled 903.
[121] 'Annual Report and Accounts', pp. 519–520.

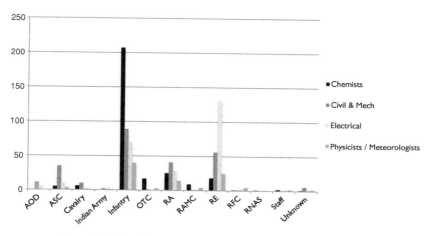

Figure 6.3 Breakdown of Royal Society's list of scientific and technical men by corps. From TNA, DSIR 10/125, Royal Society: List of Scientific and Technical Men on Active Service, August 1915.

this figure. Some chemists were eventually seconded from their original units to the RE to serve in the Special Brigade, the unit tasked with offensive and defensive gas warfare, which explains the initially high number serving in the infantry. Of the 208 chemists listed as infantry, forty-six of them would go on to serve as officers in the Special Brigade during the war.[122]

As this figure suggests, identifying and transferring skilled civilians was far from easy. Perceptions of the army's process for selecting suitably qualified men were not universally positive, while policies that involved combing out men from industry were unpopular, particularly with trade unions. The exigencies of war meant that the army could not afford to pursue a wholly bureaucratic or, conversely, a wholly personalised approach. The shift to a war economy in Britain, coupled with the army's expansion, required the development of a formal process for identifying and transferring skilled personnel. At the same time, there needed to be flexibility and sensitivity to operational requirements, which was not always popular or indeed possible. The development of this process was an important aspect of the army's learning experience, revealing instances of effective collaboration, the continuing relevance of the informal social network, and inevitable instances of friction. It was a costly process of trial and error that the army did not always get right.

[122] TNA, WO 142/334, Roll of RE Special Brigade Officers, 1919.

The army's identification and transfer of men has drawn unfavourable comparisons with the US Army's forward thinking approach, particularly with the latter's employment of psychologists and businessmen on its Classification of Personnel committee. Established in 1917, the committee provided 'an instrument to increase the value of the army's manpower through securing the most effective placement of each man'.[123] Original membership of the committee consisted almost wholly of psychologists, but a number of business specialists were appointed to ensure the 'successful prosecution of the work', including representatives from Winchester Repeating Arms Company, Western Electric, and Pennsylvania Railroad.[124] These individuals placed their experience of 'putting skilled workers where they were most needed' at the service of the War Department.[125] Drawing on this scientific and business expertise, the committee designed a programme to help army trainers identify skilled men from the incoming masses of farmers and labourers. The US Army welcomed the scheme due to 'unexpected problems such as finding enough men with clerical skills to staff division headquarters'.[126] Complex in nature, the scheme included activities such as the compilation of an index of occupations, trade testing, personnel specifications, and the preparation of tables of occupational needs for each sort of platoon, company, or regiment.

When developing its selection scheme, the US Army conducted a detailed study of the British personnel organisation.[127] Its findings suggested that the British organisation 'in some respects is far superior to ours. Special reports . . . covered their [the British] whole program of recruitment, classification, trade-testing, assignment and transfer, industrial furloughs, weekly consolidation and analysis of strength reports'.[128] American delegations were despatched to Britain to observe

---

[123] R. M. Yerkes, 'Report of the Psychology Committee of the National Research Council', *Psychological Review* 26 (2) (1919), p. 100.

[124] W. V. Bingham, 'Army Personnel Work', *Journal of Applied Psychology* 3 (1) (1919), p. 3; United States Adjutant-General's Office, *The Personnel System of the United States Army*, II (2 vols, Washington, DC: GPO, 1919), p. 19.

[125] W. V. Bingham, 'Army Always on Lookout for Specialists', *New York Times* (14 April 1918). The US army was also interested in scientific management, notably Taylorism. Upon America's entry into the war, the Chief of Ordnance, William Crozier, brought into his department 'every member of the Taylor Society on whom he could lay his hands'. See R. Kanigel, *The One Best Way: Frederick Winslow Taylor and the Enigma of Efficiency* (New York: Viking Penguin, 1997), p. 487.

[126] J. D. Keene, *Doughboys, the Great War, and the Remaking of America* (London: Johns Hopkins University Press, 2001), p. 29.

[127] The British government was aware of the types of intelligence and early psychometric testing used by the US. See TNA, NATS 1/873, America New Recruiting System, 1917.

[128] Bingham, 'Army Personnel Work', p. 9.

and report on its recruitment programme. Their aim was to gather suggestions 'that looked toward the improvement of the personnel system in America, in order that it might function more effectively in France'.[129] The US Army's findings suggested that the British had a centralised and well-defined policy for personnel selection. The truth was rather different.

Despite the existence of a pre-war Department of Recruiting and Organisation under the AG at the War Office, the British army initially embarked on a highly personalised approach to the allocation of manpower. It tried, and largely failed, to balance both industrial demands and the pressures of an overtaxed army bureaucracy. Unsurprisingly, the process was far from effective at first. The army's policy passed through three overlapping stages: ad hoc and personalised in 1914–1916, semiformalised from 1916 to 1917, before the eventual overhaul of formal departments and processes from 1917 onwards.

The early stage of this process mirrored the government's broader manpower problem. The ideal manpower planning machinery did not exist early in the war because the relative priorities of aspects of the war effort had not been determined.[130] The government strove to meet GHQ's manpower demands, ensuring that young fit men were released from industries for military service. Major-General Sir Robert Hutchison, future head of the Directorate of Organisation, recalled that the government, 'without knowledge of the difficulties of personnel, drew into the military net every man who would voluntarily come forward'. As a result, some men decided to enlist in local infantry units, denying the technical branches access to their skills. There were 'skilled mechanics and apprentices... laborers, university graduates, politicians' all serving in infantry formations.[131] At this early stage of the war, there was no uniform policy towards the transfer or identification of skilled workers. This lack of thought not only began to have a deleterious effect on British industry, but it also caused problems for RE and railway units that were expanding to meet the army's demands. According to Lyndall Urwick, a champion of scientific management, this 'unbusiness like omission to select and sort candidates intelligently on the basis of their previous record' led to chaos and inefficiency. The officering of the army could only be rescued if 'ability (*including well-proved ability in previous civil life*) is diligently and continually searched

[129] United States Adjutant-General's Office, *Personnel System*, I, pp. 381–382, 593.
[130] K. Grieves, '"Total War"? The Quest for a British Manpower Policy, 1917–18', *Journal of Strategic Studies* 9 (1) (1986), p. 80.
[131] United States Adjutant-General's Office, *Personnel System*, I, p. 684.

for'.[132] If not then the army would do worse than lose battles: it might lose the war.

The capacity to move men between formations and fronts as required was subject to the operational demands of the various forces. The army was disinclined to enforce hard and fast rules when it came to transferring men from infantry to technical branches. As Hutchison observed, 'if you want to pull a man away from a fighting organization, it is charged that you are interfering with . . . a General's winning this or that battle'.[133] At the Conference of Headmasters in December 1915, one delegate had received letters from former pupils who 'had been claimed by the Munitions Department, but their commanding officer in a Service battalion had refused to let them go'. For that headmaster, the solution was simple: better coordination and more subordination.[134] He was right, of course, but top-down involvement only came about when the situation was deemed critical. In the case of military railways, the possible extension of advanced railheads in early 1916 was contingent on additional railway troops, and that these could 'only be formed by the transfer of skilled railway men from other arms, and by the raising of additional Pioneer or Labour Battalions for railway purposes'.[135] According to an ICE report, this led military authorities to transfer eleven hundred drivers and firemen who were serving in units in France to work on the military railways.[136]

This continuing ad hoc approach added fuel to the fire in Whitehall, where criticism of the army's inefficient use of manpower was rife by mid-1916, leading to calls for the formalisation of the selection and transfer process. Christopher Addison, parliamentary secretary to the Ministry of Munitions, criticised the army's ad hoc method, noting 'there appears to be very little doubt that the War Office could get all the men they want if they combed the Armies thoroughly and systematically; and I think they ought to help themselves before coming down on us for men'. Concerns that skilled workers were not being used effectively by the army was a long-standing issue and one heightened by competition between the War Office and the Ministry of Munitions. The most contentious issues that had arisen between the two departments were the military requirement for skilled engineers and the release of men from

---

[132] L. Urwick, 'The Real Ground for Alarm', *The New Statesman*, 30 October 1915. Added emphasis. I am grateful to Dr Christopher Phillips for uncovering the identity of the author and bringing this article to my attention.

[133] United States Adjutant-General's Office, *Personnel System*, I, p. 685.

[134] Unknown, 'The Waste of Brains', *The Times*, 24 December 1915.

[135] TNA, PRO 30/66/9, Papers of Brigadier-General Sir H. Osborne Mance, QMG2 to Mance, 23 January 1916.

[136] Institution of Civil Engineers Archive [ICEA], OC 4277, H. A. Ryott, 'The Provision of Personnel for Military Railways in the War of 1914–1919' (1920), p. 8.

the army for civil industries.[137] In July 1916, the two departments came to an agreement whereby the munitions industry would make up any deficit that might occur in preliminary military demand for artificers for the army's technical corps.

Ongoing negotiations with the trade unions, notably the Amalgamated Society of Engineers [ASE], further compounded competition between the two government departments. After a series of deputations, the government and the ASE reached a formal agreement in November 1916, which stated that the 'provision of skilled mechanics for the army will in future be made by the Ministry of Munitions'. The government agreed not to apply compulsion to skilled men, hoping instead to obtain the required men for service in the technical corps through voluntary means. The trade unions agreed to 'do their utmost to provide the Ministry of Munitions with skilled men, who will undertake to serve ... either in the Artificers' Corps of the Army or as War Munitions Volunteers'.[138] The army was forced to rely on employers, lists of skilled men provided by trade unions, and patriotic goodwill, as they endeavoured to comb out men for the technical corps. It was a tall order: only nine thousand six hundred men were reallocated to skilled work in the army in November and December 1916.[139]

Pressure from the ASE, other trade unions, and voices within the army itself suggested a process far removed from the systematic one lauded by the US Army. In the first years of the war, the army relied considerably on informal transfers either by volunteering or through an individual's own personal connections. Often the expertise of these individuals was discovered through interpersonal relationships or direct petitions to higher formations and senior generals. Cowans was aware that the army needed to identify and utilise men with the appropriate skills for the task in hand and regularly sponsored such transfers. He was 'not hide-bound by any War Office red tape' and he realised, particularly where supply depots were concerned, that 'they must have men with business, rather than military, experience'.[140] Although Cowans had expressed some reservation over civilian expertise, he was still keen to secure 'men of business'. Writing to Altham in November 1915, Cowans mentioned two Territorial officers in the MEF who would be useful for labour and supply. The first officer, Pearson, was 'accustomed to dealing with large questions in regard to navvies' having 'managed all kinds of arrangements – the organisation of 50,000 men etc – so anything we

---

[137] Quoted in K. Grieves, *The Politics of Manpower 1914–18* (Manchester: Manchester University Press, 1988), p. 32.

[138] TNA, MUN 5/57/320/16, ASE Pamphlet, 20 November 1916, p. 2.

[139] Grieves, *Politics of Manpower*, p. 98.

[140] Chapman-Huston and Rutter, *Cowans*, II, p. 55.

[the Army] do ought to be child's play'.[141] Altham heeded his advice, requesting Pearson to help with labour organisation in the MEF. The second officer mentioned by Cowans was Major Vernon Willey, an officer in the Nottinghamshire Yeomanry. Willey had 'managed a very big business in America, and was manager of that Business at 25', and 'absolutely wasted as a would be soldier'.[142] Cowans was keen to impress on senior generals in both the MEF and BSF that 'more than ever I am sure you ought to get business men'. He went on in still stronger terms:

This is exactly what we keep on rubbing into you, as I am sure, when we hear of a few exceptions, there must be scores more in the Territorials and Yeomanry that are with you, like Pearson, and that man Willey... These are the sort of men that we want to get hold of, there is no doubt about it.[143]

Through Cowans and Altham's efforts, Willey was transferred from the front line to become Assistant Director of Equipment and Ordnance, and then Controller of Wool Supplies at the War Office. Willey worked alongside other citizen soldiers who had been transferred from the front line, including Captain John Bland, a Kitchener officer and partner in a wool company, and Major John Sexty, a Territorial officer and partner at a curriers in Gloucestershire.[144]

This pragmatic approach masked the reality of a failing personnel system. Addison had been right to criticise the War Office's ineffective attempts at 'combing out', which were neither thorough nor systematic. Skilled men often fell through the cracks. By late 1916, both the military and industry were suffering severely from these 'unscientific methods of recruiting'. Men were required for work in munitions factories and shipyards back in Britain, as well as in the army's technical branches. These effects were also felt in the army's subsidiary theatres. In a letter to Scott-Moncrieff, Paul remarked how

I frequently come across officers and other ranks serving in the infantry, who in civil life are engineers, contractors, clerks of works and foremen. In some cases they have been lent to us as a temporary measure by arrangement, and we have been very glad of their services; they have done excellent work. But invariably after a period their commanding officers request their return.[145]

A reorganisation of the army's personnel machinery was long overdue.

---

[141] TNA, WO 107/43, Inspector-General of Communications: Letters, Cowans to Altham, 12 November 1915.

[142] Ibid., Cowans to Altham, 23 October 1915.

[143] Ibid., Cowans to Altham, 13 November 1915.

[144] Ibid.; TNA, MUN 4/6471, Department of Surveyor-General of Supplies, 'List of Businessmen Assisting Contracts RMS', n.d. (c.1917).

[145] TNA, WO 161/42, Brigadier-General E. M. Paul to Director of Fortifications and Works (War Office), Letter 19, 8 February 1917, p. 83.

This overhaul finally came about in July 1917 with the reorganisation of the Department of Recruiting and Organisation and its transformation into the Directorate of Organisation. With the full backing of Robertson, and under the capable leadership of Major-General Hutchison, the directorate was given a free hand to use whatever means necessary to ensure that personnel was placed on an even footing. Each service arm, along with women and the Labour Corps, were allotted to a separate branch. At the time of reorganisation, many highly skilled men were not employed at their trades; men of high medical category were retained in all corps on home service duties; unskilled men of high medical category were employed in technical corps; and, in many cases, men on the Lines of Communication were of 'an unnecessarily high medical category'.[146] Such conditions had arisen owing to the voluntary recruitment system and the 'somewhat spasmodic' efforts that had been used to meet manpower demands in the early years of the war. In an attempt to alleviate these problems as well as gain accurate data on the types of tradesmen available to the army, Hutchison and his staff instituted an 'occupational card index' system in October 1917. Through this, another important by-product of civilian expertise came to the fore: the potential for increased administrative efficiency.

The directorate's card index was stored in London and had three main objectives: first, to facilitate the 'reinforcement of the army by the discovery and release of low category tradesmen in return for conditionally exempted men of category A in civil life'; secondly, to enable the selection of skilled tradesmen who were 'not employed at their trades in the Army to meet the requirements of technical units'; and finally, to identify men 'required to be released from the Army for important war service in civil life'.[147] The index recorded each man's physical location in the army, his civilian profession, who he was employed by, his previous two employers, and his home address. Whenever a man moved within Britain or overseas, his card was moved correspondingly to indicate where he went. This card index system was also trailed within each soldier's Army Book.[148]

When reflecting after the war, the directorate was of the view that, while the index was 'sound in principle', it 'failed from the outset to produce many satisfactory results, nor can it be said that at any time it saved time or money, or promoted efficiency'.[149] Such a damning indictment was based on a number of factors, ranging from the index's

[146] TNA, WO 162/6, History of Directorate of Organisation, n.d. (c.1919), p. 8.
[147] Ibid., p. 48.
[148] United States Adjutant-General's Office, *Personnel System*, I, p. 688.
[149] TNA, WO 162/6, History of Directorate of Organisation, n.d. (c.1919), p. 49.

late establishment in the war, its divided control between numerous government departments, and a failure to understand its importance. While these technologies of bureaucracy were designed to minimise individual agency, promoting instead a single collective agent, their invention and use were still subject to human fallibility. Furthermore, the increasing size of the army and, with it, the increasing volume of paperwork would forever threaten to overwhelm these existing administrative arrangements.[150] Those closest to the front line did not always understand the necessity and the contingencies for organising knowledge. Indeed, units that were 'fully engaged in duties of which they saw the immediate necessity...could spare no thought for matters of theory'.[151] This attitude was further compounded by the amount of raw data required for the index to function. This data was compiled from accurate and timely returns from the various units both at home and abroad. The problem with these returns was their sheer volume. Some formations reported having to complete thirty to forty returns per week to different branches. This duplication of effort was eventually replaced, leading to the development of a 'consolidated return'. This return was 'made as far as possible to give all the information that was required by the various branches and departments'.[152] The return was perforated allowing different branches to tear off the portion that related to their needs. These administrative measures were routine in the business world. The use of pre-printed forms, card indexes, and vertical filing systems were all designed, in theory, to increase efficiency.[153]

While the directorate's central card index was felt to be unsuccessful, other branches used indexes in various ways to great effect, attesting to the diversity of method and experience within a single military department. The directorate's AG2(o) branch, responsible for 'reinforcement' infantry officers in Britain, established its own four-coloured card index in July 1916, with almost one hundred thousand cards written out by female volunteers. For this branch, the card index was of 'the most vital importance' and one of the 'most useful institutions' not only for recording the whereabouts of officers, but also for recording specialist qualifications such as whether they had passed Staff College [psc], their

---

[150] P. Joyce, *The State of Freedom: A Social History of the British State since 1800* (Cambridge: Cambridge University Press, 2013), pp. 162, 174, 181–182.
[151] TNA, WO 162/6, History of Directorate of Organisation, n.d. (c.1919), p. 49.
[152] United States Adjutant-General's Office, *Personnel System*, I, pp. 689–690.
[153] J. Yates, 'Investing in Information: Supply and Demand Forces on the Use of Information in American Firms, 1850–1920', in P. Temin (ed.), *Inside the Business Enterprise: Historical Perspectives on the Use of Information* (Chicago: University of Chicago Press, 1991), pp. 122, 126–127.

suitability for staff employment, language proficiency, and any adverse reports.[154] The AG9 branch, responsible for personnel in the MGC, also instituted a card index in September 1916. It believed the index to be 'of immense value . . . and has been a considerable saving in correspondence and clerks, and would have been instituted by the DSD . . . for the whole army but for the difficulty of copying cards and the shortage of clerks'.[155]

These administrative measures were not limited to the Directorate of Organisation or, indeed, to the British army. The Admiralty, for example, cultivated a close relationship with Lloyd's of London from 1905, benefitting from the company's 'considerable unofficial assistance' in maritime intelligence matters.[156] BEF GHQ was beginning to embrace information technology for intelligence analysis, utilising the expertise of the Prudential Assurance Company and its Powers Samas tabulating machines to process German casualty data.[157] The 'science of statistics' was also used to great effect, particularly for supply and transport purposes. George Beharrell, a pre-war colleague of Geddes and statistician to the Transportation Directorate, emphasised the 'impossibility of successfully directing large organisations' if statistical information was not forthcoming. Statistics told 'each responsible officer what he was doing, whether he was going back or going forward, and how he compared with his opposite number in other places'.[158] Such accurate information led to increased efficiency, particularly on the railways and inland waterways. This emphasis on efficiency was evident in other parts of the army both on and beyond the Western Front. In the EEF, the ASC's Motor Transport branch transferred from a ledger-based accountancy system to a card index system in August 1916 for the 'accurate working of receipts, demands, issues, and stock-keeping'; while the army's Labour Directorate used principles of statistical forecasting and scientific management to understand labour requirements, and measure and improve output.[159]

---

[154] TNA, WO 33/3129, Interim report on Major-General Money's committee on Organization Directorate, 1919, p. 6.
[155] TNA, WO 162/6, History of Directorate of Organisation, n.d. (c.1919), pp. 20, 571, 572.
[156] N. A. Lambert, *Planning Armageddon: British Economic Warfare and the First World War* (Cambridge, MA: Harvard University Press, 2012), pp. 211–213.
[157] Beach, *Haig's Intelligence*, p. 176; L. Dennett, *A Sense of Security: 150 Years of Prudential* (Cambridge: Granta, 1998), pp. 230–232; L. Halewood, '"A Matter of Opinion": British Attempts to Assess the Attrition of German Manpower, 1915-1917', *Intelligence and National Security* 32 (3) (2017), pp. 333–350.
[158] TNA, ZPER 9/32, G. Beharrell, 'The Value of Full and Accurate Statistics', *The Railway Gazette*, September 1920, p. 37.
[159] Badcock, *Transport Services*, p. 273; TNA, WO 107/37, Report on work of the Labour force during the war, November 1919, pp. 134, 170 and Appendix Y.

Although the army had now developed a system for identifying the professions and numbers of its personnel, it also had to ensure that these men were proficient in their stated trade. The Trade Test Centre at Woolwich verified this competence.[160] Orders were issued for skilled men of engineering trades, including new recruits and those serving in non-technical units, to be sent to Woolwich for practical testing. Specialist liaison officers were attached to the centre for the purpose of examining and selecting men suitable for technical work. Each man was tested and either passed as skilled or proficient and posted to a branch in which his qualifications could be most fully employed. For the military railways, a number of men were obtained through this measure, amounting to 2,550 in 1917 and 3,805 in 1918. If a soldier was rejected as unskilled, he was either returned to his unit or posted to a technical branch as a pioneer.[161]

Though trade testing proved a useful way of confirming a soldier's qualifications, sometimes certain skills were not required. These episodes were highly contentious with the potential to foment unrest. This was particularly acute in late 1916 at the height of the army's personnel crisis. A number of MPs expressed consternation that 'the services of a number of men who have passed a trade test and obtained a skilled certificate are not utilised at all on skilled work'. In response, the financial secretary to the War Office outlined his department's policy towards skilled volunteers:

Men who have passed trade tests are posted to units in which their technical skill can be utilised *so far as such tradesmen are required in the Army*. If the number of tradesmen in any particular trade is in excess of the numbers of that trade required in the Army the surplus men are utilised in other ways for which they may be suited. This does not, of course, mean that there will not be at any given moment and in any given unit tradesmen who are not engaged in their trade . . . it is a matter of progressive adjustment.[162]

The War Office's policy on this matter was formalised in an Army Council order in August 1917, which stated that no tradesman who possessed a skill required by any of the technical corps should be allowed to remain in a unit in which his skill was 'not being utilised for the benefit of the nation'.[163] However, this did little to reduce concern. In early May 1918, one Private Harmer had voluntarily joined the Royal Air Force [RAF] as

---

[160] Regional Command Trade Test Centres were developed as the war progressed.
[161] ICEA, OC 4277, Ryott, 'Military Railways', p. 9.
[162] *Hansard*, 'Skilled Men', House of Commons debate, 8 November 1916, vol. 87 c177. Added emphasis.
[163] TNA, WO 293/7, Army Council Instructions (War Office), ACI 1303, 22 August 1917.

a mechanic. He was 'given to understand that he would be sent to Liverpool and from there to a trade centre to pass a test'. Instead, he was 'put straight into the Infantry'. Harmer's plight was debated in the House of Commons. The MP who raised the matter charged that there had been 'hundreds of similar instances'. In response, the under secretary of state for war replied that as Harmer was a 'turner', and that there were 'no requirements for men of this trade at the present time', he was placed in an infantry unit in accordance with his medical category.[164]

As the example of Private Harmer reveals, the army's operational requirements remained a constant source of friction between the government and trade unions throughout the war. In its November 1916 agreement with the ASE, the government pledged that 'every possible effort' would be made to transfer skilled men to mechanical units.[165] However, in September 1917, the ASE highlighted the 'serious position' of skilled men being posted to line regiments, rather than technical branches. According to the ASE, the government and the army were reneging on publicly agreed assurances. In short, it could place no confidence in the government, the Ministry of Munitions, or the employers themselves. Although there were measures in place to mitigate this problem, a representative of the War Office referenced 'circumstances of a special kind' that would prevent a commander from taking a man 'out of a fighting unit and put[ting] him to his trade'.[166] The army 'actively pursued' the transfer of skilled men, but this was at the whim of the 'prevalent military situation'.

The eventual establishment of a systematic personnel policy within the army was a welcome development. It was necessary and long overdue, but it was never problem-free. Individuals still fell through the cracks. Operational requirements still took precedence. While the US Army admired the centralised British approach, it was a process applied retrospectively. The army's attitude towards manpower is a discrete learning process in and of itself, but one that does not cast the army in a positive light. It was a process that relied on cooperation and close working with politicians, government departments, and industry. At various times, the army revealed itself to be parochial, rarely wavering from its purely military view of the war. Operational requirements and expediency often undermined attempts to rationalise and improve the manpower policy.

---

[164] *Hansard*, 'Voluntary Enlistment (Skilled Men)', House of Commons debate, 13 May 1918, vol. 106 c52W.

[165] TNA, MUN 5/57/320/16, Agreement between Government and ASE, 20 November 1916.

[166] TNA, MUN 5/57/320/38, Minutes of conference with Amalgamated Society of Engineers on skilled men for Army technical units, 11 September 1917, p. 4.

That it took almost three years for the army to seriously consider the rational organisation of manpower is damning. Indeed, it took for the manpower situation to reach crisis point before substantial changes were made and, even then, it was patently too little, too late. The army's attitude towards manpower reveals both the strengths and weaknesses of its preference for flexibility. Until the decision came to overhaul manpower, the army's approach was ad hoc – predicated on informal and unstructured attempts to secure expertise and personnel. This may have worked at a local level, but it was ultimately unsustainable. In this respect, the dangers of a personalised army came painfully to the fore.

Conclusions

Broadly speaking, the army recognised the importance of civilian expertise to the efficient running of the military machine. This was not a wartime phenomenon, but based on a mutually beneficial, cooperative process that had been in existence for over fifty years. However, the soldier-civilian relationship in warfare had 'never been so intermeshed as during 1914–1918 – nor the combatant-civilian distinction so blurred'.[167] The relationship between the civil and military professions offers a number of insights into the army as an organisation. First, that it was capable of recognising and implementing change, despite inevitable pockets of resistance and organisational inertia. While friction is often viewed negatively, it remains a fundamental part of any organisation. Senior figures made efforts to smooth over organisational resistance. In some cases, however, the army was right to be sceptical of civilian involvement. Change was not always positive, and civilian involvement was far from a cure-all. Secondly, it is clear that the army still valued pragmatic solutions to its problems. Despite overhauling formal departments and processes, particularly for personnel selection, the army still needed to be adaptable. Whilst a necessity, this adaptability was a double-edged sword, however: it may have been vital to meet occupational requirements, but it meant that individuals still fell through the cracks. Finally, the army's desire to seek out civilian expertise, both inside and outside the institution, highlights the importance of this knowledge to its learning process. With the wider use of civilian expertise came the adoption of administrative innovations, such as card index systems and pre-printed forms. Though not always popular with some directorates, the general willingness to adopt such methods

---

[167] H. Jones, 'The Great War: How 1914–18 Changed the Relationship between War and Civilians', *JRUSI* 159 (4) (2014), p. 90.

shows an organisation ready and willing to employ efficiency measures that were standard practice in the business world. In short, by looking beyond its boundaries and learning from non-traditional sources, the army revealed itself to be an adaptive organisation and one open to learning from different disciplines and walks of life.

While previous chapters have revealed the ways in which the army learned from its expeditionary forces, its allies, and its civilian experts, learning was not solely a case of acquiring knowledge and skills; it also involved imparting them to newcomers. Engaged in a constant process of integration, the army facilitated the adjustment of various formations and individuals, whether they were new to the organisation, or had transferred to a new location or role within it. Integration is a process designed to help newcomers learn about their new employment and adjust to a new organisation.[1] It is also known as 'learning the ropes' or 'getting up to speed'.[2] Militaries are significant practitioners of integration. Organisations like the British army have preserved their organisational memory and, indeed, their ethos over time through the continuous integration of newcomers. This has led to the army remaining the same in terms of its identity, even though its strategies, processes, and membership have changed.[3]

The integration of newcomers is a learning process in and of itself. These newly arrived individuals and formations had to learn to be part of the army for the purposes of cohesion and interoperability. This process necessarily involved organisational efforts alongside individual proactivity on the newcomer's part. We have seen how the army employed various ways and means to learn from diverse stimuli. Similarities can be detected in the approaches used to integrate newcomers. Familiar interpersonal methods including secondments and mentoring ran alongside non-interpersonal ones such as publications. An examination of this process not only sheds light on how the army attempted to integrate

---

[1] R. Korte and S. Lin, 'Getting on Board: Organizational Socialization and the Contribution of Social Capital', *Human Relations* 66 (2013), p. 409.

[2] M. R. Louis, 'Surprise and Sense Making: What Newcomers Experience in Entering Unfamiliar Organizational Settings', *Administrative Science Quarterly* 25 (2) (1980), p. 230.

[3] E. P. Antonacopoulou and W. H. Guttel, 'Staff Induction Practices and Organizational Socialization: A Review and Extension of the Debate', *Society and Business Review* 5 (1) (2010), pp. 22–23.

newcomers, but it also reveals, more importantly, how these newcomers were able, and encouraged, to self-integrate. Elements of integration have been considered in Chapter 4 with the movement of formations between theatres; this chapter takes the experience of the Australian Imperial Force [AIF] as its focus.[4] Formations of the AIF were present in a number of different operational theatres, including Egypt, Gallipoli, Palestine, and the Western Front. While not as prominent as the Indian Army in General Staff planning for a war in Europe, the AIF proves an interesting case study owing to its relative newness as a force. Unlike India, none of the Dominions, including Australia, had armies worthy of the name at the turn of the twentieth century.[5]

From humble beginnings as largely irregular forces at the outbreak of war, the units of the AIF ended the war as self-proclaimed 'shock troops', the corps d'élite of the British army. This combat effectiveness has been partly attributed to the AIF's homogeneity.[6] Like the Canadian formations, Australian divisions (on the Western Front at least) were not split up amongst British corps. Instead, they were kept together wherever possible, first in I and II ANZAC before their eventual grouping into the Australian Corps in November 1917. For some, the AIF's effectiveness was largely ascribed to its independence, resourcefulness, and classlessness.[7] According to Charles Bean, the Australian official historian, the Australian soldier was not 'a material to be treated according to pure British drill-book methods'. He was 'never at heart a Regular soldier'.[8] However, homogeneity and national identity were not solely responsible for the transformation of a largely untrained, irregular force into a high performing instrument within the British military machine. Such a transformation was contingent on successful integration. As we have seen, the army allowed for adaptation and flexibility where the acquisition of knowledge and experience was concerned, but did the

[4] The integration of Kitchener's New Armies has been considered in P. Simkins, *Kitchener's Army: The Raising of the New Armies, 1914–1916* (Manchester: Manchester University Press, 1988), pp. 163–320. Discussion of the integration of Indian formations, notably into the EEF, has been considered by J. E. Kitchen, *The British Imperial Army in the Middle East* (London: Bloomsbury, 2014), and Fox, 'Thomas Cook's Tourists'.
[5] Delaney, 'Army Apostles', p. 173.
[6] J. E. Edmonds, *History of the Great War: Military Operations, France and Belgium 1918*, V (5 vols, London: HMSO, 1947), pp. 179, 610–611.
[7] C. E. W. Bean, *Anzac to Amiens* (Canberra, ACT: Australian War Memorial, 1983 [1946]), p. 537; N. Wise, 'The Lost Labour Force: Working-Class Approaches to Military Service during the Great War', *Labour History* 93 (2007), p. 172.
[8] C. E. W. Bean, *The Official History of Australia in the War of 1914–1918: The Story of ANZAC from the Outbreak of War to the End of the First Phase of the Gallipoli Campaign, May 4, 1915*, I (12 vols, Sydney, NSW: Angus and Robertson, 1941), pp. 126–127.

same levels of flexibility apply when integrating newcomers? To what extent was the AIF empowered to self-integrate into the army?

Establishment of the Commonwealth Military Force

To answer such questions requires us to consider Britain and Australia's pre-war military relationship. Australia's defence arrangements were shaped by her isolation. Following Australia's federation in 1901, Major-General Sir Edward Hutton, a British regular officer, was appointed to command the newly formed Commonwealth Military Force [CMF] and charged with organising Australia's disparate forces into a homogeneous federal force.[9] The CMF's sole purpose was that of home defence. Predominantly civilian in nature, it only had a small cadre of permanent soldiers. The militia dominated its officer corps, with only a small number of professional officers responsible for training, administration, and technical tasks.[10] In 1912, the strength of Australia's military forces totalled 23,696. Of this number, 2,235 were full-time and 21,127 were citizen soldiers.[11]

Driven by imperial rather than national objectives, Hutton called for the creation of a professional mobile field force capable of operating overseas. Unlike the CMF, this force was to be capable of serving wherever the Australian government desired. The development of the Australian forces from federation up to 1914 was foregrounded by the struggle between 'Imperialists' (men such as Hutton and his protégé Brudenell White) and 'Australianists' (officers such as James Legge). The latter group took an independent view of Australia and desired the promotion of her domestic interests over imperial priorities. Though the idea of a field force was initially dismissed, compulsory military training was instituted in 1909, just before Kitchener's arrival to inspect Australia's defences and military organisation.[12] However, it was not until 1912 that Australia, in partnership with New Zealand, turned her attentions

---

[9] The establishment and evolution of Australia's post-federation force has been covered in detail in J. Grey, *A Military History of Australia* (Cambridge: Cambridge University Press, 2000 [1999]), pp. 63–79; A. Palazzo, *The Australian Army: A History of Its Organisation 1901–2001* (Melbourne, VIC: Oxford University Press, 2001); and C. Stockings, *Britannia's Shield: Lieutenant-General Sir Edward Hutton and Late-Victorian Imperial Defence* (Melbourne, VIC: Cambridge University Press, 2015).

[10] J. Connor, *Anzac and Empire: George Foster Pearce and the Foundations of Australian Defence* (Melbourne, VIC: Cambridge University Press, 2011), p. 14.

[11] G. H. Knibbs, *Official Yearbook of the Commonwealth of Australia, 1901–1912 No. 6* (Melbourne, VIC: McCarron, Bird, 1913), p. 1047. The remaining 334 were made up of 'Volunteers' and 'Area Officers'.

[12] Stevenson, *To Win the Battle*, p. 13.

to planning for the possibility of creating an expeditionary force for service overseas.

Much as there was a struggle between the 'Imperialists' and 'Australianists', rivalry also existed between the CMF's permanent and militia officers. Often viewed as a product of the inter-war years, reaching its zenith during the Second World War, this rivalry was in fact evident from the creation of the militia.[13] Lieutenant-General Sir James McCay's biographer, for example, notes that in the 'hot-house world' of the Australian military, McCay's 1907 appointment to the role of Director of the Australian Intelligence Corps led to conflict with permanent officers 'who . . . resented a militia officer holding such a senior position'.[14] This rivalry continued to simmer away during the First World War. Writing to Brudenell White in September 1918, Harry Chauvel remarked on 'the intrigues going on in London', blaming 'the old ill feeling amongst the Victorian militia officers against the permanent forces' and their ambition to 'get one of their own men into power'.[15]

Imperial Interoperability

Though a self-governing Dominion, Australia's defence policy and organisation were still part of the wider question of Imperial defence. This required the interoperability of British and Dominion forces. In case of major conflict, it was expected that the Empire's forces would combine to fight the common foe.[16] As Harry Crerar remarked in the inter-war period, the ideal should be that 'any Dominion formation should take its place in the Imperial Army as easily and as efficiently as a formation of the Regular or Territorial Armies'.[17] Interoperability was promoted in a number of ways: through shared publications, education and training, the establishment of an Imperial General Staff, and the loan or attachment of British officers.[18]

[13] For interwar and Second World War rivalry, see D. M. Horner, 'Staff Corps versus Militia: The Australian Experience of World War II', *Defence Force Journal* 26 (January/February 1981), pp. 13–26; G. Pratten, *Australian Battalion Commanders in the Second World War* (Melbourne, VIC: Cambridge University Press, 2009).

[14] C. Wray, *Sir James Whiteside McCay: A Turbulent Life* (Melbourne, VIC: Oxford University Press, 2002), pp. 80–81.

[15] NLA, White Papers, MS 5172 2.3/43, Chauvel to White, 9 September 1918.

[16] J. Bou, 'Ambition and Adversity: Developing an Australian Military Force, 1901–1914', *Australian Army Journal* 9 (1) (2012), p. 80.

[17] H. D. G. Crerar, 'The Development of Closer Relations between the Military Forces of the Empire', *JRUSI* 71 (483) (1926), p. 442.

[18] See B. D. Faraday, 'Half the Battle: The Administration and Higher Organisation of the AIF 1914–1918', Unpublished PhD Thesis, University of New South Wales, 1997, for a fuller exposition of these attempts at interoperability.

The Imperial conferences, particularly those of 1909 and 1911, played an important role in facilitating attempts at interoperability.[19] It was as a result of these conferences that British training manuals, including *Combined Training*, the *Field Service Pocket Book* (1906), and *FSR* were distributed to and adopted by the Dominion forces. At the 1909 conference, the Australian representative noted that the adoption of such manuals 'seems to me almost to go without saying...the *Field Service Regulations* and training manuals ought to be adopted if the principles proposed...are to work out satisfactorily'.[20] This decision went some way to establishing uniformity, as well as ensuring Dominion forces were up to date with the latest tactical and administrative methods.

Education and training were also brought into line. A number of places were set aside for Dominion officers at the two staff colleges from 1905 onwards. Brudenell White and Thomas Blamey attended Camberley and Quetta, respectively. It is perhaps no surprise that they both went on to hold senior staff appointments during the First World War: Brudenell White serving as MGGS Fifth Army, and Blamey as BGGS Australian Corps. On the outbreak of war in 1914, however, Australia could only call on thirteen *psc* officers, four of whom were British officers on loan.[21] Though limited in scope, the extension of staff college training to the Dominions allowed for the adoption of uniform procedures across the Commonwealth. The common system of staff education and training influenced the decision to adopt British promotion examinations for their regular officers, which Australia did in 1909.[22] These overarching changes to military education were further enhanced by the establishment of the short-lived *Commonwealth Military Journal* in 1911, which published articles by British and Australian soldiers on aspects such as 'infantry formations in the attack, modern musketry training, aviation, wireless telephony and night operations'.[23] Australia also had access to

---

[19] See R. A. Preston, 'The Military Structure of the Old Commonwealth', *International Journal* 17 (2) (1962), pp. 98–121.

[20] TNA, CAB 18/12A, Imperial Conference: Proceedings, vol. 1, 1909, p. 21.

[21] Out of the thirteen officers, Cyril Brudenell White, Henry Macartney, Edgar Reynolds, Cecil Foot, and John Lavarack were Camberley graduates. Edmond Brockman, Eric Harrison, Thomas Blamey, and J. C. O'Brien were Quetta graduates. John Gellibrand, Duncan Glasfurd, Charles Gwynne, and Francis Irvine were British officers that had graduated from Camberley.

[22] TNA, CAB 18/13B, Imperial Conference: Papers laid before the Conference 1911, 'Examination of the Promotion of Officers of the Permanent Forces of the Dominions', n.d., p. 9.

[23] 'Commonwealth Military Journal', *The Western Mail*, 17 June 1911. Publication of the *Commonwealth Military Journal* was suspended in 1916 for economic reasons, but also because 'officers do not require to have the theories of warfare put before them while engaged in the real thing'.

the United Services Institutes, established on the British model, in Sydney and Melbourne, where officers were able to read and discuss current military publications and literature from overseas.[24]

Along with shared publications and training, the CMF benefitted from the loan of British regular officers. These 'army apostles' were sent to the self-governing Dominions with the 'new gospel' of reform. Officers on loan were normally requested by governments to fill certain roles (if Dominion forces had no qualified personnel), or to teach.[25] The majority of officers on loan to Australia ended up on the directing staff at the Royal Military College, Duntroon, and included Colonel Charles Gwynn (Director of Military Art) and Colonel Ewen Sinclair-Maclagan (Director of Drill) – the latter going on to command the 4th Australian Division during the war.[26] Further loans were required to fill particular roles, including Duncan Glasfurd who was appointed Director of Military Training in 1912 to oversee and inspect compulsory training under the cadet scheme; Henry Clogstoun, appointed as Director of Works in 1912 to help reorganise Australian military engineers; and Harold Mackworth, appointed as Director of Army Signals.[27]

Attempts at interoperability and integration between Britain and Australia had steadily gained impetus during the few years preceding the First World War. However, one of the most important military encounters involving the two nations occurred concurrently with Australian federation: the Boer War. More than sixteen thousand Australians served, forming an integral part of the Imperial Army. For the most part, these Australian 'volunteers' served under British commanders, with some of the latter going on to play an important role in the AIF's development and integration during the First World War. These commanders included familiar names such as Rawlinson, Hamilton, Birdwood, Allenby, who had commanded a squadron of New South Wales Lancers, and Plumer, who had commanded a mixed force of Australians, Canadians, and Rhodesians at Mafeking. The latter two commanders were singled out for particular praise during the First World War. In a 1916 letter to George Pearce, Alec Godley was delighted to 'hear that the others [I ANZAC] have gone into General Plumer's army, as he had so many

[24] Grey, *Military History*, p. 77.   [25] Delaney, 'Army Apostles', pp. 174, 177–178.
[26] Seven of the eight military instructors at Duntroon were on loan from the British army. See Delaney, 'Army Apostles', p. 184.
[27] Glasfurd served as GSO1 1st Australian Division (1914–1916) and then as commander of 12th Brigade AIF (1916). He was killed in action on 12 November 1916. Clogstoun served as OC 3rd Field Company, AE (1914–1916); CRE 3rd Australian Division (1916–1918); and CRE XIII Corps (1918). Mackworth served as CO 1st Australian Division Signal Company (1914–1915); OC Signals, Dardanelles Army (1915–1916); DDAS, EEF (1916–1917); attached to AIF HQ, Cairo (1917–1918).

Australians under him in South Africa, and knew them and liked them, and they knew and liked him'.[28] Henry Gullett, the Australian official historian of the Sinai and Palestine campaign, was similarly complimentary about Allenby, recalling a visit in July 1917 to an Australian unit in the desert where the inebriated troopers struck matches on Allenby's staff car and 'almost leaned on him. The tighter they were the closer they wished to get to him'.[29]

Although they were under British command during the Boer War, some Australian officers did gain experience of staff work in British formations. The war also provided future AIF commanders and staff with the experience of operating within a larger British force. William Bridges, the original commander of both the AIF and the 1st Australian Division, had served in the Boer War in a divisional staff appointment before going on to become the first commandant of Duntroon and Inspector-General of the army. His war service brought him into contact with individuals such as Hamilton, while his staff appointments gave him credibility when dealing with British regular officers, particularly in Egypt. These personal contacts were vital. As one Dominion officer recalled, knowing personally the 'senior or opposite number in formations . . . is a factor possessing a value which needs no argument'.[30] In the 1st Australian Division, Boer War veterans were well represented in senior staff positions, with twelve of the fifteen officers having served in South Africa. The heads of the division's supporting units were all Boer War veterans except for the CRA.[31] Other notable AIF officers with Boer War experience included Brudenell White, Chauvel, Legge, John Gellibrand, and William Glasgow – all of whom would go on to hold senior appointments in the AIF during the First World War.[32]

The process of integrating Dominion forces also benefitted from the reports of the Inspector-General of Overseas Forces. These reports gave an insight into the state of each nation's force. Despite the greater alignment between Britain and her Dominions, inspections of the Australian forces in the years leading up to the outbreak of war did not make

---

[28] AWM, Papers of General Sir A. Godley, 3DRL/2233, Godley to Pearce, 27 April 1916.
[29] AWM, Papers of Henry Gullett, AWM40 69, Ts extracts from Gullett's original diaries and notebooks, 'General Murray', n.d.
[30] Crerar, 'Closer Relations', p. 445.
[31] D. M. Horner, 'The Influence of the Boer War on Australian Commanders in the First World War', in P. Dennis and J. Grey (eds), *The Boer War: Army, Nation and Empire. The 1999 Chief of Army History Conference* (Canberra, ACT: Army History Unit, 2000), pp. 178–179, 188.
[32] Brudenell White ended the war as MGGS Fifth Army; Chauvel as GOC Desert Mounted Corps, EEF; Legge as Inspector-General, Australian Military Forces; Gellibrand as GOC 3rd Australian Division; and Glasgow as GOC 1st Australian Division.

for pleasant reading. The 1912 and 1913 reports found that the forces were, by and large, as poorly trained and inefficient as they had been since federation.[33] Hamilton's inspection of the Australian forces in April 1914, though less damning, highlighted grave deficiencies in training and unit cohesion. The system in place was entirely suited to peacetime conditions, but unlikely to withstand the demands of war for more than a few weeks.[34] Referring to the Australian forces in a pitched battle, Hamilton suggested they would need a 2:1 majority to overcome regular European troops. This large margin was owing to the 'comparative lack of discipline and cohesion'. Given the limited training of recruits – sixteen days per annum, of which only eight were to be spent in camp – it is unsurprising that such deficiencies existed.[35] Of course, deficiencies were not limited to the Australian force. A comparison can be drawn with the British Territorial Force, where recruits were expected to attend annual training of between eight to fifteen days.[36] Where Australian staff officers were concerned, none of the brigade majors in Australia had received any formal staff training, while only three of six military districts had general staff officers. Faced with the prospect of rapid expansion and long-term conflict, the Australian staff and the broader training system were on the back foot on the eve of war.[37]

Formed on 15 August 1914 under the command of Bridges, the AIF initially constituted the 1st Australian Division (which Bridges also commanded) and the 1st Light Horse Brigade. As commander of the AIF, Bridges reported directly to George Pearce in Melbourne. In a September 1914 Order of Council, Bridges was given powers to promote officers, to change and vary units, to transfer officers and men, and to hire and transfer civilian employees where necessary.[38] This authority resulted in a number of clashes with senior generals, including Birdwood (GOC ANZAC) and Maxwell (GOC, Egypt). In some cases, Bridges was 'subordinate to Birdwood, in most areas Birdwood was subordinate to Maxwell, but in other areas Bridges was supreme'.[39] To simplify matters, Bridges insisted on working through Birdwood in all dealings with the base in Egypt. After Bridges's untimely death at Gallipoli in May 1915, command of the AIF initially passed to an Australian, Colonel James Legge, before he was ousted in favour of Birdwood in September

[33] Bou, 'Ambition and Adversity', p. 81.   [34] Grey, *Military History*, p. 78.
[35] AWM, AWM1 20/5, 'Report on Inspection of the Military Forces of Australia', 24 April 1914, pp. 11, 45.
[36] War Office, *Manual of Military Law* (London: HMSO, 1907), p. 699.
[37] Delaney, 'Army Apostles', p. 185.
[38] Quoted in Faraday, 'Higher Administration', p. 43.
[39] AWM, Papers of C. E. W. Bean, AWM38 3DRL/606 255/1, White to Bean, 8 May 1924.

of the same year. As with Bridges, Birdwood held dual command, as GOC of both the AIF and, in this instance, I ANZAC. As we shall see later, this caused consternation amongst generals and politicians. Birdwood remained undisputed administrative head of the AIF in all theatres, including Egypt and Britain, until the Armistice.

The AIF's command and administration remained stable after Birdwood's appointment, but a secretarial infrastructure was still required back in the UK. Although a base depot had been established in Egypt under Colonel Victor Sellheim in January 1915, the Australian wounded from Gallipoli were often transferred back to Britain. This led to the creation of the Australian Administrative Headquarters in London in October 1915, under the command first of Colonel Sir Newton Moore and, subsequently, Robert Anderson. With the evacuation of Gallipoli in January 1916 and the eventual move of Australian forces to the Western Front, AIF Headquarters was transferred to London in May 1916 where it remained for the rest of the war.

Institutional Integration in the First World War

Although the initially tangled nature of the AIF's command and administration proved problematic, it was, as its name suggests, conceived as part of the British Imperial effort.[40] This required it to be integrated effectively into a British imperial military system to enable interoperability. This was achieved through the use of institutional integration methods, ranging from command appointments, attachments and mentoring, publications, and training schools. A fundamental framework was already in place, however: many of these methods were refinements of those used pre-war, albeit expanded by an order of magnitude. These methods are already familiar to us as the means through which the army learned more broadly. In this instance, these means were employed to teach the AIF about the British army and its role within it. Although there was some resistance and scepticism towards these methods, with questions around their efficacy, the AIF, on the whole, benefitted from them. The mistakes made when integrating the Kitchener divisions, for instance, had been largely resolved, particularly by the time the AIF arrived on the Western Front in early to mid-1916. However, the often strained relationship between the Australian government and the British military resulted in persistent tensions, the consequences of which were not always in the AIF's best interests.

[40] AWM, Bean Papers, AWM38 3DRL/606 255/1, White to Bean, 8 May 1924.

High Command: Lieutenant-General Sir William Birdwood

Despite a leavening of officers conversant with the army's processes, the AIF suffered from command inexperience, particularly at brigade level and above. Of the 1st Australian Division's original cadre of 631 officers, only ninety-nine were serving or retired members of British or Australian regular forces, while 104 had previous war experience.[41] This inexperience led to the widespread employment of British and Indian Army officers to command and staff the AIF. Birdwood, an Indian Army officer, was the most senior of these appointments. Though Bridges had overall command of the AIF, Birdwood had been appointed field commander of the ANZAC in November 1914. He identified his Boer War experience as one of the reasons for his selection:

My close contact with these excellent fellows laid the foundation of my very happy relations with the Australian and New Zealand troops throughout the War of 1914–18. Indeed, it was because he realised how well we had got on together in South Africa that Lord Kitchener selected me to command the combined Australian and New Zealand Army Corps in 1914.[42]

Birdwood had served as Kitchener's military secretary during the Boer War. It is likely that he owed his appointment as much to Kitchener himself as to his 'happy relations' with the Australians. Following the Boer War, Birdwood held the position of Assistant AG, India in 1904 and QMG, India in 1912. As an officer in the Indian Army, however, he sat somewhat apart from the British military establishment. There was still a snobbish prejudice against career Indian Army officers.[43] It is possible that this may have aided him in his command of the Australian forces. He, like them, was an outsider of sorts.

Despite holding the rank of lieutenant-general, Birdwood was predominantly a tactical commander. While in close contact with political movers and shakers, Birdwood did not advise the Australian government on strategy, nor did he command a campaign. Birdwood's corps undertook tactical missions directed by higher command. His skills were centred on man management. More of a leader than a commander, Birdwood relied to a great extent on his long-standing Australian chief of staff, Brudenell White, for the day to day running of the AIF. Owing to Brudenell White's proficiency, Birdwood was prone to 'always "buzzing

[41] P. Sadler, *The Paladin: A Life of Major-General Sir John Gellibrand* (Melbourne, VIC: Oxford University Press, 2000), p. 56.
[42] W. R. Birdwood, *Khaki and Gown: An Autobiography* (London: Ward, Lock, 1941), p. 124.
[43] Morton-Jack, *The Indian Army*, pp. 116, 265.

around", looking people up, perambulating all over the place, barely ever at headquarters and not *really* exercising command at all'.[44] Still, William Hughes, the Australian Prime Minister, deemed Birdwood to be 'a man in every way competent, who knows the Australian soldier and who is respected and loved and admired by him'.[45]

Though he had a keen eye for talent and was quick to identify poor performance, Birdwood was no martinet. Monash, for example, was suitably impressed by his chief's 'wonderful grasp of the whole business of soldiering'. He went on to note how

I have been around with him for hours and heard him talking to privates, buglers, drivers, gunners, colonels, signallers and generals and every time he has left the man with a better knowledge of his business than he had before. He appeals to me most thoroughly, and I think the Australasian Army Corps is most fortunate that Kitchener chose Birdwood as their Corps Commander.[46]

Brudenell White, who would have a long association with Birdwood both during and after the war, recalled Birdwood as a 'young (49) vigorous fellow with charming quiet manners' and a 'beautiful clear and honest nature – without any warps'.[47] As far as First World War generals go, Birdwood was relatively informal with his troops, which was not always popular with some of his peers. Lynden-Bell correlated the Australians' notorious indiscipline to Birdwood's familiar approach: 'It was the custom when Birdwood visited the trenches in Gallipoli for the Australians to say, "How are you, Birdie old boy", to which he would reply, "All right, sonnies"'.[48] Nevertheless, in Birdwood the Australians had a valuable leader that was respected by the Australian government, experienced in senior administrative positions, and furnished with proven people skills.

The AIF benefitted from Birdwood's command, particularly in the early days of his tenure. He kept the force 'contented and immune from outside interference' as well as 'free from intrigue'.[49] His appointment also helped mitigate the latent factionalism between permanent and militia officers. He was not subject to the same prejudices that would influence whether he believed a militia or regular officer to be most suitable for command or promotion. His candid views on the suitability of AIF senior officers for promotion were an important aspect of his

[44] P. Pedersen, *Monash as Military Commander* (Carlton, VIC: Melbourne University Press, 1985), p. 298. Original emphasis.
[45] LHCMA, Robertson Papers, 8/4, Hughes to Robertson, 12 April 1916.
[46] AWM, Monash Papers, 3DRL/2316 1/1, Monash to wife, 13 February 1915.
[47] NLA, White Papers, MS 5172 2.1/11, White to wife, n.d (c. 24 December 1914).
[48] IWM, Lynden-Bell Papers, 90/1/1, Ts account of Gallipoli campaign, n.d., pp. 9–10.
[49] BL, Birdwood Papers, MSS Eur D686/77, Monash to Pearce, 21 June 1918.

correspondence with George Pearce and Ronald Munro Ferguson, the Australian Governor-General. His correspondence with both men was prolific. Commenting on recent brigade appointments, for example, Birdwood wrote that commands had been given to 'Elliott, Glasgow, Irving and Glasfurd. The first named I have only put in temporarily so far, as I have heard conflicting reports as to his stability'.[50] Later in the war, Birdwood commented on the relative merits of Brudenell White and Chauvel, questioning whether the latter's success in Egypt 'is due to him' as he lacked 'great character or ability'.[51]

Birdwood's eye for talent, his reputation, and leadership qualities offered order and unity to an organisation that was initially ill-equipped and poorly trained for war. More importantly, however, his appointment streamlined the command system for Australian soldiers fighting overseas. He was, after all, de facto head of the AIF in all theatres. At the War Office, Birdwood's continuing control of the AIF was seen as self-serving and threatened to foment ill feeling between Birdwood and a number of senior generals.[52] Though appreciating his generalship, one British officer thought Birdwood like a cat:

[He] always wants stroking. A little douche of cold water frightens him away. Somehow these men who pin their hopes to the favour of various big men, are more sensitive to a little wholesome criticism than they need to be.[53]

Murray noted that Birdwood had 'a distinct eye to his future . . . He wants to remain at the end of the war everything to Australia', while Allenby deemed Birdwood's control, particularly over AIF troops in Palestine, as 'an absurdity'.[54] Robertson agreed with this assessment, observing that Birdwood had 'a way of communicating with the Government of Australia and getting them to put forward suggestions made by him'.[55] As the subject of these criticisms, Birdwood was aware of these whispers and intrigues: 'there is a great deal of jealousy against me at the War Office . . . also, they never look favourably upon the Indian Army officer'.[56]

---

[50] AWM, Pearce Papers, 3DRL/2222 3/1, Birdwood to Pearce, 20 February 1916.
[51] AWM, Pearce Papers, 3DRL/2222 2/11, Birdwood to Munro Ferguson, 9 May 1917.
[52] J. D. Millar, 'A Study in the Limitation of Command: General Sir William Birdwood and the AIF, 1914–1918', Unpublished PhD Thesis, University of New South Wales, 1993, p. 3.
[53] LHCMA, Hamilton Papers, 7/7/37, Pollen to Hamilton, 19 April 1916.
[54] IWM, Murray Papers, 79/48/3, Murray to Robertson, 23 March 1916; TNA, WO 106/718, Correspondence between General Staff, War Office and Egypt, Allenby to Robertson, 19 July 1917.
[55] LHCMA, Robertson Papers, 8/1/67, Robertson to Allenby, 1 August 1917.
[56] AWM, Birdwood Papers, 3DRL/3376 33, Birdwood to Munro Ferguson, 14 February 1917.

Birdwood's push to retain command of the AIF beyond 1916 – and the Australian government's ultimate support for this decision – blocked promotion opportunities for Australian officers.[57] In the Canadian Corps, Byng had made way for a Canadian officer, Arthur Currie, in April 1917. In Palestine, Harry Chauvel had been appointed to command the Desert Mounted Corps, again in April 1917, yet Monash did not take over the Australian Corps until May 1918 with Birdwood continuing to remain as head of the AIF. Though much admired by the men he commanded, Birdwood's retention of command encroached on the culture and identity of the AIF. Following Monash's appointment to command the Australian Corps, Chauvel, although 'very glad' that Birdwood retained administrative command, railed against the Australian government's inconsistency: 'they insist on having Australians commanded in the field by Australian officers, but allow the administration to be run by a British officer!'[58]

While not always viewed favourably and felt by some to be a poor choice for command, Birdwood played an important role in the initial integration of the AIF into the wider British army. He was well connected, and willing to use those connections – both in a careerist sense, but also with a degree of altruism – to better support his force. He was respected by senior Australian government officials, including the Prime Minister and Governor-General. However, as an Indian Army officer, Birdwood was able to capitalise on his outsider status. While his appointment elicited some negative responses from officers such as Elliott, he could act with a certain degree of autonomy, as well as legitimising change within the force.

Divisional Command

Command problems also manifested themselves at the divisional level. Appointments to divisional command, particularly after the expansion of the AIF in early 1916, were complex affairs.[59] The AIF was still reliant on a handful of professional Australian officers supplemented by Imperial officers. For some Australian officers, such as Elliott, this reliance on Imperial officers was a contentious issue. Commenting on Birdwood's command, he wrote that 'he ... has not handled Australians as long as I have, and has not studied them as I have done'.[60] However, as Birdwood

[57] Connor, *Anzac and Empire*, p. 123.
[58] AWM, Chauvel Papers, PR00535 4/13, Chauvel to wife, 11 July 1918.
[59] J. Bentley, 'Champion of Anzac: General Sir Brudenell White, the First Australian Imperial Force and the Emergence of the Australian Military Culture 1914–18', Unpublished PhD Thesis, University of Wollongong, 2003, p. 268.
[60] AWM, Papers of Brigadier H. E. Elliott, 2DRL/0513 3/4, Elliott to wife, 14 April 1916.

recalled in 1917, 'Imperial officers have been employed with the AIF only when Australian officers were not available', and that the 'dearth of qualified Australian officers was due in the first instance to our being such a young force and naturally requiring experience'.[61]

The appointment of Imperial officers underscored the tension between Australia's burgeoning national identity and aspirations for political devolution, and the need for military efficiency. Even in the early years of the war, the army had to be sensitive to the AIF's needs, particularly in its dealings with the Australian government. Godley experienced such sensitivity first-hand when deciding to appoint an Imperial officer as his divisional medical officer. A pre-war 'army apostle' to New Zealand, Godley understood the tensions involved when working with Dominion governments. Required to justify his nomination to Pearce, Godley argued that it was better to have an Imperial officer to 'act temporarily' owing to the 'naturally rather amateurish' medical arrangements. A regular officer would 'start them in the right way', he reasoned. Providing they had 'sufficient military knowledge and experience to carry on the job properly', it would then be possible to appoint an Australian or New Zealand officer.[62] Although it was important for Australian commanders to learn on the job, it was just as vital that the AIF had experienced individuals to guide it during its early years.

The high officer casualties sustained at Gallipoli, coupled with the AIF's expansion, led to a dilution of experience. Though the reliance on Imperial officers lessened, there was still widespread inexperience at divisional command. By March 1916, two Imperial officers (Harold Walker and Herbert Cox) commanded the 1st and 4th Australian Divisions, and two Australians (Legge and McCay) commanded the 2nd and 5th Australian Divisions, respectively.[63] Chauvel had also been appointed to command the Anzac Mounted Division. There was now an Australian majority at divisional command level, but this did little to quell the grumblings. The appointment of Cox to the command of the 4th Australian Division was particularly contentious and brought to the fore concerns around the favouring of Imperial over Australian officers. Once again, Pearce voiced his 'general feeling of disappointment' over the appointment, particularly given the experience of Australian commanders such as Chauvel and Monash.[64] However, Birdwood defended his decision, arguing how 'very much harder it must be to select Australian officers,

[61] BL, Birdwood Papers, MSS Eur D686/57, Birdwood to Defence Department, n.d.
[62] AWM, Godley Papers, 3DRL/2233, Godley to Pearce, 16 April 1915.
[63] The 3rd Australian Division was formed in February 1916 and was eventually commanded by Major-General John Monash.
[64] AWM, Pearce Papers, 3DRL/2222 3/1, Pearce to Birdwood, 4 February 1916.

when comparatively speaking few have had consistent and regular military training throughout their lives', and also that the number of permanent officers 'in the higher ranks is naturally small'.[65] Both Godley and Birdwood's experiences provided a snapshot of the frictions faced by Imperial officers who had to negotiate the demands of politicians back in Australia and the ongoing demands of operations.

Although desert training and operations at Gallipoli had given Australian officers experience of handling larger bodies of men, this did not instantly qualify them for higher command. Though the policy was increasingly unpopular with the Australian government, the British army, sensibly, determined that relatively inexperienced Australian officers should cut their teeth at lower levels of command before they were moved to senior positions. Monash, for example, had served as a brigade commander throughout the Gallipoli campaign, but his inexperience was obvious, particularly during the August offensive.[66] Pearce acceded to Birdwood's decision to appoint Cox, suggesting confidence in the latter's judgement, but insisted on being consulted on all AIF appointments above the rank of colonel.[67] With the command and staffing of the newly formed 3rd Australian Division, Pearce was much firmer and attempted to prevent the appointment of any British officers to that division. Birdwood was astute enough to recommend Monash for command of the division, along with Harold Grimwade, another Australian, as his artillery commander, commenting that 'the experience they are gaining with troops in France will be of the very greatest value'.[68] The raising and training of the 3rd Australian Division marked a turning point in the AIF's integration into the army. Its reliance on Imperial officers was markedly reduced, with Australian officers commanding all of its combat formations.[69] In short, the army demonstrated an aptitude for integration, taking into account and responding to the mores of its Dominion contingents.

Mentoring and Attachments

Along with command appointments, the army used mentoring and attachments to great effect when integrating new formations. As well as suffusing the AIF's command structure with much-needed experience, Imperial officers became instructors, trainers, and staff officers,

[65] AWM, Pearce Papers, 3DRL/2222 3/2, Birdwood to Pearce, 24 March 1916.
[66] R. Crawley, *Climax at Gallipoli* (Norman: Oklahoma University Press, 2014), p. 205.
[67] Connor, *Anzac and Empire*, p. 65.
[68] AWM, Pearce Papers, 3DRL/2222 3/2, Birdwood to Pearce, 3 July 1917.
[69] Its three brigade commanders, for example, were pre-war militia officers who had seen service at Gallipoli.

providing the AIF with a firm grounding in the elementary aspects of soldiering.

According to Bean, the 'Australian and New Zealand officers had to rely almost entirely on themselves'.[70] While an appealing sentiment, this was untrue. Through its senior generals, the AIF could access a number of experts who helped streamline the integration process. For example, during initial desert training, Godley expressed concern over the 'weak and inexperienced' staff and poor musketry training in Chauvel's Light Horse Brigade. In order to alleviate this inadequacy, he secured an Indian Army officer to act as a musketry instructor, doing the same for Monash's 4th Australian Brigade.[71]

These personal appointments were supplemented by the wider Imperial 'mentoring' system. Building on the greater interoperability between Empire forces, the War Office attached a number of qualified staff officers and commanders – 214 in total – to the Canadian Corps alone to 'command certain components and complete the connections of the staff nervous system'. This scheme enabled the Canadians to develop their own officers to eventually take over those functions.[72] The strength of the army's mentoring system can be partly attributed to the dynamic relationship between the mentor and the mentee. It was a relationship that not only allowed for the transfer of job-related knowledge, but also equipped the mentee with the tools to navigate the politics of a complex institution.[73] The fact that the army moved towards a formalised mentoring system for both staff training and greater Dominion interoperability showed that, as an organisation, it recognised the benefits of heuristic learning as a way of transferring knowledge between professionals and novices. As one Canadian staff officer recalled, there was a 'wonderful group of staff officers around us, the pick of the British army. They were absolutely superb . . . and they taught us very much'.[74] Another remarked that 'we counted the British officers who served with us part of our organization'.[75]

In the case of the AIF, this relationship is most obvious in the 3rd Australian Division. While Pearce had insisted on an all-Australian formation where possible, here a guiding hand could be found in the guise of two regular Imperial officers: Lieutenant-Colonels George Jackson as

---

[70] Bean, *Official History*, I, p. 139.
[71] AWM, Godley Papers, 3DRL/2233, Godley to Pearce, 30 March 1915.
[72] Delaney, 'Canadian Corps', p. 953.
[73] L. Kahle-Piasecki, 'Making a Mentoring Relationship Work: What Is Required for Organizational Success', *Journal of Applied Business and Economics* 12 (1) (2011), p. 46.
[74] P. Brennan, 'Julian Byng and Leadership in the Canadian Corps', in Hayes et al., *Vimy Ridge*, p. 98.
[75] Crerar, 'Closer Relations', p. 445.

GSO1, and Mynors Farmar as AA&QMG.[76] Both had experience of serving with Australian formations: Jackson had served as GSO1 to the 2nd Australian Division, and Farmar – a pre-war graduate of the LSE's army administration course – had worked with Australian troops during his time as brigade major to the 86th Brigade (29th Division). Sellheim and Brudenell White, both pre-war associates of Farmar, had recommended him for AA&QMG, with Birdwood agreeing to this appointment 'after inquiries...concerning work in Gallipoli'.[77] These two seasoned officers remained with the division for over a year. Upon their departure, their positions were filled by Australian officers: Robert Jackson was appointed AA&QMG in September 1917, while Carl Jess took over as GSO1 in January 1918.[78]

The departure of both Jackson and Farmar was political in nature, marking the beginnings of Australianisation – a key turning point in the AIF's integration. From as early as May 1917, the Australian government was agitating for the replacement of 'Imperial officers holding high AIF appointments'.[79] The policy was finally agreed in July 1917 with a telegram from Munro Ferguson to the British Secretary of State for the Colonies requesting the 'employment of Australian officers on the staffs'.[80] Birdwood received a letter five days later demanding that the men under his command

be constituted in purely Australian formations as far as possible and with Australian officers for commands and staffs. I have ascertained... the names of over 90 officers... employed under you who are not Australian, and while appreciating thoroughly the assistance given by the British army, I consider that units under your command should now be able to provide Australian officers for these positions. I shall be glad if you will prepare a list of Imperial officers whom you can now replace.[81]

One of those ninety officers was Mynors Farmar. Writing to his wife, he confirmed that 'the politicians in Australia are clamouring for the displacement of all British officers with Australian troops, saying that they stand in the way for promotion for Australians. They look upon a Staff Officer as a sort of carpet knight, an ornamental position which

---

[76] Mynors's brother, Major-General (George) Jasper Farmar, served as DAQMG to the Canadian Corps in a similar mentoring role.

[77] Swinfen Eady Collection, Papers of Colonel H. M. Farmar, Ts memoir, n.d., pp. 52–53; Farmar to wife, 30 December 1916.

[78] Farmar was appointed AA&QMG to the 35th Division in September 1917. Jackson remained as GSO1 until his promotion to command the 87th Brigade in January 1918.

[79] BL, Birdwood Papers, MSS Eur D686/57, Trumble to Commandant AIF London, 18 May 1917.

[80] Ibid., Munro Ferguson to Long, 30 July 1917.

[81] Ibid., Defence Department to Birdwood, 4 August 1917.

their political friends will ably occupy'.[82] Monash, who had developed a close friendship with Farmar, often staying with the family whilst on leave, was 'enraged at the thought', whereas Farmar confessed himself 'heartbroken to leave the division'.[83] Along with his personal attachment to the formation, Farmar remained concerned over the lingering problems of military experience and factionalism within the AIF: 'There are so very few Australians who have the military education or experience: and also, sad to say, few who are above chicanery for advancement or advancement for their friends'.[84]

Yet, even after the launch of Australianisation, Imperial staff officers were still used to mentor Australian commanders late on in the war, underlining the ongoing significance attached to the practice. This was evident in Harry Chauvel's case. Allenby's decision to place Chauvel – an Australian who was not *psc* – in command of the DMC, a mixed corps of eleven horsed brigades, five of them yeomanry, four Australian, one New Zealand, and one Indian, was unique in the war.[85] However, both Allenby and Lynden-Bell had reservations about Chauvel's ability. They believed that Chauvel would 'do all right in command', but his lack of 'higher military training' was identified as a major weakness.[86] Although he had the capacity for command, he would 'be improved by having a trained and experienced cavalryman as BGGS'.[87] Murray had noted Chauvel's weaknesses in the 'higher strategical and tactical handling of cavalry' in late 1916.[88] Chauvel was not ignorant of his own shortcomings. Unburdening himself to his wife, he confessed to

walking on pretty thin ice with all these people, and have been very lucky to have been able to hold my own; for they are naturally very conservative and I have neither been trained in the British cavalry or [*sic*] been to the Staff College. Sometimes, at the conferences at GHQ, when I look around the room and realise that I am absolutely the only one who is not in the British regular army and cannot put *psc* after my name, I do get a bit of a funk on lest I should be caught out in a want of knowledge on some technical point.[89]

Chauvel's concerns mirrored Farmar's observations on the military education of some AIF senior commanders, suggesting that Australianisation was not always the most suitable policy.

[82] Swinfen Eady Collection, Farmar Papers, Farmar to wife, 13 August 1917.
[83] Ibid., Ts memoir, n.d., p. 56.
[84] Ibid., Farmar to wife, 13 August 1917.   [85] Badsey, *Doctrine and Reform*, p. 286.
[86] TNA, WO 106/718, Correspondence between General Staff, War Office and Egypt, Lynden-Bell to Maurice, 18 July 1917.
[87] Ibid., Allenby to Robertson, 19 July 1917.
[88] LHCMA, Godley Papers, 3/193, Murray to Godley, 14 December 1916.
[89] AWM, Chauvel Papers, PR00535 3/2, Chauvel to wife, 14 February 1918.

Despite some opposition from both Chauvel and Chetwode, Richard Howard-Vyse was brought over from France as the new BGGS.[90] Though new to the Palestine theatre, Howard-Vyse's appointment was designed to support Chauvel as he moved from the command of a column to a corps. As a *psc* officer with former service on both Allenby and Chetwode's staffs in France, Howard-Vyse was well qualified for the job. Cyril Falls recalled how Chauvel needed 'some coaching in the early days of his big command', but 'British commanders and staffs were inclined to be too patronising in this respect, to the annoyance of Australians and Canadians'.[91] While this may have been the case at first, the relationship between Chauvel and Howard-Vyse proved productive soon enough. Chauvel believed him to be 'turning out very well indeed and is an extremely nice fellow'.[92] There was regret on Chauvel's part at Howard-Vyse's eventual departure to command the 10th Cavalry Brigade in July 1918. Incidentally, Howard-Vyse's replacement was Brigadier-General Charles Godwin – another Imperial officer. Godwin was also *psc* with a wealth of staff experience. As his 'most dashing Brigadier' and someone 'whom I like very much', Godwin's appointment was well received by Chauvel.[93]

Throughout his service in the First World War, Chauvel's chief staff officers were Imperial officers. This is unsurprising given his command of a multi-national corps. His correspondence – often candid in nature – does not betray any feelings of wounded national pride at not having an Australian chief of staff. In fact, Chauvel developed close relationships with his staff and other senior Imperial officers, notably Lynden-Bell: 'the only real friend I had left at GHQ'.[94] Arguably, Chauvel's background as a permanent officer, and his experience as Australian representative to the Imperial General Staff, served him well in his dealings with his Imperial colleagues. However, the AIF in Palestine, much like the EEF, was not afforded the same attention or priority as its counterpart in France. Birdwood's mandate as commander of the AIF enabled him to exchange and transfer personnel within or between units of the force.[95] As the larger force in the principal theatre, the AIF in France was able to call on talented officers in Egypt, thus limiting Chauvel's

90 Ibid., Chauvel to wife, 29 August 1917.
91 C. Falls, *Armageddon 1918: The Final Palestine Campaign of World War I* (Philadelphia: University of Pennsylvania Press, 1964), p. 173.
92 AWM, Chauvel Papers, PR00535 4/11, Chauvel to wife, 26 October 1917.
93 AWM, Chauvel Papers, PR00535 4/13, Chauvel to wife, 15 July 1918.
94 AWM, Chauvel Papers, PR00535 4/11, Chauvel to wife, 9 September 1917.
95 AWM, Pearce Papers, 3DRL/2222 3/2, Memorandum on Birdwood's powers as GOC AIF, 3 July 1916.

opportunity to secure a qualified Australian chief of staff such as Brudenell White, Jess, or Blamey.

By war's end, the AIF was primarily commanded and staffed by Australians as a result of the policy of Australianisation. However, these commanders had learned their trade with the advice and guidance of Imperial commanders and staff officers. In 1918, Monash commanded the Australian Corps, with Blamey as his chief of staff. At divisional level, of the seven formations, four were commanded by Australians, two by Imperial officers, and one by a New Zealander; while at brigade level, pre-war Australian militia officers dominated both the infantry and mounted commands.[96]

Like command appointments, attachments and mentoring provided the AIF with handrails whilst it learned its trade. The use of heuristic learning methods was widespread throughout the army. Although Imperial officers were seconded to Australia pre-war, the decision to formalise and expand these methods was in response to the increasing civilian make-up of the army, particularly from 1915 onwards. Yet for these approaches to work, it was important that the Imperial officers – essentially 'outsiders' to the AIF's culture and ethos – were temperamentally suited to their roles as instructors or mentors. Birdwood believed that Imperial officers must 'possess very much the velvet glove'. If handled right, the men 'will do anything to fall in with one's wishes', but if handled wrong, they 'will do nothing'.[97]

The use of Imperial officers was not always popular with the AIF, yet there were instances where a successful working relationship developed between the two groups: Monash and Farmar's relationship is a good example of this, while Charles Rosenthal often called in on his former divisional commander, Cox, when the latter was appointed to the India Office in early 1917.[98] This relationship was not limited to the AIF either. Canadian and Imperial officers found relations to be both cordial and professional. They understood the seriousness of the business in which they were engaged and simply got on with it.[99]

The mentoring scheme gave the AIF access to officers who had complete command of the mechanisms and staff procedures of the army, yet this often butted up against both the AIF and Australia's conception of itself as a semi-independent force. Writing to Munro Ferguson

[96] The four Australian divisional commanders were Glasgow, Rosenthal, Gellibrand, and Hobbs.
[97] BL, Birdwood Papers, MSS Eur D686/77, Birdwood to Macready, 22 June 1916.
[98] Mitchell Library, State Library of New South Wales [ML], Papers of General Sir C. Rosenthal, MLMSS 2739, Diary entry, 17 June 1917.
[99] Delaney, 'Canadian Corps', pp. 951–952.

in May 1917, Long hoped that 'it is not the wish of your Government that none but Australian officers should serve on staffs of Australian formations as they regard the staff generally as an Imperial organisation in which officers of Dominion and British Forces shall be considered interchangeable'.[100] The Australian government declined this proposal. One of the reasons given was 'the different systems of discipline, training, and administration governing the British army and the AIF'.[101] There were indeed differences in discipline and administration between the two forces. However, where training was concerned, this excuse was patently untrue.

Publications

The importance of command appointments and mentoring cannot be understated. However, publications and their subsequent influence on training school syllabi provided a basic, yet important, foundation. Although the Australian forces had access to British publications before the war, it is debatable how familiar the Australian officer would have been with these documents. As Bridges had dryly commented at the 1910 General Staff conference, *FSR* was about as useful to most Australian militia officers as 'the cuneiform inscriptions on a Babylonian brick'.[102] This belief correlates with Bean's view that Australians were not 'a material to be treated according to pure British drill-book methods'.[103] However, for the AIF to integrate and become a working part of the army, it needed to familiarise itself with these publications – a necessity that it took seriously.

According to Bean, initial training 'was simply the old British Army training. Little advice came from the Western Front'.[104] This was far from the case. The experiences of the Western Front exerted a powerful influence on the AIF and its commanders. One of Birdwood's first actions as field commander was to request 'copies of any instructional pamphlets you [the War Office] may have on points of training...on experience gained up to date in the war'. He subsequently followed this up with an urgent request for

Notes from the Front vols one and two 1500 copies of each. He [Birdwood] considers they would be invaluable and wants sufficient for issue to each officer of

[100] BL, Birdwood Papers, MSS Eur D686/57, Long to Munro Ferguson, 11 August 1917.
[101] Ibid., Trumble to Commandant AIF London, 18 May 1917.
[102] TNA, WO 279/496, General Staff officers conference, 17–20 January 1910, pp. 53–54.
[103] Bean, *Official History*, I, pp. 126–127.   [104] Ibid., p. 139.

his command. If more are available they could with advantage be distributed to NCOs also. He would also like three hundred copies each of Lecture by [Brigadier-General R. A. K.] Montgomery, *Notes on Artillery in the Present War*, and *Notes on the Use of Plane Tables with Artillery*, for use of artillery officers and higher commanders.[105]

On 2 April 1915, the 4th Australian Brigade received *Notes on Artillery in the Present War*, suggesting that certain formations of the AIF were made aware of the latest developments and were most likely trained in them, too.[106] This 'experience gained in France' was also disseminated in the form of lectures. Monash recalled a lecture by an Imperial staff officer on grenade training which referred to rifle grenade tactics then used on the Western Front.[107] Rosenthal, on the other hand, described a lecture on artillery based on 'a pamphlet issued by the War Office giving details of the front'. The effect of the lecture reinforced the seriousness of the task ahead, and led him to reflect on 'how few of us will return to Australia'.[108]

Along with the most recent publications, Birdwood also procured specimen maps from France, copies of the latest BEF Standing Orders for corps, division, and brigade, as well as *FSR* and all manner of War Manuals.[109] The appointment of Imperial officers proved particularly useful in conveying the latest British best practice. They already had a working knowledge of these central publications, providing strong foundations upon which the AIF could base its future training and development. One of Godley's divisional conferences in January 1915 drew attention to the fact that 'officers on the continent do not read *Field Service Regulations* Part II sufficiently'. If the men were short of rations or equipment then it would be 'the fault of senior officers in not having read their *Field Service Regulations Pt II* which tell you how to obtain everything, and deal with any administrative difficulty'.[110] The same conference also highlighted the need for every officer and senior NCO to read the 'various Notes and Pamphlets from the Front'. It is unsurprising

[105] AWM, Birdwood Papers, 3DRL/3376 11/12, Telegram, Delhi to War Office, 2 December and 24 December 1914.
[106] AWM, Monash Papers, 3DRL/2316 3/7, 'Notes on Artillery in the Present War'.
[107] AWM, Monash Papers, 3DRL/2316 3/38, 'Notes from a Lecture on Grenade Training Given by a Lt-Col J. Duncan', 16 March 1916.
[108] ML, Rosenthal Papers, Diary entry, 30 December 1914.
[109] AWM, Birdwood Papers, 3DRL/3376 11/12, Telegram, GOC Egypt to WO, 1 January 1915.
[110] AWM, Monash Papers, 3DRL/2316 3/6, 'Notes for GOCs Conference', 23 January 1915.

that, in a letter to his wife, Monash admitted that 'what is keeping me so busy is in getting to learn the ropes'.[111]

Notwithstanding the perennial issue of whether these publications were actually read, it is clear that the army expected the AIF to base its training around them to promote greater uniformity. The Australians took the publications seriously. In February 1916, the training of machine gun companies in the MEF was 'to be carried out on a common system in order to standardise knowledge', with reference to the latest publications from France.[112] Divisional conferences in 1916 often referred to existing publications, such as *SS109* and numerous translated publications from the French army.[113] Furthermore, Brudenell White's own papers contain a wealth of official SS pamphlets alongside Army and formation-specific publications, including the Fifth Army's 'Memorandum on Trench to Trench Attack by a Battalion Commander', and the 1st Australian Division's 'Artillery in Trench Warfare'.[114] A memo in Monash's papers warned of the dangers of 'reading *FSR I* unintelligently' and included a list of references from *FSR* and *Infantry Training* relating to infantry in open warfare. More importantly, this memo highlighted the need to 'read and try to apply' the principles within these manuals and suggested that, if the meaning was obscure, officers should 'ask for instances to be given by application of theory'.[115] One historian has suggested that the cultural, political, and institutional separation from Britain granted the Dominion forces a degree of flexibility not afforded to Imperial forces; that the lack of philosophical rigidity provided the AIF with a high level of learning flexibility, allowing lessons to be analysed and very quickly disseminated and applied.[116] This pragmatism was by no means unique to the Dominion forces, however. The very nature of the army's publications, along with its pragmatic attitude towards learning, encouraged a degree of flexibility in the tactical implementation of the publications throughout its various parts. The AIF was required to follow British guidance for the purposes of uniformity and interoperability, but units – both in the AIF and the wider British army – had the autonomy to experiment with tactics, techniques, and procedures.

---

[111] AWM, Monash Papers, 3DRL/2316 1/1, Monash to wife, 10 February 1915.
[112] AWM, AWM25 877/3, Training of Machine Gun Companies, Feb-April 1916, Memo, CGS MEF to GOC I ANZAC, 24 February 1916.
[113] AWM, Monash Papers, 3DRL/2316 3/41, Personal Notes on 2nd Division Conference, 23 June 1916.
[114] AWM, White Papers, 3DRL/1400 4/7.
[115] AWM, Monash Papers, 3DRL/2316 3/43, 'Notes on Conditions of Trench and Open Warfare', 18 August 1916.
[116] Bentley, 'Champion of Anzac', p. 300.

As the AIF gained experience, it took advantage of the autonomy that the British system permitted. In a memo to Brudenell White in February 1917, the commandant of the I ANZAC school questioned whether they were 'right in sticking to the 1914 book as to the advanced guard and infantry methods and formations? Should we not practice on the basis of a larger infraction on the enemy's front, the close support of mounted troops, by means of armed motor cars, busses, etc?'[117] His suggestion, while focused on tactical techniques, contested the guidance emanating from the top of the army, which recommended that 'the pre-war manuals remain in force', and that 'it is the duty of Commanders to see that the principles laid down in the manuals are adhered to'.[118] The commandant believed in the need for uniformity to a point. He agreed that 'the efficient carrying out in practice of all the latest methods, memorandum, experience from recent fighting... should be on absolutely clear cut lines'. But, for him, variety of method should be allowed, reflecting the needs and challenges of local conditions.[119] There was a need for standardisation and uniformity, but not to the point of being doctrinaire.

Training Schools

As previous chapters have revealed, the publications produced during the war fed into the army's various courses and schools of instruction across its operational theatres. During the AIF's initial desert training in early 1915, the system was in its infancy, leading to a greater reliance on individual commanders for the training of units. The inexperience of the newly raised Australian formations required them to learn the basics of soldiering from scratch. They were also required to adopt the new British company organisation.[120] Small unit training, particularly at platoon and company level, had to be extended before progressive and formation training could take place. The monotony of basic training was a source of frustration for the individual soldier thirsting for front line action. As one NCO observed, 'the men are fed up of it all and will not improve much more in fact I consider they are going backwards now they have been disheartened, constant promises and nothing coming of any of them'.[121]

---

[117] AWM, White Papers, 3DRL/1400 4/7, Ross to White, 4 February 1917.
[118] AWM, AWM25 947/76, Infantry Training France 1917 Memo, GHQ to GOCs Army, 6 May 1917.
[119] AWM, White Papers, 3DRL/1400 4/7, Ross to White, 4 February 1917.
[120] AWM, Papers of Lance-Corporal H. Gibson, PR03311, Gibson to family, 31 January 1915.
[121] AWM, Papers of Lance-Corporal F. O'Brien, PR83/26, O'Brien to family, 26 March 1915.

The extension of company training meant that battalion and brigade level training could not commence until February 1915. These larger exercises were overseen and umpired by senior commanders. Unfortunately, they were not always successful. Brudenell White admitted to 'feeling depressed' as a result of a poor divisional manoeuvre, whereas 2nd Australian Brigade's night attack in March 1915 was 'not good'.[122] Comments on the Australian and New Zealand Division's operations also highlighted significant deficiencies, some fundamental in nature, including the inadvisability of laying down 'hard and fast rules', indifference towards communications, and an 'injudicious' distribution of troops.[123] To compound matters still further, some formations completed progressive training quicker than others resulting in fluctuations in preparedness between formations. Monash recalled how 'we [4th Australian Brigade] have already taken part in three large Divisional Field operations with every man out and spread out over miles of country – while in the case of those who left Australia with Bridges, they have not, so far, although they have been in Egypt ten weeks, had a single day's Brigade training, much less Divisional training'.[124] In fact, Bridges's 1st Australian Division never got to the stage of divisional manoeuvres. The usefulness of these large-scale manoeuvres proved limited given the nature of terrain and the type of warfare experienced at Gallipoli.[125] The only tangible benefit of this desert training lay in the establishment of a tactical foundation upon which the units could build. However, training could not make up for the lack of experience, particularly at the junior levels of command, nor could it rectify weaknesses in staff work.

During the AIF's operations at Gallipoli, the training establishments in Egypt were overhauled to improve the training of AIF reinforcements and future drafts. These improvements can be largely attributed to the work of a British regular officer, Major-General James Spens (GOC, Cairo District). It was Spens's work that laid the foundations for the Australian and New Zealand Training Centre at Tel-el-Kebir. Spens was outside Australian jurisdiction, reporting instead to Maxwell, yet he established a system whereby each of the AIF's brigades at the front were represented by a battalion at the depot.[126] Staffed by British regular

---

[122] NLA, White Papers, MS 5172 1/3/21, Diary Entries, 5 March 1915 and 12 March 1915.

[123] AWM, Monash Papers, 3DRL/2316 3/6, 'Umpire's Notes on Divisional Operations', 19 February 1915.

[124] AWM, Monash Papers, 3DRL/2316 1/1, Monash to wife, 13 February 1915.

[125] P. Pedersen, 'The AIF on the Western Front: The Role of Training and Command', in M. McKernan and M. Brown (eds), *Australia: Two Centuries of War and Peace* (Canberra, ACT: AWM, 1988), pp. 169–170.

[126] Stevenson, *To Win the Battle*, p. 93.

officers, these battalions were designed to provide replacement personnel, producing good results from September 1915 onwards.

Following the evacuation from Gallipoli, AIF troops reorganised into four divisions in preparation for service on the Western Front.[127] To facilitate the training of reinforcements for these divisions, the training centre at Tel-el-Kebir came under GHQ control and was placed under the command of Major-General Steuart Hare, a British regular, in April 1916. Hare was supported by a number of regular British officers as instructors. Hare's remit was to 'take in hand the thorough and systematic training of all troops', but he was encouraged to correspond with Australian and New Zealand Headquarters on matters he considered necessary.[128] The situation he found at Tel-el-Kebir was far from satisfactory. Not only were there concerns around the discipline of Australian troops, but there was uncertainty around the command hierarchy. For the purposes of command and training, it was recommended that all of the AIF's training units come under Hare's command, with Colonel Reginald Spencer-Browne, the centre's Australian commandant, taking responsibility for the units' administration.[129] It was also recommended that training at the centre should be confined to company exercises.[130]

Once again, we see the authority and requirements of the British army butting up against those of the Australian government. Hare was unconvinced by the dual nature of the arrangement, recalling that 'Spencer-Browne is quite pleasant about it, but as I am responsible to GHQ for the training of all troops in the camp, and he is under me and yet is responsible to Gen[eral] Sellheim, the position is an impossible one'. The reason why this system eventually worked was due to Spencer-Browne's willingness to subjugate his authority to Hare. It was through personal accommodation and compromise that progress was achieved. However, if Spencer-Browne departed and a 'cantankerous and pigheaded man took his place', the system threatened to become unworkable.[131] For the Australian government, Spencer-Browne's subordination to Hare represented a direct infringement on the AIF's autonomy, particularly when concerns were raised over the former's suitability. Writing to Pearce,

---

[127] AWM, AWM25 721/78, Circular Memos re: reorganisation of AIF, February–April 1916.

[128] AWM, AWM255 88, Establishment of Australia and New Zealand Training Centre at Tel-el-Kebir, Lynden-Bell to Hare, 12 April 1916.

[129] AWM, AWM25 721/52, Suggested Organisation Tel-El-Kebir Training Centre, April 1916, Memo, 'Modus Vivendi for ANZ Training Centre' n.d., p. 1.

[130] AWM, AWM255 88, Establishment of Australia and New Zealand Training Centre, Lynden-Bell to Hare, 6 May 1916.

[131] IWM, Papers of Major-General Sir S. W. Hare, 09/86/1, Diary Entries, 15 and 18 April 1916.

Godley acknowledged that the centre was on a 'better footing', but Spencer-Browne's 'limitations do not admit of his satisfactorily training and administering such a large body of men. What is really wanted is a good, live, young, active, energetic Major-General. Possibly this may be supplied by the War Office in England'.[132]

Along with the reorganisation of the training centre, the AIF had access to a range of formal training classes, which ran under the auspices of the Imperial School of Instruction at Zeitoun. Besides courses for training officers and NCOs, it also ran machine gun, Lewis gun, signal and telephone, artillery, Stokes gun, and bombing classes.[133] To ensure equal training opportunities, the Imperial School was brought under the control of GOC Egypt with 50 per cent of vacancies allotted to the ANZAC.[134] Bringing the school under the command of GOC Egypt increased the potential for uniformity of training across formations still in Egypt. These higher level courses, which focused on the training of instructors and specialists, were designed to supplement divisional schools and individual training at unit level. The latter warranted particular attention given the dilution of experience after Gallipoli and the expansion of the AIF. In an attempt to mitigate the consequences of expansion, the ANZAC staff issued a series of circular memoranda to provide guidance on the most valuable types of training. These memoranda advocated 'section, platoon, company and specialist training', but 'too much close order drill must be avoided'.[135] Lectures and hints were aimed at young or recently promoted officers to ensure that their training kept the men interested. As one pamphlet outlined, 'owing to the limited military experience of many of the company and platoon commanders, it has been noticed that some of them soon get to the end of their ideas regarding training and then devise exercises which are of little value'.[136]

Both British and Australian higher commands raised concerns around the efficacy of the training conducted. Birdwood confessed he did not 'truthfully feel that any of them [4th and 5th Australian Divisions] are thoroughly trained divisions, and they are not equal in this respect to the two I took with me to the Peninsula last April'.[137] The British high command was far from charitable in its own assessment. In a private letter

[132] AWM, Godley Papers, 3DRL/2233, Godley to Pearce, 31 May 1916.
[133] Murray, *Despatches*, p. 8.
[134] AWM, AWM25 877/1, Courses of Instruction at ISI Zeitoun, GOC Egypt to GOC I ANZAC, 22 February 1916.
[135] AWM, AWM25 941/2 PART 2, Training Infantry – Egypt 1915–1916, 'Training Memo No. 1', 5 April 1916.
[136] AWM, Monash Papers, 3DRL/2316 3/38, 'Some Hints on Training', 21 March 1916.
[137] AWM, Birdwood Papers, 3DRL/3376 11/2, Birdwood to Wigram, 16 March 1916.

to Robertson in March 1916, Murray saw the Australians' 'lack of discipline and the inefficiency of their officers', as well as their 'enormous conceit in themselves' as considerable handicaps.[138] This evaluation was formalised in his official report on the efficiency of the 4th and 5th Australian Divisions in which Murray deemed the officers 'poor in military knowledge, and herein lies the chief trouble both as regards infantry and artillery. With good regular officers who know how to train and command them, the infantry would soon be turned into a magnificent fighting force'.[139] However, no regular officers were available to command the new Australian formations and, even if there had been, such a move would have meant negotiating a political minefield. Maxwell was inclined towards leniency in his own assessment. He suggested that the shortage of trained officers was due to the high casualties at Gallipoli, as well as there being 'no smart regular battalion to set a standard by'. For him, 'a Territorial Division in the making' was not conducive to the learning of discipline or soldiering.[140] Birdwood, fully aware of the limitations within the AIF's command structure, informed Pearce that he hoped 'to send all our young officers . . . to regular training schools either in England or France, before taking up their duties with the regiments. This will be a tremendous boon to us, and will ensure regiments [are] getting men who are, at all events, tolerably trained in the many details of company officers' work'.[141] This was a clear acknowledgement of the AIF's dependence on the army's training infrastructure and training methods.

Upon its eventual arrival in France, the AIF made considerable use of British training schools, particularly for the training of company commanders, platoon sergeants, and various specialists.[142] Notwithstanding their dominant position in Egypt, the I and II ANZAC were now just two out of eighteen corps in the BEF. More than ever, they had to adhere to the British way of working. Lieutenant-Colonel John Peck, for example, was the first Australian officer to attend Bonham-Carter's senior staff school. Bonham-Carter recalled that, when he first arrived, Peck was 'like a nervous foal bucking and blowing through his nostrils in his anxiety and fear that he would be treated with lack of friendliness or courtesy by a lot of stiff regular staff officers'.[143] However, Peck 'found himself

---

[138] IWM, Murray Papers, 79/48/3, Murray to Robertson, n.d (c. March 1916).

[139] AWM, AWM252 A108, 'Reports on Degree of Efficiency of Australian Divisions Prior to Leaving Egypt', 30 May 1916.

[140] LHCMA, Robertson Papers, 4/5, Sir John Maxwell to Robertson, 7 March 1916.

[141] AWM, Pearce Papers, 3DRL/2222 3/2, Birdwood to Pearce, 19 May 1916.

[142] AWM, AWM4 1/44/8, 2nd Australian Division GS War Diary, 29 March 1916. The I ANZAC school did not open until 11 November 1916.

[143] CAC, Bonham-Carter Papers, BCHT 9/2, Autobiography, n.d., p. 26.

among the friendliest and most generous minded lot of men he had ever met. He wanted to apologise for his former ideas and ignorance, and that no Australian would be allowed to run down the "Imperial" Army in his presence'.[144]

Through the use of military publications and the training school system, the British army promoted uniformity of method across its organisation. The AIF benefitted from these two institutional methods of learning during its own integration process. In the main, the AIF was required to conform to the British way of working, particularly in the opening phases of the war. However, enough flexibility existed within this institutional system to allow for innovation, individuality, and even divergence at the tactical level. As each commander trained his own formation, the possibility for divergence and individuality was increased. Nevertheless, this training was carried out within the formal parameters laid down in pamphlets such as *SS152*. As with schools in the other theatres, the various AIF training schools were modelled on *SS152*'s template. For the AIF to function as a working part of the broader army, this shared template was vital. Although 'the spirit of criticism and independence' allowed for great innovation and creativity in the AIF's tactical thinking, it is important to recognise that the AIF's learning process was intertwined with that of the entire army.[145]

Self-Integration

From its initial establishment to its blooding at Gallipoli, the AIF was subject to a fairly prescriptive, institutional integration process, which combined both personal and non-personal sources. Imperial officers were prevalent at all levels of command, and also played a role as specialist instructors. Memos abounded, gently reminding AIF officers to consult *FSR* or one of the many SS pamphlets published during the war. This degree of oversight was to be expected while the AIF learned the fundamentals of war.

While Gallipoli provided it with combat experience, it also led to a dilution of experience. This resulted in Imperial officers remaining in command positions. As the force gained in experience, the degree of prescription decreased. For the purposes of interoperability, the AIF was still expected to utilise existing publications and training infrastructure. However, its growing experience, particularly from May 1916 onwards, resulted in greater autonomy and a lighter touch from its Imperial overseers. Boosted later by the policy of Australianisation, it was this growing

[144] Ibid.   [145] Bentley, 'Champion of Anzac', p. 300.

experience that gave the AIF the opportunity and, arguably, the confidence to self-integrate.

The process of self-integration describes how newcomers proactively acquire knowledge and build relationships within a new organisation. Embracing both liberal and horizontal approaches to learning, commanders and formations within the AIF sought to gain an understanding of the wider army and their role within it. While institutional practices dominated the force's initial training and integration, it is possible to detect an increasing degree of self-integration running alongside these institutional methods, which ramped up when AIF formations reached the Western Front. In many cases, self-integration involved making use of existing institutional systems, such as imitating publications or schools, or forging new relationships. However, there were instances where self-integration was more inventive.

After being invalided from Gallipoli, Rosenthal appealed to the War Office to be sent on a 'trip' around the Western Front during his period of recuperation. Incessant in his demands to the War Office, Rosenthal was a man who took his soldiering profession seriously. Between his arrival in England in mid-October 1915 and his eventual departure for the Western Front on 1 December, he had petitioned the War Office at least four times. During his trip to France, he was billeted with the 1st Division, spending time with both General Staff and artillery headquarters. His diary contains numerous and often quite specific details on establishments, enemy dispositions, gun emplacements, and the various fuzes in use within the 1st Division and IV Corps more broadly. Rosenthal was impressed with what he saw, particularly where training was concerned:

Attended lecture at night given by an Engineer captain regarding construction and maintenance of trenches. I gave them details of our trench work at Gallipoli. Lecture held in large Residence set apart for instructional purposes. Any officers who in the immediate future are to have command of companies etc are withdrawn from units and put through a thorough course, inspecting the fronts during the day and receiving instructions from lectures at night.[146]

This opinion was reinforced during his tour around the 1st Division's courses of instructions:

Selected and proved officers and NCOs are appointed as Instructors and a proportion of men from each battalion is put through a fortnightly course of instruction. I saw all varieties of hand grenades and bombs successfully thrown in actual trenches specially prepared . . . General Staff gave me book on bombs etc.[147]

[146] ML, Rosenthal Papers, Diary entry, 6 December 1915.
[147] Ibid., 10 December 1915.

In total, his tour lasted twelve days and provided him with much food for thought. He had spent time with the heavy artillery, the neighbouring French artillery, at training schools, and also in the front line trenches near Mazingarbe and Hulluch. Rosenthal noted the kindness of the 1st Division who had 'given me every facility for observing the frontage here and there'. Prior to his departure, the 1st Division and IV Corps also provided him with samples of shells and fuzes, aerial photographs of Loos, and 'maps etc, so that all future movements of troops in this area I shall be able to follow with ease when I have returned to Gallipoli'. Upon returning to his formation, which was now based at Tel-el-Kebir, Rosenthal shared these maps with his subordinates, and discussed the findings of his trip with colleagues.[148]

As well as underlining the degree of proactivity required for self-integration, Rosenthal's trip also marked him out as a 'thinking officer'. The relationships that he built up with both Major-General Sir Arthur Holland (GOC, 1st Division), and Brigadier-General Garnier Cartwright (CRA, 1st Division) would be renewed at various points during the conflict either through proximity in the front line or at gunner conferences. Holland was a particularly useful contact. He was well respected by General Sir Henry Wilson, while his expertise and innovation in artillery training was recognised by Allenby, Haig, and Robertson.[149] Rosenthal recognised this, as did Winterbotham in 1914 and Gillman in mid-1917 when visiting Holland's I Corps training schools.

Where possible, attempts were made locally to try and integrate British and Australian officers in a more social setting. On Christmas Day 1915, Rosenthal was aboard a troop ship bound for Cairo. The size of the dining saloon usually necessitated Australian officers dining at 6pm, followed by the British at 7pm. However, on that special day, 'we divided the officers into groups with an equal number of British and Anzac officers, thus ensuring a better knowledge of each other'.[150] The importance of getting to know one another was another means of harnessing the army's social ethos in support of operational cohesion and effectiveness.

Localised attachments also took place in the front line, proving their enduring worth as a means of acquiring and disseminating knowledge. The Australians were familiar with this practice as they were employed in a similar capacity to instruct incoming Kitchener Army divisions

---

[148] Ibid., 8–12 December 1915 and 10 January 1916.
[149] See K. Jeffery, *Field Marshal Sir Henry Wilson: A Political Soldier* (Oxford: Oxford University Press, 2006), p. 159; LHCMA, Robertson Papers, 7/6, Robertson to Haig, 25 September 1916.
[150] ML, Rosenthal papers, 25 December 1915.

at Gallipoli.[151] Arranged by individual commanders as a way of self-integrating, units were able to benefit from the rapid transmission of experience and information from long-serving, often British, formations on the Western Front. In March 1916, for example, officers and men from each battery in the 1st Australian Division were attached to the 9th Division's artillery for instruction. In April of the same year, five officers and twenty ORs were attached to the 28th Brigade.[152] The AIF divisions that arrived on the Western Front in June 1916 took advantage of the experience already gained by the 1st and 2nd Australian Divisions in a similar fashion. Rosenthal, then temporary commander of the 4th Australian Division, actively liaised with the divisional and artillery headquarters of the 1st and 2nd Divisions, as well as the New Zealand Division, regarding the 'attachment of officers and men for instruction'.[153]

The 3rd Australian Division received far more systematic training than its sister divisions with full use made of the army's manuals and wider training infrastructure, yet it too showcased a number of methods of self-integration. Not only did Monash have two Imperial staff officers to support him, he also had access to the existing schools system as well as his own experience of fighting on the Western Front to draw on. As a commander, Monash was preoccupied with practicality: the AIF had '20 months experience of war [and] there will not be a minute wasted in teaching things the men will afterwards have to unlearn. My 6 weeks in France will be a powerful help to me in this respect'.[154] Having witnessed first-hand the benefits of the school system, he took full advantage of it, sending his officers and NCOs to Army schools and courses – both in Britain and France – to be trained as instructors.[155] In one of his first conferences as commander, Monash outlined his attitude towards training and instruction, noting the importance of getting 'instructors away to courses and carry[ing] on instruction of others concurrently', as well as pressing for the 'higher training of officers at divisional school in subjects such as reconnaissance, order and message writing'.[156] He was also desirous for 'experienced officers' from France, in order to benefit from their 'better understanding of requirements'.[157] Using the I

[151] AWM, Birdwood Papers, 3DRL/3376 11/6, Birdwood to Kitchener, 18 August 1915.
[152] TNA, WO 95/1734/2, 9th Division GS War Diary, 31 March 1916 and 14 April 1916.
[153] ML, Rosenthal Papers, MLMSS 2739, Diary entry, 19 June 1916.
[154] AWM, Monash Papers, 3DRL/2316 1/1, Monash to wife, 22 July 1916.
[155] AWM, Monash Papers, 3DRL/2316 3/43, Report by Major-General Sir Francis Howard, 27 August 1916.
[156] AWM, Monash Papers, 3DRL/2316 3/42, Notes from Conference with Monash, 21 July 1917.
[157] NLA, White Papers, MS 5172 2.4/25, Monash to White, 22 August 1916.

ANZAC's circular memoranda as a template, the 3rd Australian Division issued its own version: the 'training circular'. These circulars were easily digestible, distilling basic tenets on the importance of training schools, use of the bayonet, and how to be an effective platoon commander.[158] Acting as building blocks, these circulars also made reference to official pamphlets, which were to be consulted once these basic principles were understood.

To supplement these institutional methods, heuristic learning was also practised with the establishment of 'The Bustard' trench system at Lark Hill on Salisbury Plain. The 3rd Australian Division dug 'The Bustard' between August and September 1916 for the purpose of familiarising troops with trench conditions, including the experience of live-fire training. Monash aimed for a system where brigades could 'go to live for several days...and then carry out a complete relief'.[159] This system would be used to simulate assaults, practice reliefs, and consolidate positions. During his own training at The Bustard, one Australian signaller recalled the rather punishing routine experienced by the infantry who were 'busily engaged in different sham fights and bayonet charges... orders came from the brigade saying certain movements were to be performed, and despite any weather had to be carried out'.[160] Drawing upon his own experience, Monash was keen to add realism and atmosphere wherever possible, hoping to involve the artillery and RFC during exercises.[161] He was taking no chances with the preparation of his force. In the weeks prior to the division's departure for France, a complex 'stunt' was arranged involving the detonation of a mine, infantry consolidation, supported by RFC contact planes, and a creeping barrage.[162] The decision to establish this working trench system demonstrated greater autonomy and training sophistication within the AIF. While not perfect, it at least gave the men of the 3rd Australian Division a taste of manning a muddy trench system in the pouring rain.

Although Monash was given a free hand in the training of his command, he was still subject to quality control through a series of inspections by British regular officers. These officers included Generals Sir Henry Sclater (GOC, Southern Command), Sir Francis Howard

---

[158] AWM, Monash Papers, 3DRL/2316 3/42.

[159] NLA, Papers of General Sir J. Monash, MS 1884 71/481, Monash to Birdwood, 2 August 1916.

[160] AWM, Papers of A. E. Forbes, PR03583, Diary, October 1916, pp. 23–24.

[161] M. Molkentin, 'Training for War: The Third Division A.I.F. at Lark Hill, 1916', AWM Summer Scholarship Paper, 2005, p. 26.

[162] AWM, Monash Papers, 3DRL/2316 3/43, Artillery Group Operation Order No. 2, 2 November 1916.

(Inspector of Infantry), and Field Marshal Sir John French (CinC, Home Forces). In a letter to his wife, Monash complained that his division was 'being inspected to death, and it does disturb the training so'.[163] However, such inspections were necessary in order to identify areas for improvement. In August 1916, Howard's tour drew attention to the 'elementary stage' of bayonet training in the 3rd Australian Division owing to 'the different systems obtaining in Australia and with us'. Howard went on to suggest the value of despatching British instructors to Australia in order to 'guide it in the right lines'.[164] For the most part, Howard's review was favourable, and concluded with the remark that 'the Division promises so well that if left intact and supplied with rifles it should be ready to go out fully trained in the class of warfare now obtaining by the 3rd week in October at the latest'.[165] Howard's prediction was not far off the mark: the 3rd Australian Division arrived on the Western Front in November 1916.[166]

Efforts at self-integration and improvement were also evident in the EEF's DMC. Chauvel and Howard-Vyse sought to improve the quality of the corps's newly commissioned Australian Light Horse officers with the establishment of a 'School for Young Officers'.[167] Based on *SS152*'s guidance, the school sought to instruct 'lately commissioned officers...in their duties as officers, and in the tactics of troop leading'.[168] It aimed to supplement instruction provided at the GHQ schools at Zeitoun, as well as that found in divisional schools and courses of instruction. Convinced of its necessity, GHQ authorised the establishment of the school, which opened on 18 February 1918. The majority of its instructors were drawn from Australian formations, and priority was given to those officers who had been commissioned from the ranks to help them acclimatise to the rigours of command.[169] Its establishment not only highlights the army's flexibility in responding to demand, but also serves as yet another example of AIF commanders and units utilising existing army infrastructure to ensure the continued and efficient training of their officers. Despite these intentions, as well as the infrastructure and expertise at the AIF's disposal, the constraints of time and the demands of war remained major challenges. Yet in the face of these

[163] AWM, Monash Papers, 3DRL/2316 1/1, Monash to wife, 3 September 1916.
[164] AWM, Anderson Papers, PR83/020, Monash to Anderson, 22 November 1916.
[165] AWM, Monash Papers, 3DRL/2316 3/43, 'Report on 3rd Australian Division by Major-General Sir Francis Howard', 27 August 1916.
[166] AWM, AWM4 1/46/1, 3rd Australian Division GS War Diary, 24 November 1916.
[167] AWM, AWM25 877/12, Establishment of School for Young Officers, Howard-Vyse to CGS EEF, 17 January 1918.
[168] Ibid., Howard-Vyse to GOC Australian Mounted Division, 13 April 1918.
[169] Ibid., Howard-Vyse to COs, 31 January 1918.

challenges, the AIF did not simply maintain its success in integrating, but built on it to become a corps d'élite.

Conclusions

In an address to his senior officers in the 3rd Australian Division, Monash declared that success came down to a 'community of ideals, aims [and] purposes'; that 'uniformity of view' was a vital precursor to success in battle.[170] Monash was correct in that uniformity of training and method was essential for the purposes of interoperability and unit cohesion. However, this was by no means the whole story. Rather than pursuing a doctrinaire approach in its dealings with the AIF, the army was sensitive to the various new sub-cultures that existed within its organisation, along with the particular social, cultural, and political mores of national contingents. In the case of the AIF, these mores were not always easy to negotiate. This sensitive attitude revealed an overwhelming preference for autonomy and initiative that continued to reinforce the army's pre-war ethos. Of course, institutional integration methods were used to great effect, providing building blocks and enabling the AIF to learn the ropes. These methods incorporated both interpersonal and non-interpersonal means. This blended approach not only shows that the AIF was not treated 'according to pure British drill-book methods', but it is also testament to the army's increasingly sophisticated understanding of learning and knowledge sharing.[171]

The army did not have a standardised approach to integration. Though there was commonality in the methods used, the process was kaleidoscopic, varying between theatres, forces, and, often, formations. The army was reasonably effective at gauging when it needed to intervene and when it needed to step back – a motif present throughout its wartime learning experience. By refusing to enforce a standardised process, the army increased the likelihood that formations would develop their own personalised and, arguably, more effective approach. AIF formations and their commanders were encouraged to self-integrate, arranging their own attachments schemes, along with hands on measures, such as the development of 'The Bustard' system. While self-integration may seem inevitable in a hierarchical bureaucracy, the actions of these AIF formations actually underscored the army's institutional flexibility. Tactical innovation, in particular, was encouraged, allowing

---

[170] AWM, Monash Papers, 3DRL/2316 3/42, Notes on 'Three Talks to Senior Officers', 15 October 1916.
[171] Bean, *Official History*, I, p. 126.

for the character and individuality of formations to shine through. The success of this combined institutional and individual integration process is evident. As one general remarked, 'it is not possible to turn civilians into trained commanders in a few months – the wonder is that they have picked up so much and done as well as they have!'[172]

[172] AWM, Birdwood Papers, 3DRL/3376 2/4, Plumer to Birdwood, 14 April 1917.

Conclusion
Learning to Fight

I would like to emphasise how to study history. The real value is not a remembrance of dates or numbers or details, but first and foremost the study of human nature. For successful war depends on a knowledge of human nature and how to handle it.[1]

– General Sir John Shea

Logically, no doubt, the campaigns in Syria and Palestine, which caused the final overthrow of the Turkish military powers in the great war between the Central Powers of Europe and the rest of the civilised world, ought to be dealt with as part of a whole which should include the campaigns in Dardanelles, Macedonia, in Mesopotamia and the Caucasus, in Arabia, Palestine and Syria. Even so the story would be only part of a greater whole, directly influenced by varying policies in the main theatre of war, by the shifting strategic views of statesmen, by sea power and a hundred other considerations.[2]

– Major-General Guy Dawnay

When the guns fell silent on 11 November 1918, the British army had fought across the fields of France and Flanders, the deserts of Mesopotamia and the Sinai, the mountains of Italy and Salonika, the craggy cliffs of Gallipoli, and the savannah of East Africa. It had expanded from a small, professional force into a mass, multi-national citizen army. It had fought not only with fists and bludgeons, but also with brains and rapiers. In short, at war's end, it was a military both experienced and transformed.

Learning within the army was more complex than previous historians have allowed. It was expansive. It encompassed more than just operational and tactical considerations. The army proved to be effective and institutionally capable of learning and adapting both on and beyond the Western Front. It was willing and able to draw on and use the expertise

---

[1] LHCMA, Shea Papers, 6/3a, 'The Study of Military History as Exemplified by the Palestine Campaign 1917–18', n.d.

[2] IWM, Dawnay Papers, 69/21/1, Lecture on Gallipoli and Palestine, n.d, p. 1.

240

of its allies and enemies, as well as that from other disciplines and walks of life. The overall effectiveness of its process for learning was contingent on a number of different factors. The army's ethos enhanced its ability to learn and adapt. It also influenced its approach to learning. Out of necessity, it was required to prioritise, blend, and, at times, modify different ways and means for learning. This diversity of approach was underpinned by its organisational flexibility, which enabled it to integrate civilians, combat formations, and national contingents. Through a combination of this flexibility and its ethos, the army promoted a culture of innovation across its operational theatres where individuals were given the opportunity to influence institutional behaviour.

Fundamental to the army's learning effectiveness was the influence of its two-stranded pre-war ethos, comprising the social and the intellectual. This proved an important and enduring framework throughout and beyond the First World War. Though the army expanded and changed almost beyond recognition, both the social and intellectual ethos, evident before 1914, survived intact. Its enduring nature was, in part, due to wider social and cultural aspects. It was shaped by the values of civil society. In some respects, civilians who joined the army already had a latent understanding of it. Its survival was also ensured through implicit and explicit means. The regular army still dominated the highest levels of command. CinCs and senior generals were able to impress this ethos on to lower levels of command. Attachments and mentoring schemes offered another implicit way of instilling this ethos, as seen with the integration of the AIF formations. Publications and training schools promoted it explicitly. Pre-war manuals such as *Infantry Training* and *FSR* were used throughout the war, and, where possible, regular army instructors were sought to run training schools across the various expeditionary forces.

This ethos provided the army with flexibility. It was vital in the creation of a fertile environment for learning. It enabled the army to recalibrate its approach to learning quickly in response to its increasingly civilian composition. Such an approach stands in stark contrast to Paul Kennedy's belief that the army 'did not encourage open discussion and reassessment', remaining wedded to 'cultural norms of loyalty, defence, and unthinking courage'.[3] It also challenges Williamson Murray's assertion that 'the bureaucratic framework and the culture of the pre-war period ensured that learning took an inordinate amount of time'.[4] The army

---

[3] Kennedy, 'Britain in the First World War', in Millett and Murray (eds), *Military Effectiveness*, pp. 53–54.

[4] W. Murray, *Military Adaptation in War* (Cambridge: Cambridge University Press, 2011), p. 22.

realised early on in the war that principles and pragmatism were adequate for those who had military experience, but for newcomers they were not enough. It therefore embarked upon a far more systematic approach to knowledge capture and dissemination. This also extended to the subsidiary theatres. While this policy was criticised by detractors post-war, who accused the army of encouraging the impression that there was 'a stereotyped right answer', it was a necessary response to the influx of citizen soldiers.[5] Although knowledge was often disseminated in a standardised format, it still remained for each force to decide whether to ignore or adapt the instructions it received. The various expeditionary forces and, indeed, the corps and divisions within them were not unitary. They each had their own idiosyncrasies and ways of operating. On the Western Front, for instance, Third Army (initially commanded by Allenby and then Byng) and Fourth Army (under Rawlinson) were innovation hubs. Innovators like Hemming and Maxse were encouraged by a leadership constellation that identified their talents and smoothed over initial resistance to their ideas. In short, the army was a culture of sub-cultures when it came to learning. Yet, these sub-cultures and idiosyncrasies were still consonant with the values and norms of the army's wider ethos.

This ethos also influenced the army's ways and means of learning. The relationship between learning and ethos was one of reciprocal interdependence. In this respect, the study supports Foley and Catignani's respective research into the impact of culture on learning. The army's ways and means of learning were interlocking and often mutually supportive. However, by separating out these two areas, we are rewarded with a more complex and expansive view of learning in time of war. Too often are the army's methods for learning, such as SS pamphlets and training schools, conflated with its ways of learning. By understanding the latter, we are able to understand better why it prioritised or developed certain methods for learning. This study's networked model of military learning offers a new way of examining the learning process. It moves us away from the formal-informal dynamic that has been the mainstay of existing scholarship. It reveals the interconnectedness of different types of learning, whether formal or informal, individual or organisational, bottom-up or top-down. It also forces us to take note of the blockages and the constraints that existed within this network. Recognising that learning can only occur in an organisation rich in connections and relationships requires us to acknowledge the role of the

---

[5] LHCMA, Kirke Papers, 4/4, 'Notes by Major-General Arthur McNamara on Training', May 1932, p. 2.

individual within the organisation and their ability to influence organisational behaviour.

Where the army's methods for learning are concerned, this study provides a point of departure from Foley's assertion that the British army prioritised informal methods. Shaped by its ways of learning, the army's methods were diverse, constituting institutional and individual, systematic and incidental, printed and pictorial, oral and visual. These means were used in different ways, at different times, and in different combinations. In the opening months of the war, the army pursued an initially ad hoc approach, but it was not long before it recognised the need for a central knowledge repository. Even so, this repository was evolving, reflecting the army's institutional flexibility. Publications were amended to reflect battlefield developments or in response to the changing learning needs of its readership. While the deluge of publications and training schools across all theatres suggests a heavy-handed, interventionist approach, this was far from the case.

Though publications and training schools remained in force throughout the war, informal methods were by no means any less important or any less prevalent. As in other large organisations and indeed with modern militaries today, individuals turned to each other, gathering knowledge unofficially. By doing so, the problem of knowledge lag could be partially mitigated, enabling individuals to access up to date tactical information without having to wait for its formal codification. The social strand of the army's ethos underpinned such connections between individuals, whether through shared military service, attendance at the same public school, or other social circumstances. The army recognised and attempted to exploit these exchanges whether through smoking meetings, conferences, or the phenomenon of 'smartening friction'.

Of course, the army was not able to capture all incidental exchanges. The casual interactions between former colleagues, or between members of neighbouring divisions might facilitate rapid adaptation, but it also proved a weakness. The use of social networks exacerbated the tendency of the army to lose or forget knowledge.[6] In some instances, we see individuals and groups of individuals taking matters into their own hands, often through unofficial publications. Within some branches, such as mining and signalling, this resulted in some success. The development of *Mining Notes* provided a rapid, systematic way of codifying incidental exchanges, capturing low level experiences, and disseminating them both vertically and horizontally. Rather than solely focusing on the topdown distribution of SS pamphlets, an examination of other methods,

---

[6] Catignani, 'Coping with Knowledge', p. 59.

such as *Mining Notes* and more incidental exchanges, has shown that both Foley's and Kollars's conceptions of horizontal learning are equally applicable to the British army.

While revealing the army's adaptability, these varying approaches to learning also reveal additional organisational tensions: ad hocism versus standardisation, principles versus prescription, and diversity versus uniformity. The publication of *SS152*, for example, typified these tensions with its simultaneous call for uniformity and diversity of method; while the army's vacillation between ad hoc and systematic approaches to personnel selection provides another example. These tensions were far from 'unproblematically compatible'.[7] They were ever-present – a pre-war hangover, a scratch in the vinyl that the army was forced to revisit over and over again, but was never able to resolve fully. Instead, it tried to find ways of mitigating these tensions, encouraging formations and individuals to innovate within institutional parameters. This was a very British response. Derided by outsiders as evidence of a 'lack of firmness' and an 'exaggerated respect for individuality', it is unsurprising that this approach led to considerable diversity of method even within the more systematic approaches, such as training schools and publications.[8]

This flexible approach to learning and innovation was not stumbled upon by accident, nor was it limited to a particular expeditionary force. It was a deliberate policy and one facilitated by the army. Whether through the self-integration of the AIF to the appointment of civilian experts, with or without military rank and uniform, it was contingent on the local situation in each force. A one size fits all approach across all theatres would have been both ineffective and a positive danger. Within the army's various expeditionary forces, the pace of learning and innovation varied. However, their respective experiences had an important influence beyond the confines of their own theatres. In his final despatch, Allenby wrote that operations in Palestine 'have thus been part of a studied whole, and not an isolated campaign'.[9] Dawnay echoed his thoughts after the war, noting that 'the crowning victory at Damascus' could be traced 'back to the ruins of the Dardanelles campaign', and that 'the course of events in the near East was wholly dependent on, and largely dictated by, the situation in the main theatres'.[10] Personnel, matériel, and expertise flowed between these disparate locations. Innovations from the Western Front found their way to subsidiary theatres, while expertise from these smaller theatres, in turn, found their way back to training schools in France and the UK. Through a combination of systematic

---

[7] Collini, 'Idea of "Character"', p. 49.   [8] Greenhalgh, *Liaison*, p. 123.
[9] *London Gazette*, Issue 31498, 8 August 1919, p. 10193.
[10] IWM, Dawnay Papers, 69/21/1, Lecture on Gallipoli and Palestine, n.d, pp. 1, 16.

and incidental exchanges, a cross-theatre learning network developed during the course of the war. Expeditionary forces often amended recommended syllabi in response to differing tactical and geographical circumstances, while formations interpreted and adapted publications to reflect their local situations. In line with Espagne and Burke's respective discussions on the history of transfers, we can see how knowledge was understood or interpreted in different ways by different individuals or groups.[11] By exerting agency and acting as vectors, individuals selected what appealed to them, or what they thought they needed. As a result, knowledge was adapted and put to use in ways not originally intended.

In short, the army had to be responsive, sensitive, and flexible to the needs of its constituent forces. This responsiveness was particularly important for organisational learning. In Part I of this study, organisational learning was defined as 'the process of improving actions through better knowledge and understanding'.[12] Broadly speaking, the army learned in two ways: first, through the learning of its members, and secondly, through integrating or interacting with individuals with new knowledge. By doing this, the army promoted a culture of innovation that went beyond the efforts of men such as Maxse and Geddes. These two men were merely examples of, rather than exceptions to, the rule.[13] The army showed a willingness to interact with, and reach out for, the advice of those with recognised expertise, whether they were civilians or soldiers. As a result, individuals were given the opportunity to influence institutional behaviour. However, this culture of innovation was greater than a single person's independent relationship with the organisation. Rather, it was the interdependence of individuals that proved key. For change to take place, a network of individuals was required. Though one person may have come up with an innovative idea, it was for those in higher command to embrace a role that involved selecting, supporting, and spreading these ideas. CinCs such as Allenby, Haig, and Milne were vital to the promotion of change and innovation whether through the introduction of new weapons technologies, the employment of civilian transport experts, or the introduction of new artillery tactics. As CinCs, they were empowered and willing to promote a learning environment within their forces. This environment was aided by a number of individuals – entrepreneurs and facilitators – who sat between the innovator and the higher command to smooth over organisational resistance. Using their own personal and professional networks, these individuals

[11] Espagne, *Transfert*, pp. 1–2; Burke, *Encyclopédie to Wikipedia*, pp. 86–87.
[12] Fiol and Lyles, 'Organizational Learning', p. 803.
[13] This, again, stands in stark contrast to Kennedy's assertion that there were structural problems within the British army of the First World War. See Kennedy, 'Britain in the First World War', in Millett and Murray (eds), *Military Effectiveness*, pp. 51, 52–53, 63.

built up effective working relationships with others in different parts of the organisation, enhancing trust and providing legitimacy. It was through this network, across all levels of the army, that a culture of innovation pervaded the entire institution.

External expertise and initiatives were a key part of this culture. The army was not an insular organisation, nor was it averse to change or new knowledge. It could not afford such attitudes when fighting a war against a rival military-industrial system. Chemical warfare, military mining, signals technology, and inland water transport all resulted from the army's decision to listen to outsiders, whether civilians or individuals from allied nations. The employment of civilian experts to head up transport missions and the implementation of efficiency measures, routine in the business world, provide additional examples of this outward-facing attitude. With the exception of some local difficulties, the army embraced such measures, willingly incorporating the language of business and efficiency into its day to day processes. These measures permeated throughout the army, both on and beyond the Western Front; from the card indexes of the Directorate of Organisation, to the 'science of statistics' in the Transportation Directorate, to the EEF's ledger-based accounting system. Though fraught with acute cultural and political tensions, the army also looked to its allies for innovations. Instances of collaboration were clear at a local level, or between individuals with a pre-existing relationship. It is unsurprising that some of the most fruitful collaborations occurred in a scientific context where artillery and communication technologies were concerned. Exposure to allied methods, whether operational, tactical, or technological, forced the British to reflect on their own practice. It is here that we can detect a weakness in the army's culture of innovation: individuals often saw what they wanted to see. For those 'thinking officers', men such as Montgomery, Cavan, and Currie, shortcomings in British practice were apparent. For others, national pride and arrogance hindered attempts to learn vital lessons that had been paid for in blood.

While a culture of innovation was promoted, it was not perfect. The army did much to provide ways of capturing and disseminating learning, benefitting from new technologies and ways of thinking, but some units and their commanders focused on learning in the best way they could. Decisions were often irrational, contributing to significant casualties on the battlefield. Arrogance, intolerance, and Blimpish pockets were inevitable. The reactionary attitudes of individuals such as Stuart-Wortley, Clayton, and Maxwell was used by contemporaries such as Lloyd George as a stick with which to beat the seemingly conservative army. Their individual resistance was tantamount to organisational conservatism. Yet, to be conservative is to 'prefer the familiar to the unknown, to prefer the tried to the untried, fact to mystery, the actual to the possible'. The possibility of change is seen as 'a threat to identity . . . an emblem of extinction' and, for conservatives, is met with a 'cool and critical' disposition.[14] The army may have been critical at times, but it did not sacrifice potential innovation to maintain the status quo. As one officer commented, 'I found officers of high rank almost too receptive to novel proposals, especially when they were based on anything mysterious or scientific'.[15]

Accusations of conservatism were far from the norm, far less widespread, and far from unique to the British military. Some commentators have suggested that the French army was 'unintelligent' and suffered from a tendency towards over-centralisation, which hindered its ability to adapt quickly.[16] While there was, indeed, friction and suspicion within the French army – the experiences of Weiss and Cotton offer a good example here – it, too, learned in a way analogous to the British. Its system was organic. Grand Quartier Général, much like the British high command, was tasked with managing and controlling the brutal changes that confronted it. It acted as a pump, 'intelligently circulating good ideas and encouraging the replacement of less than good ideas'.[17] Like the British, it was reliant on a command structure that understood and acted on the feelings and ideas of the men in the field, a network of individuals to bear these ideas, and an effective training structure to spread them across the organisation.[18]

Similar concerns were apparent within the corporate world. Indeed, for large businesses like Brunner Mond, Armstrong Whitworth, and Krupp, the war was far from plain sailing, leading to significant, often unwanted, adjustment and upheaval. Some departments or products were mothballed, machinery was constantly readjusted, labour diluted, while new manufacturing technologies and products were demanded and devoured by the military-industrial machine.[19] The war required both militaries and businesses to change. However, this was not easy.

---

[14] M. Oakeshott, *Rationalism in Politics and Other Essays* (London: Methuen, 1962), pp. 169, 170, 172.

[15] C. H. Foulkes, *Gas! The Story of the Special Brigade* (London: William Blackwood, 1934), p. 102.

[16] D. Porch, 'The French Army in the First World War', in Millett and Murray (eds), *Military Effectiveness*, p. 225; B. I. Gudmundsson, *Stormtroop Tactics: Innovation in the German Army, 1914–1918* (Westport, CT: Praeger, 1989), p. 173.

[17] Krause, *Early Trench Tactics*, p. 165.   [18] Goya, *La Chair*, p. 417.

[19] J. I. Watts, *The First Fifty Years of Brunner, Mond & Co 1873–1923* (Northwich: Brunner Mond, 1923), pp. 52–55, 59; Anon., *The War Work of Sir W. G. Armstrong, Whitworth & Company Ltd* (London: Arden Press, n.d. [c. 1919]), pp. 1–2, 18, 23–24; H. James, *Krupp: A History of the Legendary German Firm* (Princeton, NJ: Princeton University Press, 2012), pp. 135–141.

Change required individuals to modify their beliefs, look beyond the boundaries of their communities, and break with long-standing routines. Change is often perceived as threatening, particularly for those who feel that their role or prestige might be at risk. The army was aware of such threats. However, rather than idly sitting by, higher command helped prepare for change. It levered the army's ethos, focusing on cohesion, communication, and collaboration, whilst also encouraging innovators to find their own ways of making change more palatable.

In summary, through a combination of its pre-war ethos and increased fluidity in wartime, the army displayed organisational and cultural flexibility, allowing for high levels of learning and adaptation. This was not limited to a single formation, branch, or expeditionary force. It was an institutional undertaking. Unsurprisingly, the process was necessarily complex and far from even. The methods used to realise it were not always precise, nor were they always effective. However, with its preference for practical solutions, the army was prepared to look beyond its boundaries, considering non-traditional methods, as it sought to reckon with the challenges of modern war.

Learning, and the change that accompanies it, is a complex process. By examining the army institutionally, this book has revealed the extent to which its learning process was influenced by other institutions and agencies that sat outside the military organisation. This speaks to the intricacy of a process that has, for the most part, been previously understood in a rather inward-looking, insular context. By thinking about learning as a collaborative process, predicated on a rich array of connections and relationships, it is possible to understand the links between certain individuals and institutions that enabled this process to function. By focusing on the process rather than the outcome, the importance of factors such as organisational culture, human agency, as well as institutional and individual resistance come to the fore. These factors, particularly those relating to human nature, have often been neglected in analyses of the army's learning process, which has encouraged a view of increasing competence. The reality was much more complicated and fraught.

Part of this tension was not so much to do with the resistance of elites, but the sheer amount of knowledge generated. It is, therefore, unsurprising that the army would look to the world of big business for knowledge management solutions in order to process and make sense of this information. However, while it is tempting to anthropomorphise the army, assigning it learning qualities, its essence and ability to learn was embodied in its individuals, rather than its formal processes. Although this book has sought to enhance our understanding of learning in the

British army of the First World War, it also has implications for our broader understanding of military innovation. It is clear that recognising and exploring the links between theatres and formations help us to understand how learning, adaptation, and the difficulties associated with them, occur institutionally. It has also shown that a vectored view of learning and innovation is too simplistic. The importance of organisational culture and the networked interplay of approaches deserves greater attention. While Kollars's 'tolerance of creativity' has proved to apply to the British army, the evidence suggests that the army went beyond tolerance and actively cultivated creativity. By moving away from the usual focus on front line units and employing a holistic analysis of the army, we can see that a considered, pragmatic approach to adaptation took place across the military institution. Organisational and operational fluidity is not limited to those militaries fighting in modern, counter-insurgency operations. Even in an unlimited, total war, the British army displayed fluid tendencies. While by no means a 'flat' organisation, it was willing to listen to dissenters, promote self-reliance, and subvert the chain of command where necessary.

Although this study has considered how the army learned in wartime, its findings also have implications for our understanding of how large organisations negotiate and respond to change. The army experienced some of the same challenges and barriers faced by all organisations, notably resistance to change, 'not invented here' syndrome, and the need to integrate newcomers. Though the army was unique in its function and role, the difficulties it faced in terms of learning and adaptation were not. Before and during the First World War, parallels were drawn between the army and business. In 1907, Mackinder had called for the army administrator to be transformed into a 'soldier businessman', while Cowans was likened to a 'Managing Director', Haig a 'master sales manager', and the whole army an 'amazing business institution'.[20] The army's regulations and training pamphlets were akin to company journals, allowing for the dissemination of job-related information along with the promotion and projection of corporate identity, corporate culture, and organisational power.[21]

In some respects, the British army of the First World War was similar to a multi-national franchise, with a series of decentralised outlets around the world. The army experienced similar concerns to those that confronted such corporations, namely the reluctance to adopt a one size

[20] Funnell, 'Social Reform', p. 70; Marcosson, *Business of War*, pp. viii–ix, 2, 160.
[21] M. Heller, 'British Company Magazines, 1878–1939: The Origins and Functions of House Journals in Large-Scale Organisations', *Media History* 15 (2) (2009), esp. pp. 158–160.

fits all policy, the importance of promoting a shared culture, and the problem of geographical dispersion.[22] With its pre-war experience of fighting across the globe, the army refined or developed a number of ways to overcome these concerns. The use of liaison officers, secondments, and attachments allowed for subsidiary theatres to benefit from innovations taking place on the Western Front. Less tangible, however, was the importance of its ethos or corporate culture. This encouraged an entrepreneurial attitude and a non-parochial mind-set, mitigating the potential liabilities associated with bureaucracy and stagnation. Corporate culture determines how an organisation responds to change. For the army of the First World War, it determined how it identified lessons, how it innovated, and, ultimately, how it learned to fight.

[22] L. M. Lucas, 'The Role of Culture on Knowledge Transfer: The Case of the Multinational Corporation', *The Learning Organization* 13 (3) (2006), pp. 271–272.

Bibliography

UNPUBLISHED PRIMARY MATERIAL

I OFFICIAL DOCUMENTS

Australian War Memorial, Canberra
AWM 1   Pre-Federation and Commonwealth Records
AWM 4   Australian Imperial Force unit war diaries, 1914–1918
AWM 25   Written records, 1914–1918 war
AWM 27   Classified files
AWM 252   Records arranged according to AWM Library subject classification, 1914–1918
AWM 255   Written records, 1914–1918 war, second series

The National Archives of the United Kingdom, Kew
CAB 18   Committee of Imperial Defence: Miscellaneous Reports and Papers, 1875–191
CAB 24   War Cabinet and Cabinet: Memoranda, 1915–1939
CAB 25   Supreme War Council: Papers and Minutes, 1917–1919
CAB 37   Cabinet Office: Copies of Cabinet Papers, 1880–1916
CAB 45   Official War Histories Correspondence and Papers
DSIR 10   National Physical Laboratory: Registered Files
FO 371   General Correspondence from 1906 to 1966
MT 23   Admiralty, Transport Department: Correspondence and Papers
MUN 4   Records of the Central Registry
MUN 5   Munitions Council: Historical Records Branch
NATS 1   Ministry of National Service: Records
RAIL 1014   Great Western Railway Collection
WO 27   Adjutant-General and Army Council: Inspection Returns, 1750–1914
WO 32   Registered Files (General Series)
WO 33   Reports, Memoranda, and Papers (O and A Series)
WO 95   First World War and Army of Occupation War Diaries
WO 106   Directorate of Military Operations and Military Intelligence: Correspondence and Papers
WO 107   Quartermaster-General's Department: Correspondence and Papers
WO 114   Adjutant-General's Department: Strength Returns of the Army

WO 123	Army Circulars, Memoranda, Orders, and Regulations, 1711–1992
WO 142	Ministry of Munitions, Trench Warfare, and Chemical Warfare Departments: Reports and Papers
WO 158	Military Headquarters: Correspondence and Papers, First World War
WO 161	Miscellaneous Unregistered Papers, First World War
WO 162	Adjutant-General's Department: Papers
WO 163	War Office Council, later War Office Consultative Council, Army Council, Army Board and Their Various Committees: Minutes and Papers, 1806–1980
WO 181	Directorate of Military Survey and Predecessors: Papers
WO 256	Field Marshal Sir Douglas Haig, Western Front: Diaries
WO 279	Confidential Print
WO 293	Army Council: Instructions
ZLIB 21	Minutes of Proceedings of Institution of Civil Engineers
ZPER 9	Railway Gazette International: Periodicals

Royal Artillery Historical Trust, Salisbury Plain
MD 2818   Memorandum on Army Training during the Individual Training Period, 1912–1913

II PRIVATE PAPERS

Australian War Memorial, Canberra
Papers of Brigadier-General R. M. Anderson, PR83/020
Papers of C. E. W. Bean, AWM38 3DRL/606
Papers of Field Marshal Lord Birdwood, 3DRL/3376
Papers of General Sir H. Chauvel, PR00535
Papers of Brigadier H. E. Elliott, 2DRL/0513
Papers of A. E. Forbes, PR03583
Papers of Lance-Corporal H. Gibson, PR03311
Papers of General Sir A. Godley, 3DRL/2233
Papers of Henry Gullett, AWM40/69
Papers of Lieutenant G. L. Makin, 1DRL/0473
Papers of General Sir J. Monash, 3DRL/2316
Papers of Lance-Corporal F. O'Brien, PR83/26
Papers of Senator Sir G. F. Pearce, 3DRL/2222
Papers of General Sir C. B. B. White, 3DRL/1400

British Library, Manuscript Collections, London
Papers of Field Marshal Lord Birdwood, MSS Eur D686

Churchill Archives Centre, University of Cambridge
Papers of General Sir Charles Bonham-Carter
Papers of Lord Rawlinson

Imperial War Museum, Department of Documents, London
Papers of Field Marshal Lord Chetwode, PP/MCR/C1
Papers of Brigadier-General E. Craig-Brown, Con Shelf 1/4

Papers of Major-General G. P. Dawnay, 69/21/1
Papers of Lieutenant-General A. N. Floyer-Acland, 12635
Papers of M. S. Fox, 76/49/1
Papers of Lieutenant-Colonel V. M. Fergusson, PP/MCR/111
Papers of Major-General Sir S. W. Hare, 09/86/1
Papers of Lieutenant-Colonel H. H. Hemming, PP/MCR/155
Papers of Major W. R. Kermack, PP/MCR/214
Papers of Major-General Sir A. L. Lynden-Bell, 90/1/1
Papers of General Sir F. I. Maxse, PP/MCR/C42 and 69/53/13
Papers of Brigadier-General R. Micklem, 87-8/1
Papers of General Sir A. Murray, 79-48/2-3
Papers of Major T. C. Owtram, 83/17/1

Institution of Civil Engineers Archive, London
Report on 'The Provision of Personnel for Military Railways in the War of 1914–
    1918', OC 4277

Liddell Hart Centre for Military Archives, King's College London
Papers of Field Marshal Viscount Alanbrooke
Papers of Field Marshal Viscount Allenby
Papers of General Sir W. H. Bartholomew
Papers of General Sir J. T. Burnett-Stuart
Papers of Brigadier-General T. Capper
Papers of Brigadier-General F. A. S. Clarke
Papers of Lieutenant-Colonel H. Darlington
Papers of Brigadier-General Sir J. E. Edmonds
Papers of Major-General Sir C. H. Foulkes
Papers of Major-General J. F. C. Fuller
Papers of General Sir A. Godley
Papers of General Sir I. S. M. Hamilton
Papers of Brigadier-General P. Howell
Papers of Sergeant C. F. Jones
Papers of Lieutenant-General Sir L. E. Kiggell
Papers of General Sir W. M. St G. Kirke
Papers of Captain Sir B. H. Liddell Hart
Papers of Field Marshal Sir A. A. Montgomery-Massingberd
Papers of General Sir R. O'Connor
Papers of Field Marshal Sir W. R. Robertson
Papers of General Sir J. S. M. Shea
Papers of Major W. G. Wallace

Liddle Collection, University of Leeds
Papers of Sir J. F. Evetts, Liddle/WW1/GS/0533

Mitchell Library, State Library of New South Wales, Sydney
Papers of Major-General Sir C. Rosenthal, MSS 2739

Modern Records Centre, University of Warwick, Coventry
Papers of Sir William Guy Granet, MSS.191

The National Archives of the United Kingdom, Kew
Papers of Brigadier-General H. O. Mance, PRO 30/66/9

National Army Museum, Chelsea
Papers of Captain N. E. Drury, 7607-69
Papers of Captain R. S. Hawker, 1988-09-86
Papers of Sir G. Macauley, 8008-72
Papers of Colonel R. Macleod, 8112-9
Papers of Lord Rawlinson, 5201-22-18
Papers of Royal Munster Fusiliers, 7603-69-1
Papers of Lieutenant-Colonel A. Weston Jarvis, 1999-03-43

National Library of Australia, Canberra
Papers of General Sir C. B. B. White, MS 5172
Papers of General Sir J. Monash, MS 1884

Private Collection of Katherine Swinfen Eady
Papers of Colonel H. M. Farmar

Royal Artillery Historical Trust, Salisbury Plain
Papers of Lieutenant-General Sir H. C. C. Uniacke, MD 1160
Papers of General Sir W. Gillman, MD 1161
Papers of Major-General Sir H. H. Tudor, MD 1167

PUBLISHED PRIMARY MATERIAL

I GOVERNMENT PUBLICATIONS

British Parliamentary Papers, 1905 (Cd.2252). Order in Council defining the
    duties of the Inspector-General of the Forces
British Parliamentary Papers, 1907 (Cd.3696), Army. Report of the Advisory
    Board, London School of Economics, on the first course at the London
    School of Economics, January–July 1907
British Parliamentary Papers, 1910 (Cd.5213), Army. Report of the Advisory
    Board, London School of Economics, on the fourth course at the London
    School of Economics, October 1909–March 1910

II PARLIAMENTARY DEBATES

Civil Services and Revenue Departs Estimates, 1913–14, House of Commons
    debate, 29 May 1913, *Hansard*, vol. 53 c457
Skilled Men, House of Commons debate, 8 November 1916, *Hansard*, vol. 87
    c177
Voluntary Enlistment (*Skilled Men*), House of Commons debate, 13 May 1918,
    Hansard, vol. 106 c52W

III OFFICIAL PUBLISHED MATERIAL

Australia
Bean, C. E. W., *Anzac to Amiens* (Canberra, ACT: Australian War Memorial,
    1983 [1946])

The Official History of Australia in the War of 1914–1918: The Story of ANZAC from the Outbreak of War to the End of the First Phase of the Gallipoli Campaign, May 4, 1915, I (12 vols, Sydney, NSW: Angus and Robertson, 1941)

The Official History of Australia in the War of 1914–1918: The Australian Imperial Force in France, 1916, III (12 vols, Sydney, NSW: Angus and Robertson, 1941)

Knibbs, G. H., *Official Yearbook of the Commonwealth of Australia 1901–1911 No. 5* (Melbourne, VIC: McCarron, Bird, 1912)

Official Yearbook of the Commonwealth of Australia 1901–1912 No. 6 (Melbourne, VIC: McCarron, Bird, 1913)

Canada

Wise, S. F., *Canadian Airmen and the First World War: The Official History of the Royal Canadian Air Force* (Toronto, ON: University of Toronto Press, 1980)

France

Ministère de la Guerre, *Les Armées Françaises dans la Grande Guerre,* 6/1 Annex Vol I (Paris: Imprimerie Nationale, 1932)

Service Géographique de l'Armée, *Rapport sur les Travaux Exécutés du 1er Aout 1914 au 31 Decembre 1919: Historique du Service Géographique de l'Armée pendant la Guerre* (Paris: Imprimerie du Service Geoographique de l'Armée, 1936)

Germany

Reichsarchiv, *Der Weltkrieg 1914 bis 1918: Die Kriegführung an der Westfront im Jahre 1918,* XIV (14 vols, Berlin: E. S. Mittler & Sohn, 1944)

Great Britain

Edmonds, J. E., *History of the Great War: Military Operations, France and Belgium 1918,* V (London: HMSO, 1947)

Egyptian Expeditionary Force General Headquarters, *Action of 6th Mounted Brigade at El Mughar* (Cairo: Government Press, 1918)

Falls, C. F., *History of the Great War: Military Operations, Egypt and Palestine* (2 vols, London: HMSO, 1930)

History of the Great War: Military Operations, Macedonia (2 vols, London: HMSO, 1933)

Fourth Army Headquarters, *Attack on Zenith Trench,* 1916

General Headquarters, *SS109 Training of Divisions for Offensive Action,* 1916

SS152 Instructions for the Training of the British Armies in France, 1917

SS177 Instructions on Wiring, 1917

SS191 Inter-communication in the Field, 1917

General Staff, *Field Service Regulations, Part I: Operations* (London: HMSO, 1909)

Field Service Regulations, Part 2: Administration (London: HMSO, 1909)

Ministry of Defence, *Transforming the British Army: An Update – July 2013* (London: Ministry of Defence, 2013)

Advantage through Innovation: The Defence Innovation Initiative (London: Ministry of Defence, 2016)

War Office, *Combined Training (Provisional)* (London: HMSO, 1902)
  Infantry Training (London: HMSO, 1905)
  Manual of Military Law (London: HMSO, 1907)
  Statistics of the Military Effort of the British Empire during the Great War 1914–1920 (London: HMSO, 1922)

United States of America
Adjutant-General's Office, *The Personnel System of the United States Army*, I (2 vols, Washington, DC: Government Printing Office, 1919)
Department of Defense, *Quadrennial Defense Review 2014* (Washington, DC: US Department of Defense, 2014)

IV DIARIES, MEMOIRS, UNIT HISTORIES

Addison, G. H., *The Work of the Royal Engineers in the European War, 1914–19: The Organization of Engineer Intelligence and Information* (reprint, Uckfield: Naval and Military Press, 2006 [1926])
Badcock, G. E., *A History of the Transport Services of the Egyptian Expeditionary Force, 1916–1917–1918* (London: Hugh Rees, 1925)
Baring, M., *Flying Corps Headquarters 1914–1918* (London: William Blackwood, 1968)
Beadon, R. H., *R.A.S.C.: History of Supply and Transport in the British Army*, II (2 vols, Cambridge: Cambridge University Press, 1931)
Birdwood, W. R., *Khaki and Gown: An Autobiography* (London: Ward, Lock, 1941)
Boraston, J. H. (ed.), *Sir Douglas Haig's Despatches (December 1915–April 1919)* (London: J. M. Dent, 1919)
Buchan, J., *Francis and Riversdale Grenfell: A Memoir* (London: Thomas Nelson, 1920)
Callwell, C., and Headlam, J., *History of the Royal Artillery from the Indian Mutiny to the Great War* (Woolwich: Royal Artillery Institute, 1931)
Champion de Crespigny, C., *Forty Years of a Sportsman's Life* (London: Mills and Boon, 1910)
Dudley Ward, C. H., *The 74th (Yeomanry) Division in Syria and France* (London: John Murray, 1922)
Fay, S., *The War Office at War* (London: Hutchinson, 1937)
Foulkes, C. H., *Gas! The Story of The Special Brigade* (London: William Blackwood, 1934)
Greenhalgh, E. (ed.), *Liaison: General Pierre des Vallières at British General Headquarters* (Stroud: The History Press, 2016)
Halpern, P. G. (ed.), *The Keyes Papers: Selections from the Private and Official Correspondence of Admiral of the Fleet Baron Keyes of Zeebrugge, Vol. 1, 1914–1918* (London: Navy Records Society, 1972)
Hesketh-Prichard, H. V., *Sniping in France 1914–18* (London: Hutchinson, 1920)
Hughes, M. (ed.), *Allenby in Palestine* (Stroud: Sutton, 2004)
Institution of Royal Engineers, *History of the Corps of Royal Engineers*, V (London: Longman's, 1952)

History of the Corps of Royal Engineers, VI (London: Longman's, 1952)

The Work of the Royal Engineers in the European War, 1914–19: Egypt and Palestine – Water-Supply (Chatham: W&J Mackay, 1921)

Lawrence, T. E., *Seven Pillars of Wisdom* (reprint, London: Book Club Associates, 1974 [1922])

Lloyd George, D., *War Memoirs*, II (2 vols, London: Odhams Press, 1938 [1936])

Luxford, J. H., *With the Machine Gunners in France and Palestine* (London: Whitcombe and Tombes, 1923)

Lyttelton, N., *Eighty Years: Soldiering, Politics, Games* (London: Hodder and Stoughton, 1927)

Marshall, W. R., *Memories of Four Fronts* (London: Ernest Benn, 1929)

Morrison, F. L., *The Fifth Battalion, Highland Light Infantry in the War 1914–1918* (Glasgow: MacLehose, Jackson, 1921)

Murray, A. J., *Sir Archibald Murray's Despatches June 1916 – June 1917* (London: J. M. Dent, 1920)

Ogilvie, D. D., *The Fife and Forfar Yeomanry 1914–1919* (London: John Murray, 1921)

Priestley, R. E., *The Work of the Royal Engineers in the European War, 1914–19: The Signal Service (France)* (reprint, Uckfield: Naval & Military Press, 2006 [1921])

Robertson, W. R., *From Private to Field Marshal* (London: Constable, 1921)

Robinson, P. (ed.), *The Letters of Major General Price Davies VC, CB, CMG, DSO* (Stroud: The History Press, 2013)

Sandilands, H. R., *The 23rd Division 1914–1919* (London: William Blackwood, 1925)

Syk, A. (ed.), *The Military Papers of Lieutenant-General Frederick Stanley Maude, 1914–1917* (Stroud: The History Press, 2012)

Townsend, C. E. C., *All Rank and No File: A History of the Engineer and Railway Staff Corps RE, 1865–1965* (London: The Engineer and Railway Staff Corps, RE [TAVR], 1969)

Young, M., *Army Service Corps 1902–1918* (Barnsley: Leo Cooper, 2000)

V NEWSPAPERS AND MAGAZINES

Country Life
London Gazette
The New Statesman
New York Times
The Spectator
The Times
The Western Mail

SECONDARY MATERIAL

I ARTICLES AND CHAPTERS

Antonacopoulou, E. P., and Guttel, W. H., 'Staff Induction Practices and Organizational Socialization: A Review and Extension of the Debate', *Society and Business Review* 5 (1) (2010), pp. 22–47

Bailes, H., 'Patterns of Military Thought in the Late Victorian Army', *Journal of Strategic Studies* 4 (1) (1981), pp. 29–45

Ball, S. J., 'Harold Macmillan and the Politics of Defence', *Twentieth Century British History* 6 (1) (1995), pp. 78–100

Beach, J., 'Issued by the General Staff: Doctrine Writing at British GHQ, 1917–1918', *War in History* 19 (4) (2012), pp. 464–491

Beadon, R. H., 'The Business Man and the Army', *Journal of the Royal United Services Institute* 62 (1917), pp. 286–296

Berthoin Andal, A., and Krebsbach-Gnath, C., 'Consultants as Agents of Organizational Learning: The Importance of Marginalia', in M. Dierkes, A. Berthoin Andal, J. Child, and I. Nonaka (eds), *Handbook of Organizational Learning and Knowledge* (Oxford: Oxford University Press, 2007), pp. 462–483

Bingham, W. V., 'Army Personnel Work', *Journal of Applied Psychology* 3 (1) (1919), pp. 1–12

Black, J., 'A More Vigorous Prosecution of Public Works: The Reforms of the Indian Public Works Department', *Accounting History* 6 (2) (2001), pp. 91–119

Bonham-Carter, C., 'Suggestions to Instructors of Recruits', *Army Review* 7 (1) (1914), pp. 119–127

Bou, J., 'Ambition and Adversity: Developing an Australian Military Force, 1901–1914', *Australian Army Journal* 9 (1) (2012), pp. 71–87

Brennan, P., 'Julian Byng and Leadership in the Canadian Corps', in G. Hayes, A. Iarocci, and M. Bechthold (eds), *Vimy Ridge: A Canadian Reassessment* (Waterloo, ON: Wilfrid Laurier University Press, 2007), pp. 87–104

Buchanan, R. A., 'Engineers and Government in Nineteenth-Century Britain', in R. Macleod (ed.), *Government and Expertise: Specialists, Administrators and Professionals, 1860–1919* (Cambridge: Cambridge University Press, 1988), pp. 41–58

Carney, R. N., and Levin, J. R., 'Pictorial Illustrations *Still* Improve Students' Learning From Text', *Educational Psychology Review* 14 (1) (2002), pp. 5–26

Catignani, S., 'Coping with Knowledge: Organizational Learning in the British Army?', *Journal of Strategic Studies* 37 (1) (2013), pp. 30–64

'"Getting COIN" at the Tactical Level in Afghanistan: Reassessing Counter-Insurgency Adaptation in the British Army', *Journal of Strategic Studies* 35 (4) (2012), pp. 513–539

Close, C., 'British Survey on the Western Front: Discussion', *Geographical Journal* 53 (4) (1919), pp. 271–276

C. N. W. (pseud.), 'The Making of the New Unit', *Journal of the Royal United Services Institute* 61 (1916), pp. 598–607

Collini, S., 'The Idea of "Character" in Victorian Political Thought', *Transactions of the Royal Historical Society* 35 (1985), pp. 29–50

Cozzi, S., '"When You're a Long, Long Way from Home": The Establishment of Canadian-Only Social Clubs for CEF Soldiers in London, 1915–1919', *Canadian Military History* 20 (2011), pp. 45–60

Cowan, R., and Foray, D., 'The Economics of Codification and the Diffusion of Knowledge', *Industrial and Corporate Change* 6 (3) (1997), pp. 595–622

Crerar, H. D. G., 'The Development of Closer Relations between the Military Forces of the Empire', *Journal of the Royal United Services Institute* 71 (483) (1926), pp. 441–455

Cresswell, T., 'Mobilities II', *Progress in Human Geography* 36 (5) (2012), pp. 645–653

Cross, R., Parker, A., Prusak, L., and Borgatti, S. P., 'Knowing What We Know: Supporting Knowledge Creation and Sharing in Social Networks', *Organizational Dynamics* 30 (2) (2001), pp. 100–120

Crossan, M. M., Lane, H. W., and White, R. E., 'An Organizational Learning Framework: From Intuition to Institution', *Academy of Management Review* 24 (3) (1999), pp. 522–537

Daddis, G. A., 'Eating Soup with a Spoon: The US Army as a "Learning Organization" in Vietnam', *Journal of Military History* 77 (2013), pp. 229–254

Delaney, D., 'Army Apostles: Imperial Officers on Loan and the Standardization of the Canadian, Australian, and New Zealand Armies, 1904–1914', *War in History* 23 (2) (2016), pp. 169–189

'Mentoring the Canadian Corps: Imperial Officers and the Canadian Expeditionary Force, 1914–1918', *Journal of Military History* 77 (2013), pp. 931–953

DiBella, A., 'Can the Army Become a Learning Organization? A Question Reexamined', *Joint Force Quarterly* 56 (1) (2010), pp. 117–122

Di Manno, S., '"Hier sur tous les fronts … Demain sur tous les mondes" Mobilisation météorologique et reconfigurations disciplinaires, militaires et aéronautiques durant la Première Guerre mondiale', *Cahiers d'histoire. Revue d'histoire critique* 127 (2015), pp. 117–133

Dye, P., 'France and the Development of British Military Aviation', *Air Power Review* 12 (1) (2009), pp. 1–13

Easterby Smith, M., 'Disciplines of Organizational Learning: Contributions and Critiques', *Human Relations* 50 (1997), pp. 1085–1113

Eraut, M., 'Informal Learning in the Workplace', *Studies in Continuing Education* 26 (2) (2004), pp. 247–273

Espagne, M., 'La notion de transfert culturel', *Revue Science/Lettres* 1 (2013) (Published Online 1 May 2012. DOI: 10.4000/rsl.219), pp. 1–9

Farrell, T. G., 'The Dynamics of British Military Transformation', *International Affairs* 84 (4) (2008), pp. 777–807

'Improving in War: Military Adaptation and the British in Helmand Province, Afghanistan, 2006–2009', *Journal of Strategic Studies* 33 (4) (2010), pp. 567–594

Fiol, C. M., and Lyles, M. A., 'Organizational Learning', *Academy of Management Review* 10 (4) (1985), pp. 803–813

Foley, R. T., 'A Case Study in Horizontal Military Innovation: The German Army, 1916–1918', *Journal of Strategic Studies* 35 (6) (2012), pp. 799–827

'Dumb Donkeys or Cunning Foxes? Learning in the British and German Armies during the Great War', *International Affairs* 90 (2) (2014), pp. 279–298

Foley, R. T., McCartney, H., and Griffin, S., '"Transformation in Contact": Learning the Lessons of Modern War', *International Affairs* 87 (2) (2011), pp. 253–270

Fox, A., '"Thomas Cook's Tourists": The Challenges and Benefits of Inter-Theatre Service in the British Army of the First World War', *Journal of Historical Geography* (Published Online 10 July 2017. DOI: 10.1016/j.jhg.2017.06.012)

Fox-Godden, A., 'Beyond the Western Front: The Practice of Inter-Theatre Learning in the British Army, 1914–1918', *War in History* 23 (2) (2016), pp. 190–209

'"Hopeless Inefficiency"? The Transformation and Operational Performance of Brigade Staff, 1916–1918', in M. LoCicero, R. Mahoney, and S. Mitchell (eds), *A Military Transformed? Adaptation and Innovation in the British Military, 1792–1945* (Solihull: Helion, 2014), pp. 139–156

Funnell, W., 'National Efficiency, Military Accounting and the Business of War', *Critical Perspectives on Accounting* 17 (2006), pp. 719–751

'Social Reform, Military Accounting and the Pursuit of Economy during the Liberal Apotheosis, 1906–1912', *Accounting History Review* 21 (1) (2011), pp. 69–93

Gooch, J., 'The Creation of the British General Staff, 1904–1914', *Journal of the Royal United Services Institute* 116 (1971), pp. 50–53

'The Weary Titan: Strategy and Policy in Great Britain, 1890–1918', in W. Murray, M. Knox, and A. Bernstein (eds), *The Making of Strategy: Rulers, States, and War* (Cambridge: Cambridge University Press, 1994), pp. 278–307

Gourvish, T. R., 'The Rise of the Professions', in T. R. Gourvish and A. O'Day (eds), *Later Victorian Britain 1867–1900* (Basingstoke: Macmillan, 1988), pp. 13–35

Graham, S., 'When Infrastructures Fail', in S. Graham (ed.), *Disrupted Cities: When Infrastructures Fail* (London: Routledge, 2010), pp. 1–26

Greenhalgh, E., 'The Viviani-Joffre Mission to the United States, April-May 1917', *French Historical Studies* 35 (4) (2012), pp. 627–659

Grieves, K., 'The Transportation Mission to GHQ', in B. Bond et al. (eds), *Look to Your Front: Studies in the First World War* (Staplehurst: Spellmount, 1999), pp. 63–78

'"Total War"? The Quest for a British Manpower Policy, 1917–18', *Journal of Strategic Studies* 9 (1) (1986), pp. 79–95

Halewood, L., '"A Matter of Opinion": British Attempts to Assess the Attrition of German Manpower, 1915–1917', *Intelligence and National Security* 32 (3) (2017), pp. 333–350

Hansen, M. T., Nohria, N., and Tierney, T., 'What's Your Strategy for Managing Knowledge', *Harvard Business Review* 77 (2) (1999), pp. 106–116

Harkness, K. A., and Hunzeker, M., 'Military Maladaptation: Counterinsurgency and the Politics of Failure', *Journal of Strategic Studies* 38 (6) (2015), pp. 777–800

H. B. R. (pseud.), 'A Memory of a Side-Show', *Army Quarterly* 3 (1) (1921), pp. 77–87

Heffernan, M., 'Geography, Cartography and Military Intelligence: The Royal Geographical Society and the First World War', *Transactions of the Institute of British Geographers* 21 (3) (1996), pp. 504–533

Heller, M., 'British Company Magazines, 1878–1939: The Origins and Functions of House Journals in Large-Scale Organisations', *Media History* 15 (2) (2009), pp. 143–166

Heyck, T. W., 'Myths and Meanings of Intellectuals in Twentieth-Century British National Identity', *Journal of British Studies* 37 (2) (1998), pp. 192–221

Hogan, J., 'Genderised and Racialised Discourses of National Identity in Baz Lurhman's "Australia"', *Journal of Australian Studies* 34 (1) (2010), pp. 63–77

Høiback, H., 'What Is Doctrine?', *Journal of Strategic Studies* 24 (6) (2011), pp. 879–900

Horner, D. M., 'The Influence of the Boer War on Australian Commanders in the First World War', in P. Dennis and J. Grey (eds), *The Boer War: Army, Nation and Empire: The 1999 Chief of Army History Conference* (Canberra, ACT: Army History Unit, 2000), pp. 173–190

Hoyle, R. W., 'Introduction', in R. W. Hoyle (ed.), *Our Hunting Fathers: Field Sports in England after 1850* (Lancaster: Carnegie, 2007), pp. 1–40

Humphries, M. O., '"Old Wine in New Bottles": A Comparison of British and Canadian Preparations for the Battle of Arras', in G. Hayes, A. Iarocci, and M. Bechtold (eds), *Vimy Ridge: A Canadian Reassessment* (Waterloo, ON: Wilfrid Laurier University Press, 2007), pp. 65–86

Hussey, J., 'The Deaths of Qualified Staff Officers in the Great War: "A Generation Missing"?', *Journal of the Society for Army Historical Research* 75 (304) (1997), pp. 245–259

Jack, E. M., 'Survey in France during the War', *Royal Engineers' Journal* 30 (1) (1919), pp. 1–27

Joly de Lotbinière, A. C., 'Obituary: Major-General Sir Philip Twining', *Royal Engineers' Journal* 31 (4) (1920), pp. 219–224

Jones, H., 'The Great War: How 1914–18 Changed the Relationship between War and Civilians', *Journal of the Royal United Services Institute* 159 (4) (2014), pp. 84–91

Kahle-Piasecki, L., 'Making a Mentoring Relationship Work: What Is Required for Organizational Success', *Journal of Applied Business and Economics* 12 (1) (2011), pp. 46–56

Keiger, J. F. V., '"Perfidious Albion"? French Perceptions of Britain as an Ally after the War', *Intelligence and National Security* 13 (1) (1998), pp. 37–52

Kennedy, P., 'Britain in the First World War', in A. R. Millett and W. Murray (eds), *Military Effectiveness, Vol. 1, The First World War* (Cambridge: Cambridge University Press, 2010 [1988]), pp. 31–79

Kesner, R. M., 'Builders of Empire: The Role of the Crown Agents in Imperial Development, 1880–1914', *Journal of Imperial and Commonwealth History* 5 (3) (1977), pp. 310–330

Kim, D. H., 'The Link between Organizational and Individual Learning', *Sloane Management Review* 35 (1) (1993), pp. 37–50

King, W. B. R., 'Geological Work on the Western Front: Discussion', *The Geographical Journal* 54 (4) (1919), pp. 201–215

Kirke-Green, A. H. M., 'Canada in Africa: Sir Percy Girouard, Neglected Colonial Governor', *African Affairs* 83 (331) (1984), pp. 207–239

Kochanski, H., 'Planning for War in the Final Years of Pax Britannica, 1889–1903', in D. French and B. Holden Reid (eds), *The British General Staff: Reform and Innovation c. 1890–1939* (London: Frank Cass, 2002), pp. 9–25

Kollars, N. A., 'War's Horizon: Soldier-Led Adaptation in Iraq and Vietnam', *Journal of Strategic Studies* 38 (4) (2015), pp. 529–553

Kollars, N. A., Muller, R. R., and Santora, A., 'Learning to Fight and Fighting to Learn: Practitioners and the Role of Unit Publications in VIII Fighter Command 1943–1944', *Journal of Strategic Studies* 39 (7) (2016), pp. 1044–1067

Korte, R., and Lin, S., 'Getting on Board: Organizational Socialization and the Contribution of Social Capital', *Human Relations* 66 (3) (2013), pp. 407–428

Kumar, K., 'English and French National Identity: Comparisons and Contrasts', *Nations and Nationalism* 12 (3) (2006), pp. 413–432

Lambert, A. D., 'Sir Julian Corbett, Naval History, and the Development of Sea Power Theory', in N. A. M. Rodger, J. Ross Dancy, B. Darnell, and E. Wilson (eds), *Strategy and the Sea: Essays in Honour of John B. Hattendorff* (Woodbridge: Boydell, 2016), pp. 190–200

Lambert, F. J., 'Internationalisme Scientifique et Révolution Quantique: Les Premieres Conseils Solvay', *Revue Germanique Internationale* 12 (2010), pp. 159–173

Lester, A., 'Imperial Circuits and Networks: Geographies of the British Empire', *History Compass* 4 (1) (2006), pp. 124–141

Levin, J. R., 'On Functions of Pictures in Prose', in F. J. Pirozzolo and M. C. Wittrock (eds), *Neuropsychological and Cognitive Processes in Reading* (New York: Academic Press, 1981), pp. 203–228

Levitt, B., and March, J. G., 'Organizational Learning', *Annual Review of Sociology* 14 (1988), pp. 319–338

Lewis, A. C., and Grosser, M., 'The Change Game: An Experiential Exercise Demonstrating Barriers to Change', *Journal of Management Education* 36 (5) (2012), pp. 669–697

Linssen, W., and Raymaekers, P., 'Engineering Institutions and Networking in Nineteenth-Century Belgium and Britain', *Proceedings of Institution of Civil Engineers* 166 (EH1) (2013), pp. 25–35

Lloyd, E. H., 'Work in Connection with the Suez Canal Defences in 1916, Which Was Undertaken by the Egyptian Ministry of Public Works Officials for and in Conjunction with the Royal Engineers', *Minutes of Proceedings of Institution of Civil Engineers* 207 (1919), pp. 349–373

Louis, M. R., 'Surprise and Sense Making: What Newcomers Experience in Entering Unfamiliar Organizational Settings', *Administrative Science Quarterly* 25 (2) (1980), pp. 226–251

Lowe, R., 'Plumbing New Depths: Contemporary Historians and the Public Record Office', *Twentieth Century British History* 8 (2) (1997), pp. 239–265

Lucas, L. M., 'The Role of Culture on Knowledge Transfer: The Case of the Multinational Corporation', *The Learning Organization* 13 (3) (2006), pp. 257–275

Lyon, H. G., 'Meteorology during and after the War', *Monthly Weather Review* 42 (2) (1919), pp. 81–83

Macleod, R., 'The Chemists Go to War: The Mobilization of Civilian Chemists and the British War Effort, 1914–1918', *Annals of Science* 50 (5) (1993), pp. 455–481

'Sight and Sound on the Western Front: Surveyors, Scientists, and the "Battlefield Laboratory", 1915–1918', *War and Society* 18 (1) (2000), pp. 23–46

Mangan, J. A., and McKenzie, C., 'Martial Conditioning, Military Exemplars and Moral Certainties: Imperial Hunting as Preparation for War', *International Journal of the History of Sport* 25 (9) (2008), pp. 1132–1167

Martin, J., 'The Transformation of Lowland Game Shooting in England and Wales in the Twentieth Century: The Neglected Metamorphosis', *International Journal of the History of Sport* 29 (8) (2012), pp. 1141–1158

McGuire, D., and Gubbins, C., 'The Slow Death of Formal Learning: A Polemic', *Human Resource Development Review* 9 (3) (2010), pp. 249–265

McKenzie, C., 'The British Big-Game Hunting Tradition, Masculinity and Fraternalism with Particular Reference to the "Shikar Club"', *The Sports Historian* 20 (1) (2000), pp. 70–96

McPherson, M., Smith-Lovin, L., and Cook, J. M., 'Birds of a Feather: Homophily in Social Networks', *Annual Review of Sociology* 27 (2001), pp. 415–444

Miles, H. S. G., 'Army Administration', *Journal of the Royal United Services Institute* 68 (429) (1923), pp. 23–44

Moreman, T. R., 'The British and Indian Armies and North-West Frontier Warfare, 1849–1914', *Journal of Imperial and Commonwealth History* 20 (1) (1992), pp. 35–64

Moureu, C., 'La Chimie et La Guerre: Science et Avenir', *La Revue d'Infanterie* 340 (58) (1921), pp. 188–204

O'Toole, P., and Talbot, S., 'Fighting for Knowledge: Developing Learning Systems in the Australian Army', *Armed Forces & Society* 37 (1) (2011), pp. 42–67

Pedersen, P., 'The AIF on the Western Front: The Role of Training and Command', in M. McKernan and M. Brown (eds), *Australia: Two Centuries of War and Peace* (Canberra, ACT: AWM, 1988), pp. 167–193

Perry, N., 'The Irish Landed Class and the British Army, 1850–1950', *War in History* 18 (3) (2011), pp. 304–332

Petter, M., '"Temporary Gentlemen" in the Aftermath of the Great War: Rank, Status and the Ex-Officer Problem', *Historical Journal* 37 (1) (1994), pp. 127–152

Phillips, C., 'Henry Wilson and the Role of Civil-Military Cooperation during the Planning of British Mobilisation for War, 1910–1914', *Ex Historia* 5 (2013), pp. 115–135

Philpott, W., 'L'histoire militaire un siècle après la Grande Guerre', *Revue Française de Civilisation Britannique* 20 (1) (2015), pp. 1–7

Poell, R. F., Chivers, G. E., Van der Krogt, F. J., and Wildemeersch, D. A., 'Learning-Network Theory: Organizing the Dynamic Relationship between Learning and Work', *Management Learning* 13 (1) (2000), pp. 25–49

Pope-Hennessy, L. H. R., 'The British Army and Modern Conceptions of War', *The Edinburgh Review* 213 (436) (1911), pp. 321–346

Porch, D., 'The French Army in the First World War', in A. R. Millett and W. Murray (eds), *Military Effectiveness, Vol. 1, The First World War* (Cambridge: Cambridge University Press, 2010 [1988]), pp. 190–228

Preston, R. A., 'The Military Structure of the Old Commonwealth', *International Journal* 17 (2) (1962), pp. 98–121

Prott, V., 'Tying Up the Loose Ends of National Self-Determination: British, French and American Experts in Peace Planning, 1917–1919', *Historical Journal* 57 (3) (2014), pp. 727–750

Rasmussen, A., 'Tournant, Inflexions, Ruptures: Le Moment Internationaliste', *Mil Neuf Cent. Revue d'Histoire Intellectuelle* 19 (1) (2001), pp. 27–41

Razzell, P. E., 'Social Origins of Officers in the Indian and British Home Army', *British Journal of Sociology* 14 (3) (1963), pp. 248–260

Reynolds, D., 'Britain, the Two World Wars, and the Problem of Narrative', *Historical Journal* 60 (1) (2017), pp. 197–231

Richardson, T., 'Borders and Mobilities: Introduction', *Mobilities* 8 (1) (2013), pp. 1–6

Rose, E. P. F., 'Groundwater as a Military Resource: Pioneering British Military Well Boring and Hydrogeology in World War 1', in E. P. F. Rose and J. D. Mather (eds), *Military Aspects of Hydrogeology: Geological Society Special Publication 362* (London: Geological Society, 2012), pp. 105–138

Roussel, Y., 'L'Histoire d'une Politique des Inventions', *Cahiers pour L'histoire du CNRS* 3 (1989), pp. 19–57

Sandford, A. H., *Key to Infantry Training 1914* (Melbourne, VIC: Critchley Parker, 1915)

Sandiford, K. A. P., 'Cricket and the Victorian Society', *Journal of Social History* 17 (2) (1983), pp. 303–317

Sankey, C. E. P., 'Bridging-Operations Conducted under Military Conditions', *Proceedings of Institution of Civil Engineers* 192 (1913), pp. 77–126

Seligmann, M., 'Hors de Combat? The Management, Mismanagement and Mutilation of the War Office archive', *Journal of the Society for Army Historical Research* 84 (337) (2006), pp. 52–58

Sheffield, G. D., 'The Australians at Pozières: Command and Control on the Somme, 1916', in D. French and B. Holden Reid (eds), *The British General Staff: Reform and Innovation c. 1890–1939* (London: Frank Cass, 2002), pp. 112–126

Sheffy, Y., 'Chemical Warfare and the Palestine Campaign, 1916–1918', *Journal of Military History* 73 (3) (2009), pp. 803–844

Simon, H. A., 'Bounded Rationality and Organizational Learning', *Organization Science* 1 (2) (1991), pp. 125–134

Simpson, A., 'Launcelot Kiggell and Herbert Lawrence', in D. T. Zabecki (ed.), *Chief of Staff: Napoleonic Wars to World War 1*, I (2 vols, Annapolis, MD: Naval Institute Press, 2008), pp. 199–206

Simpson, L. S., 'Railway Operating in France', *Journal of the Institution of Locomotive Engineers* 12 (1922), pp. 697–728

Sloan, G., 'Haldane's Mackindergarten: A Radical Experiment in British Military Education?', *War in History* 19 (3) (2012), pp. 322–352

Stancombe, M., 'The Staff Corps: A Civilian Resource for the Military', *Proceedings of Institution of Civil Engineers* 157 (5) (2004), pp. 22–26

Stephens, G. N., 'The Medical Work of the Italian Expeditionary Force', *Journal of the Royal United Services Institute* 64 (1919), pp. 647–659

Strachan, H., 'The British Army, Its General Staff and the Continental Commitment, 1904–1914', in D. French and B. Holden Reid (eds), *The British General Staff: Reform and Innovation c. 1890–1939* (London: Frank Cass, 2002), pp. 75–94

'The First World War as a Global War', *First World War Studies* 1 (1) (2010), pp. 3–14

Sunderland, D., 'The Departmental System of Railway Construction in British West Africa, 1895–1906', *Journal of Transport History* 23 (2) (2002), pp. 87–112

Swap, W., Leonard, D., Shields, M., and Abrams, L., 'Using Mentoring and Storytelling to Transfer Knowledge in the Workplace', *Journal of Management Information Systems* 18 (2001), pp. 95–114

Unknown, 'Annual Report and Accounts', *Proceedings of Institution of Automobile Engineers* 9 (1915), pp. 518–535

Unknown, 'Évolution des Methods de Tir des Artilleries Alliées Pendant la Guerre', *Revue d'Artillerie* 87 (January–June 1921), pp. 538–549

Unknown, 'Review of *Detailed History of the Railways in the South African War, 1899–1902*', *Royal Engineers' Journal* 2 (1) (1905), pp. 133–135

Unknown, 'Roll of Honour', *Proceedings of Institution of Automobile Engineers* 9 (1914), pp. 537–540

Van der Kloot, W., 'Lawrence Bragg's Role in the Development of Sound-Ranging in World War I', *Notes and Records of the Royal Society* 59 (2005), pp. 273–284

Various, 'The "Cavalry Journal" Committee', *The Cavalry Journal* 9 (January 1914)

Various, 'Discussion: Bridging-Operations Conducted under Military Conditions', *Minutes of Proceedings of Institution of Civil Engineers* 192 (1913), pp. 127–134

Various, 'Discussion: The Work of the Royal Engineers in the Great War', *Minutes of Proceedings of Institution of Civil Engineers* 210 (1920), pp. 84–90

Wheatley, M. J., 'Can the US Army Become a Learning Organization?', *Journal for Quality and Participation* 17 (2) (1994), pp. 50–55

Wilson, P. H., 'Defining Military Culture', *Journal of Military History* 72 (2008), pp. 11–41

Winterbotham, H. S. L., 'British Survey on the Western Front', *The Geographical Journal* 53 (4) (1919), pp. 253–276

Wise, N., 'The Lost Labour Force: Working-Class Approaches to Military Service during the Great War', *Labour History* 93 (2007), pp. 161–176

Yates, J., 'Investing in Information: Supply and Demand Forces on the Use of Information in American Firms, 1850–1920', in P. Temin (ed.), *Inside the Business Enterprise: Historical Perspectives on the Use of Information* (Chicago: University of Chicago Press, 1991), pp. 117–154

Yerkes, R. M., 'Report of the Psychology Committee of the National Research Council', *Psychological Review* 26 (2) (1919), pp. 83–149

II BOOKS

Alderson, E. A. H., *Pink and Scarlet* (London: William Heinemann, 1900)

Amenta, E., Nash, K., and Scott, A., *The Wiley-Blackwell Companion to Political Sociology* (Oxford: Wiley-Blackwell, 2012)

Andersen, C., *British Engineers in Africa, 1875–1914* (London: Pickering and Chatto, 2011)

Anderson, B., *Imagined Communities: Reflections on the Origins and Spread of Nationalism* (new edn, London: Verso, 2006 [1983])

Anon., *The War Work of Sir W. G. Armstrong, Whitworth & Company Ltd* (London: Arden Press, n.d. [c.1919])

Badsey, S., *Doctrine and Reform in the British Cavalry 1880–1918* (Aldershot: Ashgate, 2008)

Ballantyne, T., *Orientalism and Race: Aryanism in the British Empire* (London: Palgrave Macmillan, 2001)

Baynes, J., *Far From a Donkey: The Life of General Sir Ivor Maxse* (London: Brassey's, 1995)

Beach, J., *Haig's Intelligence: GHQ and the German Army, 1916–1918* (Cambridge: Cambridge University Press, 2013)

Beckett, I. F. W., *Victorians at War* (London: Hambledon Press, 2003)

Beeby Thompson, A., *Emergency Water Supplies* (London: Crosby Lockwood, 1924)

Berberich, C., *The Image of the English Gentleman in Twentieth-Century Literature* (Aldershot: Ashgate, 2007)

Blaxland, J., *The Australian Army from Whitlam to Howard* (Melbourne, VIC: Cambridge University Press, 2014)

Boff, J., *Winning and Losing on the Western Front: The British Third Army and the Defeat of Germany in 1918* (Cambridge: Cambridge University Press, 2012)

Bowman, T., and Connelly, M., *The Edwardian Army: Recruiting, Training, and Deploying the British Army, 1902–1914* (Oxford: Oxford University Press, 2012)

Brown, I. M., *British Logistics on the Western Front 1914–1919* (Westport, CT: Praeger, 1998)

Burke, P., *A Social History of Knowledge: From the Encyclopédie to Wikipedia* (Cambridge: Polity, 2012)

Chapman-Huston, D., and Rutter, O., *General Sir John Cowans GCB GCMG: The Quartermaster-General of the Great War* (2 vols, London: Hutchinson, 1924)

Clausewitz, C., *On War*, trans. M. Howard and P. Paret (London: Oxford World Classics, 2007)

Colley, L., *Britons: Forging the Nation 1707–1837* (London: Pimlico, 2003 [1992])

Connelly, M., *Steady the Buffs! A Regiment, a Region, and the Great War* (Oxford: Oxford University Press, 2006)

Connor, J., *Anzac and Empire: George Foster Pearce and the Foundations of Australian Defence* (Melbourne, VIC: Cambridge University Press, 2011)

Crawley, R., *Climax at Gallipoli* (Norman: Oklahoma University Press, 2014)

Davenport, T., and Prusak, L., *Working Knowledge: How Organizations Manage What They Know* (Boston: Harvard Business School, 1998)

Dennett, L., *A Sense of Security: 150 Years of Prudential* (Cambridge: Granta, 1998)

Dunlop, J., *The Development of the British Army, 1899–1914* (London: Methuen, 1938)

Erickson, E., *Ottoman Army Effectiveness in World War I: A Comparative Study* (London: Routledge, 2007)

Falls, C., *Armageddon 1918: The Final Palestine Campaign of World War I* (Philadelphia: University of Pennsylvania Press, 1964)

French, D., *The British Way in Counter-insurgency, 1945–1967* (Oxford: Oxford University Press, 2011)

    Military Identities: The Regimental System, the British Army, and the British People, c. 1870–2000 (Oxford: Oxford University Press, 2005)

    Raising Churchill's Army: The British Army and the War against Germany, 1919–1945 (Oxford: Oxford University Press, 2000)

    The Strategy of the Lloyd George Coalition 1916–1918 (Oxford: Clarendon Press, 1995)

Fuller, J. F. C., *The Foundations of the Science of War* (London: Hutchinson, 1926)

Gale, T., *The French Army's Tank Force and Armoured Warfare in the Great War: The Artillerie Spéciale* (London: Routledge, 2013)

Glazer, A. M., and Thomson, P. (eds), *Crystal Clear: The Autobiographies of Sir Lawrence and Lady Bragg* (Oxford: Oxford University Press, 2015)

Gooch, J., *The Italian Army and the First World War* (Cambridge: Cambridge University Press, 2014)

    The Plans of War: The General Staff and British Military Strategy, c. 1900–1916 (London: Routledge, 1974)

Gordon, A., *The Rules of the Game: Jutland and British Naval Command* (London: John Murray, 2005 [1996])

Goya, M., *La Chair et L'Acier: L'Armée Française et L'Invention de la Guerre Moderne 1914–1918* (Paris: Tallandier, 2004)

Grant, P., *Philanthropy and Voluntary Action in the First World War: Mobilizing Charity* (London: Routledge, 2014)

Greenhalgh, E., *The French Army and the First World War* (Cambridge: Cambridge University Press, 2014)

    Victory through Coalition: Britain and France during the First World War (Cambridge: Cambridge University Press, 2005)

Grey, J., *A Military History of Australia* (Cambridge: Cambridge University Press, 2000 [1999])

Grieves, K., *The Politics of Manpower, 1914–18* (Manchester: Manchester University Press, 1988)

   Sir Eric Geddes: Business and Government in War and Peace (Manchester: Manchester University Press, 1989)

Griffith, P., *Battle Tactics of the Western Front: The British Army's Art of Attack, 1916–1918* (London: Yale University Press, 2000 [1994])

Gudmundsson, B. I., *Stormtroop Tactics: Innovation in the German Army, 1914–1918* (Westport, CT: Praeger, 1989)

Hall, B. N., *Communications and British Operations on the Western Front, 1914–1918* (Cambridge: Cambridge University Press, 2017).

Harmsworth, A. C. W. (1st Viscount Northcliffe), *Lord Northcliffe's War Book* (New York: George H. Doran, 1917)

Harris, J. P., *Men, Ideas, and Tanks: British Military Thought and Armoured Forces, 1903–1939* (Manchester: Manchester University Press, 1995)

Harris, P., *The Men Who Planned the War: A Study of the Staff of the British Army on the Western Front, 1914–1918* (Farnham: Ashgate, 2015)

Holden Reid, B., *A Doctrinal Perspective 1988–98* (Camberley: SCSI, 1998)

Huggins, M., *The Victorians and Sport* (London: Palgrave Macmillan, 2004)

Hughes, T., *Tom Brown's School Days* (London: Macmillan, 1900 [1857])

James, H., *Krupp: A History of the Legendary German Firm* (Princeton, NJ: Princeton University Press, 2012)

Jeffery, K., *Field Marshal Sir Henry Wilson: A Political Soldier* (Oxford: Oxford University Press, 2006)

Jones, S., *From Boer War to World War: Tactical Reform of the British Army, 1902–1914* (Norman: Oklahoma University Press, 2012)

Joyce, P., *The State of Freedom: A Social History of the British State since 1800* (Cambridge: Cambridge University Press, 2013)

Kanigel, R., *The One Best Way: Frederick Winslow Taylor and the Enigma of Efficiency* (New York: Viking Penguin, 1997)

Keene, J. D., *Doughboys, the Great War, and the Remaking of America* (London: Johns Hopkins University Press, 2001)

Kochanski, H., *Sir Garnet Wolseley: Victorian Hero* (London: Hambledon Press, 1999)

Krause, J., *Early Trench Tactics in the French Army: The Second Battle of Artois, May–June 1915* (Farnham: Ashgate, 2013)

Lambert, N. A., *Planning Armageddon: British Economic Warfare and the First World War* (Cambridge, MA: Harvard University Press, 2012)

Liddell Hart, B. H., *Thoughts on War* (London: Faber and Faber, 1944)

Lupfer, T. T., *The Dynamics of Doctrine: The Changes in German Tactical Doctrine during the First World War* (Fort Leavenworth, KS: Combat Studies Institute, 1981)

Luvaas, J., *The Education of an Army: British Military Thought, 1815–1940* (London: Cassell, 1965)

Mandler, P., *The English National Character: The History of an Idea from Edmund Burke to Tony Blair* (New Haven, CT: Yale University Press, 2006)

Marcosson, I. F., *The Business of War* (London: The Bodley Head, 1918)

Mason, T., and Riedi, E., *Sport and the Military: The British Armed Forces, 1880–1960* (Cambridge: Cambridge University Press, 2010)

Moreman, T. R., *The Army in India and the Development of Frontier Warfare, 1849–1947* (Basingstoke: Macmillan, 1998)

Morton-Jack, G., *The Indian Army on the Western Front: India's Expeditionary Force to France and Belgium in the First World War* (Cambridge: Cambridge University Press, 2014)

Murray, W., *Military Adaptation in War* (Cambridge: Cambridge University Press, 2011)

Oakeshott, M., *Rationalism in Politics and Other Essays* (London: Methuen, 1962)

Palazzo, A., *From Moltke to Bin Laden: The Relevance of Doctrine in the Contemporary Military Environment* (Canberra, ACT: Land Warfare Studies Centre, 2008)

Seeking Victory on the Western Front: The British Army and Chemical Warfare in World War I (London: University of Nebraska Press, 2000)

Parker, P., *The Old Lie: The Great War and the Public-School Ethos* (London: Constable, 1987)

Paul, H. W., *From Knowledge to Power: The Rise of the Scientific Empire in France, 1860–1939* (Cambridge: Cambridge University Press, 1985)

Pedersen, P., *Monash as Military Commander* (Carlton, VIC: Melbourne University Press, 1985)

Pegler, M., *Sniping in the Great War* (Barnsley: Pen and Sword, 2008)

Perry, B., *The Amateur Spirit* (Boston: Houghton Mifflin, 1915 [1904])

Porter, P., *Military Orientalism: Eastern War through Western Eyes* (New York: Columbia University Press, 2009)

Posen, B., *The Sources of Military Doctrine: France, Britain and Germany between the World Wars* (Ithaca, NY: Cornell University Press, 1984)

Pugh, J., *The Royal Flying Corps, the Western Front, and the Control of the Air, 1914–1918* (London: Routledge, 2017)

Pratt, E. A., *British Railways and the Great War* (London: Selwyn and Blount, 1921)

Radley, K., *We Lead, Others Follow: First Canadian Division 1914–1918* (St Catherines, ON: Vanwell, 2006)

Ramsey, M. A., *Command and Cohesion: The Citizen Soldier and Minor Tactics in the British Army, 1870–1918* (Westport, CT: Praeger, 2002)

Robbins, S., *British Generalship during the Great War: The Military Career of Sir Henry Horne (1861–1929)* (Farnham: Ashgate, 2010)

British Generalship on the Western Front 1914–18 (Abingdon: Frank Cass, 2005)

Robins, G. U., *Lays of the Hertfordshire Hunt and Other Poems* (London: Arthur L. Humphreys, 1916)

Rosen, S. P., *Winning the Next War: Innovation and the Modern Military* (London: Cornell University Press, 1991)

Russell, J. A., *Innovation, Transformation and War: Counterinsurgency Operations in Anbar and Ninewa Provinces, 2005–2007* (Stanford, CA: Stanford University Press, 2011)

Sadler, P., *The Paladin: A Life of Major-General Sir John Gellibrand* (Melbourne, VIC: Oxford University Press, 2000)

Scruton, R., *England: An Elegy* (London: Pimlico, 2001)

Simkins, P., *From the Somme to Victory: The British Army's Experience on the Western Front, 1916–1918* (Barnsley: Pen and Sword, 2014)

Snyder, J., *The Ideology of the Offensive: Military Decision Making and the Disasters of 1914* (Ithaca, NY: Cornell University Press, 1984)

Spiers, E., *The Late Victorian Army, 1868–1902* (Manchester: Manchester University Press, 1992)

Stevenson, R., *To Win the Battle: The 1st Australian Division in the Great War, 1914–18* (Melbourne, VIC: Cambridge University Press, 2013)

Strong, P., and Marble, S., *Artillery in the Great War* (Barnsley: Pen and Sword, 2011)

Travers, T., *The Killing Ground: The British Army, the Western Front, and the Emergence of Modern War 1900–1918* (reprint, Barnsley: Pen and Sword, 2003 [1987])

Ulrichsen, K. C., *The First World War in the Middle East* (London: Hurst, 2014)

The Logistics and Politics of the British Campaigns in the Middle East, 1914–22 (London: Palgrave Macmillan, 2011)

Watts, J. I., *The First Fifty Years of Brunner, Mond & Co 1873–1923* (Northwich: Brunner, Mond, 1923)

Wilkinson, S., *The Brain of an Army* (2nd edn, London: Archibald Constable, 1895)

Wray, C., *Sir James Whiteside McCay: A Turbulent Life* (Melbourne, VIC: Oxford University Press, 2002)

III UNPUBLISHED DISSERTATIONS AND THESES

Bentley, J., 'Champion of Anzac: General Sir Brudenell White, the First Australian Imperial Force and the Emergence of the Australian Military Culture 1914–18', Unpublished PhD Thesis, University of Wollongong, 2003

Evans, N., 'From Drill to Doctrine. Forging the British Army's Tactics, 1897–1909', Unpublished PhD Thesis, University of London, 2007

Faraday, B. D., 'Half the Battle: The Administration and Higher Organisation of the AIF 1914–1918', Unpublished PhD Thesis, University of New South Wales, 1997

Ford, M., 'The British Army and the Politics of Rifle Development, 1880 to 1986', Unpublished PhD Thesis, University of London, 2008

Geddes, A., 'Major-General Arthur Solly-Flood, GHQ and Tactical Training in the BEF, 1916–1918', Unpublished MA Dissertation, University of Birmingham, 2007

Millar, J. D., 'A Study in the Limitations of Command: General Sir William Birdwood and the AIF, 1914–1918', Unpublished PhD Thesis, University of New South Wales, 1993

Mitchell, S. B. T., 'An Inter-Disciplinary Study of Learning in the 32nd Division on the Western Front, 1916–1918', Unpublished PhD Thesis, University of Birmingham, 2013

Phillips, C., 'Managing Armageddon: The Science of Transportation and the British Expeditionary Force, 1900–1918', Unpublished PhD Thesis, University of Leeds, 2015

IV MISCELLANEOUS

King, A., 'The Ethos of the Royal Marines: The Precise Application of Will',
      Report Commissioned by the Royal Marines, 2004, https://ore.exeter.ac.uk/
      repository/bitstream/handle/10036/58653/RMethos4.pdf
Leonard, G., 'The Limits of Decision Making: Accounting, Budgets, Tactical
      Efficiency and the Choices of the British General Staff, 1908–1913', paper
      presented at 13th World Congress for Accounting Historians, Newcastle-
      upon-Tyne, July 2012
Molkentin, M., 'Training for War: The Third Division AIF at Lark Hill, 1916',
      AWM Summer Scholarship Paper, 2005

V INTERNET SOURCE

Oxford Dictionary of National Biography, Oxford University Press, 2004, online
      edn, www.oxforddnb.com

Index